OXFORD PSYCHOLOGY SERIES

Editors: Donald E. Broadbent
James L. McGaugh
Nicholas J. Mackintosh
Michael I. Posner
Endel Tulving
Lawrence Weiskrantz

OXFORD PSYCHOLOGY SERIES

Elements of episodic memory

Endel Tulving
Professor of Psychology
University of Toronto

OXFORD PSYCHOLOGY SERIES NO. 2

CLARENDON PRESS · OXFORD
OXFORD UNIVERSITY PRESS · NEW YORK
1983

Oxford University Press, Walton Street, Oxford OX2 6DP
London Glasgow New York Toronto
Delhi Bombay Calcutta Madras Karachi
Kuala Lumpur Singapore Hong Kong Tokyo
Nairobi Dar es Salaam Cape Town
Melbourne Wellington
and associate companies in
Beirut Berlin Ibadan Mexico City

© Endel Tulving, 1983

British Library Cataloguing in Publication Data
Tulving, Endel
    Elements of episodic memory.—(Oxford
    psychology series; 2)
    1. Cognition   2. Memory
    I. Title
    153.4   BF311
    ISBN 0-19-852102-2

Library of Congress Cataloging in Publication Data
Tulving, Endel.
    Elements of episodic memory.
    (Oxford psychology series; no. 2)
    Bibliography: p.
    Includes index.
    1. Memory.   2. Recollection (Psychology)
I. Title.   II. Series.
BF371.T84 1982   153.1   82–8241
ISBN 0-19-852102-2

Typeset in Times Roman 10/12 (Linotron 202),
by Syarikat Seng Teik Sdn. Bhd.,
Kuala Lumpur, Malaysia
Printed in Great Britain by
The Thetford Press Limited, Thetford, Norfolk

Preface

Ten years ago I published a paper in which I proposed that a distinction might be drawn between two kinds of memory—episodic and semantic. Episodic memory is concerned with unique, concrete, personal experiences dated in the rememberer's past; semantic memory refers to a person's abstract, timeless knowledge of the world that he shares with others. Distinctions of this kind had been quite familiar to philosophers interested in problems of memory, but their implications for the psychological study of memory had not been explored. I thought that the adoption and the analysis of the distinction might be useful in that it 'could aid in the solution of a number of outstanding problems of human memory'.

This book begins with a progress report on the distinction. The first of the three main parts of the book discusses the shortcomings of the 1972 formulation, presents a somewhat more complete characterization of the two forms of memory, considers empirical evidence relevant to the distinction, and formulates a conclusion in the form of the hypothesis that episodic and semantic memory can be regarded as functionally different yet closely interacting memory systems. Although the two systems share a number of features, they are also sufficiently different to encourage their separate study. The potentialities and actual accomplishments of such separate study of episodic memory are discussed in the remainder of the book.

In the second main part of the book, a general theoretical framework for the study of episodic memory is outlined. The 'elements' of episodic memory in the title of the book refer to the major components of this framework, although, in adopting the term, I also had in mind the rudimentary nature of our knowledge, as well as the book's concern with the fundamentals of episodic memory. Since, contrary to the opinion I expressed in the 1972 essay, relatively little research has been directly focused on phenomena of episodic memory, and most of it has been concerned with the rememberer's knowledge of the semantic contents of learning episodes, serious systematic study of episodic memory still lies mostly in the future. The general framework presented in the second part of the book may help research workers in this future enterprise.

The third main part of the book describes a number of specific laboratory phenomena that I and my colleagues, as well as students of memory in other institutions, have studied over the past ten years or so, phenomena that can be interrelated within the general framework outlined in the second part of the book. While the material in the first two main parts of the book is mostly new, much of the material in the third part has already been published in the form of journal articles and book chapters.

There is, however, some new information that may be of interest even to readers who are quite familiar with previous research on topics such as encoding specificity, recognition failure of recallable words, and the relation between recognition and recall. All of this material, old and new, is here brought together in a systematic form.

In planning and writing the book, I was acutely aware of my own limitations in resolving the inevitable conflict between writing for the general psychological reader and writing for the expert in the field. I could not see how, within the scope of the book, I could communicate with a person who has not studied the literature on memory in great detail and at the same time say something that is not totally uninteresting to the person who has. I decided in favour of writing in a rather general and broad way even though this entailed the risk of being criticized by experts as dealing with the problems at a superficial or shallow level. It is always possible, of course, to take any one of the many phenomena, experiments, or theoretical notions mentioned in the book and delve in minute detail into its logic or methodology, factual status, and theoretical significance. But such discussions are of interest to relatively few individuals, and are best conducted in the pages of professional journals. In this book I thought it was more important to try to help the reader to see the forest than the trees.

Another feature of the book is somewhat idiosyncratic. This reflects my own conviction that scientific research is not only a social but also a highly personal enterprise, particularly in a developing science such as the science of memory. Although in the final analysis it does not matter how a particular scientific fact or idea is arrived at, who the actors were in the drudgery, drama, or accident of its creation, and what personal clashes and conflicts paved the way to its formulation, the personal element is always implicitly present in the final product of research. I frequently have great difficulty in understanding what my colleagues say, as they undoubtedly have difficulty in understanding me. On such occasions I have often felt that knowing something about an author's metatheoretical convictions, beliefs, and values would help me to understand his way of doing science. Hence my decision to share some of my own personal prejudices and biases with the reader. I have tried to achieve this objective by adopting a format that would enable the reader who wishes to do so to have his science 'straight'.

The book is written at two levels, which are distinguished by two styles of type. The main text, approximately 80 per cent of the total, and appearing in the larger size of roman type, like the one used here, is a treatment of the substantive problems of interest; it discusses the psychological science of memory. Where debatable matters are presented in the main text, all standard criteria and methods of adjudication apply. Interspersed with the main text are sections appearing in a smaller size of sans serif type that contain commentary on the main text. These sections consists of personal observations of various kinds, informal remarks on what has been discussed in the main text, some personal-historical titbits, some thoughts that are too speculative to be put in the main text, and various comments of other kinds that reveal my metatheoretical convictions. The commentary part may be thought of as having more to do with the psychology and sociology of science than with science as such. It can be passed over by anyone who has misgivings about mixing affect of practitioners of science with the effects of the practitioners' labours.

To illustrate the nature of the material covered in the commentary sections of the book, let me mention an episode I remember that set me thinking about writing a book. A number of years ago, a friend of mine, a respected and honoured psychologist, told me about a young colleague of his who was shortly going to be considered for tenure and promotion. My friend said that he was a very capable person, bright, hard-working, with many excellent ideas, and a demonstrated record of research accomplishment, but that, unfortunately, 'he had not written his book yet'. For this reason, his prospects for tenure were not totally unblemished.

At the time of our conversation, I had been in the psychological research business for a long time, had published a number of papers in various journals, had been promoted to full professor, and even imagined that some of the things that I had found in my experiments were not completely uninteresting. But I, too, had not written my book yet. Trying to conceal my embarrassment, I changed the topic of conversation, but I never quite recovered from the emotional impact of the casual comment of my friend. From that day on I started thinking about writing 'my book'.

This book has gone through several drafts and has changed its nature considerably in the process. The first draft was written in 1976–7 during a year of leisure made possible by an award, the Izaak Walton Killam Memorial Scholarship, from the Killam Committee of Canada Council. A second draft was completed during the following year, which I spent at the University of Oxford as a Commonwealth Visiting Professor. Without the award from the Killam Committee and the freedom provided by the visit to Oxford, which was initiated through the efforts of several people there, especially Professor Lawrence Weiskrantz, the book would not have come into being. I am very grateful to both the Killam Committee and my colleagues in Oxford.

The research that I describe in the book would not exist without generous support that I have received from the Natural Sciences and Engineering Research Council of Canada (formerly the National Research Council of Canada) and the National Science Foundation of the United States. Nor would it exist without the stimulation provided by the Ebbinghaus Empire and the help and collaboration of many students and colleagues, notably Eric Eich, Arthur Flexser, John Gardiner, Gregory Jones,

Stephen Madigan, Robert Mathews, John Ogilvie, Marcia Ozier, Donald Thomson, and Sandy Wiseman. Others, assistants or colleagues, have been helpful with particular points and issues that have come up in the book. They include Bennet Murdock, David Olton, Jaan Puhvel, Norman Slamecka, Michele Stampp, Linda Tulving, Gwendolyn Turner, and Olga Watkins.

Four very good friends—Fergus Craik, Henry (Roddy) Roediger, Daniel Schacter, and Michael Watkins—have played an influential role in shaping my thoughts about memory as well as having given me a lot of encouragement for writing the book, and for writing it in my own way. Each of them also read the complete draft of an earlier version of the book and, through gentle but perceptive criticism, provided a great deal of valuable advice that has helped to improve the final product.

Carol Macdonald deserves special mention. Over the years she typed close to a million words in getting the various drafts of the book from the dictated tapes on to paper, a remarkable accomplishment by any standards. In the process she converted many a mumble into meaningful phrases, helped to tidy up my grammar, and provided invaluable help with definite articles, a part of the English language that I have never quite mastered.

I am deeply grateful to these students, assistants, colleagues, and friends. Whatever merit the book may turn out to have is largely attributable to my good fortune of having been associated with them.

E. T.

Toronto, Canada
May 1982

Contents

1

Study of memory

Remembering past events is a universally familiar experience. It is also a uniquely human one. As far as we know, members of no other species possess quite the same ability to experience again now, in a different situation and perhaps in a different form, happenings from the past, and know that the experience refers to an event that occurred in another time and in another place. Other members of the animal kingdom can learn, benefit from experience, acquire the ability to adjust and adapt, to solve problems and make decisions, but they cannot travel back into the past in their own minds.

The kind of memory that is involved in remembering past events is called episodic memory. This is what this book is about. Episodic memory represents only a small part of a much larger domain of memory. It is the form most familiar to the proverbial man in the street, yet it has received little direct attention from psychologists or other scientists. Philosophers have speculated about many issues related to episodic memory, but psychologists have not. Such a somewhat paradoxical state of affairs has come about because of the failure, until most recent times, to distinguish between the episodic and other forms of memory. Psychologists have studied memory for almost a hundred years now, and although it can be argued that many of their studies were concerned with episodic memory, the argument is not entirely justified. Since students of memory did not draw the distinction between episodic memory and other forms, they were unaware of the fact that their scientific curiosity was directed at phenomena representing different mixtures of memories.

Progress in memory research

Few problems that inquiring minds have attempted to resolve by the methods of science have resisted understanding as stubbornly as have problems of memory. Philosophers, looking at phenomena of memory through the window of their own minds, have speculated about its nature for over two thousand years. Physiologists and brain scientists have been busy trying to discover and understand the nature of neural processes and the function of brain centers that give rise to memories. Psychologists have mapped a good part of the territory of memory through thousands of experiments in which memory performance has been measured under controlled conditions, and, with the aid of ideas borrowed from philosophy and other branches of knowledge, have tried to formulate theories of memory. Despite all these efforts, and despite a great deal of evidence that we feel is relevant to the understanding of memory, our general insights into the nature and workings of memory, until most recently, were not greatly different from what they were, say, a hundred years ago. It is only in the last twenty years or so that we seem to have broken out of the stranglehold of the past, and have made what can be regarded as genuine progress.

The progress has occurred on several fronts. In this book we will be concerned with one of them: understanding how people remember experienced events. We now know a good deal about the remembering of events that we did not know only thirty or forty years ago. This knowledge has been derived from the application of new methods that were unknown to early students of memory and, more important, from the application of general ideas about the workings of the human mind that have allowed us to raise problems and suggest solutions to them that would not have been possible in earlier times.

Before launching into the description of the progress in the study of memory in the book, I should try to explain how my present orientation is related to two earlier statements I have made about progress in the study of memory. The first time I dared to assume the role of a critic evaluating the field of memory and verbal learning was some twelve years ago when my colleague Stephen Madigan and I joined forces in writing a chapter for the *Annual Review of Psychology* (Tulving and Madigan 1970). Our overall conclusion was that progress in the study of memory since Aristotle's time had been somewhat disappointing. The second time I had an occasion to consider our field from the perspective of an outsider observing it over a long time span was a few years ago when I participated in a symposium on memory organized to commemorate the 500th anniversary of the University of Uppsala. Again my assessment was that genuine progress in understanding memory was not overwhelming (Tulving 1979*a*). Although I realize that the vast majority of the readers of this volume have been and will be spared any knowledge of these earlier indiscretions, and that they therefore are not in a position to discern any discrepancy between the conclusions then and now, for the sake of public record I should try to explain the apparent conflict.

The extent of progress I can see in our field depends on the time span under consideration. If we look at the last twenty or thirty years, we have good reasons to be quite satisfied; if we look farther back, it is more difficult to feel happy about what has happened. This somewhat paradoxical statement is illustrated graphically in Fig. 1.1. It shows a wave-like curve that represents the changes in our understanding of memory that have taken place from Aristotle's days to our own. Historical time is shown on the abscissa, on an inverted logarithmic scale taking the present as the starting point, and the ordinate shows positive and negative changes in our knowledge, measured in undefined subjective units. Needless to say, the curve represents only my own view of the matter; most people who have studied the history

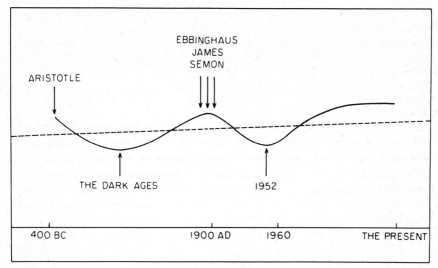

ARISTOTLE

EBBINGHAUS
JAMES
SEMON

THE DARK AGES

1952

400 BC   1900 AD   1960   THE PRESENT

Fig. 1.1 Progress in the understanding of memory through the ages.

of the subject and know what is going on today undoubtedly have different ideas for such a curve of progress. Keeping in mind the highly idiosyncratic origin of the curve, let us note a few things about it. The general trend, as I hope the reader can detect, is upward, although the slope of the main line is not entirely impressive. Superimposed on the long-range trend are the much more readily noticeable ups and downs. The gradual decline following the ancient Greek philosophers represents conventional views about the intellectual history of the western world and needs no special comment. Nor does the reversal of this trend somewhere around the seventeenth or eighteenth century. The decades around the turn of the present century were good years for the study of memory. Ebbinghaus (1885) had developed methods for making controlled observations about learning and forgetting; William James (1890) had distilled the wisdom of the philosophical past into many sharp and insightful ideas about the human mind; and Richard Semon (1904, 1921), a German scientist whose name is almost unknown to the students of psychology today, published two important volumes on memory, espousing ideas that pointed to a very promising future (Schacter, Eich, and Tulving 1978; Schacter 1982). Unfortunately, that future did not arrive until much later. The study of memory, like the study of many other manifestations of the human mind, fell victim to the view that psychology was a science of behavior rather than a science of the mind. Psychologists began studying learning of responses and lost interest in remembering of experiences. And since the two sciences of psychology—one of behavior, and the other of knowledge—have yet to merge into a unitary whole, studying behavior gives us no more understanding of knowledge than studying knowledge helps us to understand behavior.

The shift of emphasis from memory to learning is one reason why my curve takes a plunge after Ebbinghaus, James, and Semon, and reaches its local lowest point somewhere around 1952. That was the year of the publication of McGeoch and Irion's influential book entitled *The psychology of human learning*. It summarized the then current knowledge about human learning. The word 'memory' did not appear in it, except as a part of the label of 'memory span'; Semon's name was not mentioned; Sir Frederic Bartlett's name appeared only once; and that of Clark Leonard Hull, whose experimental work was largely based on observations of lower organisms but whose theory of behavior was supposed to apply to all, was mentioned in over sixty different places in the book. For these reasons alone I am inclined to think of 1952 as a bad year for memory.

My second and more directly relevant reason for taking McGeoch and Irion's (1952) book as a benchmark against which to judge the progress we have made, and for thinking of it as representing a low point, has to do with two fundamental principles of memory. The portents and accomplishments in the study of memory throughout history can be evaluated by the simple expedient of observing how closely the dominant theoretical ideas at any given time have embodied or done justice to the principles. I have done essentially just that in drawing the curve in Fig. 1.1. The early 1950s represent the low point because the then prevalent theory of learning— emphasizing acquisition of responses to stimuli governed by the laws of reinforcement, the laws of association, or both—made little allowance for the two principles. Conversely, the more recent upswing in the curve of progress reflects the facts that the principles have been discovered now and taken into account by most experimenters and theorists.

The first of the two principles might be called the principle of 'goodness of encoding'. It holds that what a person remembers about an event, and how well the event is remembered, depends in an important manner not just on what that event is but on how it is perceived, thought about, reacted to, or 'encoded' at the time the rememberer witnesses it. The second principle might be called the principle of retrieval. It holds that what a person remembers about an event, and how well, depends not only on the nature of the event and its encoding, but also on the conditions prevailing at the time of its attempted recollection, particularly that component of the conditions that we refer to as retrieval information. A great deal of the discussion of problems of memory in this book revolves around the separate and joint operations of the two principles in determining what people remember.

The progress we have made in the study of memory has not been attributable as much to striking new discoveries than to a gradual elimination of wrong and unfruitful ideas. In this respect the science of memory follows in the footsteps of more mature sciences. George Sarton (1959) has pointed out that the growth of science has always entailed 'the gradual purification of its methods and even of its spirit'. Practitioners in many fields of science have always made mistakes; 'their knowledge has improved only because of their gradual abandonment of ancient errors, poor approximations, and premature conclusions' (Sarton 1959, p. xi). In the science of memory, too, we have made 'mistakes of every kind'; whenever we can detect one and rectify it, we can claim that progress has been made.

Memory as a warehouse

Let us illustrate the nature of the kinds of wrong ideas that have stood in the path of progress for a long time with the following historical observation. In 1807, a nobleman from Baden, M. Gregor von Feinaigle, visited Paris in order to deliver a lecture on his 'new' memory system. The event was described briefly in the June 1807 issue of the *Philosophical Magazine*. The lecture included a description of Feinaigle's model of memory, which in the *Philosophical Magazine* was rendered as follows: 'The memory may be compared to a warehouse stored with merchandise. A methodological arrangement of the contents of such a repository enables its owner to find any article that he may require, with the utmost readiness.'

This brief statement has a modern ring to it, and helps to remind us how little our general thinking about memory has changed over time. Spatial analogies of memory are still popular in our day (Roediger 1980), and the successful operation of memory is greatly dependent upon the organization of the material in the store (Tulving and Donaldson 1972; Puff 1979). The 'owner' of the memory system, when trying to remember something, knows what it is that he wants from memory, and can recognize it after finding it. This is the basic idea underlying the generation/recognition theories of retrieval that we shall briefly discuss later on in the book (pp. 243–9). Finally, recovering something from the memory store is like lifting a package off the shelf in the warehouse: what the searcher finds depends entirely on what it is. This idea is prevalent in many 'activation theories of retrieval' about which I also have something to say later on (pp. 178–9).

The orientation towards the study of memory that the reader will find in this book is somewhat different from that of a number of other contemporary views, as well as different from Gregor von Feinaigle's warehouse-memory. First, I assume that there is no such thing as 'the memory'; rather, we have to distinguish between different forms of memory. Second, retrieval of information is not like finding an object methodically stored away in a particular place. Third, to assume that the rememberer knows what it is that he wants is to beg the question about retrieval: if the nature of the 'desired' object is already known, why is it necessary to 'find' it? Finally, what a person recollects about an experience is not determined by the memory trace of that experience. The memory trace is only one important co-determinant of recollection; the other equally important one is the retrieval information that is used in the process of actualizing the trace.

These disagreements with Feinaigle, and with those who hold similar ideas today, represent some of the main themes of this book. We shall pursue these and many other themes under three general headings, corresponding to three main parts of the book: (i) the episodic/semantic distinction; (ii) general abstract processing system; and (iii) synergistic ecphory. In the first part, I shall argue that episodic memory represents a functionally separate memory system that closely interacts with other systems to bring about recollection of events. In the second part, an overall framework for the study of episodic memory is outlined. In the third, experimental research is described that points to the important role that the interaction between encoding and retrieval processes plays in determining outcomes of individual acts of remembering.

Unitary memory?

On the very first page of his book, published in 1812 under the title of *The new art of memory*, Gregor von Feinaigle adopted Dugald Stewart's definition of memory: 'Memory is that faculty that enables us to treasure up, and preserve for future use, the knowledge we acquire.' This old definition is surprising only because of the obscurity of its immediate source. Otherwise, it is a definition that would not be out of place in any introductory textbook today. We might quibble about the term 'faculty', but otherwise it represents as good a brief definition as any. Nevertheless, we can expand the definition to cover a wider range. At or near one end of the range are definitions that assign the term to phenomena which demonstrate the influence of some experience or behavior at a later time. A definition of this kind would embrace a huge variety of phenomena that are known to people in everyday life or that have been studied by psychologists in the laboratory: classical conditioning, instrumental conditioning, verbal conditioning, concept formation, language learning, verbal learning, learning of emotions, learning of addictions, learning of attitudes, learning of preferences, as well as acquisition, retention, and utilization of all sorts of knowledge, habits, and skills. Near the other end of the range of definitions are those that assign the term to present subjective experience that an individual feels to be related to a particular event that he witnessed, or in which he participated, in the past.

A general theory of memory, broadly defined, would embrace all phenomena that could be subsumed by any definition covered by the range of possible definitions. Improvement with practice in sensory-perceptual tasks—detection of stimuli near sensory thresholds, discrimination of small differences in stimuli, localization of stimuli in space, and the like—would have to be included. So would sharpening and honing of skills such as walking, talking, playing the piano, saying the alphabet backwards, reading upside-down type, deciding that a string of letters is a word, answering affirmatively to questions such as 'Is a spaniel a dog?' All this in addition to acquisition of conditioned responses of all kinds, learning a first or second language, developing social graces, and remembering one's past life. What kind of a theory could encompass them all?

Seeking for general theories of memory is like seeking for a general theory of, say, locomotion. Memory has to do with the after-effects of stimulation at one time that manifest themselves subsequently at another time; locomotion is concerned with the change of position of a living creature from one location to some other location. Consider now the problem facing the theorist of locomotion when he contemplates the variety of forms of locomotion that his theory has to handle. A very small sample would include an ameba moving by changing the shape of its entire protoplasmic mass, an earthworm literally eating itself through the ground, a protozoan drawing itself through water by beating its flagella, a mollusk gliding along a track of slime that it itself secretes, a Portuguese man-of-war relying on its gas-filled float to propel itself across water like a sailboat, and many different insects that swim, run, jump, burrow, or fly from one place to another, not to mention spiders, snakes, monkeys, and human infants. There exists an almost endless variety of specific mechanisms that evolution has bred to provide its creatures with mobility. What do all these forms of locomotion—the swimmings, crawlings, walkings, runnings, flyings, jumpings, wigglings, glidings, slidings, and jet propulsions—have in common, other than the fact that they get the creature from one point to another under its own steam, and that it spends energy in doing so?

What do the almost equally endless variety of forms of memory in the broad sense have in common, other than that they can be subsumed under the definition, and that they manifest one of the basic characteristics of intelligent matter?

Suppose that we gave up, at least for the time being, the search for a general theory of memory, and instead decided to seek understanding of the many manifestations of memory in smaller domains. How should we go about the task? Where should we begin?

A reasonable plan of action would call for the development of a taxonomy of memory, the construction of a classification system that would permit us to break the vast domain of memory phenomena into separate but related smaller units, try to make sense of the manifestations of memory within these units, and then construct more ambitious and comprehensive theories of memory by integrating particular theories to the extent that it proves feasible.

The construction of any scheme of classification is simple in principle and very difficult in practice. Ideally we would group all the phenomena of memory into different categories in such a way that each phenomenon is more similar to other phenomena in its category than it is to any other phenomenon outside the category. Then we would repeat the operation at the level of categories, forming them into higher-level categories, and so on, ending up with a neat hierarchical classification of all phenomena.

The problems with this scheme are few in number but they are nasty. Even now the number of known facts about memory that could be regarded as phenomena is exceedingly large, and it keeps growing; and we do not know how to measure the similarity of phenomena so that we can reliably classify them. Even in zoology, where the problem of classification is much simpler because it is based on visible structures, there is no general agreement on many details of the system. In the science of memory, where the basis of classification would be based on functional characteristics of memory phenomena, the task would be far more difficult.

The other alternative is to work from the top down: divide the whole domain of memory into a small number of smaller domains, and subdivide these further as the need for it becomes apparent for whatever reason. This is the approach adopted for our present purposes. This book is about a small domain of memory, episodic memory, corresponding roughly to the narrow definition of memory given above (p. 6). Two other subdivisions of memory that can be identified at the present time are semantic memory and skills.

The first of the three major parts of the book will be devoted to the discussion of the proposal that episodic and semantic memory are functionally different; that they represent separate, albeit related, systems. A large part of the discussion will be concerned with examining the differences between the systems, and with the nature of their relation. My general conclusion will be that the episodic-memory system is functionally different from semantic memory.

Episodic/semantic distinction

The first step we take in subdividing the domain of memory is to distinguish between procedural and propositional memories. This distinction has been proposed by a number of theorists. For instance, Kolers (1975b), taking his lead from Scheffler (1965) suggested a separation between operational or procedural memory on the one hand and semantic or substantive memory on the other. A corresponding division is that between skills and knowledge. The category of operational or procedural memory consists of a huge number of perceptual-motor skills and cognitive skills; and the latter category, which I label 'propositional memory', consists of an equally huge variety of knowledge that can be represented and expressed symbolically.

Both procedural and propositional memories satisfy the broad definition: an individual's present experience or behavior is influenced by an earlier experience or behavior. But the two categories also differ. An individual can demonstrate his procedural knowledge of a particular kind in only one way: by performing a task that entails the skill. Demonstration of propositional knowledge, on the other hand, can take many, behaviorally quite different, forms. A second distinction concerns the truth value of the two kinds of knowledge: skilful procedures acquired by a person are neither true nor false; whereas questions of veridicality do arise with respect to one's knowledge of the world and one's relation to it. A third distinction concerns the form of acquisition of the two categories of knowledge: procedural knowledge usually requires extensive periods of practice, whereas propositional knowledge can frequently be acquired on a single brief occasion. Finally, one of the most salient characteristics of skilled behavior is absence of thought from its execution, it is 'automatic'; expression of propositional knowledge, on the other hand, usually requires directed attention.

Propositional memory can be further subdivided into episodic and semantic memories. One is involved in the recording and subsequent retrieval of memories of personal happenings and doings, the other with knowledge of the world that is independent of a person's identity and past. The distinction has been discussed by a number of thinkers under various names; in 1972 I brought it to the attention of psychological students of memory.

The 1972 distinction, which is discussed in Chapter 2 in this book, was not very well thought out. It was impressionistic, incomplete, and somewhat muddled, whatever evidence existed to support it was all anecdotal. Nevertheless, it did create some interest, and a number of experimenters and theorists have pursued the implications of the proposed distinction. As a result of the thought spent on the problem, and the collaborative effort of many people, we are now in a better position to discuss and evaluate the proposed distinction again.

Chapter 3 presents an extended and updated version of the 1972 paper. Episodic and semantic memory are conceptualized as two *systems* that differ with respect to (a) the kind of information processed by them, (b) characteristics of their operations, and (c) their applications in real life as well as the memory laboratory. The original list of a few essential differences between the two forms of memory is expanded to include 28 different diagnostic features, hypothesized differences between the systems.

The nature of the distinction is further discussed in Chapter 4. Questions are raised as to the nature of the distinction. Is it merely a heuristic one? Is it limited to the kinds of information the two memories deal with? Can we contemplate the possibility that the two systems are functionally different? What does it mean to say that two systems are functionally different? How could we evaluate the hypothesis that they are? How do we adjudicate the dispute between those who hold memory to be a unitary entity and those who believe in the reality of functional differences?

A number of experimenters have tried to test the validity of the hypothesized distinction between episodic and semantic memory experimentally.

Some other evidence relevant to the issue has emerged from clinical observations of severe impairment of memory in brain-damaged patients. In Chapter 5 we review this evidence. The evidential basis for the distinction is still quite sparse, and the results, not surprisingly, are somewhat mixed. Nevertheless, on the basis of the evidence that is available now, the tentative conclusion that episodic and semantic memories represent different functional systems can be regarded as a reasonable hypothesis.

Although the results from empirical investigations of the problem of the distinction are encouraging, some other data have also been reported that complicate the issue. Certain kinds of 'priming' effects, a type of learning without awareness, have been found in the same experiments that have provided support for the distinction. These priming effects do not seem to be readily explainable in terms of either episodic or semantic memory. Their existence, therefore, suggests the need for either a modification of the distinction, or its extension. One form of the extension is already implied in the distinction between procedural and propositional memory: it is possible that data discrepant with the episodic/semantic distinction can be accounted for in terms of procedural memory. Another possibility, quite speculative at this time, lies in the postulation of 'free radicals' in memory, bits of symbolic knowledge originally constructed as a part of an experienced episode that become detached from the episode and lead an independent existence of their own. Some parallels between the episodic/semantic distinction and a similar distinction that has emerged from work with animals will also be discussed in Chapter 6.

The upshot of the extended discussion of the episodic/semantic distinction in the first part of the book is that episodic memory is a distinctive functional system, justifying its experimental and theoretical study and analysis separately from other forms of memory. Insofar as students of memory have largely refrained from drawing a conscious and deliberate distinction between episodic and semantic memory in their work, relatively little work has been done that speaks directly to problems of episodic memory. Most of the research has been of a hybrid kind, dealing with a mixture of effects of the two memory systems.

General Abstract Processing System

One of the most compelling and salient characteristics of remembering of past events is the individual's subjective awareness of remembering: when a person recollects something that has happened to him in the past, he recognizes the experience as remembering; 'knows' that the present experience refers to a past event and, rightly or wrongly, 'knows' it to be true. The study of episodic memory, therefore, would be expected to have something to say about this subjective experience, about its underlying processes, and about its psychological antecedents and consequents. Yet there is almost nothing in the psychological literature on memory that deals with these issues. In Chapter 7 I speculate about the reasons for such a state of affairs.

If we wish to study episodic memory in its own right, and include the rememberer's recollective experience as one of the critical constructs in our conceptualizations of remembering, we need an overall pretheoretical framework within which we can pursue individual problems. Such a framework is described in the second main part of the book, comprising Chapters 7, 8, and 9. The framework is dubbed the General Abstract Processing System. Its schematic outline is presented in the second part of Chapter 7, and its various components are described at greater length in the other two chapters.

The basic unit of episodic memory is an individual act of remembering that begins with the witnessing or experiencing of an event or episode and ends with its subjective remembering (recollective experience), with the conversion of the remembered information into some other form, or both. The general framework for the study of episodic memory is described with respect to such an act of remembering.

The framework specifies a number of components of remembering and their interrelations. The components are of two kinds, observable events and hypothetical constructs. The components are referred to as *elements* of episodic memory; they constitute the basic units into which a complete act of remembering can be decomposed.

The elements of episodic memory can be divided into two main categories: elements of encoding and elements of retrieval. Chapter 8 is devoted to the discussion of the first category, Chapter 9 to the second. The central element in the first category is that of encoding: the process that converts the information about an experienced event, in a particular setting and at a particular time, into an engram, or memory trace. The central element of the retrieval process is ecphoric information, a synergistic product of the engram and the retrieval cue, episodic information and semantic information, or a product of the past and the present. Ecphoric information determines the rememberer's recollective experience of the past episode, as well as its convertibility into other forms of experience or overt behavior.

The general framework of episodic memory described in the second part of the book serves three functions. First, it can be used to define episodic memory: episodic memory is a class of psychological phenomena that fit into the framework as described. Second, it provides guidance to experimenters and theorists in the selection of problems to study, description of variables manipulated and relations observed, and in the interpretation of findings and phenomena at a rather general level of abstraction. Third, the framework can be thought of as an intellectual challenge for the students of memory. Although most of its constituent ideas are accepted by memory

theorists today, there is a great deal of room for improvement. Its usefulness and validity must be continually evaluated, its elements and relations among them thought about and analyzed, and parts of it, or all of
it, replaced with better ideas whenever the present ones are found to be
inadequate. There is no doubt that the framework will change with time;
the present version constitutes simply a convenient starting point for such
an undertaking.

Synergistic ecphory

Since 'memory is extraordinarily complicated' (Jenkins 1979, p. 430), and
since we have no reason to believe that episodic memory is much simpler,
there exist many particular problems that can be raised and studied within
the general framework. In the third part of the book, comprising Chapters
10 to 14, we will discuss some of these problems. The selection is not
entirely random: I have selected experiments and attendant theoretical
speculations with which I happen to be most familiar. We can subsume
much of this research under the label of 'synergistic ecphory', after one of
the central ideas that has emerged from it and that has guided the enterprise. 'Ecphory' is one of the elements of episodic memory, a component
of the process of retrieval; 'synergistic' refers to the joint influence that
the stored information (the engram) and the retrieval information (the cue)
exert on the construction of the product of ecphory (ecphoric information).
   Synergistic ecphory is a concept that can be contrasted with somewhat
different ideas theorists have had about the nature of the retrieval process.
I classify these alternative ideas under the label of 'activation theories of
retrieval'. Both associationistic theories and search-and-find theories of
retrieval fit under the label: in both, what the rememberer remembers,
and how well he remembers a particular experience, are determined by
the characteristics of the after-effects of the initial encoding as retained in
the system to the moment of attempted retrieval. The synergistic ecphory
view, on the other hand, holds that these after-effects tell only one half
of the story, and that for a complete understanding of the 'what' and the
'how' of retrieval we must also take into account the substantive contribution made by non-episodic information present at retrieval. The episodic
engram provides part of the 'raw materials' for the construction of ecphoric
information and the rememberer's recollective experience, as well as the
information that the subjective experience relates to a past event; the
non-episodic retrieval information provides the other part, as well as the
information that the experience of the past is taking place in the present.

Many thinkers and psychologists have for a long time known, or at least
suspected, that a simple activation theory of remembering is incomplete, and
that something else is needed to account for the experience. Associative

views have particularly been singled out for criticism in this regard. Consider, for instance, the following summary of observations made about associative processes in memory. The law of association, or the law of suggestion, is known to exert the 'most extensive influence over the phenomena and processes of the mind'. If two objects have been seen 'in conjunction, or in immediate succession, at any one time—then the sight or thought of one of them afterwards is apt to suggest the thought of the other also; and the same is true of the objects of all the senses'. The succession of associated ideas takes place with such 'speed and facility' that 'many of the intermediate terms, though all of them undoubtedly present to the mind', flash by so quickly and evanescently as to 'pass unnoticed'. For instance, 'in the art of reading, the ultimate object is to obtain possession of the author's sentiments or meaning; and all memory of the words, still more of the component letters, though each of them must have been present to the mind', remains unnoticed. 'The mind is too much occupied with the information itself, for looking back on the light and shadowy footstep of the messenger who brought it, which it would find difficult if not impossible to trace', besides, there is no practical reason to retain the form in which the information was received ... Although such an account of the association can account for many familiar mental phenomena, it cannot explain 'the phenomena of memory'. One idea can be awakened by another, and in this sense the law of association makes it possible for us to 'understand how it is that certain ideas, suggested by others which came before it, are now present to the mind'. But association cannot explain our conviction that the awakened idea represents one that we had before.

The central theme of the third part of the book is closely related to the ideas expressed in this passage. It is not without interest, therefore, to observe that the passage was not written by a contemporary student of memory who shares the ideas that some of us at Toronto hold dear. Indeed, it may come as a surprise to some readers that the passage was written by T. Chalmers one hundred and fifty years ago (Chalmers 1833). We might think that it is high time that cognitive psychologists turn their talents to solving the problem of episodic memory for which activation theories are inadequate.

The early research that has culminated, not entirely rationally, in thoughts about synergistic ecphory is described in Chapter 10. The important insight that was derived from this research had to do with the fact that goodness of remembering was determined jointly by encoding and retrieval processes and the information on which the processes acted. The study of encoding/retrieval interactions was carried out under the banner of 'encoding specificity'. In Chapter 11, I describe a sample of experiments and their results that have shown that encoding specificity applies in a wide variety of situations. Like the early work that we did at Toronto, this other research has been concerned with people's memory for miniature events under laboratory conditions: recalling or recognizing familiar words seen or heard in a particular place at a particular time. The wide generality of conditions under which the encoding specificity principle has been shown to hold has important implications for some of the previously popular ideas about memory. These ideas, denied or excluded by the experimental findings, are also briefly discussed in Chapter 11.

Encoding specificity ideas have come under criticism, sometimes heavy criticism, from several quarters. These criticisms are briefly reviewed and rebutted in Chapter 12. On analysis, most of them only *seem* to be damaging to encoding specificity. Some criticisms are based on questionable and sometimes unwarranted assumptions; others have neglected to take into account all relevant experimental facts.

An interesting phenomenon that is known in the literature under the name of recognition failure of recallable words is discussed in Chapter 13. The phenomenon—that an individual cannot recognize a word he or she studied earlier but can recall it to some other cue—served initially not only to extend the domain of encoding specificity, but also to disprove the then prevailing generation/recognition theory of retrieval. That theory was subsequently modified and brought in line with the offending data. More recently, the phenomenon of recognition failure has been studied from the point of view of interest in the nature of internal representation of information, and the relation between recall and recognition in the actualization of the stored episodic information.

The relation between recall and recognition is pursued in somewhat greater detail in the final chapter of this book. Recall and recognition, and the relation between them, is fitted into the framework of the General Abstract Processing System. An experiment is reported whose results were in conflict with some of my own earlier assertions about the nature of the relation between recall and recognition; and a revised version of the ideas is presented. Our ideas that recall and recognition are more similar than different have been reconciled with the ideas of others that recall and recognition are more different than similar, all within the general framework.

The final chapter also describes what I call the 'synergistic ecphory model of retrieval'. It relates episodic trace information to (semantic) retrieval information, recognition to recall, and qualitative differences in recollective experience to quantitative differences in memory performance. In a modest way, the model measures the progress we have made in the study of memory.

Part 1
Episodic/semantic distinction

2
Inchoate distinction

Ebbinghaus said that psychology is a young science with a long history. The same could be said about the distinction between episodic and semantic memory. Douglas Herrmann, in a talk presented to the Ebbinghaus Empire at the University of Toronto in April 1981, claimed that the distinction can be traced back to Aristotle. Yet, as an object of interest in the science of memory it is only ten years old.

Among the best-known proponents of the distinction is Henri Bergson (1911) who discussed in some detail two memories which he said are 'profoundly distinct'. One was habit, a 'set of intelligently constructed mechanisms' that enables people to adapt themselves to their environment; the other was true memory, coextensive with consciousness, 'truly moving in the past', and capable of marking and retaining the dates and order of happenings (Bergson 1911, p. 195).

Bertrand Russell strongly endorsed Bergson's distinction. He claimed that despite the difficulty 'in distinguishing the two forms of memory in practice, there can be no doubt that both forms exist' (Russell 1921, pp. 166–7). Bergson's and Russell's influence on philosophers concerned with problems of memory has been profound. Many take the distinction more or less for granted, characterizing it as 'common usage'. Thus, for instance, Furlong (1951) points out that when a person says he remembers seeing someone post a letter, the remembering is quite different from the person's 'remembering' the square root of a number. 'In the former case the mind looks back to a past event: we recollect, reminisce, retrospect; there is imagery. In the latter case this looking-back is absent, and there is little or no imagery. We have retained a piece of information; that is all. There is retentiveness but not retrospection' (Furlong 1951, p. 6). Furlong suggests that the major distinguishing features of the 'retrospective memory' are its 'reference to context in time and space, and the attendant imagery', and that retrospective memory becomes gradually the 'non-retrospective type' as the context fades.

The Swiss psychologist Claparède (1911), discussing the feelings of familiarity in recognition, contrasted two kinds of mental connections: those established between representations, and those established between representations and the self. He suggested that the activation of connections of the first kind does not produce any feelings of familiarity or recognition, and that only those 'between the perception and the feeling of me-ness' are capable of doing so (1911, p. 63).

Yet another example of the long history of the distinction is found in Reiff and Scheerer's (1959) two primary 'forms of memory': 'those *with* the experience of an autobiographic index, to be called *remembrances*; and those *without* the experience of an autobiographic index to be called *memoria*' (p. 25). They suggested that the important feature distinguishing the two primary forms of memory is that 'remembrances are always accompanied by the experience of personal continuity through time, while in memoria this experience is absent' (p. 25).

All these distinctions are forerunners of the contrast between episodic and semantic memory. Some other dichotomous classifications of memory are not quite so. Thus, for instance, Arthur Koestler's contrast between abstract and picture-strip memories (1969), which is included in Hintzman's (1978, Fig. 12.4) list of writers who have proposed similar distinctions, refers to different degrees of clarity and veridicality of memories. Koestler lumps together personal events and acquired knowledge: 'The bulk of what we remember of our life history, and of the knowledge we have acquired in its course, is of the abstractive type' (Koestler 1969, p. 261). Similarly, we must wonder about Schachtel's (1947) contrast between autobiographical and practical memory, another entry in Hintzman's list. Despite the suggested labels, it does not quite match the episodic/semantic distinction, because Schachtel contrasts only different types of 'material' remembered and thinks of the distinction as an 'artificial abstraction' (Schachtel 1947, p. 5). Douglas Herrmann has a long list of other contrasts that could be thought of as similar to the contrast between episodic and semantic memories but which in fact are not.

Recollection of events and recall of facts

In writing the paper in which I discussed episodic and semantic memory (Tulving 1972) I was most directly influenced by Reiff and Scheerer's ideas. Yet my predilection for two rather different kinds of memory went back a little farther, and my views were affected by my background and work in experimental psychology of memory.

As a student of psychology in the early 1950s I knew, as did other students, that verbal learning was one of the dullest subjects in the whole field. I had the good fortune to escape taking any courses in it. The Department of Psychology at Toronto, where I did my undergraduate work, was not very strong in experimental psychology, and at Harvard, where I did my graduate work, no one was interested in verbal learning. But I was aware of the distinction between general and personal memory. In my role as a teaching fellow to E. G. Boring in Psychology I, in the fall term of 1954, I had to read the textbook of the course. It was edited by Boring, Langfeld, and Weld, and it contained a chapter on remembering, imagining, and reasoning, written by T. A. Ryan. With the authority expected of the author of an introductory text, Ryan informed the reader that remembering is of two kinds: one of personally experienced past events that are *recollected*, and the other of general facts, which are *recalled*. We recollect how the car in which we were riding skidded into the ditch, whereas we recall a chemical formula or the name of the author of *Huckleberry Finn*. Since the distinction made perfect sense to me, I did not give it much further thought at that time.

Nor did I give much thought to exactly what it was that subjects were doing in the verbal-learning experiments that I found myself doing after I had returned to a teaching position at Toronto. In these experiments, we gave students words to study, retain, and recall, usually over a number of trials (e.g. Tulving and Thornton 1959; Tulving and Patkau 1962; Tulving 1962*a*, *b*). These were verbal *learning* experiments, and the word 'memory' did not occur in them. If someone had asked me at that time whether our subjects were recalling or recollecting the words, I probably would have dismissed the query as irrelevant.

But Ryan's distinction must have had something to do with the fact that when I stumbled into single-trial experiments I began thinking of words that subjects learned as to-be-remembered *events*, rather than, as conventional wisdom had it, to-be-remembered *items* (Tulving 1968*a*, 1969). At first the distinction did not carry with it any strong theoretical convictions. But I do remember being pleased with it, because it seemed to lend a certain air of ecological respectability to list-item experiments: memory processes involved in remembering mini-events (appearances of familiar words in unfamiliar lists) were likely not to be altogether different from the processes involved in larger events in real life. Thus, quite deliberately, we began talking about *event memory*, *event information*, and *event-memory experiments* (Thomson and Tulving 1970), and about specific encoding patterns and cognitive environments of *perceived events* (Tulving and Thomson 1971).

After a while it seemed self-evident that what the subjects had to do in our single-trial list-item experiments was to remember the occurrence of word events rather than learning or recalling the items. Surely, when the subject reproduced the name of the word he had seen in the list, he did not express his knowledge of the meaning or spelling of the word, but rather his awareness of the fact that the word had appeared in a particular place at a particular time, namely in the studied list. And what was the appearance of a word in a particular place at a particular time if not an event?

The realization that many verbal learning experiments were concerned with event memory rather than 'memorization of items' gradually shifted some old problems into a new focus, and also taught me an important lesson. The lesson was that the words we use to describe what we do as observers and experimenters are exceedingly important in shaping our theoretical thoughts, rather than just the other way around. From that time on I became very much more interested in the language we use in talking about memory and other aspects of the mind than I had been before. One of the immediate consequences of thinking of word-events in memory experiments was my 'discovery' of what many wise philosophers from Heraclitus on had known all the time: events do not repeat themselves, there is never another event exactly like a given one. *Items* may be repeated, within a list or on

different trials, producing events that have certain things (the nominal identity of the item) in common while differing in other respects (occurring at
different times in different places). Another 'discovery' had to do with the
relation between the learner's response and the internal cognitive state that
it represented: identical responses could reflect different kinds of awareness.
Thus, for instance, making a free-association response, such as 'chair', to a
stimulus word, such as 'table', does not mean the same thing as the same
response made to a question such as, 'What was the word that appeared
beside the word "table" in the list you just studied?'

In 1970, Bob Glaser and Jim Voss at the Learning Research and Development Center of the University of Pittsburgh asked me, together with
Wayne Donaldson, a faculty member at the Center, to organize a conference
on the topic of organizational processes in memory. The two-day conference
was held at the University of Pittsburgh in March 1971. We had invited a
number of active researchers to participate who were likely to say something
interesting on the subject. As usual, in order to entice them to participate,
they were given a completely free hand in selecting their own particular topics, as long as these had some relation to the subject of the conference. Thus
it happened that three papers presented at the meeting had to do not with
memory but with what I, in my naiveté, thought of as understanding of language. These were papers by Rumelhart, Lindsay, and Norman (1972);
Kintsch (1972); and Collins and Quillian (1972). Concern for memory processes, I thought, crept into their discussion of how people comprehend
language, answer questions, make inferences, know facts, and solve
problems—the topic of the three chapters, broadly perceived—simply
because all these mental activities, like all other mental activities, depend on
and involve memory. Since the authors of two of the three chapters—
Rumelhart *et al.* and Kintsch—wanted their theories of language understanding to account for acquisition and recall of word lists as well, it was not possible for me, or any other person similarly inclined, to argue that their
efforts—interesting and exciting and full of promise, like all new things—
seemed to have much less relevance to remembering events than they
themselves seemed to think.

The authors of all three chapters explicitly used the expression 'semantic
memory' in describing their work, borrowing the term from Quillian (1966).
That designation, therefore, seemed appropriate for talking about the contents of the three chapters. On the assumption, however, that 'semantic
memory' was not quite the same thing as recollecting the car skidding into the
ditch, it created the problem of how we were to think about, and refer to, the
memory that was not 'semantic'.

I did not give a paper at the Pittsburgh conference. My own interests had
shifted from organizational processes to the fascinating problem of the interaction between storage and retrieval, I was doing experiments on the recall
of unique word-events, and I did not think I had much to say on the topic of
the conference. However, after finding myself in deep puzzlement about the
conceptual status of the newly emerging field of semantic memory, and
remembering Hilgard's (1956, p. 460) dictum that the reduction of persistent
differences to uniformity may sometimes reflect only a 'foolhardy desire for

scientific parsimony', I decided to add a chapter of my own to the book that described the conference proceedings, a chapter in which I was going to point out what I thought were some of the 'persistent differences' between semantic memory and the other kind. This was the essay on the distinction between episodic and semantic memory (Tulving 1972).

Episodic memory, I suggested, is a system that receives and stores information about temporally dated episodes or events, and temporal-spatial relations among them. Since people are quite capable of remembering both meaningless and meaningful events, events *could* be stored in the episodic system solely in terms of their 'perceptible properties' (Tulving 1972, p. 385), although the 'important role that the semantic system plays in storage and retrieval of episodic memory information' (p. 392) also had to be assumed in light of a great deal of relevant evidence. The act of retrieval of information from either the episodic or the semantic system would constitute an event that would be registered in the episodic store thereby changing its 'contents'. I also thought that the episodic system is 'probably quite susceptible to transformation and loss of information' (p. 386).

Semantic memory, I suggested, 'is the memory necessary for the use of language. It is a mental thesaurus, organized knowledge a person possesses about words and other verbal symbols, their meaning and referents, about relations among them, and about rules, formulas, and algorithms for the manipulation of the symbols, concepts, and relations' (p. 386). Perceptible properties of 'input signals' are not registered in semantic memory, only their 'cognitive referents'. I also suggested that retrieval of information from the semantic system would leave its contents unchanged, and that, in general, the semantic system is less susceptible to loss of information than the episodic system.

So much for the summary of the distinction. A somewhat more detailed discussion of the two forms of memory revolved around five issues: (a) nature of stored information, (b) autobiographical versus cognitive reference, (c) conditions and consequences of retrieval, (d) vulnerability to interference, and (e) interdependence of the two kinds of memory.

Associative continuity and transsituational identity

The contrast between the two kinds of memory, with respect to each of these five issues, can be illustrated by comparing the concepts of 'association' and 'item' in a meta-theoretical world in which memory is one, as it was in experimental psychology before 1972, with a world in which the distinction is at least assumed if not accepted.

Consider two situations. In one, a person is asked to study and remember an A–B pair of words, and his knowledge of the pair subsequently tested by presenting word A as a cue for the recall of word B. We can describe this as an episodic-memory task, and characterize the nature of the subject's task as that of learning the association between A and B. In the other situation we present to the subject the stimulus word A and ask him to respond with the first related word that occurs to him. And let us assume that in this 'free-association' task the subject responds with the word B. We might characterize the situation as one in which a previously acquired A–B association was 'activated'.

Now, how do we think about the relation between the A–B association in the episodic paired-associate recall task and the A–B association in the semantic free-association task? Or, a question more relevant to our present purposes, how did memory experiments and theorists think of this relation before 1972?

It turns out that the question is not easy to answer, because it was seldom raised in this form. Few relevant statements had been explicitly made on the problem (e.g. Russell 1961). Yet implicitly most theorists who relied on associative concepts seemed to hold that the two A–B associations were in some sense the same. For instance, given that a person already 'possessed' a strong association between two words such as EAGLE and BIRD, not only would the person be highly likely to respond with BIRD to the stimulus word *eagle* in the free-association task, but he would also readily learn the *eagle*– BIRD pair in the paired-associate recall task. The strength of the pre-experimental association between two words was regarded as an important determinant of the ease with which the association could be learned and recalled in what we now call an episodic task. Similarly, the other important property of associations, directionality or asymmetry, was also assumed to be highly correlated in situations such as the free-association and the paired-associate learning tasks. Thus, given that the *eagle*– BIRD association was stronger than the *bird*– EAGLE association in the free-association situation, it was expected to be learned more readily in the paired-associate task as well.

The assumption that the large if not perfect transferability of a given association across situations was attributable to the identity of the association in different situations was so much a part and parcel of the theoretical thinking of the associative school that it did not even have a distinctive name. Why should it, if it is not going to be contrasted with anything else? An A–B association is obviously different from an X–Y association, and also different from an A–C association, and an C–B association, even from a B–A association, if we take directionality into account, but equally obviously an A–B association is the same as an A–B association, and why should this simple state of affairs deserve a special label? We do not have a special label to designate the fact that the book on our desk is the same book as it was in the library from which we borrowed it, or that our friend Josephine is the same person even if we see her in two different settings. The book has a name, as does Josephine, and as does an association (e.g. A–B, or *eagle*– BIRD), but the 'fact' that they retain their identity in different situations does not.

When our research group began wondering about the relation between two kinds of association—those existing by virtue of people's knowledge of language and manifesting themselves in situations such as free-association tasks, and those that people had to learn in memory experiments—we referred to them as pre-experimental and experimental, or pre-experimentally and experimentally established (e.g. Tulving and Osler 1968). And a little later, Donald Thomson and I decided to refer to the idea that pre-experimental and experimental associations entailing identical terms are essentially the same across different situations as the hypothesis of *associative continuity* (Thomson and Tulving 1970) Rejection of the hypothesis implies that the relation between an experimentally established A–B association and a pre-experimentally established A–B association is not one of identity, but something else. The distinction between episodic and semantic memory provided some guidance as to the direction in which the nature of the relation was to be sought.

When students of memory began thinking in terms of and speaking the language of information processing, they replaced associations with items, or chunks of items, as basic functional units (e.g. Broadbent 1958; Miller 1956*a*, *b*; Shepard and Teghtsoonian 1961; Murdock 1961; Waugh and Norman 1965). The basic attitude towards identity of associations was initially carried over into the new conceptual schemes: an item presented to the learner for study at one time was regarded as identical with the same item presented later on in the same situation, as well as in different situations. Gradually, however, a difference emerged: some theorists began talking about informational units in the short-term store as copies or replicas of the corresponding units in long-term memory (e.g. Atkinson and Shiffrin 1968; Shiffrin and Atkinson 1969). These copies were at first thought of as faithful reproductions of the master elements in permanent memory, but since the short-term store was assumed to be separate from the long-term store it became possible to think of the two as not necessarily sharing all characteristics. For instance, it was possible to think that pre-experimental associations that characterized a word in long-term memory were not automatically copied into the replicas of the word stored as a result of their study in a particular list (Thomson and Tulving 1970).

Before the completion of the transition from conventional associationism to the idea that to-be-remembered items were to-be-remembered events, however, the assumption that a given item was the same across situations was implicitly held by most theorists. For instance, the 'correct' item implicitly generated by the rememberer to a recall cue was assumed to be identical with the item that had been studied in the list, as well as identical with the corresponding 'old' test item in recognition memory (e.g.

Bahrick 1969, 1970; Kintsch 1970). Like the hypothesis of associative continuity, this assumption had no distinctive identifying label. In order to
differentiate between it and our own ideas, Donald Thomson and I
referred to it as the assumption of *transsituational identity* (Thomson and
Tulving 1970).

It was against this background of thought of associations as continuous
between tasks, and of items as identical across situations, that I speculated
about differences between episodic and semantic memory systems. In
some sense, the distinction I proposed was as much a denial of the commonly held assumptions about associative continuity and transsituational
identity as it was an assertion about the potentially heuristic usefulness of
the idea that memory for events is not quite the same thing as memory for
associations or items.

Temporal co-occurrences and semantic relations

Keeping in mind an A–B association learned in a laboratory experiment
and an A–B association revealed in a free-association test, let us compare
episodic and semantic memory with respect to the five issues dealt with in
the 1972 essay.

First, consider the nature of stored information. The information stored
in episodic memory is about temporal co-occurrence of two words, A and
B, whereas in semantic memory it entails a meaningful relation between
the two words. The individual who has learned the A–B association in a
memory experiment knows that the two words occurred side by side in a
particular list on a particular occasion; the individual who produces the
response B to the stimulus A in the free-association test expresses his
knowledge of the semantic properties of the two items. In both the recall
and free-association tests the individual might make exactly the same
response to the same stimulus, for instance responding with BIRD to the
stimulus word *eagle*, but in one case this expresses his knowledge of a specifically dated event involving the co-occurrence of the two words, whereas
in the other the response is based on the respondent's timeless knowledge
of the meanings of the two words. An individual not familiar with the language could still remember the co-occurrence of two words, treating them
as nonsense items, and might therefore be capable of responding correctly
in the episodic-memory test, whereas knowledge of the language is a necessary condition for the person to be able to make an appropriate response
in the semantic-memory task of free association.

Second, consider what episodic and semantic associations represent, or
what they 'refer to'. An A–B association learned in an episodic-memory
experiment possesses an autobiographical reference; it represents an event
that the learner has personally witnessed; the A–B association handled by
the semantic system, on the other hand, exhibits only 'cognitive' reference.

The response BIRD to the stimulus *eagle* in the paired-associate recall task is predicated on the learner's memory for the list that he learned on a particular occasion: the mini-event of the temporal co-occurrence of the two words could be remembered only as a part of the larger event of learning the list. If a learner had forgotten that he ever learned a list containing the *eagle*–BIRD association, he could not remember the association. Conversely, his ability to respond with BIRD to *eagle* in the recall task implies memory not only for the mini-event but also for the larger episode of learning the list. Such an autobiographical reference is absent in situations in which the *eagle*–BIRD association is activated in a semantic task. The individual is as likely to respond with BIRD to *eagle* when he is instructed to guess what most other people would say in response to *eagle* as he is in a situation in which the instructions call for the first response that occurs to him. Thus, whereas the correctness or appropriateness of the response in the paired-associate recall task requires its referral to a particular part of the rememberer's personal past, the acceptability of the response in the semantic free-association task can be judged in terms of the semantic structure of the language, as reflected in the responses made by other members of the language community in the same situation.

Third, the two types of memory differ with respect to conditions and consequences of retrieval. As to the conditions under which retrieval takes place in episodic memory, specification of the date and place of the to-be-remembered event is a necessary component of the question or cue provided to the rememberer. A similar specification would be meaningless in a situation in which the person has to respond to the question in terms of his semantic memory. When we ask the rememberer, 'What is the word that appeared with *eagle*?' he would be fully justified in asking in return, 'When?' or 'Where?' or both. When we ask him, 'What is the square root of 9?' or 'What is the relation between *eagles* and BIRDS?' the counter-question of 'When?' or 'Where?' would be meaningless, or worse. With respect to consequences of retrieval, recall of the event of the co-occurrence of *eagle* and BIRD, whether covertly or overtly, usually can be expected to enhance the probability that the event could be remembered on a subsequent occasion, whereas covert thinking about, or overt expression of, particular bits of semantic knowledge, such as the relation between *eagle* and BIRD, usually makes little difference to the person's ability to reply to the same question in the future.

The fourth issue in the 1972 essay had to do with the vulnerability of episodic and semantic memories to interference. The suggestion was that episodic memories are more vulnerable to interference than semantic memories. Like other presumed differences between the two systems, this one too was mostly a result of armchair speculation. But there also existed some experimental evidence that seemed to be relevant. It was possible to entertain the thought, in light of this evidence, that the well-established phenomena of associative interference demonstrated in list-learning experiments (e.g. Postman 1961) did not exist, or at least were less prominent, in situations involving semantic associations. It is very easy to demonstrate the loss of A–B associations learned in one list by having learners learn a second list of A–C associations—different responses learned to the same stimuli. Yet Slamecka (1966) showed that experimental acquisition of A–C associations had no interfering effect on recall of pre-experimentally acquired A–B associations. On the basis of this evidence it looked as if learning temporal co-occurrences of words did not affect their semantic relations. Another bit of relevant evidence comes from experiments such as the one reported by Bower (1972*a*) in which it was shown that people can learn a new association much more readily to a stimulus item designating a known person than one referring to an unknown one. According to the basic tenets of interference theory, it should be more difficult to learn a new response to a stimulus (such as a known person) with which many responses are already associated (about whom we know many things), and easy to do so for a stimulus (an unknown person) that is a source of few potentially competing associations. There are, of course, other possible interpretations of findings such as those reported by Slamecka (1966) and Bower (1972*a*), and I did not think of the data as 'proof' of the distinction. But they were suggestive.

The last issue dealt with in the 1972 paper had to do with the interdependence between the two systems. I assumed that most of the time the two systems interact closely, each influencing the processing of information in the other in many situations. But I also thought that such interdependence was optional rather than obligatory, since it was possible to imagine conditions under which an individual could remember the co-occurrence of stimulus-items not previously encountered, and hence not represented in semantic memory. For instance, an individual could remember a novel association between an unfamiliar taste and an unfamiliar odor, or between an unfamiliar face and an unfamiliar name. In these situations, the involvement of the semantic system in the acquisition and retention of episodic information is likely to be minimal. The interdependence between the two systems, I thought, is also likely to be slight in situations in which people learn experimental associations between familiar words in list-learning experiments. Thus, learning the experimental *eagle*–BIRD pair in a list would not change what the learner knows about the meaning of these words: temporal co-occurrence does not change the structure of semantic memory. In brief, the general assessment of the interdependence between the two systems was that the effect that one system has on the other is variable rather than constant: it should be possible to identify situations in which the interdependence is pronounced as well as those in which it is negligible.

Shortcomings of the 1972 formulation

In this chapter I am referring to the 1972 distinction as inchoate, because that is what is was: rudimentary, imperfect, incomplete, and rather disorganized. One of the main purposes of the essay, as I saw it, was to pose questions about the nature of the relation between the two forms of memory. Although I was partial to the hypothesis that they represent different systems, it was not possible at that time to present strong arguments, let alone evidence, in favor of the hypothesis. Hence my summary statement: what I had done in the essay was to 'present a case for the possible heuristic usefulness of a taxonomic distinction between episodic and semantic memory as two parallel and partially overlapping information processing systems' (Tulving 1972, p. 401).

With the wisdom of hindsight it is easy to see the weaknesses and shortcomings of the distinction in the 1972 essay. We will briefly review some of them here.

One weakness of the 1972 paper had to do with its neglect of the similarities of the two systems. It did not seem worth while to spend much time on telling the readers something that they presumably already knew, namely that memory is memory. This is why I rather cursorily dispatched the commonality of episodic and semantic systems in a single sentence: 'Let us think of episodic and semantic memory as two information processing systems that (a) selectively receive information from perceptual systems . . . or other cognitive systems, (b) retain various aspects of this information, and (c) upon instructions transmit specific retained information to other systems, including those responsible for translating it into behavior and conscious awareness' (Tulving 1972, p. 385).

In retrospect it looks as if a little more emphasis on the similarities and parallels between episodic and semantic memory might have been useful in that it might have prevented some subsequent misunderstanding from arising. Since I did not give that emphasis, some readers interpreted the suggested division between the two forms of memory in too extreme a form, as if the 1972 formulation had been to the effect that the two have nothing to do with one another.

Another problem had to do with the implied exhaustiveness of the primitive taxonomy implicit in the distinction: it was possible to read the essay to imply that there are no other forms of memory than episodic and semantic. This shortcoming of the paper had its roots in my preoccupation with the implications of the three chapters on semantic memory to the effect that semantic memory was simply an extension of the other kind, the 'non-semantic' memory that had been studied since Ebbinghaus. My chapter was an attempt to present an alternative hypothesis. In the process, I failed to say anything about the relation between episodic and

semantic memory on the one hand and memory for skills and skillful
behavior, on the other. The discussion of episodic and semantic memory
made no reference to the potentially important distinction between propositional and procedural knowledge, it was only concerned with the former. Retained effects of learning experiences that manifest themselves in
improvement of skillful performance of all kinds, therefore, did not fit into
the taxonomy. If memory is defined as retention and utilization of acquired
knowledge, then the knowledge of how to knit a sweater, tell a claret from
a burgundy, read Cyrillic script, and thousands of other such learned ways
of responding to and interacting with the environment entail memory, but
this memory cannot be classified as either episodic or semantic. The taxonomy of memory implied in the 1972 paper was incomplete.

Yet another difficulty had to do with the designation of the two systems.
The term 'episodic' seems to have caused relatively little difficulty, at least
judging by the reaction to it. It does convey a reasonably accurate description of the kind of information or knowledge to which it refers: not only
is 'episode' one of the synonyms of 'occurrence', it is also defined in the
dictionary as 'an event that is distinct and separate although part of a larger
series'. Thus we can think of a person's life as consisting of successive
episodes as readily as we can think of the appearance of words, pictures,
or other items in a to-be-remembered list as miniature episodes, embedded
within a larger episode of reading or listening to the list. The term 'episodic
memory' seems slightly better than a possible alternative that I as well as
others had used before, namely 'event memory', since it avoids the use of
a noun as an adjective, and its sound is more pleasant. The relative brevity
of the term gives it an advantage over another possible alternative, namely
'autobiographical' memory, that, despite its historical precedents, further
suffers because of its connotation of a literary account of one's life. Whatever the reasons—and I concede that the arguments I have given are not
terribly compelling—the fact remains that the term of 'episodic memory'
seems to have been generally accepted as reasonably appropriate.

It is 'semantic memory' that in retrospect seems to have represented a
less happy choice. Its connotations are simply not quite right for the realm
of phenomena to which it is supposed to refer. In many ways a better
expression would be 'knowledge of the world', which indeed has been used
by many writers. Then the contrast would be between *memory* and *knowledge*, requiring no use of adjectival modifiers at all. In this case we would
be back where William James was in 1890.

The main problem with the term 'semantic' is that it is derived from
linguistics, and that it makes people think of the meaning of words and
other symbols. We know many things about the world that are neither
meaningful nor readily expressible in words or other symbols. Attempts
have been made to suggest other terms in lieu of 'semantic memory'. Thus,
for instance, Hintzman (1978) proposed the term 'generic memory', and

Estes (1976*a*) suggested the label of 'categorical memory'. Both have advantages over the term 'semantic', and if we could set the clock back ten years we could select either of these expressions. Because of the widespread acceptance of the distinction between episodic and semantic memory, however, and because most people now correctly think of semantic memory as knowledge of the world, it may be both difficult and unnecessary to start revising the terminology.

In thinking of a suitable label for the type of memory that was not 'semantic', I considered several possibilities, but finally decided to adopt the term 'episodic' from Munsat (1965) who had a whole chapter under the title 'Non-episodic memory' in his interesting philosophical discussion of the concept of memory. Munsat himself did not distinguish between 'episodic' and 'non-episodic' memories, but the idea of 'episodic memory' is clearly implied by 'non-episodic memory'.

I had little choice about the term 'semantic memory', as I mentioned earlier, because the term had been used by all three sets of authors who wrote chapters on semantic memory in the 1972 volume. However, the lack of choice concerning the term 'semantic' did encourage me to look for an -ic adjective as the designation for the memory that was not semantic.

Personal episodes and their 'semantic' contents

Perhaps the most serious problem with the 1972 formulation of the distinction had to do with the lack of clear and definite ideas regarding the relation between autobiographical episodes and what might be called their 'contents'. I had somewhat preremptorily classified the large majority of laboratory experiments on memory that had been done up to that time as experiments on episodic memory. The reasoning was that in these experiments the subjects were tested for their knowledge of what they had seen or heard at a particular time in a particular situation, that this knowledge concerned co-occurrences of verbal symbols, and that the information acquired did not bring about changes in the subjects' semantic memory. I had also assumed that subjects had to remember the learning episode in order to be able to remember some part of it, such as a pair of to-be-remembered words, and that one could make safe inferences about the subjects' remembering of the learning episode on the basis of their ability to recall the material learned.

All these are questionable assumptions, or at least they point to problems whose complexity cannot be brushed aside with a few superficial statements or assumptions. I shall take up some of these problems later on in the book, although I will not be able to say much about them even now, because the realization that critical problems of this kind exist is of relatively recent origin.

At this juncture, it may be worth while to illustrate the nature of some

of the problems, by drawing on an interesting observation made by Warrington and Weiskrantz (1974). I shall describe the observation more fully
later in the book (p. 000), and, therefore, only summarize it in very
general terms here.

Warrington and Weiskrantz found that densely amnesic patients who
have great difficulty remembering recently studied material can nevertheless make use of information that they have acquired in the course of the
episode of studying the material. For instance, a patient may not be able
to identify an 'old' test word in recognition memory as a copy of a word
he saw earlier in the list, but he can produce the name of the word in
response to a perceptual or graphemic fragment of it more readily than he
could have done in the absence of the learning experience.

The Warrington–Weiskrantz effect brings into sharp focus the related
issues of the rememberer's awareness of a learning episode, his knowledge
of his own knowledge, and the objective effect of the learning episode on
the performance of a present cognitive task. In exactly what sense did
Warrington and Weiskrantz's amnesic patients 'remember' the words they
did not recognize but could efficiently produce in the word-fragment completion task? The patients' behavior suggests that they can utilize knowledge acquired on a particular occasion without being aware that they are
doing so, that is, without knowledge of their own knowledge. But if so,
are we justified in assuming that any other 'correct' memory performance
in an episodic-memory task necessarily conveys evidence about the individual's remembering the episode?

One possibility of 'explaining' the Warrington–Weiskrantz effect is to
assume that their patients' episodic memory is impaired but semantic memory is not, and that the efficient performance on the word-fragment completion test reflects the utilization of information that has been stored in
semantic memory. People do learn all sorts of things from personally experienced episodes that become part of their semantic memory, and we know
that the utilization of this knowledge is not predicated on, and usually does
not require, the retention of information about the learning episode itself. In
fact, a number of theorists (e.g. Kinsbourne and Wood 1975; Rozin 1976)
have suggested that amnesia is a condition in which episodic memory is
selectively impaired while semantic memory is less or not at all affected. The
Warrington–Weiskrantz effect thus would seem to provide direct support for
the episodic/semantic account of the amnesic syndrome.

There are several reasons why such a straightforward explanation should
not be adopted uncritically. First, the episodic/semantic theory of amnesia
has difficulty accounting for a number of amnesic phenomena (Schacter and
Tulving 1982; Warrington and Weiskrantz 1982). Second, there is no evidence that the Warrington–Weiskrantz effect implies transfer of information
to, or some change in, the amnesic patients' semantic memory. Third, if we
accepted the idea that utilization of information acquired on a particular
occasion, under conditions where the person cannot remember the occasion,

is mediated by the semantic-memory system, we might be tempted to assume that there is no fundamental distinction between episodic and semantic memory. For reasons to be discussed in Chapters 3 and 5, I am reluctant to do so.

The Warrington–Weiskrantz effect neatly illustrates the (possible) fallacy of the assumptions that (a) the rememberer must remember (be consciously aware) of an episode in order to be able to make use of (recall? recollect?) the information acquired in it, and (b) laboratory experiments in which people learn and retain verbal materials, or other kinds of isolated pieces of symbolically expressible knowledge, tap only the episodic-memory system. Now it seems somewhat more reasonable to separate the remembering of a personal episode from the knowledge of its 'semantic' contents, and to think that the former is mediated by, and reflects the operation of, the episodic system; whereas the latter is governed by the principles applying to, and reflects the operations of, the semantic system. By these criteria, most of the 'episodic-memory' experiments that have been done in psychological laboratories since Ebbinghaus tell us more about semantic memory than episodic memory. Indeed, one could argue that the scientific study of episodic memory, although initiated, is still waiting to be pursued seriously and vigorously.

Despite the shortcomings of the 1972 formulation, it did serve the function of encouraging students of memory to think about the implications of the distinction, and to seek and be alert to evidence potentially relevant to the question of whether episodic and semantic memory just appear to be different in some ways or whether they really are. In the next three chapters we look at the distinction from the point of view of our current knowledge. The ten years that have passed since the initial formulation have made it possible for us to engage in a somewhat more thorough and systematic analysis.

3
Argument for differences

In this chapter and the next two, I present and elaborate the proposal that episodic and semantic memory should be regarded as separate albeit closely interacting systems. We know more about episodic and semantic memory now than we did ten years ago, and therefore it is possible to discuss the issue in a somewhat more organized fashion. In discussing the matter, I follow the good advice of Roger Bacon who said that there are two methods of acquiring knowledge, argument and experiment. In this chapter I present the argument for the differences of the two systems; in Chapter 5, we shall examine relevant empirical and experimental evidence. The contents of this chapter, like the 1972 paper, represent what are essentially armchair speculations, casual observations, and fruits of intuition. Many specific arguments can be taken as starting points for further thought and analysis, and perhaps as an object of experimental study. Some of the arguments will undoubtedly turn out to be wrong, although it is not clear at the present time which ones they are.

Similarities

Before we go on to consider the differences between the systems, let us quickly summarize their similarities. These similarities are well known to all students of memory, as well as to most rememberers, but it may be worth recording them here for the sake of completeness of the account. Moreover, explicit mention of the similarities will help to temper the conclusion that I will arrive at, to the effect that episodic and semantic memories are different systems. When I argue for the differences, I do not wish to imply that the two systems have nothing in common, or that they are 'completely separate' or 'sharply different', whatever these expressions might mean.

Episodic and semantic systems are both *memory* systems: they have to do with the acquisition, retention, and utilization (conversion) of information and knowledge. A great deal of acquired information reaches the system through the senses, and much of it results from observations and other 'purely mental' activity. Retention of information in both systems is generally thought of as passive and automatic, it requires no ongoing effort or expenditure of energy. In both systems, information originally stored may be modified and altered as a result of related mental activity. The individual is usually not aware of the knowledge he possesses; this awareness is brought about by the retrieval of the information.

Retrieval of information from both systems is instigated by stimuli, questions, or cues. It is highly selective: a particular question or cue will activate or actualize only a very small amount of the total information that is potentially available for retrieval. People are not consciously aware of the retrieval process; only the products of retrieval become introspectively available. A great deal of the retrieved information from both systems can be described verbally. Some knowledge in both episodic and semantic systems, however, cannot readily be expressed in symbolic form: try to describe in words the face of a person you know well, or even a simple familiar object, such as a rocking chair, without referring to its function.

The similarities and parallels between episodic and semantic systems become particularly clear when we compare them with another memory system, that concerned with the acquisition and utilization of procedures and skills. The distinction between episodic and semantic memory on the one hand and memory for procedures and skills on the other is probably as important in the taxonomy of memory systems as that between episodic and semantic memory. Let us classify episodic and semantic memory as two systems of *propositional memory*, and think of the memory for procedures and skills as *procedural memory* (cf. Winograd 1975). I shall assume the separation between propositional and procedural memory as a fundamental given, although I can imagine how some psychologists may wish to disagree with the assumption.

The idea that the information stored in both episodic and semantic systems is represented, or representable, in the form of propositions is an old one (e.g. Clifford 1890). It has been elaborated in a sophisticated and detailed fashion in a number of contemporary theories of memory (e.g. Anderson and Bower 1973; Kintsch 1972; Rumelhart *et al.* 1972).

The format of representation of information underlying skills is unknown; but it is generally agreed that whatever it is, it is not propositional in nature. Terms such as habits, plans, and motor programs have been used to refer to the unknown substratum. The study of skills goes back to early pioneers such as Bryan and Harter (1897); improvement of sensory-perceptual skills lies at the root of many forms of non-propositional learning (Gibson 1953), and the important role that skills play in cognitive activities has been emphasized by several contemporary theorists (Kolers 1975*a*, *b*, 1976; Neisser, Novick, and Lazar 1963; Hirst, Spelke, Reaves, Caharack, and Neisser 1980; Chase and Ericsson 1981).

The propositional base of both episodic and semantic memory means that it is meaningful to ask questions about veridicality of knowledge stored in and retrieved from either system. Similar questions about procedural knowledge are meaningless. Furthermore, propositional knowledge can be thought about, contemplated introspectively, attended to internally; procedural knowledge cannot. Communication of knowledge retrieved from either the episodic or the semantic system to an external observer usually depends on the employment of natural language or some other symbol system; procedural knowledge can be communicated through non-symbolic behavior. Both episodic and semantic memories can be frequently acquired in a single act of perception or thought, whereas the acquisition of skills usually requires intensive practice.

As an illustration of the difference between the operations of the semantic-memory system and the procedural-memory system, consider the following thought experiment. You present the following list of items to a subject with a request to classify each item as a word or non-word as fast as he can: jargonelle, warrender, preconise, elyphoric, ornithurous, variosity, merganser, desponation, spirantize, facility, premotion, favorance. You record the subject's response and the decision latency for each item.

In this list, as it happens, all odd-numbered items represent words and all even-numbered items non-words, the definition of a 'word' being that it is an entry in the *Oxford English Dictionary*. The proportion of words and non-words correctly identified by the subject could be regarded as a measure of his performance on this semantic-memory task. This measure tells you something about the *information* stored in the subject's semantic memory. The decision time provides a measure of his *skill* in using that information in performing the task.

The two measures, one of semantic knowledge, the other of the skill in performing the task, are independent in the sense that repeated testing of the subject with the same list or comparable lists will not produce any changes in his semantic memory, nor in any measure of that knowledge, but it will change his skill in performing the task, reflected in the reduction of the decision time over successive test trials.

The results of the thought-experiment show that changes resulting from a particular kind of practice occur in one system, procedural memory, but not in the other, propositional memory. Similar demonstrations, both in the form of thought-experiments as well as real ones, can be, and have been, produced in comparisons of episodic memory and procedural memory. For instance, long after the learning of a paired-associate list is complete, in the sense that the subjects can respond with perfect accuracy, the latency of the response continues to decrease (e.g. Peterson 1965).

Having taken a quick look at the similarities and parallels between episodic and semantic systems, and their differences from the system or systems of procedural memory, we are now ready to start considering the ways in which episodic and semantic memory differ from one another.

Differences in information

A summary of features that distinguish episodic and semantic memory is shown in Table 3.1. The entries in the table are discussed and elaborated in what follows here. The diagnostic value of the features listed varies over

Table 3.1
Summary of differences between episodic and semantic memory

Diagnostic feature	Episodic	Semantic
Information		
Source	Sensation	Comprehension
Units	Events; episodes	Facts; ideas; concepts
Organization	Temporal	Conceptual
Reference	Self	Universe
Veridicality	Personal belief	Social agreement
Operations		
Registration	Experiential	Symbolic
Temporal coding	Present; direct	Absent; indirect
Affect	More important	Less important
Inferential capability	Limited	Rich
Context dependency	More pronounced	Less pronounced
Vulnerability	Great	Small
Access	Deliberate	Automatic
Retrieval queries	Time? Place?	What?
Retrieval consequences	Change system	System unchanged
Retrieval mechanisms	Synergy	Unfolding
Recollective experience	Remembered past	Actualized knowledge
Retrieval report	Remember	Know
Developmental sequence	Late	Early
Childhood amnesia	Affected	Unaffected
Applications		
Education	Irrelevant	Relevant
General utility	Less useful	More useful
Artificial intelligence	Questionable	Excellent
Human intelligence	Unrelated	Related
Empirical evidence	Forgetting	Analysis of language
Laboratory tasks	Particular episodes	General knowledge
Legal testimony	Admissible; eyewitness	Inadmissible; expert
Amnesia	Involved	Not involved
Bicameral men	No	Yes

a wide range. Some of the listed features may turn out to be irrelevant to the distinction, others may be and remain questionable, and still others may prove to provide highly significant evidence related to the distinction. At the present time, however, all of them should be considered as *hypotheses*, as possible starting points of discussion and evaluation rather than as marks on the final tally sheet.

The major weakness of armchair reflection on any problem lies in the absence of rules by which the results of the armchair thinker's contemplation of an issue can be judged to pertain to the world more than to himself.

It is quite possible, therefore, that individual readers may disagree with some of the claims that I will make in discussing the differences. But to the extent that we consider them as hypotheses that may be amenable to empirical tests, present agreements and disagreements are not particularly crucial.

The features of the two systems have been divided into three broad categories in Table 3.1. One has to do with the kind of information, or knowledge, handled by the two systems, the second concerns the operations of the systems, and the third pertains to what I, in the absence of a better term, have referred to as 'applications'. This division, like the selection of features to be considered, is somewhat arbitrary and therefore debatable. But I thought that at least an attempt to divide the potentially distinguishing features into different categories was useful, even if wrong in detail, since many people have tended to concentrate only on the kinds of information handled by the two systems, the characteristics of 'memories' that people have when they remember episodes or when they retrieve something from the semantic system. The three divisions of features indicate that there is more to the distinction than just the characteristics of these 'memories'. Thus, suggested differences in the properties and functioning of the two systems, as well as differences in 'applications', might be regarded as providing evidence against the hypothesis that the distinction between episodic and semantic memories refers to nothing more than two different types of information that the memory system handles.

Source

Much of the information and knowledge that is registered in both systems is derived from the external environment through the senses, although some may be provided internally by thoughts, introspection, imagination, and other 'higher' mental processes. But the two systems differ in the *immediate* source of the information they receive. A 'mere sensation' of some perceptual inhomogeneity in an otherwise homogeneous perceptual field is sufficient as a source of information into the episodic system, whereas such a meaningless and uninterpreted change in the perceptual environment is unlikely to be registered in the semantic system.

Feedback from information-seeking perceptual activities and goal-directed behavior may have priority of entry into the episodic system, but the perception and activity need not be meaningful, or not even a natural part of some ongoing series, in order to be registered. Occurrences of simple visual and auditory stimulus events, even if they are not readily identifiable and have no known purpose, can be registered in the system as sensory experiences that occurred in a particular place at a particular time (King 1972). In a laboratory experiment, in which a person is exposed to a series of to-be-remembered items, the *omission* of an item in the series, the occurrence of a 'blank', is an *event* that is registered in the episodic system even if it is not encoded in relation to existing knowledge, and even if the meaning of the occurrence is unknown.

Mere sensation of an input signal, on the other hand, is not sufficient for registering the corresponding information in the semantic system. For information to be stored in semantic memory, the content of the occurrence of the episode must be understood and comprehended, that is, related to existing knowledge. When a subject in a psychological experiment sees two words side by side, and is asked to remember the pair, he may be perfectly capable of recalling the pair in a later test, but it is unlikely that his knowledge, understanding, or comprehension of the words constituting the pair are changed as a consequence of their mere co-occurrence. Similarly, a person may hear a train whistle as it rushes by, and may well remember it, but the event does not change the semantic system: the person's knowledge of trains or whistles remains unchanged.

Both the episodic and semantic memory systems register only change; if some information already exists in the system, the same information is not entered again. A meaningless co-occurrence of two perceptual elements is registered in the episodic system, as long as there is no record already in existence of such an event, in that particular place at that particular time. The fact that the engine of a train can whistle may also be entered into the semantic system, if the system does not already contain such knowledge.

Units

The prototypical unit of information in the episodic system is an *event* or an *episode*. An event is something that occurs in a particular situation. It has always a beginning and an end in time, and the interval between the two temporal boundaries is filled with some activity, frequently but not always by one or more 'actors'. Events recorded in the episodic system always involve the rememberer, either as one of the actors or as an observer of the event. A person can witness or participate in events directly or vicariously. The remembering of vicariously experienced events—for instance, watching a play, reading a novel, or even comprehending a disembodied sentence such as 'a shabbily dressed man in his late fifties jumped off the Golden Gate bridge early this morning'—is governed by the same general principles that apply to the remembering of directly experienced events.

The *segmentation* of the stream of experience into events is governed by perceptual and cognitive skills acquired over a lifetime. The segmentation process not only orders events in time—one event precedes or follows another—but also creates events nested within others, as well as events that overlap partially in time. Simple events, such as seeing a flash of light or hearing an unfamiliar sound, can be easily described in terms of a particular change in the individual's perceptual environment. Complex events, such as a two-month-long trip round the world, are rich in detail and virtually impossible to describe in their entirety. Simple events can be described in terms of their perceptible properties alone, whereas the description of complex events requires interpretation of their components in terms of semantic memory.

It is much more difficult to name the basic units of information and knowledge in semantic memory. The problem lies in the fact that there are many 'basic' units that have been mentioned by the philosophers, psychologists, and cognitive scientists who have tried to describe that aspect of the human mind that we refer to as 'knowledge'. The suggestion that the prototypical units of knowledge in the semantic system are facts, or ideas, or concepts, or rules, or propositions, or schemata, or scripts, or something else, or some combination of these, does not do much justice to the fruits of all the past deliberations, but it does serve the purpose of differentiating the semantic units from the episodic units. Facts and other units of semantic memory, like events, can be described in propositional form, although sometimes the translation of propositions into verbal expressions is not easy.

Given the much greater complexity of semantic memory than episodic memory, and given the short amount of time that psychologists have systematically studied semantic memory, we should not despair of our present inability to specify 'the' basic unit of our knowledge of the world. For the time being, we shall have to live with the working hypothesis that what constitutes the 'basic' unit of semantic memory depends on the situation in which knowledge is actualized and the use to which it is put.

Organization

Organization of knowledge in the episodic system is temporal: one event precedes, co-occurs, or succeeds another in time. The organization is also relatively loose, in the sense that the initially precisely recorded information about an event can be easily changed or lost. Such change or loss of temporal information tends to affect short-lived simple events more drastically than extended complex events. A person may not remember the temporal relations between two short events in a longer series, but have little difficulty temporally placing one series in relation to another.

The organization of knowledge in the semantic system is governed by a wide variety of relations. For the lack of a good descriptive generic term that could serve as a label for all these relations, I am using the term 'conceptual' to describe the organization of semantic memory and to contrast it with the organization of episodic memory. Conceptual organization of semantic memory is tight: individual facts and ideas, once assigned to an appropriate place in the overall semantic structure, do not wander around freely in the structure. One consequence of this state of affairs is that, relative to the episodic system, most errors of utilization of knowledge from the semantic system are those of omission rather than commission.

Differences in the organization of the two systems have been noted by Estes (1976*b*) and by Lockhart, Craik, and Jacoby (1976), among others. Estes suggests that episodic memories are 'relatively unorganized', with the consequence that 'the constituent elements cannot be called up readily and systematically on command', whereas 'semantic or categorical memories are organized into a system that permits efficient retrieval' (Estes 1976*b*, p. 64).Lockhart *et al.*, reacting to my 1972 suggestion that episodic memory is structured in temporal and spatial terms, proceeded 'to offer the more radical suggestion that episodic memory has *no* inherent structure' (Lockhart *et al.* 1976, p. 82).

Reference

The suggestion that events in the episodic system are organized in time could also be expressed by saying that each event in the episodic system is referred to a particular instant, date, or period in time. But the referent is not chronological time or calendar time; rather, at the occurrence of the event, it is the rememberer's personally experienced time, and at recollection, his personal past.

William James considered the personal reference of memories as the most important defining feature of memory, which for him was what we here refer to as episodic memory. He expressed the matter in his inimitable fashion as follows:

And to 'refer' any special fact to the past epoch is to think that the fact *with* the names and events which characterize its date, to think it, in short, with a lot of contiguous associates. But even this would not be memory. Memory requires more than mere dating of a fact in the past. It must be dated in *my* past. In other words, I must think that I directly experienced its occurrence. It must have that 'warmth and intimacy' which were so often spoken of in the chapter on the Self, as characterizing all experiences 'appropriated' by the thinker as his own (James 1890, p. 650).

Claparède, the Swiss psychologist whom I mentioned earlier (p. 18), in connection with his distinction between two kinds of 'mental connection' in remembering, talked about connections 'established *mutually between representations*, and those established between *representations* and the *me*, the personality. In the case of purely passive associations or idea-reflexes, solely the first kind of connection operates; in the case of voluntary recall and recognition, where the *me* plays a role, the second kind of connection enters' (1911, p 71).

The role of episodic memories in defining an individual's personal identity has been discussed by both philosophers (e.g. Grice 1941; Shoemaker 1959) and psychologists (e.g. Greenwald 1981).

The knowledge recorded in the semantic system has no similar necessary connection to the knower's personal identity. Instead, it refers to the universe, or certain parts thereof, that may, although they need not, include the owner of the memory system. In many cases the knowledge an individual possesses may be connected to the external world only indirectly, rather than directly, but even the most abstract and abstruse bits of knowledge stand in the referential relation to the real world.

Veridicality

A person in the witness box says: 'Just as I entered the room, I saw the accused raising the gun, pointing it at the victim, and shooting him dead. The whole scene is clearly before my eyes; I doubt that I will ever forget it.' The witness knows that his memory is true, indeed, he is absolutely convinced of it. The strong feeling of the veridicality of the memory somehow is immediately given in the recollective experience, it is an integral part of the past event remembered now. The belief that the memory of the event corresponds to the actual event, or that it faithfully reflects those aspects of the event that are now remembered, need not be inferable from other knowledge. The basis of such a belief is a deep mystery. Since the rememberer usually has no way of comparing his memory of the event with the original, the belief cannot be based on the results of a comparison process. Moreover, since it is quite possible for a person to 'remember' as true something that in fact is false, it is not possible for us to argue that the belief in the veridicality of a remembered event represents simply the retention of something recorded at the time when the original event took place.

Retrieved semantic knowledge seldom possesses the intensely felt subjective veridicality that characterizes episodic memories. We know that something we know about the world is true but the judgment is usually based on our assessment of the relation of the fact to other related facts in semantic memory. When others tell us that something we have known about the world is wrong, we may be persuaded by the evidence that speaks to the issue; we do not struggle against changing our beliefs. When the same external referees point out a similar discrepancy in our memory belief concerning a particular past episode that we clearly remember, our subjective feeling of veridicality of the recollective experience remains unchanged even when we intellectually accept the verdict of others.

Differences in operations

We will next consider a number of possible differences between the episodic and semantic systems that have less to do with the type of information handled and more with the properties and *modus operandi* of the systems. The line between the informational and functional characteristics of the system is a fine one. Some of the features discussed under 'information'—for instance, the problem of veridicality of retrieved knowledge—might have been discussed with equal justification under the 'operations'. In some sense, we are just looking at two sides of the same coin when we separate the information handled by the system from the way it is handled. Yet some of the items considered under the heading of 'operations' do represent characteristics of the system that are independent of the information.

The caveat I made earlier still applies: the discussion that follows is speculative. The discussed differences represent hypotheses rather than firm assertions of any kind.

Registration

The process of registration of information into the two systems is closely related to the question of the source of the two kinds of information we discussed earlier. Here I wish to emphasize the point that the registration of information into the episodic system is more direct than that into the semantic system. The episodic system is capable of recording and retaining information about perceptible properties of stimuli that can be apprehended immediately by the senses. It is in this sense that we could say that registration in the episodic system is 'experiential'.

The information registered in the semantic system, on the other hand, is frequently given to us in symbolic form, expressed in natural or some other language. What is registered in the semantic system is not perceptible properties of the input signals, but rather the information about the cognitive referents of the signals. Episodic memory registers what we might call immediate, or first-hand knowledge, whereas semantic memory records mediate or second-hand knowledge.

Bertrand Russell, among others, discussed this difference between episodic and semantic memory some time ago. He thought that sensation, immediate memory, and 'true memory' all lie on one continuous dimension. All these various forms of experiencing, Russell said, 'give knowledge which is, in some degree and with appropriate limitations, independent of extraneous evidence. But most of the knowledge of people with any degree of education is not of any of these kinds. We know what we have been told or have read in books or newspapers; here words come first, and it is often necessary to realize what the words mean' (Russell 1948, p. 112).

The point is that language plays a much more important role in recording information into the semantic system than into the episodic system. This, of course, does not mean that human beings and other organisms cannot acquire knowledge about the world without relying on language, any more than it means that all semantic memory is language-bound. But language greatly facilitates transmission of knowledge from one person to another, as well as from one generation to the next, and hence a great deal of knowledge that we have of the world has been acquired in this form.

Temporal coding

We have already discussed the temporal organization of the information in the episodic system and the conceptual organization in the semantic system. With respect to the functional properties of the system, this distinction resolves into one according to which the episodic system has the capability of keeping track of the temporal succession and dating of incoming information, and retaining this information over time, whereas the semantic system has no such capability.

When an event occurs, its encoding may include reference to other similar or related events, and the corresponding information is recorded as part of the trace of the event. The rememberer can judge the relative recency of two events, since the original trace of the earlier event does not include any reference to the occurrence of the later one, whereas the original trace of the later event may include a reference to the earlier one. Although this 'pure' state of affairs may be affected by the process of recoding (which we will discuss on page 164), at least it does provide a potential basis for judgments recency of events. Direct estimation of relative recencies of two unrelated events is difficult, because the relevant information is unlikely to be recorded in the system at the time of the occurrence of the events; relative recency discrimination of related events, on the other hand, is easier (Tzeng and Cotton 1980).

The semantic system handles temporal concepts as it does others, with reference to the world that exists independently of the individual. In that world events have temporal relations, but these relations have nothing to do with personal time. Whereas temporal relations of events in episodic memory are recorded experientially in subjective time, propositions entailing temporal relations in semantic memory are represented symbolically in abstract time. To illustrate: a student in the history of psychology class is told that Freud was born at Freiberg, Moravia, in 1856; a week later he learns that Pavlov was born at Ryazan in 1849. In his personal time, the event of having found out about Freud's birthdate precedes the comparable event of learning about Pavlov's birthdate. However, in response to the appropriate question, he may be able to express his knowledge that Pavlov's birth preceded Freud's.

Affect

Relatively little psychological work has been done, or thought expanded, on the problem of the relation between affect and memory, and what work has been done has been mute on the role of affect in, or relation of affect to, the two forms of memory we are discussing here (e.g. Bower 1981; Rapaport 1950; Zajonc 1979). However, both on the basis of casual observations as well as intuition, it makes sense to assume that only episodic memory has affective components, or at least that affect plays a more important role in the episodic than in the semantic system. Personal experiences are often 'emotional', or take place while the person is in a particular mood, and information about the state of the rememberer may be recorded as part of the memory trace of the event. This affective component of the memory trace may then play a role in the retrieval of information about the event (Bower 1981). A person may also read about material, or vicariously experience events, that arouse an emotional state, and the information thus acquired may be 'emotional' to the extent that the episodic affect is conditioned to the semantic content of the episode.

In light of the importance of the problem of the relation between affect and memory, and the important and interesting work that has recently been done (e.g. Bower 1981; Zajonc 1980), it seems safe to predict that a fertile ground of discovery awaits psychologists who decide to study the role of affect in episodic and semantic memory.

Inferential capability

By inferential capability I mean the capability of a system to extract more information from an input than is explicitly provided. Since extraction of something that is not in what is given is logically impossible, the 'extraction' process is better thought of as addition of information from the store to the information conveyed by the input, and treating the addition as a part of the original.

The episodic system is relatively limited in its inferential capability. If you wish to remember that the great idea about practice effects in reaction time came to you while you were listening to Sibelius's Second Symphony at a concert in the town hall on a Wednesday night in the early summer, you had better remember that event as it happened; it cannot be deduced from the rest of your episodic memory, nor from your knowledge of the world. Similarly, if you wish to remember that this idea came to you *after* you had read the interesting book about prediction and understanding in science at one sitting one Sunday afternoon in the garden, you better do that in that form, too; the order of the two episodes cannot be inferred from any other knowledge. On the other hand, if you are told that 'three turtles rested on a floating log, and a fish swam beneath them', you also know that the fish swam beneath the log, even though that information was not in the message you received (Bransford, Barclay, and Franks 1972). The statement that the inferential capability of the episodic system is limited means that events are what they are, they occur when they occur, and knowledge about their contents and temporal dates to other events need not be deducible from other knowledge. However, to the extent that some daily events are part of a regular routine, inferences can be made about them on the basis of the knowledge of the routine stored in semantic memory. Moreover, to the extent that episodes 'contain' some factual or semantic content, inferences about the contents of episodes can be made on the same basis that apply to semantic memory.

Whenever it looks as if episodic information is retrieved through inferences, it turns out that inferences are made on the basis of knowledge of
the world. For instance, Kolers and Palef (1976) found that people made
faster negative than positive responses to questions about whether they
had visited certain cities. Such efficient 'knowing not' implies that negative
responses are not given as a consequence of failure of finding the named
city in a list of cities that the respondent in fact had visited. Kolers and
Palef interpreted their results as implicating certain analytical procedures.
Thus, a respondent can make a fast negative response when asked about
a city in a country, or on a continent, that he has not visited. The response
to a question about episodic memory is based on an inference made on
the basis of knowledge of geography.

Similarly, Brown, Lewis, and Monk (1977) have described three experiments demonstrating that subjects in a recognition-memory situation correctly reject highly memorable distractors more confidently than they
reject less memorable items. It is as if the subjects reasoned that if the
highly memorable item (for instance the name of a family member) had
in fact occurred in the list, they certainly would have remembered it. Since
they do not, it must be a distractor. The Brown *et al.* finding illustrates
inferential reasoning in an episodic-memory task, but inferences are based
on the subjects' knowledge about how their memory works; the finding
illustrates the operation of meta-memory (Flavell and Wellman 1977).

The semantic-memory system possesses a rich inferential capability.
Because of the tightly organized conceptual knowledge structures that
characterize the semantic system, and the availability of implicit and
explicit rules for making inferences, it is quite possible for the rememberer
to know many things that were never entered directly into his semantic
system. Evidence shows that people are capable of making inferences even
from the subtlest of cues (e.g. Harris and Monaco 1978; Loftus and Zanni
1975).

Context dependency

Context dependency refers to the tendency for the processing of a unit of
information (e.g. its encoding, or retrieval) to be influenced by other units
of information that are present at the time of processing. It is generally
thought that the operation of the episodic system is more context-dependent than the operation of the semantic system. It has sometimes been proposed that the principal characteristic of the episodic system lies in its
handling of 'contextualized' knowledge, and that the semantic knowledge
is 'decontextualized'.Thus, for instance, Kintsch has suggested that 'episodic memory is context-dependent, in the sense that it is available only
in the presence of rather specific contextual retrieval cues. On the other
hand, semantic memory refers to general knowledge. The original context
of acquisition, and hence the personal reference, is no longer of any sig-

nificance, because general knowledge can be retrieved and used in a wide variety of contexts' (Kintsch 1980, p. 596). Experimental evidence, too, has been produced in support of the proposition that context plays a more important role in episodic than semantic encoding (e.g. Ehrlich 1979).

I am listing context dependency as one of the possible differentiating features of episodic and semantic memory, although I am not convinced that the picture is as clear as is sometimes assumed. Although context dependency in episodic memory can readily be demonstrated, similar demonstrations are not unknown in semantic-memory tasks (e.g. Conrad 1974; Marcel 1980; McKoon and Ratcliff 1979; Schvaneveldt, Meyer, and Becker 1976). 'Context' has many meanings, and its manipulations and variations in experiments can take many forms. Even within a particular memory system, certain changes in context may affect one kind of memory performance and not another. For instance, changes in both the drug state (e.g. Eich 1980), and in the physical environment (e.g. Baddeley 1976, pp. 74–5; Godden and Baddeley 1975; Smith, Glenberg, and Bjork 1978) can be shown to affect recall but not recognition.

The question of whether episodic and semantic systems can be differentiated in terms of context dependency is a complex one and unlikely to be decisively resolved one way or another. My own present impression is that context dependency may not turn out to be an important diagnostic: in many ways, acquisition and utilization of our knowledge of the world may be as context-dependent as is our knowledge of the past.

Vulnerability

Information stored in the episodic system is more vulnerable—it is changed, modified, and lost more readily—than is the information in the semantic system. There are several reasons for such a state of affairs. First, a great deal of the information in the semantic system is overlearned, in contrast to much of the information in the episodic system that is based on single episodes. Second, the relatively looser organization of the information in the episodic than in the semantic system may contribute to its greater vulnerability. Third, the richness of combinations of cognitive elements characterizing any particular episode, in comparison with the much more streamlined and abstract knowledge-packages in the semantic system, may be regarded as yet another source of the ease with which information in the episodic system is modified, recoded, and erased.

As is the case with many of the other differences we are discussing here, the hypothesis of differential vulnerability to interference of the two systems holds only in a statistical sense. This means that if we could measure the vulnerability of all the information in both systems, and express the result on some absolute scale, the episodic system would show greater vulnerability. Or even if we could somehow identify prototypical bits of episodic and semantic knowledge, we would expect to find that the former are changed and forgotten more readily than the latter. It is perfectly possible, of course, that many episodes and aspects of episodes are re- membered better than many parts of semantic knowledge.

Access

Access to, or actualization of, information in the episodic system tends to be deliberate and usually requires conscious effort, whereas in the seman- tic system it tends to be automatic. A perceptual change in the person's environment—appearance of a stimulus object, a change in the current situation, a verbal utterance or instruction, and so on—is immediately, and in the first instance, responded to and interpreted in terms of semantic knowledge. The same stimulus reminds a person of a particular episode only when the individual's mind is in a particular state; the episodic system must be in the 'retrieval mode' before a stimulus change in the environ- ment can serve as an effective retrieval cue to stored episodic information.

For instance, if you meet a friend unexpectedly, your likely reaction to the encounter will consist of wonderment why the friend, in terms of what you know about him or her, should be in that particular place at that par- ticular time. The sight of the friend is less likely to immediately trigger the memory of any particular previous occasion where you met him or her. An even clearer illustration of differential access to the two systems is pro- vided by people's reactions to words. When we hear words in conversation, or read them in print, or even when we encounter single words in psy- chology experiments, we become aware of their meaning instantly and effortlessly, but do not usually think of episodes from the past that could be described in the words we see or hear. It is a relatively simple matter, however, to set up a situation in which the presentation of single words has the effect of making people recollect particular events from the past (Crovitz and Schiffman 1974; Robinson 1976; Teasdale and Fogarty 1979). Instructions from others, certain physiological and emotional states, as well as the absence of goal-directed cognitive activity may place the epi- sodic system into the 'retrieval mode', with the consequence that particular stimulus events, which provide automatic access to semantic codes, are treated as retrieval cues setting off the more deliberate retrieval process in episodic memory.

Retrieval queries

The general form of the retrieval query directed at the episodic system is, 'What did you do at time *T* in place *P*?' 'Doing' referred to means cognitive activities—seeing, hearing, perceiving, imagining, thinking—as well as all sorts of overt behavior. Note that the query specifically refers to the person to whom it is directed: 'What did *you* do?'

Variants of the general query in experimental situations include instruc- tions such as (a) 'What objects did you see on the table?' (b) 'What word was (did you see) beside *earthquake*?' and (c) 'Did you hear the sentence Aardvarks eat ants?' The time and place of the occurrence of the events in these questions is an implicit part of the query.

In real life the queries addressed to rememberers of episodes also represent variants of the same general form: 'What did he say then?' 'What happened after she left?' 'Were they surprised?', and so on, all questions implying a particular place and a particular time, and the rememberer's presence there.

The general form of the query directed at the semantic system, on the other hand, is, 'What is X?' where X refers to an object, a concept, a property or characteristic, a relation, a situation, and so on. The questions are satisfactorily answered by naming X, assigning it to a category, describing one or more of its prominent characteristics, comparing it with Y, and so on. Neither the question nor the answer need to imply anything at all about the respondent's personal activity entailing X on a particular occasion. Many variants of the general form of the retrieval query addressed to the semantic system, too, are possible, including questions to which the respondent can answer with a simple Yes or No.

Retrieval consequences

Answering a question about an episode tends to (a) change the information that was stored about the episode, or to 'recode' its memory trace, and (b) make it more likely that the same question, or one related to it, can be answered on a subsequent occasion. Retrieval of information from episodic memory in response to implicit or self-generated queries—'thinking about' or reviewing the event in one's mind—produces consequences comparable to those resulting from responses to explicit questions.

Retrieval of information from semantic memory produces less readily detectable consequences. Knowledge in the semantic system is not changed as a consequence of its actualization. Forgetting, of course, occurs in the semantic system as it does in the episodic, and actualization of a given bit of semantic knowledge may counteract the effects of the processes responsible for forgetting. But in general the retrieval consequences in semantic memory are negligible.

Access time to information in semantic memory may be reduced as a consequence of retrieval. When one and the same retrieval query is addressed to the system, the answer may require progressively less time (e.g. Anderson and Ross 1980; Jacoby 1978). This finding may reflect the enhanced efficiency of cognitive skills involved in responding to retrieval queries, it may indicate that after the initial response subsequent answers to the question are based on information retrieved from the episodic system, or both. Changes in the amount of time required for answering retrieval queries need not imply changes in the knowledge or its organization in the semantic system.

Retrieval mechanisms

Retrieval mechanisms refer to the nature of processes that are involved in and responsible for actualization of latent knowledge. Since virtually nothing is known about them, I can do no better than speculate about the possibility that retrieval mechanisms might be different in episodic and semantic memory.

In the episodic system, the mechanism entails a synergistic process in which the information available in the retrieval environment, including the retrieval cue, is *combined* with the information stored in episodic memory to bring about a product that contains information from both sources. I have more to say about these speculative thoughts in Chapters 9 and 14. In semantic memory, on the other hand, retrieval mechanism may entail a process in which the retrieval query or cue serves primarily an instigating function, and the process serves to actualize the dispositional knowledge-structures, or to bring about their 'unfolding' in a manner governed primarily by the nature of stored knowledge.

Although differences in retrieval mechanisms in episodic and semantic memory may exist and be eventually identified, at the present time we also have good reasons to believe that the similarities between the two kinds of retrieval mechanisms are likely to be at least as noticeable as their differences. Whatever differences may be found are likely to be differences in degree rather than in kind. If so, retrieval mechanisms would not constitute a critical diagnostic.

Recollective experience

Remembered events are felt by rememberers to be personal experiences that belong to the autogenous past, whereas 'actualized' knowledge from semantic memory represents an impersonal experience bound to the present moment. Remembered past events somehow 'belong' to the rememberer; even when not accompanied by the feeling of 'warmth and intimacy' of which William James spoke, they tend to have a definite affective tone that is uniquely and unmistakably one of the salient attributes of recollective experiences. A similar feeling tone is missing in the actualization of knowledge of things we know about the world, even when these 'things' refer to personally significant objects or people we know. We may, of course, react with 'warmth and intimacy' to the physical presence of these objects or people, or thoughts about them; the feelings are missing from our *knowledge* of them as a part of the world.

Retrieval report

Because of the close connection between terms such as 'remember' and 'know' in our language, they are frequently used interchangeably when people express their knowledge. But by and large, the terms are used differently when we report to outsiders on the knowledge we have retrieved from the episodic or semantic system. We tend to use the word 'remember' for episodes, and the word 'know' for semantic memories. You remember the red car travelling at approximately forty miles an hour when it hit the pedestrian on the crosswalk, you remember visiting the hospital, you remember the smile on a friend's face when you told him about your adventure, and you remember seeing a particular word in a list in a memory experiment. Thus, you remember what you did (saw, heard, observed, felt, thought, and so on) on an earlier occasion. We may use the term 'know' when we refer to episodic memory, but such usage typically serves to alert the listener to some special implication of the statement, such as extreme confidence in the veridicality of the memory, an inference based on something remembered, and the like.

When we talk about our knowledge of the world, however, we do usually use the term 'know'. You know that grass is green and that no light is emitted by black holes, that after winter comes spring and that the velocity of sound is much greater in water than in air, that sugar tastes sweet, and that desferoxamine may help people with Alzheimer's disease. Again, the use of 'remember' carries special implications. For instance, if you say that you remember that the speed of sound is greater in water than in air, you emphasize the fact that you have not yet forgotten the fact once learned in school. If you say that you remember that sugar tastes sweet, you are telling your listener that you have not tasted it for a very long time. But if someone tells you that he 'remembers' that water is a colorless liquid, or that most people sleep at night, you are fully justified in wondering about the state of his mind.

Developmental sequence

Most writers on the topic assume that our semantic knowledge is based on episodic experiences. Listen, for instance, to Kintsch: 'There is the problem of how general knowledge (semantic memory) develops on the basis of particular experiences (episodic memory)' (Kintsch 1974, p. 79). A comparable statement appears in a discussion of children's conceptual development: 'The fact that conceptual knowledge in the child appears to be based upon personal experiences or 'episodes' may well mean that semantic memory has its origins in and grows out of episodic memory' (Anglin 1977, p. 253).

Yet several writers have suggested that both phylogenetically and ontogenetically semantic memory develops *before* episodic memory. Kinsbourne and Wood (1975), for instance, have pointed out that people learn 'word meanings and other such semantic information before there is any evidence of episodic remembering', and that even if we assumed the view of a unitary memory, 'its capability for episodic remembering represents a more advanced state of the system than does its capability for semantic remembering' (Kinsbourne and Wood 1975, p. 284).

Similar observations were made by Schachtel (1947) who, in the course of his discussion of the intellectual development of infants and children, emphasized the importance of the processes of differentiation and specialization. He then went on to say: 'Memory is a relatively late product of this whole process of differentiation and specialization. Autobiographical memory—that is the ability for voluntary recall of one's past life—is one of the latest developments in childhood, which is not surprising since it is part of the awareness of self, a capacity found only in man, and even in adult man usually not very well developed.' Schachtel also suggested that the child's concept of self 'hardly develops before the third year' (p. 15), long after the child has accumulated a tremendous amount of knowledge about the world around him.

The absence of episodic memory in young children may be related to their inability to keep track of the order of events in their personal past. This inability is reflected in their tendency to refer to the past with a single word such as 'yesterday' (Fraisse 1963, p. 159). The difficulty that children have with the temporal organization of their personal memories has also been described by Piaget: 'When a child of between two and four years old wants to retell the story of the walk, a visit to some friends, or his adventures on a journey, a multitude of juxtaposed details stumble forth incoherently; each one is associated with others in couples or little successions, but their overall order escapes the habits of our mind' (Piaget 1946, p. 261, cited in Fraisse 1963, pp. 159–60).

In connection with the problem of the development of human episodic memory, it is interesting to speculate about the implications of certain observations made by Douglas (1975) concerning the effects of hippocampal damage to spontaneous alternation behavior in young rats. In the spontaneous-alternation paradigm, the animal is given two test trials a day in a T-maze in the absence of any external reward. In this free-choice task, tame adult rats show a consistent preference on the second trial for the arm of the maze not chosen on the first trial, selecting the opposite alley approximately 85 per cent of the time.

We may think of the spontaneous-alternation paradigm as a test or manifestation of episodic memory: for the animal to choose the opposite arm of the maze, it is necessary for it to 'remember' which of the two arms it entered on the preceding trial.

Douglas relied on three separate pieces of evidence to arrive at the conclusion that the alternation behavior typical of an adult rat is critically dependent on the functions of the hippocampus. First, the typical alternation behavior—that is, the choice of the previously unselected arm some 85 per cent of the time—develops only slowly after birth. Young rats (less than 18 days old or so) exhibit chance performance only, selecting the previously unselected arm of the maze 50 per cent of the time; however, by the time they have reached about 45 days of age, they show the normal adult alternation behavior. Second, bilateral hippocampal lesions completely eliminate alternation behavior. The third piece of evidence comes from experiments such as Altman and Das (1966) who observed post-natal changes in the neuroanatomy of the hippocampus in rats and mice.

If we think of alternation behavior as a manifestation of episodic memory, we can reach the conclusions that (a) episodic memory is absent in very young rats, (b) it develops slowly after birth, reaching the adult level of maturation at about 45 days, and (c) this maturational progression is governed by neuroanatomical changes in the hippocampus.

Douglas, indeed, did suggest that a development of the ability for alternation behavior similar to that in rats takes place in humans: the pattern of alternation behavior typical of adults can be observed in older children but not in younger. The critical age is approximately 48 months. Below that age most children perseverate, that is, choose the same response on the second trial that they chose on the first, whereas above that age most children tend to alternate, selecting the previously unselected response.

Childhood amnesia

A possible difference between episodic and semantic memory, not altogether unrelated to some other suggested distinctions, was mentioned by Schachtel (1947) who pointed out that the well-known phenomenon of childhood amnesia applies only to what he called, as Freud and Proust had done before him, 'autobiographical' memory. Schachtel said that, 'It is only with regard to this memory that the striking phenomenon of childhood amnesia and the less obvious difficulty of recovering any past experience may be observed. There is no specific childhood amnesia as far as the remembrance of words learned and of objects and persons recognized is concerned' (Schachtel 1947, p. 5). It may well be, of course, as Schachtel himself points out, that the difference here is attributable to the frequent review and use of the general knowledge, coupled with less frequent recovery of information about the personal past. But since differential retrieval-induced recoding effects may in themselves be regarded as attributable to functional differences between the two systems, Schachtel's observation concerning childhood amnesia may still be considered relevant.

Differences in applications

Education

Children and people of all ages go to school in order to learn skills and knowledges that they need for life. They do not go to school in order to acquire a storehouse of temporally dated personal memories. At least so it is in theory. In practice, as we well know, most people remember their personal experiences from their school days, things that they did outside school and people they knew, much better than they remember the contents of their courses and lessons.

I have met people who, upon hearing that I teach psychology at the University of Toronto, volunteer the information that they, too, 'once' took one or more courses in psychology. Sometimes, when I have asked them, 'What courses?' they cannot tell. They do not remember the name of the course, the subject matter it covered, the professor's name, or any other thing about the course. An optimist might think that even these people still have retained some tacit knowledge from the experience, things that they know even though they cannot verbalize them; pessimists will have their suspicions confirmed that schools and universities are devices for keeping children out of their parents' hair and young people out of the overcrowded labor market.

In my 1972 paper, I very briefly considered the implications of the episodic/semantic distinction for the applicability of psychologists' knowledge of learning and remembering processes to education. 'If it is true that past research in human learning and memory has been concerned primarily with episodic memory, and if it is true that classroom learning has little to do with students' remembering personally experienced events, then it is not surprising that empirical facts and theoretical ideas originating in the verbal learning and human memory laboratories have little bearing on theory and practice of acquisition of knowledge' (Tulving 1972, p. 401).

This judgment, in retrospect, seems a bit harsh. Understanding of the principles governing the remembering of events may not have much relevance to classroom education, but since many verbal learning and memory experiments have been concerned with the acquisition, retention, and transfer of verbal and other symbolic contents of events, past research has not been entirely irrelevant. Explicit acknowledgement of the distinction between episodic and semantic memory, nevertheless, may make a positive contribution to the improvement of education and the betterment of learning in classrooms.

Even more useful, however, may turn out to be the distinction between propositional and procedural memories. Skills and procedures learned in school—reading, writing, and arithmetic, and their higher-level equivalents—are better retained and more useful to people in life than is most of the propositional knowledge. A person who has learned how to learn and study in school, how to use sources of information, how to solve problems, and other similar skills, is much better equipped for what awaits him or her after school than is a hypothetical individual who has perfectly memorized everything in the curriculum.

General utility

Knowledge of the world, by and large, is more useful to people than are personal memories.

The evidence for this claim comes from an imaginary experiment. In the experiment, subjects were deprived of the use of either their episodic or their semantic memory system; their ability to function in the day-to-day envi-

ronment and workaday world were observed and measured, and their introspective feelings about the severity of deprivation noted. The subjects
represented a large random sample from the general population between
the ages of 10 and 75. The design of the experiment was within-subjects:
each subject served twice in each of the two conditions of the experiment,
according to an A–B–B–A design. The details of the experimental manipulation of the temporary but otherwise complete suppression of the activity
in the two memory systems still represent classified information, and cannot
be divulged at this time. But the results of the experiment were clear: both
the assessment of the subjects' behavior and their introspective reports
showed that loss of the use of the episodic system turned out to be less of
a handicap than the loss of the use of the semantic-memory system. Indeed,
many subjects could not function at all when they were deprived of the use
of their semantic-memory system.

Artificial intelligence

Although some theorists are optimistic about the prospects of endowing
computers with episodic memories (e.g. Schank and Kolodner 1979) I am
sceptical. I rather doubt that computers' memories can ever even approximate people's remembering of personal events. Consider, for instance,
Schank and Kolodner's wish to converse with the computer about its visit
to a museum and meeting an important person there. We can certainly tell
computers a great deal about visiting museums, and meeting important
people, and we can even tell them that they themselves have done both.
Eventually we may be able to do it so well that the computer could hold
an intelligent conversation with human beings on these topics. Nevertheless, we know that computers would only be manipulating certain symbols
according to certain rules, they would be talking only about words, rather
than about original experiences organized temporally in their personal past
and related to their sense of personal identity, or continuity in subjective
time. A computer telling us about meeting Pope John Paul II at the
Museum of Modern Art in New York city is like a child telling us about
accompanying Alice on her trip to Wonderland: we believe that some
information from the system is used to produce a particular output, but
we would not expect to be able to verify the existence of the real-world
referents of the units of information as expressed, even if we could travel
backwards in time.

   Great strides, however, have been made in endowing computers with
semantic memories in a form that makes it possible for them to utilize their
knowledge in the peculiarly human form, and to communicate this knowledge to humans in the humans' language. Indeed, if we scan the column
of key words and phrases under the heading of 'semantic' in Table 3.1, or
review what has been said about the semantic system in this discussion of
differences between the two systems, we can readily see how well the
description of semantic memory characterizes the artificial intelligence of

computers. (For an interesting discussion of some other differences between computer and human memories, the reader is referred to Estes (1980).)

Human intelligence

The relation of human intelligence to the distinction between episodic and semantic memory should be mentioned, if for no other reason then as a complement to the discussion of artificial intelligence. Memory ability has traditionally been regarded as a component of intelligence, although not a very important component. For understandable reasons, students of intelligence have not as yet considered the distinction between episodic and semantic memory in their theories (e.g. Sternberg and Detterman 1979). Intuition tells us that intelligence, in most if not all of its definitions (Sternberg 1979), is more closely related to semantic than episodic memory. Future research may provide empirical tests of this hypothesis.

Empirical evidence

The two memory systems differ with respect to the kind of empirical evidence that psychologists rely on in studying them. Evidence relevant to the understanding of episodic memory is provided by forgetting: discrepancies between the rememberer's knowledge of a past event now and the knowledge of the same event on a subsequent occasion. Psychologists have something worth while to say about memory only because there is usually a discrepancy between what an individual remembers at one time, say immediately after 'learning', and at some later time. Changes in what the individual remembers, and how well he remembers some specified part of the original experience, provide empirical water for the theoretical mill. If there were no discrepancies between initial experiences and consequent memories, or early memories and late memories, then psychologists would have no more to say about episodic memory than they do about recording devices such as cameras and video-tape recorders. Students of episodic memory are greatly concerned with accuracy of retrieval; they infer properties of the system from the number and type of errors revealed in memory performance.

Since the study of semantic memory is still in its infancy, it is not yet entirely clear what is, or what should be, the evidential basis for theoretical statements about semantic memory. What is clear is that it is not the same as that of episodic memory. Students of semantic memory do not correlate what the person perceives or remembers now with what he remembers later on. Forgetting, however conceived, is of little interest to the student of semantic memory. Semantic-memory theorists are concerned with the analysis of meanings of words, meanings of sentences, relation of verbal utterances to the real world, and drawing of inferences from verbal statements, as well as some other issues (Smith 1978). A good deal of information about the workings of semantic memory is derived from intuition, introspection, and relatively casual questioning of others (e.g. Collins and Quillian 1972; Rumelhart *et al.* 1972). Other evidence comes from experiments in which people sort words into meaningful categories (e.g. Miller 1969), express their familiarity with letter strings (e.g. Rubenstein, Garfield, and Millikan 1970), name objects (e.g. Lachman 1973; Lachman, Shaffer, and Hennrikus 1974), verify the truth of sentences (e.g. Anderson and Bower 1973; Meyer 1973; Smith, Shoben, and Rips 1974), and the like. A large bulk of this work has to do with people's knowledge of language; it would be difficult to do with non-verbal organisms.

Laboratory tasks

Given the close relation between the two systems, it is probably as difficult to find 'pure' episodic-memory tasks and 'pure' semantic tasks as it is to find sodium and chlorine as free elements in nature, although their compound, NaCl, is found in abundance. Most experienced and remembered events have factual contents whose characteristics are greatly influenced by semantic memory; performance on semantic tasks, on the other hand, may be influenced by episodic information.

Nevertheless, an initial classification of tasks is possible on the basis of our present understanding of the nature of the two systems. The general rule is this: if successful performance on the task is not possible in the absence of retained information from a particular episode, the task is classified as an 'episodic' task; if successful performance on the task is possible in the absence of information from any particular episode, the task is classified as a 'semantic' one. By this rule, conventional recall and recognition tasks, in which the rememberer must produce the name, or identify as 'old', a copy of an item encountered on an earlier occasion in a particular situation, are classified as episodic. On the other hand, situations in which the individual has to assign words or objects to particular categories, classify letter strings as words or non-words, or identify words from their graphemic fragments represent semantic tasks.

Dependent variables in most episodic-memory experiments have been concerned with the discrepancy between input into and output from the system, that is, with the accuracy of 'reproduction'; the dependent variable in most experiments on semantic memory to date has been reaction time, that is, the time necessary to initiate or to complete a response. Reaction time has been used in those episodic-memory experiments in which the subjects always respond and the responses are regarded as 'correct'; proportions of correct responses have been used as a dependent variable in semantic-memory experiments in which subjects' responses are not always 'correct'.

Legal testimony

According to generally accepted rules of evidence in courts of law, testimony of eyewitnesses must concern matters pertaining to the case of which they have personal knowledge. Usually the court is not interested in what the witness knows about those parts of the world that are related to the particular case about which it is trying to establish the truth, in the legal sense. The hearsay rule excludes second-hand knowledge as acceptable evidence. The law of evidence is exceedingly complex (e.g. Cross 1974; Wigmore 1961), and even its individual elements cannot be readily summarized. Nevertheless, we would not be too far off the mark if we concluded that courts of law are willing to accept as evidence only some of the witnesses' episodic knowledge and none of their semantic knowledge. Yarmey (1979, p. 23) puts it simply: 'The hearsay rule says that the witness must testify only about matters that he has seen, heard, touched, tasted, or smelled. If a witness reports second-hand knowledge of what he has heard others say, his testimony is considered hearsay evidence.'

The testimony of the so-called expert witnesses, of course, is taken from their knowledge of the world. Thus, the relevance of the distinction between episodic and semantic memory to legal testimony could also be expressed by saying that for the testimony of eyewitnesses to be relevant it must be based on episodic memory, for that of expert witnesses, on semantic memory.

The general definition of the hearsay rule is that any statement that has been made outside the courtroom and offered as potentially relevant to the truth of the matter is hearsay and inadmissible. Whether or not a statement of this kind is defined to be hearsay, however, depends on whether it is or is not offered to prove the asserted facts. For example, assume that an accused charged with murder gives testimony that the victim had threatened to kill the accused. If this statement is offered as proof of the intentions of the victim, now dead, the evidence would be ruled hearsay, because it expresses the witness's (the accused's) knowledge of the world, or a small part thereof, namely the putative intentions of another person. If, on the other hand, the statement is offered as proof that the accused heard the statement and as a consequence feared for his life, it is not hearsay and is ruled admissible. This latter statement expresses the defendant's memory of a personal event and its consequences for him.

The legal interpretation of a statement as hearsay or not, in the sense just discussed, in some ways parallels the distinction that can be made between episodic and semantic classification of one and the same verbal statement, depending upon the question asked, rather than, as in the legal case, on the intention of the assertion made. When you are told that 'Aardvarks eat ants', and then are asked a question about aardvarks' eating habits, you will answer it by relying on semantic memory; if you are asked about what you were just told, you will answer the question in terms of your episodic knowledge.

Amnesia

Severely disturbed memory capacity resulting from brain damage affects primarily the episodic-memory system. Indeed, 'pure' anterograde amnesia is typically defined in terms of the patient's inability to remember recently experienced events even though their knowledge of the world is relatively unimpaired (Kinsbourne and Wood 1975, 1982; Wood, Ebert, and Kinsbourne 1982). The relation between the episodic/semantic distinction and different kinds of amnesia has been discussed at some length elsewhere (Schacter and Tulving 1982), and I shall mention some relevant evidence in Chapter 5. In general, we can expect that amnesic syndromes and other neuropsychological phenomena will provide an important source of evidence for distinguishing between episodic and semantic memory. Jerome Bruner, it discussing the distinction between what he called *memory with record* and *memory without record*, a distinction quite similar to that between episodic and semantic memory, also thought of the differences in underlying mechanisms: 'Why do certain past encounters get carried with a tag of specificity while others get converted into skills or rules or generic modes? They clearly must be quite different neural mechanisms, as we know from neuropathology. Apraxias and amnesias are not much akin' (Bruner 1969, p. 254).

Bicameral men

The later phylogenetic and ontogenetic development of episodic than semantic memory is illustrated by the absence or incomplete development of the episodic-memory system in Jaynes's bicameral men: 'The beautiful Muses . . . were the hallucinatory sources of memory in late bicameral men, men who did not live in a frame of past happenings, who did not have 'lifetimes' in our sense, and who could not reminisce because they were not fully conscious' (Jaynes 1976, p. 371). We can only assume that the semantic-memory system of bicameral men was indistinguishable from that of the human beings populating the earth in the twilight years of the second millennium AD.

4
Debate about memory

The advantages and disadvantages of armchair speculations of the kind discussed in Chapter 3 are very much the same as those of theft over honest toil, to use the colorful phrase borrowed by Stevens (1951) from Bertrand Russell (1920, p. 71). Relatively little time is needed to produce a satisfying outcome; the apparent fruits of the labor far outweigh the effort involved; no special, difficult to acquire, skills are needed; and the loot can be safely enjoyed at least by the perpetrator of the deed, although, if he wishes to share it with others, questions are likely to be raised about its source and legitimacy.

The speculations gathered in Chapter 3 are unlikely to settle the issue of the nature of the relation between episodic and semantic memory. But the exercise is probably not completely useless. It serves at least three functions. First, it provides a hint of the magnitude of the issue concerning the nature of the relation between episodic and semantic memory; it also contains a warning that no simple or quick answers can be expected to the many questions that will emerge in the attempts to clarify the issue. Second, it provides a starting point for more detailed analyses of the differences and similarities between the two forms of memory. Some of the diagnostic signs listed in Table 3.1 (p. 35) refer to characteristics of the systems that may not be particularly amenable to decisive empirical investigations; others might be studied with great profit. Moreover, the existence of an initial listing of potential differences between the two systems may encourage additions to and replacements in it. Third, it may help to clear up some of the misunderstandings about the distinction that have crept into the literature. Many of these misunderstandings are based on considerations of only limited aspects of the distinction. Let us briefly consider some of them.

The speculations that we discussed in Chapter 3 suggest that the difference between episodic and semantic memory is not limited to differences in the kind of information or the kind of knowledge they handle. The assumption that they do is one of the most frequent misunderstandings. For instance, Ortony (1975), in an otherwise admirably lucid defense of the distinction against criticisms offered by Schank (1975), limits the distinction to types of knowledge: 'A distinction between episodic and semantic memory represents a difference not so much between different kinds of *memory* but between different kinds of *knowledge* in memory. It is the contents of memory that we distinguish, not the memory itself' (p. 66). I should like to argue that the distinction is between two memory *systems* rather than merely between two kinds of information. The two systems, as we saw earlier (p. 32), have certain features in common (e.g. they receive, retain, and transmit information) and they differ with respect to some other characteristics, as suggested in Chapter 3.

Other misunderstandings are based on even more limited views of the distinction. Thus, for instance, Baddeley has suggested that 'it is questionable whether a distinction based on anything as subjective and phenomenological as personal reference is either viable or appropriate' (Baddeley 1976, p. 317). Wickelgren has argued that people's inability to remember particular contexts in which they acquired a good deal of their semantic knowledge can be explained by the process of associative interference, and therefore we need not 'assume separate memory systems for semantic and episodic information' (Wickelgren 1977, p. 233). And Muter, on the basis of the results of an experiment demonstrating recognition failure of recallable bits of semantic knowledge, analogously to similar findings in episodic memory, suggested that 'perhaps, on grounds of parsimony, the qualitative distinction between episodic memory traces and semantic memory traces should be abandoned' (Muter 1978, p. 12). I should like to suggest that there is more to the differences between the two memory systems than just the question of personal reference or memory of the contexts of remembered events, and that the distinction is not incompatible with the idea that some similarities exist between the two systems, perhaps including similarities of certain aspects of the retrieval process.

Admittedly, the rejections of the distinction on the basis of consideration of limited aspects of the systems were made at a time when the listing of the differences between them as given in Table 3.1 was not available. It is possible, therefore, that the writers who have argued in support of a unitary memory system might have thought differently about the matter had the list been known to them. It is also possible, however, that some students of memory might still be inclined to opt for the unitary view of memory and ignore the long list of suggested differences, because they are, after all, based on nothing more than speculations.

In the next chapter, we shall turn to Roger Bacon's second method of gaining knowledge, namely experiment. Some empirical evidence exists that speaks to the issue, and we will examine and evaluate it. Before we do so, however, we shall try to settle two items of preliminary business in this chapter. First, we shall briefly consider some agreements and disagreements among theorists with respect to the distinction. If we are going to be putting questions to Nature in the form of experiments the questions should have to do with disagreements and uncertainties rather than with matters that seem to be beyond dispute. Second, we will make an attempt to set down some rules of the game of empirically distinguishing one kind of memory system from another. No amount of evidence is going to help us settle the issue on empirical grounds if we do not agree on the rules by which the outcomes of experiments are related to the theoretical problem on hand.

Agreements

Let us briefly consider some ideas concerning the distinction on which reasonably good agreement seems to exist at this time.

Heuristic distinction

First, almost everyone seems to be willing to accept the distinction between episodic and semantic memory as a heuristic device that helps us to classify and describe experiments and observations. The heuristic use of the terms 'episodic' and 'semantic' does not imply commitment to any particular theory about the nature of the distinction. It does, however, aid communication, and it serves as the first step to deeper questions.

Consider the two terms as labels for different memory tasks. In a typical 'free-association' task, the subject is given a single word as a stimulus and he has to respond with another single word. The relation of the response to the stimulus may reflect the subject's knowledge of the world, his linguistic 'habits', or some particular personal experience. If we restricted the subject's freedom in this type of situation, we might gain more valuable evidence than in situations in which different kinds of responses and their relations to the stimulus words are all mixed up. Most of the responses given by subjects in nominally 'free' association tasks turn out to be related to stimuli on semantic grounds, although people can be readily instructed to respond to the stimulus in terms of a personal experience (e.g. Crovitz and Schiffman 1974; Robinson 1976; Teasdale and Fogarty 1979; Bower 1981). The diagnostic possibilities of the task, noted not only by Galton (1880) but also Cattell (1887), were fully realized by Carl Jung (1973, originally published 1909). In Jung's method, subjects were given two successive tests: in the first, they typically gave responses semantically related to stimuli, and in the second, under instructions to reproduce their earlier responses, we can assume that most of their responses were episodic. A clear distinction between episodic and semantic associations in the 'free' association task might have helped Jung in his use of the technique: the nature of patients' emotional problems might have been more readily reflected in their episodic responses to stimulus words than in their 'free' responses that in fact usually were based on linguistic and semantic knowledge. Be it as it may, the heuristic distinction could be brought to bear on the free-association task and the interpretation of the data obtained from it.

The heuristic use of the distinction could also serve as a source of particular interpretations of experimental findings that might not be thought

of otherwise. Consider, for instance, the oft-quoted experiment by Drachman and Leavitt (1972) in which they tried to adjudicate between two rival
explanations of memory impairment in the aged, namely impairment as
storage versus retrieval deficit. Drachman and Leavitt found that their two
groups of subjects, one with a mean age of 22 and the other of 67 years,
differed on learning of supraspan digit sequences as well as in both free
and cued recall of words; they did not differ on single-trial digit span or
on what Drachman and Leavitt called 'retrieval by category' or 'retrieval
from old storage'. Their general conclusion was that memory impairment
in the aged does not represent just a retrieval deficit, and that a 'disorder
of storage' is a more likely underlying condition. Had the distinction
between episodic and semantic memory tasks been available to Drachman
and Leavitt, they could have economically described the outcome of their
experiment as showing no differences between young and old subjects in
immediate memory and semantic memory, but showing differences in
episodic memory.

Other illustrations of the heuristic use of the concepts of episodic and
semantic memory in interpreting data from experiments published before
the distinction was introduced to experimental psychologists can also be
given. For instance, Slamecka (1966) found that learning of A–B pairs
consisting of unrelated words did not produce any interference in the subjects' ability to retrieve normative primary associates to the A members
of the learned pairs. Slamecka interpreted his findings in terms of the high
'strength' of the pre-experimentally established normative associations.Had
the distinction between episodic and semantic memory been available in
1966, he could also have described the results as showing that episodic
A–C associations have no demonstrable effect on semantic A–B associations.

A potentially interesting case from the point of view of the distinction
between episodic and semantic memory in the heuristic sense has to do
with the observations made by Penfield and his associates on memories
induced by the electrical stimulation of the brain (Penfield and Perot 1963).
Penfield distinguished between three forms of memory, which he referred
to as 'racial memory', 'conditioned reflexes', and 'experiential memory'.
Racial memory is possessed by animals; conditioned reflexes 'preserve the
skills, the memory of words, and the memory of non-verbal concepts';
experiential memory refers to the 'possibility of recalling the stream of
consciousness with varying degrees of completeness' (Penfield 1975,
p. 63). Penfield thought that the reports of his patients during electrical
stimulation of the left temporal cortex gave evidence of experiential memory. He summarized the matter as follows: 'Sometimes the patient
informed us that we had produced one of his "dreamy states" and we
accepted this as evidence that we were close to the cause of his seizures.
It was evident at once that these were not dreams. They were electrical

activations of the sequential record of consciousness, a record that had been laid down during the patient's earlier experience. The patient "re-lived" all that he had been aware of in that earlier period of time as in a moving-picture "flashback" ' (Penfield 1975, p. 21).

Sensitized to the difference between episodic and semantic memory, one can read the verbatim statements made by the patients providing 'flash-back' responses, as recorded by Penfield and Perot (1963), and come to the conclusion that a large majority of them do not refer to episodic mem-ories at all. One notable exception is patient M. M. (Penfield and Perot 1963, pp. 648–51), who did use words that could be interpreted as refer-ring to episodic memory. The statements made by most other patients do not contain descriptions of temporally dated and spatially located personal experiences.

Since 1972, a number of writers have explicitly referred to the epi-sodic/semantic distinction in interpreting their data. Petrey (1977) has sug-gested that the syntagmatic–paradigmatic shift in children's free associations (Entwisle 1966) becomes understandable if we think of it as reflecting a shift from episodic to semantic memory as the basis for responding. Gilhooly and Gilhooly (1979) found that picture-naming and word-completion to bigram cues are, and that free recall and recognition in adult subjects are not, affected by the age at which the children were likely to have acquired the words; they interpreted these results in terms of the distinction between episodic and semantic memory, and in terms of the further division of semantic memory into lexical and encyclopedic memories (Lachman 1973). Ojemann (1978) produced mild electrical stim-ulation of left frontal-parietal-temporal cortex in six patients who were undergoing intracranial operations for intractable epilepsy. At the time of the stimulation, the subjects engaged in one of two tasks: (a) naming a pictured object, or (b) recalling the name of the object seen 10 seconds earlier. The finding that there was no relation among specific locations of stimulation that affected performance on the two tasks was interpreted to suggest that 'language processes, including generalized word memory, utilize areas of cortex separate from those involved in short-term memory for specific, episodic verbal material . . . '(Ojemann 1978, p. 336). Russell and Beekhuis (1976) interpreted differences in memory performances of normal subjects and psychotics in terms of the episodic/semantic distinc-tion, and Caine, Ebert, and Weingartner (1977) concluded that memory impairment of patients suffering from Huntington's disease 'lie particularly in the realm of episodic memory' (p. 1087). Moeser (1976, 1977) reported a series of experiments showing that neither children nor adults could make inferences based on information in episodic memory unless the rel-evant information was all stored as a part of the same episode. Under-wood, Boruch, and Malmi (1978) found no correlation in individual subjects' memory performances between episodic- and semantic-memory tasks. And, to complete our sample of illustrative studies, we should note an experiment by Herrmann and McLaughlin (1973) that, as far as I have been able to ascertain, was the first published experiment whose results were related to the episodic/semantic distinction. Herrmann and McLaughlin viewed their results 'as consistent with the hypothesis that episodic information . . . is stored separately from semantic information . . .in long-term memory' (p. 174).

In the experiments mentioned here, as well as in other similar ones in the literature, the episodic/semantic distinction has been used in the heuristic mode. The results of the experiments were *described* in the general form of 'episodic-memory performance differed from the semantic-memory performance', with the terms 'episodic memory' and 'semantic memory' defined rather broadly, in terms of tasks, materials, or experimental manipulations. As purely descriptive statements, these kinds of conclusions are non-controversial, as long as the meaning of the two terms is understood.

Different information

Closely related to the heuristic distinction between episodic and semantic memories is one based on the nature of to-be-remembered information, material, or knowledge. Episodic information is picked up by the learner on a particular occasion, at a particular time in a particular place, and when the learner is questioned about it later, the circumstances under which the information was acquired must be specified. Material learned in list-learning and other similar experiments, by this convention, is thought of as episodic information, even if it has extra-episodic references or possesses semantic structure. Semantic information has no such association with a particular occasion of acquisition; instructions for its retrieval need not, and indeed cannot, stipulate the conditions of acquisition as one of the defining features of the information to be recovered.

Students of memory who are willing to contemplate the distinction as a heuristic have no objections to the distinction between episodic and semantic memory in terms of different types of information, either. The acceptance of the distinction in these terms, like the acceptance of the heuristic distinction, implies no commitment to the two forms of memory as representing different systems. It is perfectly possible to have one and the same memory system handle episodic and semantic information. Anderson and Ross (1980) who reject the functional distinction between episodic and semantic memories, accept the distinction between the two forms of memory in terms of different types of information. They characterize it as a 'content distinction' (p. 463), and say that it may be useful in that it may provide new insights—new ways of looking at issues and new ways of generating novel ideas. It is difficult to see how anyone would not share these sentiments.

Semantic contents of episodes

Yet another proposition on which general agreement exists concerns the semantic contents of experienced and remembered episodes. Imagine that late one night a friend telephones you. When you pick up the receiver, he says, 'Aardvarks eat ants', and then hangs up. The friend calling you on the telephone, at a particular time, with you in a particular place, and saying something to you, is an episode, probably a memorable one. The utterance is the semantic contents of the episode. You can ask many different questions about the episode and interpret it in a number of different ways, depending upon your knowledge of the world, including your friend; you can also ask questions about the utterance and interpret it in terms of your relevant semantic knowledge, and regardless of whether you remember the utterance as a part of, or independently of, the episode.

The agreement on the existence and utilization of information from semantic contents of episodes is important in so far as it should help to minimize certain misunderstandings. Consider, for instance, the question: after you have received the telephone call with the interesting message from your friend, and someone asks you, 'What do aardvarks eat?' is your answer derived from episodic or semantic memory? The answer to the question is, 'Either one, the other, or both'. In a single instance of this sort it is impossible to tell, although it may be possible to set up carefully controlled experiments that provide better answers to the same general kind of question.

People are capable of learning many things about the world through their own personal interaction with the world. Some of this knowledge is stored in semantic memory in the form of 'scripts' (Schank and Abelson 1977). For instance, if you have been to many dinners in 'old' Oxford colleges you may have a well-formulated script that 'contains' all sorts of relevant information about such dinners. The script permits you to answer relevant questions—for example, do they say grace before dinner?—as well as behave appropriately when you find yourself in the situation. On the other hand, if you have only been to one such dinner, you may still be able to answer many of the same questions on the basis of your recollection of the particular event.

The point of the discussion is that once we accept the possibility of semantic contents of particular episodes, we should always keep in mind the possibility that questions that are assumed to be directed at the semantic system could be answered in terms of the information retrieved from the episodic system.

Interdependence of the systems

Whether or not we accept the functional distinction of episodic and semantic memories, or whether we only entertain the distinction as a hypothetical possibility, it is difficult to imagine how anyone would seriously wish to resist the idea that the two systems are closely interdependent and interact with one another virtually all the time. I devoted a short section to the 'interdependence of the two systems' in my 1972 essay (pp. 391–3). I pointed out that our knowledge of the interdependence was, not surprisingly, somewhat meager, since relevant issues had simply not been raised in the absence of the distinction. I also mentioned that evidence existed 'for the important role that the semantic system plays in storage and retrieval of episodic memory information' (Tulving 1972, p. 392).

The issue of interrelation or interdependence of the two systems is related to the existence of semantic contents of episodes. The problem is sometimes also talked about as one of 'transfer' between the two systems. It is worth special mention at this point for the simple reason that there seems to be some uncertainty about it in the literature. Consider, for instance, a study by Perlmutter, Harsip, and Myers (1976). They did two experiments in which they found that reaction time in cued recall was influenced by the frequency of stimulus words in the language, as well as by the shape of the distribution of normative associates of stimulus words. They said that these findings 'seem most parsimoniously explained by the hypothesis that semantic knowledge plays a role in retrieval of episodic memories' (p. 367). This conclusion seems to be in reasonably good agreement with my own speculations that the semantic system plays an 'important role' in retrieval of episodic-memory information (Tulving 1972, p. 392). Yet, Anderson and Ross (1980, p. 446) point to the Perlmutter *et al.* study as evidence against the distinction; they say that 'it is difficult to see' why the differences in semantic information that may have affected the episodic traces of learned pairs 'would be encoded in the episodic trace'. Is this a statement to the effect that semantic information should play no role in encoding of to-be-remembered verbal material? Is it a claim that given the close interrelation between the systems we should adopt the view of unitary memory? Or is it something else?

Until such time that someone will explicitly argue against the proposition that episodic and semantic systems are similar in a number of ways, as we saw earlier (p. 32), as well as closely inter-related, we should regard the proposition as one of the basic agreements. Exactly how close the interrelation is, and what form it takes in different situations, may emerge as important research problems one day. I say 'may', because the questions are predicated on the acceptance of episodic and semantic memory as different systems.

Open questions

There are undoubtedly other issues pertaining to the episodic/semantic distinction on which most interested students would agree, but the small set we have discussed covers some of the more important ones. We now turn our attention to matters on which some disagreement seems to exist and that, therefore, constitute open questions. The length of the list of open questions depends on the detail into which we wish to go. I will mention only three that seem to be in the limelight at the present time: functional distinction between the systems, episodic/semantic distinction as a continuum, and the relation of lexical memory to the distinction.

Functional distinction?

Probably the most basic issue on which we find disagreement today concerns the problem of whether episodic and semantic memories represent different functional systems. A number of theorists have already taken a position on the issue, others are likely to do so in the future, and still others may decide to continue keeping an open mind about it. Be it as it may, it is an issue that is likely to be vigorously debated and fought over in the coming years.

I think of episodic and semantic memory as functionally different. To say that two systems are functionally different does not mean, as the preceding discussion has tried to make clear, that (a) the systems are completely separate, (b) they have nothing to do with one another, (c) there are no similarities between them, or (d) they serve completely separate functions. It does mean that one system *can* operate independently of the other, although not necessarily as efficiently as it could with the support of the other intact system. The operations of one system could be enhanced without a similar effect on the operations of the other; similarly, the activity of one system could be suppressed without a comparable effect on the activity of the other. The functional difference also implies that in important, or at least in non-negligible, ways the systems operate differently, that is, that their function is governed at least partially by different principles.

Whether it is possible to establish the functional differences between episodic and semantic memory systems to everyone's satisfaction by psychological methods alone remains to be seen. The history of the psychological science of memory has shown that theorists can be very ingenious in explaining, at one level or another, within their own favorite theory, phenomena that are regarded as crucial by a rival theory. The flexibility of the standards by which the adequacy of explanations is evaluated, or at least the lack of agreement as to the relevant criteria and their weights in such evaluation, may well render the debate about episodic and semantic memory as fruitless as have been many other debates about memory.

I am more optimistic about the possibility of distinguishing between the two systems on neuroanatomical and neurophysiological grounds. As we saw earlier (p. 62), some relevant evidence is already available and interpretations of these data relevant to the episodic/semantic distinction have been offered. Relevant evidence from clinical cases of brain damage leading to impairment of memory (e.g. Cermak 1981, Victor, Adams, and Collins

1971; Mair, Warrington, and Weiskrantz 1979; Squire 1982) could be complemented by the results from animal experiments that afford better control over the characteristics of the lesions. Particularly relevant to the debate about episodic and semantic memory are the results of experiments done by Olton and his associates, since Olton's distinction between working and reference memory is analogous to the distinction between episodic and semantic memory (e.g. Olton, Becker, and Handelmann 1979; Olton and Papas 1979; Olton and Feustle 1981). If neuroanatomical and neurophysiological correlates of episodic and semantic memory systems could be identified, the issue of the functional difference between the two systems would become redundant.

Episodic/semantic continuum?

Another open question has to do with the continuity of the two systems. A number of theorists who are willing to adopt the episodic/semantic distinction in general terms nevertheless are not quite willing to accept the idea that the two systems are in some sense separate, and prefer to think of them as constituting a continuum.

Schachtel, who drew a distinction rather similar to that between episodic and semantic memory in his classic paper on childhood amnesia (Schachtel 1947) did not perceive the two forms of memory as sharply distinct. After discussing the usefulness or even the necessity of the distinction, he softened the suggestion: 'Yet the separation of the "useful" from the "autobiographical" memory is, of course, an artificial abstraction. Actually this distinction of the contents of remembered material is not clear-cut, and the two types of material indicated by it are continuously and everywhere interrelated' (p. 5).

Similar suggestions have been made by Craik (1979), Jacoby and Craik (1979), Naus and Halasz (1979), and Kintsch (1980), among others. Craik, for instance, has pointed out that 'When the structure of the memory system is considered, the implied break between two memory systems is unsatisfactory. Whereas the occurrence of a specific event is tied to a particular time and place, there may well be clusters of events that share many features of the context; there are scripts of "things to do" in particular settings, and this type of knowledge seems intermediate between the representation of individual episodes and the representation of context-free general knowledge of the world' (1979, p. 451). Craik suggests, as a solution, the idea of 'a continuum of representation, running from highly context-specific episodes at one extreme to abstract generalized knowledge at the other' (p. 451).

The idea of the two forms of memory as representing the end points of a continuum inevitably raises the question, 'a continuum of what?' The suggestions for the continuum refer primarily to the continuum of information, or representations, characterizing individual bits of episodic and semantic knowledge that a person may retrieve on a particular occasion, from highly concrete, particular, temporally dated events on the one hand to the 'truly general knowledge' (Kintsch 1980, p. 596) on the other. In this limited sense of the idea of a continuum, derived from introspective evidence, one cannot and need not object to it. Memories of individual episodes almost invariably do have some meaningful content, or at least possess components that can be identified with corresponding information in semantic memory. Furthermore, later in the book, in Chapters 9 and 14, I will suggest that retrieval information, which frequently is derived from or through the semantic system, contributes to what I shall call ecphoric information that determines the contents of recollective experience as well as its clarity, detail, and subjective certainty. To the extent that the contribution made to ecphoric information by retrieval information can vary, the idea of remembering involving both episodic and semantic information is perfectly reasonable.

The idea that the episodic/semantic distinction represents nothing more than a continuum, however, must be rejected. A series of graded 'mixtures' of episodic and semantic components constituting retrieved memories or bits of knowledge in and of itself is not inconsistent with, and does not constitute logical proof against, two separate systems that co-operate in producing a particular outcome. The engine and the brakes of an automobile are clearly differentiable systems, although their existence could not be deduced merely by observing the accelerated, steady, and decelerated movements of the automobile. In the realm of anatomy, no one doubts the separate existence of flexsor and extensor muscles despite the fact that they jointly produce all sorts of continua of smooth motion. And in psychology we distinguish among many varieties of perceptual-motor skills whose execution depends on the interaction of perceptual and motor systems. The skills may vary over a wide range in terms of the relative contributions of the two systems, but the existence of such continua does not speak against the separation of the two systems, nor is it inconsistent with the anatomical separation between primary sensory and motor areas of the brain.

I sometimes wonder about the reasons for postulating episodic/semantic continua. Is it an expression of the desire for parsimony? (One can think of the idea of a unitary memory system as motivated by parsimony, although it may represent simply an incorrect, primitive idea that we have inherited from the past and accepted uncritically.) Does it reflect an unwillingness to make too radical a break with the past? Or is the idea of the continuum a 'compromise solution' that might be at least partly acceptable to the proponents of both the unitary view of memory and to those who think of the episodic/semantic distinction as real?

Compromises do have some value in human affairs, but more so in some enterprises than others. Many scientists know, both by studying the history of science and through personal experience, that one should maintain a sceptical attitude about compromise solutions. Ramón y Cajal, the histologist and neuroanatomist, in his interesting autobiography, expressed his opinion on the matter as follows: 'Unfortunately, I was then largely under the influence of the ideas of Duval, Hayen, and other French histologists (who denied that the white corpuscles passed through the walls of the blood vessels) and was led to a conciliatory or compromising solution, erroneous, as are almost all intermediate opinions in science' (Ramón y Cajal 1937, p. 276).

Lexical memory

Most writers who have speculated about lexical memory think of it as a part of semantic memory, or at least as a form of propositional ('knowing that') memory (Collins and Loftus 1975; Kintsch 1980; Miller 1969, 1972; Lachman 1973; Schank 1975). The idea makes intuitive sense: knowledge about words, their meaning, rules for combining them into sentences, and other aspects of our knowledge of language must be stored somewhere. Yet, we should regard the relation of lexical memory to the episodic/semantic distinction as an open question.

Should we distinguish between lexical memory and (mental) lexicon? If we talk about lexical memory, do we have in mind a memory 'system' of the kind that episodic and semantic memories are claimed to be? If so, what properties does lexical memory share with episodic and semantic memory? Which of its properties are different? Could we make up a list of diagnostic features for lexical memory, and how would that list be similar to or different from the list in Table 3.1 (p. 35)? If, on the other hand, we decide not to claim a 'system status' for lexical memory, and instead talk about the lexicon as a part of semantic memory, what kind of a part is it? We can say, of course, that the semantic memory 'contains' knowledge about words, but it also contains knowledge about many other things, like people's faces and voices, appearances of objects and places, melodies of songs, and tastes of foods (e.g. Estes 1978, p. 264). What would be the theoretical significance of assigning particular names to the assemblages of these separate classes of objects of semantic knowledge, analogously to assigning a name to the 'lexicon'?

'Language is complicated', Miller and Johnson-Laird (1976, p. 690) have said, and it would be difficult to argue with the claim that this is an understatement. But is the complication an inherent property of language, or is it derived from something else? If we think of natural language as a device that has evolved for the purpose of communicating information and knowledge from one mind to another, it also becomes reasonable to attribute the complication of language to the characteristics of human knowledge and memory it serves. The actual, intended, desired, or imagined states of the world of which people can possess knowledge and which they may have reasons to talk about can be very large in number. A complicated symbol system, and a set of complex rules, may be necessary to handle them all.

Instead of thinking of lexical memory or the mental lexicon as a part of the contents of semantic memory, we may wish to think of natural language as a means of expressing knowledge, or converting it from one form to another. Lexical units, then, would have no special status in semantic memory (knowledge of the world), and knowledge of the use of the lexical information would be regarded as a component of procedural memory (p. 33).

Lexical memory thus conceived—as a complex skill, or memory for procedures—would apply to, or be a part of, both episodic and semantic memory systems: information about personal episodes as well as knowledge of the world can be stored in propositional form, and a good deal of it, even if not all, can be expressed in language. Thus, for instance, there is nothing especially 'semantic'—as against 'episodic'—about the sentence verification task, the mainstay of contemporary semantic-memory research (Kintsch 1980). Consider the task of verifying the two following sentences: (a) Some Estonians you know are women, and (b) Some Estonians are women (cf. Smith, Rips, and Shoben 1974). In one case you would use language to express your episodic knowledge, in the other you would rely on your linguistic skills to communicate to the experimenter something about your knowledge of the world. But, are you also relying on an additional memory system called 'lexical memory'? If so, in what sense? If not, when do we use 'lexical memory'?

If we entertain the hypothesis that 'lexical memory' is not a part of the informational 'contents' of semantic memory, but rather a part of procedural memory, serving both the episodic and semantic systems, what do we do about words? Are words not 'contents'? They are, but in a relatively unimportant sense. Any object of cognition can be represented in the semantic-memory system: an object, an idea, a letter of the alphabet, a finger movement, a tennis stroke, the sound of a short burst of noise, and so on ad infinitum. All these objects of cognition have certain properties: they can, therefore, be described in propositional form. Words, too, can be described in terms of properties such as appearance, sound, significance, and name (Nelson 1979). Most of these features of words as objects of cognition are irrelevant to the function they serve as components of the skilful procedure of communication. The essence of any natural language—like that of other languages—does not consist of the lexical units, but the syntactic, semantic, and pragmatic rules of operation.

'Lexical memory' stands in the same relation to both episodic and semantic memory as chessmen stand in relation to the game of chess: useful but not necessary. Two chess masters can play the game without looking at the board or touching any chessmen, communicating the moves to each other through notational signs only. We can even imagine that the notational signs in the form of written or spoken signals are only a useful but not a necessary part of the game. If the masters could read each other's minds, they could play a fascinating game with an unpredictable outcome in the absence of any chessmen or their notational surrogates. Episodic and semantic memory systems, too, could operate in the absence of symbolic means of describing the input into them or communicating the products of retrieval from them.

Schank (1975) has questioned the distinction between semantic and episodic memories, claiming that it is 'a false one' (p. 255). Instead, he distinguishes between lexical memory 'which contains all of the information about words, idioms, common expressions etc., and which links these to nodes in a conceptual memory, which is language free' (pp. 255–6). The hypothesis of lexical memory as cognitive skill serving both episodic and semantic memory in a certain sense parallels Schank's classificatory scheme.

In this section, I have mostly raised questions about lexical memory rather than trying to provide any answers. Since little systematic thought has been devoted to the question of the relation of 'lexical memory' to the episodic/semantic distinction, the answers to the question will become more rational as we proceed with the study of memory. In the meantime, the question about lexical memory must remain open.

Rules of the game

Let us now turn our attention to the rules by which empirical evidence is related to the issue of the distinction between episodic and semantic memory. In light of the complexity of the issue, as we have already noted, individual experiments and other empirical observations will not be decisive in settling it; evidence accumulated from many observations and sources, on the other hand, can turn out to be critical. Experimental outcomes and empirical observations alone, however, are only partly relevant; other matters that lie outside the realm of empirical facts also enter the picture. Among these are the rules by which empirical data are related to the theoretical issue. In this section I shall briefly discuss these rules.

Rules of any game are created as a part of the game and they change over time. Students of memory do not sit down to figure out what kinds of rules would be useful to have and then publish the fruits of their thoughts. They make up the rules in conjunction with the empirical research that they perceive as relevant to the theoretical problem of interest, in this case the episodic/semantic distinction. Since the existing literature concerned with the distinction is still rather limited, the rules discussed here are few in number. Future research undoubtedly will generate many additional methods involving different rules and directed at different aspects of the distinction.

I shall discuss the rules under the labels of (a) simple transfer, (b) transfer comparison, (c) experimental dissociation, (d) pathological dissociation, (e) developmental dissociation; and (f) brain states. These labels are somewhat arbitrary and not entirely satisfactory, but they do serve the function of distinguishing among different kinds of logic that have been applied to the task of distinguishing episodic and semantic memory. It is important to keep the different kinds of logic in mind when evaluating evidence; it makes a difference whether, for instance, similar conclusions emerge from studies using the same logic, or whether different conclusions are drawn from experiments involving different methods and logic.

The key concepts in the discussion of the methods and rules of the game are (a) episodic or semantic information, and (b) episodic or semantic task. Episodic information has to do with temporally dated personal experiences, whereas semantic information concerns the individual's knowledge of the world independently of particular episodes. An episodic task is one in which episodic information is required for its successful accomplishment, whereas in a semantic task semantic information is sufficient.

Simple transfer

If activity of one system results in some change in the other, 'transfer' of information from one system to the other can be said to have occurred. Since the systems interact closely all the time, since factual or semantic contents of episodes frequently are transferred to the semantic system, and since encoding and retrieval operations in the episodic system are typically affected by semantic memory, the fact that transfer of information from one system to the other has occurred frequently has no diagnostic value. But it may do so under special circumstances.

Anderson and Ross (1980) did several experiments in which one of the critical questions had to do with the effect of the episodic acquisition of one proposition on the verification of a related semantic proposition. Anderson and Ross argued that, according to the episodic/semantic distinction, 'access to information in semantic memory . . . should not be influenced by what is stored in episodic memory' (p. 446). If it does, the finding would constitute evidence against a functional distinction between the two systems. Thus they had their subjects learn sentences such as 'A spaniel retrieves a ball', and then measured the amount of time that the subjects required to verify the proposition that spaniels are dogs. The verification time was compared with the verification time of a semantic proposition that was unrelated to any of the previously studied episodic sentences.

I am calling Anderson and Ross' method, or rule, 'simple transfer', because they looked only at the effect of an earlier episodic task on a subsequent semantic task, assuming that the finding of no effect would support the distinction, whereas the finding of an effect would support the unitary view of memory.

Transfer comparison

In a second type of experiment, the effects of two variables, one episodic, the other semantic, are compared on a single task. The effect of the episodic manipulation on the task is equivalent to the simple transfer rule; the introduction of the semantic variable adds another dimension to the design and makes the comparison of episodic and semantic 'transfer' effects possible. The logic relating the outcome of such an experiment to the distinction can be summarized as follows: if performance on the transfer task differs for the episodic and semantic (first-stage) variables, the distinction between the two systems is supported; the absence of any difference would weaken the distinction.

The rule of transfer comparison has been used in experiments by Herrmann and McLaughlin (1973); Herrmann and Harwood (1980); and McKoon and Ratcliff (1979). Herrmann and McLaughlin, and Herrmann and Harwood compared the effects of episodic and semantic associations between two words in a pair on the speed of the words' episodic recognition. McKoon and Ratcliff studied the effect of episodic and semantic associations between two words in a pair on the priming facilitation in a semantic task, and, in separate experiments, the priming facilitation in an episodic task.

Experimental dissociation

Experiments following the logic of experimental dissociation involve the manipulation of a single variable and comparison of the effects of the manipulation in two different tasks, one episodic, the other semantic. Dissociation is said to have occurred if it is found that the manipulated variable affects subjects' performance in one of the two tasks, but not in the other, or affects the performance in different directions in the two tasks. Thus, dissociation refers to the absence of a positive association between dependent variables of two different tasks. The finding of dissociation would be regarded as support for the distinction between episodic and semantic memory, whereas the finding that the effects of the manipulated variable are positively correlated in the two tasks would provide no support for the distinction.

The rule of experimental dissociation was employed in a series of experiments by Jacoby and Dallas (1981), although these authors were not directly concerned with the distinction between episodic and semantic memory, as well as in experiments by Kihlstrom (1980). Two different experiments described by McKoon and Ratcliff (1979), when considered together, also conform to the method of experimental dissociation, and therefore yield relevant evidence.

A powerful refinement of the method of experimental dissociation is provided by the method of double dissociation, described by Shoben *et al*. (1978). It represents an extension of the method of experimental dissociation through the addition of another variable. Thus, in this design there are two tasks, an episodic one and a semantic one, and *two* experimentally manipulated variables. The hypothesis of the distinction between the two systems is consonant with the finding that the manipulation of the two variables yields different forms of dissociation: one of the manipulated variables affects performance on episodic but not semantic task, whereas the manipulation of the other variable produces an opposite outcome, having an effect on the semantic but not the episodic task.

Pathological dissociation

The logic of this method is rather similar to that of experimental dissociation, except that instead of manipulating a particular variable experimentally, the experimenter allows Nature to perform the relevant manipulation, in the form of disease or accident. Thus, in the minimal design, the performance of two groups of subjects or patients is compared on two tasks, one episodic, the other semantic. The two groups of subjects correspond to different levels of the manipulated variable in the method of experimental dissociation. The logic of the method of pathological dissociation is analogous to that of experimental dissociation: the distinction between episodic and semantic systems is supported by the finding that the performance of the two groups differs on one of the tasks but not on the other, or goes in the opposite direction in the two tasks; the absence of such dissociation would be regarded as lack of evidence for the distinction.

Evidence that can be regarded or interpreted as relevant to the episodic/semantic distinction based on the rule of pathological dissociation has been reported by Kinsbourne and Wood (1975), Warrington and Weiskrantz (1974, 1978), and Schacter and Tulving (1982). An experiment by Cohen and Squire (1980) demonstrates a dissociation between an episodic-memory task and one involving learning of cognitive skills. Since I do not wish to include cognitive skills under the rubric of semantic memory (p. 33), Cohen and Squire's experiment is not directly relevant to our present purposes.

Developmental dissociation

The method of developmental dissociation is identical with that of pathological dissociation, except that the subject groups are defined in terms of stages of normal development (for instance, children versus adults, or 40-year-olds versus 75-year-olds). No experiments have yet been reported in the literature using this design. But Eysenck (1975) has discussed findings from memory experiments comparing the performance of older and younger subjects in a variety of situations and concluded that older people's memory is more impaired on episodic than semantic tasks.

The methods of pathological dissociation and developmental dissociation necessarily entail the use of separate groups of subjects to represent different levels of the 'manipulated' condition: a person suffering from brain damage, or a 75-year-old person, cannot be assigned to a group other than his own. Experiments reported in the literature that have used the methods of simple transfer, transfer comparison, or experimental dissociation have relied mostly on within-subjects designs. The issue of within-subjects versus between-subjects designs may be relevant, and generalizations from one type to the other should be made with caution, if the subjects' performance on a task requires, or is dependent on, the adoption of a particular mode of operation, and if switching from one mode to another produces unwanted interference.

It is important to note that the logic of dissociations (experimental, pathological, and developmental) is essentially a pretheoretical one: the interpretation of the outcomes of experiments based on methods of dissociation does not require any particular theory of memory. We need not know what is entailed in encoding and storage of information in one or the other system, we can do without a deep understanding of retrieval processes, we do not have to rely on a theory of how some psychoactive drugs affect the workings of the brain or the cognitive system, nor do we need a theory of, say, amnesia, in order to draw relevant conclusions from experiments conforming to the methods discussed. If, for instance, an experiment based on the method of experimental dissociation produces an outcome supportive of the distinction, the evidence is relevant regardless of whether we know or do not know why that particular pattern of results was observed. Similarly, negative outcomes—lack of observed dissociation—are relevant to the issue regardless of presence or absence of compelling theoretical accounts of the processes and mechanisms responsible for any particular outcome.

Brain states

A somewhat different method of distinguishing episodic and semantic memory systems entails direct measurement of brain states of individuals engaged in episodic and semantic memory tasks. If the patterns of brain activity differ in a systematic and orderly fashion for the two classes of tasks, the hypothesis of the distinction is supported; persistent failures to discover neurophysiological correlates of episodic and semantic remembering would weaken the distinction. A promising beginning in the use of the method of brain states has been made by Wood, Taylor, Penny, and Stump (1980).

Application of rules

Given the reasonably straightforward logic and rules by which we can relate experimental and empirical observations to the problem of the distinction between episodic and semantic memory, one might imagine that adducement of evidence relevant to the distinction can usually proceed without difficulties. This is not always true. Several kinds of difficulties can arise in practical situations in which the rules are applied.

One kind of difficulty lies in the availability of alternative explanations of empirical facts. Any set of data in the developing science of memory can be interpreted in many different ways and the participants in the debate do not always agree as to the best, most useful, or most adequate explanation. In experiments designed to shed light on the distinction between episodic and semantic memory, too, observed outcomes can be interpreted in many ways. A dissociation of performance in episodic and semantic tasks, supportive of the hypothesis of the distinction, can almost always be accounted for without postulating the existence of two separate systems. Similarly, the absence of a dissociation can usually be accounted for in terms of hypotheses other than that of a unitary memory system.

Although there exist no easy solutions to these problems, arising out of the complexity of our subject matter and the flexibility of our theorizing, the situation is not complete unmanageable. Acceptability of alternative explanations can be evaluated in terms of criteria such as generality, simplicity, 'depth', and 'freedom from *ad hockery*' (Langley and Simon 1981). Thus, for instance, if many different complex *ad hoc* explanations are provided to explain observed dissociations from different experiments, the simple and general explanation of the dissociations in terms of the distinction between memory systems may come to be preferred by most practitioners.

Another difficulty has to do with the decision concerning the occurrence of dissociations. I defined as dissociations those interactions between the manipulated variable (or subject groups) and tasks in which the variable was associated with performance on one task and not the other, or where it was associated with the performance on the two tasks in opposite directions. Thus, 'dissociation' is equivalent to 'crossover interaction' (Loftus 1978). What is excluded as a dissociation is not only the absence of any interaction, but also the interaction in which the effect of the manipulated variable is greater on one task than on the other. In this latter case, a simple explanation can always be invoked that the interaction results from the particular scale values of the dependent variables (N. H. Anderson 1977; Garner 1980).

But how close should the data from any particular experiment be to the 'ideal' pattern of dissociation for the experimenter to conclude that dissociation was obtained? Suppose that, in a particular experiment conforming to the method of experimental dissociation, we find that the independent variable has a very large effect on the performance in the episodic task and a very small, but statistically reliable, effect on the semantic task. Should we still conclude that the dissociation does not exist, because some mathematical transformation can be found that will eliminate the interaction, or should we take a more lenient attitude? My own feeling is that at the present stage of our knowledge, or lack thereof, we probably need not assume an exceedingly puritanical attitude. Since the two systems interact closely, it would be unreasonable to expect that variables or conditions that have a pronounced effect on performance mediated by one system have no effect whatsoever on the other. In the human nervous system crystal-pure dissociations are probably an exception rather than a rule. Insistence on such purity in experimental outcomes, therefore, may not serve us well in the long run.

Episodic and semantic tasks

One of the difficulties in relating empirical findings to the issue of the distinction lies in the uncertainty concerning episodic and semantic-memory tasks. When I talked about the meaning of the concept of functional differences between the systems (p. 66), I referred to the separately identifiable and controllable activities of the systems. The use of 'episodic' and 'semantic' memory tasks represents one method of tapping the two systems. To the extent that the two systems interact, it is not always easy to find or create situations in which only one of the two systems contributes to the observed memory performance.

The general current practice is to regard a task as episodic if the subject could not perform adequately on the task without having had a particular experience or having learned the material on a particular occasion. A semantic task, on the other hand, is one on which adequate performance is possible in the absence of learning of the relevant material on any particular occasion. In other words, episodic tasks are those for which the learning of the material in a particular episode is *necessary*, whereas semantic tasks are those for which general pre-experimental knowledge of the world is *sufficient*.

There are two immediate problems with episodic and semantic tasks thus defined. First, since both encoding and retrieval of episodes are influenced by semantic memory—a matter that will be discussed in Chapters 8 and 9—performance on most episodic tasks is influenced by both the episodic and semantic systems. Second, even if performance on a semantic task does not require episodic information, it is possible that in certain situations it is facilitated by the availability of information from a particular episode.

An example borrowed from Jacoby (1978) illustrates the second of these two problems. A person is asked to 'recall' the sum of two numbers, such as 39 and 14. The task can be solved quite adequately in terms of information and computational rules 'stored in' semantic memory. If the same question is presented to the person a short time later, he can repeat the same operation and 'retrieve' the required information from semantic memory. However, if we assume that the results of the earlier computation have been stored in episodic memory, then at least in principle the person has two ways of answering the question: perform the computation again in semantic memory, or retrieve the answer to the earlier question from episodic memory. This state of affairs makes it difficult to interpret certain outcomes of the experiment. Suppose, for instance, that the amount of time required for the person to produce the answer is measured, and that the amount of time is less on the second trial than on the first. One interpretation of the finding would be that the earlier episode of answering the question has changed the accessibility of the information in semantic memory, whereas another interpretation is that the accessibility of information in semantic memory is unchanged but the 'semantic' task is solved on the second trial by retrieving the results of the earlier operation from episodic memory.

The existence of this and similar difficulties in applying the rules of the game does not mean that the relevance of empirical findings must always remain uncertain. It does mean that students of memory interested in the issue must keep the complex nature of the process and the possible complications in studying it firmly in mind and design their experiments accordingly. The objective is always to do experiments that yield 'clean' data, whose replicability and generality can be demonstrated, and to avoid doing experiments whose outcomes complicate rather than clarify the issue. In the next chapter we shall have a chance to see how well these objectives have been achieved in the initial experiments that have been directed at, or can be perceived to be relevant to, the debate about episodic and semantic memory.

5
Empirical evidence

In this chapter we shall examine and discuss empirical evidence concerning the episodic/semantic distinction. The evidence is derived from experiments that were especially designed to speak to the issue of distinction, as well as experiments whose results happen to be relevant. I shall also mention some pertinent clinical observations.

The brief summary presented here can provide the reader only with the flavor of the research. Many experiments that have been done are quite complex, and it would be difficult if not impossible to delve into the details of their designs, methods, and findings. The interested reader is encouraged to consult the original articles for full details.

The general conclusion I am going to draw from this survey is that by and large the evidence favors the hypothesis of a functional separation between the episodic- and semantic-memory systems. Some evidence from the experiments, however, is problematic for the distinction. That evidence, and their implications for a taxonomy of memory systems, will be discussed in the next chapter.

Simple transfer

Three experiments, based on the logic of what I referred to as simple transfer (p. 72), have been reported by Anderson and Ross (1980). I will here briefly discuss Anderson and Ross's first experiment; the results of the other two experiments were not materially different from those of the first.

The experiment consisted of two phases. In the first, the study phase, subjects committed to memory a number of simple sentences, such as 'A spaniel is a dog', 'A plumber pets a dog', 'A rose is not a drawer', and 'A bee is an insect'. In the second, the test phase, they were presented with word pairs, such as SPANIEL–DOG, or ROSE–INSECT; their task was to decide as quickly as possible whether or not the left-hand word was an instance of the category designated by the right-hand word. Thus, the correct response to SPANIEL – DOG would be Yes, and to ROSE – INSECT, No.

The major experimental variable was the relation of the study-phase proposition to the implied propositions of the word pairs in the test phase. Four types of relation defined four conditions in the design: (a) Control condition—no known relation; (b) Practice condition—identical relation; (c) Interference condition—identical instance or identical category; and

(d) Spurious connection condition—identical argument with a different relation. These relations can be illustrated with respect to a common test pair SPANIEL–DOG in the four conditions. In the corresponding Control condition, subjects would memorize no sentence including the words 'SPANIEL' or 'DOG'; in the Practice condition, they would study the sentence, 'A spaniel is a dog'; in the Interference condition, they would study sentences such as 'A spaniel retrieves a ball', or 'A plumber pets a dog'; in the Spurious connection condition, they would study a sentence such as 'A spaniel sniffs a dog'. Comparable study-phase sentences would define the same four kinds of relation for the false test pair of ROSE–INSECT.

Another experimental variable was 'test block': verification times of both true and false test pairs in the four conditions defined by the study-phase to test-phase relations were measured four times, in four successive blocks of test trials.

The purpose of the experiment was to 'test whether there is a functional basis for the semantic–episodic distinction' (Anderson and Ross 1980, p. 450). The relevant evidence was going to be provided by transfer from episodic to semantic memory, measured in terms of the amount of time required for verification of test pairs as true or false. The critical comparison entailed verification times in the Control and Interference conditions. Anderson and Ross expected to find negative transfer in the Interference condition; they argued that such a finding would represent 'good evidence against a functional basis for the distinction' (p. 446).

Table 5.1
Verification latencies (ms) in Anderson and Ross (1980, Exp. 1)

Condition	True statements		False statements	
	Block 1	Block 4	Block 1	Block 4
Control	912	598	1066	639
Practice	762	583	902	683
Interference	841	614	932	684
Spurious	823	624	958	688

The results of the experiment are summarized in Table 5.1, which presents the mean verification times of 'true' and 'false' test pairs representing the four types of study/test relations, for both the first and last test blocks. The most striking finding concerns the reduction of verification times from the first to the last block: with the data averaged over all other conditions, the mean verification time dropped from 900 ms in the first block to 640 ms in the fourth block. Moreover, test blocks interacted with study/test relations: the differences among conditions were larger in the first block than in the last.

The results and their statistical analysis provided little evidence for the expected negative transfer in the Interference condition. Only in the fourth block, and only for 'false' pairs, did negative transfer occur. For the most part, verification latencies were *shorter* in the Interference than the Control condition. That is, by and large the data showed positive instead of negative transfer in the Interference Condition.

Undaunted by these adverse facts, Anderson and Ross proceeded to declare that their three experiments provided new evidence against the episodic/semantic distinction. This conclusion was based on the finding of transfer effects, mostly positive, in other conditions of the experiments, as well as on the finding of general practice effects—reduction of response times across test blocks—of the sort illustrated in Table 5.1.

It would probably be uncharitable to interpret Anderson and Ross' conclusion as a victory of rational thought over empirical facts. After all, not all facts may always mean what they seem to mean, and we may not get very far in our theoretical enterprise if we abandon every theory at the first glimpse of empirical trouble. A certain degree of flexibility in interpreting experimental outcomes may well have to be a part of the overall strategy.

Nevertheless, Anderson and Ross's treatment of the data does raise the question regarding the kind of evidence that would convince the unitary-memory theorists of the usefulness of the episodic/semantic distinction. If it sometimes seems reasonable to dismiss evidence that goes against the unitary view simply because some other evidence exists that supports it, then it is possible that all contrary evidence can be ignored. It would be interesting to hear from unitary-memory theorists as to the kinds of empirical evidence that they would accept as against their views. It would be equally interesting to hear from them as to the rules of the game by which empirical facts are brought to bear upon the theoretical issue. If we cannot agree on the rules, the debate about taxonomy of memory will necessarily remain inconclusive: Participants can 'solve' the problem of the episodic/semantic distinction on the basis of their own private rules. If so, the question is beyond the pale of science.

While we are talking about the rules of the game, I should admit to puzzlement on another matter in Anderson and Ross's analysis of their data. Although it is relatively inconsequential in the broader picture, it does illustrate the kind of difficulty that we are likely to experience in settling the issue of the distinction. The analysis concerned the data from Anderson and Ross's Experiment 2. For the 'true' judgments, they found a mean verification time of 767 ms in the Practice condition, 781 ms in the Control condition, and 787 ms in the Interference condition. Pooling the data from the Control and Interference conditions, they next tested the mean of these two conditions against the mean of the Practice condition. On the basis of a 'marginally significant difference' between the two means, they concluded that performance in the Practice condition was superior to that in the Control condition, that is, that there was positive transfer in the Practice condition (p. 457). We are witnessing here an almost magic transformation of a 14 ms difference between two experimental conditions, with an SE of 8.4 ms, into a finding that the authors interpret as supporting the view of unitary memory. Given this sort of flexibility of the rules of statistical inference, can we be very optimistic about the prospects of settling the issue of the relation between episodic and semantic memory on a commonly acceptable basis?

Anderson and Ross's results are less relevant to the episodic/semantic distinction than they think. The major problem is that the existence of transfer effects, as well as the existence of practice effects across test blocks, in experiments such as theirs, do not tell us anything about *what* it is that is transferred from the study (or an earlier retrieval) episode to a subsequent semantic task. Is new information stored in, or added to, semantic memory? If so, what is it? All we know from Anderson and Ross's experiments is that episodic study of the material affects the time necessary to answer questions of the kind that can be answered on the basis of information in semantic memory. But what does the reduced verification time signify, apart from demonstrating the 'ubiquitous law of practice effects' (Newell and Rosenbloom 1981)? After memorization of a sentence the learner can recall it, when instructed to do so, or complete it when a part of it is given; Anderson and Ross's results show that he is also able to verify a related proposition in less time. But it is difficult to argue that the operation of learning the sentence has resulted in any 'transfer to' semantic memory, in the sense of changing its contents or its organization, in a way in which a statement such as 'Did you know that aardvarks eat ants?' would do for a person who does not yet know this fact, or a statement such as 'The first space shuttle was named after the man who discovered America', would do for a person who does not know what the shuttle's name was.

The question of what is transferred from the study episode to the semantic task posed by Anderson and Ross, and the answer to it by unitary-memory theorists, are important, because it is known that transfer (or priming) effects in semantic-memory tasks, attributable to a study episode, can be found under conditions where what is transferred is completely unrelated to episodic-memory information. Relevant data have been reported by Jacoby and Witherspoon (1982) and Tulving, Schacter, and Stark (1982). I will have more to say about it in Chapter 6 (pp. 104–9). Given such facts, it is possible to entertain the hypothesis that in a situation such as that described by Anderson and Ross, too, transfer occurs, but that what has been transferred is uncorrelated with the information stored in the episodic system. If so, how would the unitary-memory theorist interpret these data? How does transfer of something that is unrelated to the episodic-memory information constitute evidence in favour of a single memory system?

I interpret the Anderson and Ross data as largely irrelevant to the problem of the distinction between episodic and semantic memory. We do not know what is transferred in their experimental situation, nor do we know whether, or how, what is transferred is related to the information in episodic memory. Simple transfer experiments of the kind described by Anderson and Ross are inadequate for providing useful evidence for the continuing debate.

Transfer comparisons

An experiment explicitly designed to test the hypothesis of 'the existence of separate semantic and episodic stores', conforming to what was referred to earlier as the method of transfer comparison, has been reported by Herrmann and Harwood (1980). It consisted of two stages. In the first, subjects committed to memory six sets of conceptually categorized words; in the second, their reaction time was measured in an episodic recognition task involving pairs of words as test items. Some test pairs contained two 'old' words, words seen in the previous acquisition set; some pairs contained an 'old' word and a 'new' word, one not seen in the acquisition set; in some test pairs both words were 'new'. In the second phase, the subjects' task was to indicate as quickly as possible which of the three types of test pairs a given pair represented.

The critical data concerned recognition latencies for test pairs in which both words were in fact 'new'. The influence of two variables, one episodic, the other semantic, on recognition latencies for the 'new' pairs was examined. The semantic variable was category belongingness: the two test words belonged either to the same conceptual category or to different categories. The episodic variable was what Herrmann and Harwood referred to as 'relatedness', with the two values of the variable being 'related' and 'unrelated'. 'Related' pairs consisted of words belonging to categories that had appeared in the acquisition set, whereas 'unrelated' words belonged to conceptual categories that had not been represented in the acquisition set. The two variables, semantic category and episodic relatedness, were crossed orthogonally, forming a 2 × 2 design.

The results of the experiment are shown in Table 5.2. The data represent mean reaction times (in seconds). The important finding is the interaction between the semantic and episodic variables: semantic category belong-

Table 5.2

Recognition latencies for 'new' pairs (s) in Herrmann and Harwood (1980)

Semantic category	Episodic relation Present	Absent
Same	2.42	1.93
Different	2.88	1.96

ingness made a difference to the decision latencies for episodically related words in test pairs, but no difference to episodically unrelated words.

Herrmann and Harwood interpreted their data as inconsistent with the hypothesis of a unitary storage system, and as consistent with the hypothesis of two separate storage systems. We can summarize their reasoning as follows. In a task in which the subject has to make episodic recognition decisions about two items, reaction time is influenced by the organization of the information in the episodic store. If both items of a test set are 'stored together', then the presentation of one of the items 'primes' (facilitates) access to the other. The difference between same and different semantic-category words in the episodic 'related' condition reflects the effect of such priming. Is this priming effect attributable to the pre-experimentally established organization of words (semantic categories) or to episodically determined organization (study of the categorized words in the first stage of the experiment)? The finding that there was no difference in decision latencies for the same and different semantic categories in the episodic 'unrelated' condition rules out the pre-experimentally established organization as a source of the priming effect, and implies that the priming effect observed in the episodically 'related' conditions (latencies of 2.42 and 2.88 seconds) reflected the belongingness of the words in test pairs to the same or different *episodic* categories. In terms of the logic of the method of transfer comparison, we have here, then, a pattern of results demonstrating that an episodic variable does, and a comparable semantic variable does not, affect subjects' performance on one and the same task. This pattern supports the distinction between the two systems.

Experimental dissociations

We will consider four experiments under the heading of experimental dissociations: Shoben *et al.* (1978); McKoon and Ratcliff (1979); Jacoby and Dallas (1981); Kihlstrom (1980).

Shoben et al. experiment

Shoben *et al.* did two experiments explicitly designed to 'assess the validity of the distinction between episodic and semantic memory' (Shoben *et al.* 1978, p. 304). I shall discuss only their second experiment, since its design was an improvement over that of the first one.

Shoben *et al.* studied the effect of two variables—'relatedness' and 'fanning'—on both an episodic task (sentence recognition) and a semantic task (sentence verification). The experiment was based on the logic of double experimental dissociation: it was designed to demonstrate dissociation of both episodic and semantic variables and episodic and semantic tasks.

In the sentence *verification* task, subjects were shown simple statements consisting of subject and predicate terms—for example, 'A canary is yellow', or 'A donkey has wings'—and they had to decide whether the statement was true or false. Time to make the decision, reaction time, was the dependent variable. In the sentence *recognition* task, sentences of the same form, both true and false, were presented to the subjects, and they had to decide whether or not they had seen the sentence in the previous part of the experiment. Again, reaction time for making the decision was measured.

One of the two variables that was manipulated was selected in the expectation that it would show an effect on the semantic task of sentence verification and no effect on the episodic task of sentence recognition. The variable was semantic relatedness between the subject and predicate terms of a sentence. For instance, the sentence 'Tigers have stripes' represents a high degree of semantic relatedness, whereas 'Tigers have thighs' represents a low degree. The second independent variable was selected in the expectation that it would show an effect on the episodic task of sentence recognition but no effect on the semantic task of sentence verification. The variable was 'fanning', defined in terms of the number of propositions learned about a concept. Thus, for instance, if a subject in the experiment learns that 'Tigers have stripes', 'Tigers have thighs', 'Tigers have fingers', and 'Tigers have cars', he has learned a total of four propositions about tigers, two true ones and two false ones, and the four propositions constitute 'Fan-4' condition.

The experiment involved two experimental sessions separated by several days. In the first session, verification times for 48 sentences were measured over five test blocks. Upon the completion of this stage, subjects were given all 48 sentences, told to go home, memorize them all, and return for the second session a few days later. When they returned, their recall of the learned sentences was tested, and then the critical part of the second session, measurement of reaction time for recognition, was given. In the recognition test, the 48 memorized target sentences were mixed with 96 previously unseen distractor sentences.

Mean reaction times for verification and recognition of the 48 'old' sentences are shown in Table 5.3. These data are pooled for true and false sentences. Statistical analysis of the data supported the conclusion that verification times were influenced by the semantic relatedness variable but

Table 5.3
Response latencies (s) in Shoben et al. *(1978, Exp. 2)*

Task	Relatedness Related	Unrelated	Fanning Fan-1	Fan-3
Semantic verification	1.23	1.16	1.18	1.21
Episodic recognition	1.36	1.41	1.26	1.50

not by fanning, whereas recognition was influenced by fanning but not by relatedness. After discussing possible objections to their intended interpretation, Shoben *et al.* concluded that the double dissociation observed in the experiment 'seems most easily handled by a model that draws a distinction between semantic and episodic representations' (p. 316).

The Shoben *et al.* study has been criticized by McCloskey and Santee (1981) on several grounds. One problem that Shoben *et al.* had, according to McCloskey and Santee, had to do with their manipulation of the 'fanning' variable in terms of the HAM (Anderson and Bower 1973) process model of retrieval. If one does not accept the HAM model, the argument continued, the fanning data obtained by Shoben *et al.* can be explained without postulation of different episodic and semantic representations. Similarly, the relatedness effect obtained by Shoben *et al.* could be explained in terms of different processes operating in episodic and semantic tasks, rather than differences in representation of information. McCloskey and Santee also reported an experiment demonstrating that semantic relatedness affects reaction time of correct rejection responses in the episodic recognition task.

McCloskey and Santee's criticism of the Shoben *et al.* article is primarily directed at Shoben *et al.*'s explanation of the double dissociation in terms of differences in episodic and semantic information. It is not clear that their criticisms have the same relevance to the idea of episodic and semantic memory as different systems of receiving, retaining, and transmitting information. Their assumption that the semantic verification and episodic recognition judgments are mediated by different processes, for instance, is not necessarily incompatible with the idea of episodic and semantic memory as different systems.

Be it as it may, McCloskey and Santee say that they regard the episodic/semantic distinction 'as a potentially useful way of classifying different types of knowledge and not as a description of two separate memory systems' (p. 71). The problem with McCloskey and Santee's conclusion lies in their separate and different explanations of the effects of the two independent variables manipulated in the Shoben *et al.* experiment. If this strategy is generally adopted, and separate explanations proposed for every new finding of dissociations in episodic and semantic tasks, we will end up with as many explanations as we have facts. One of the advantages of the episodic/semantic distinction is that it provides a unifying framework within which the individual explanations might be integrated.

McKoon and Ratcliff experiment

McKoon and Ratcliff (1979) described a total of four experiments. Their individual experiments conformed to the method of transfer comparison which we discussed earlier (pp. 73; 83). But it is possible to regard their Experiments 1 and 4 as parts of a larger experiment whose design satisfies the conditions of the method of experimental dissociation: the effect of the same experimental manipulations on performance in an episodic and a semantic task can be compared. In both experiments, McKoon and Ratcliff measured priming effects, they used the same experimental materials and the same overall procedure, and all experimental conditions of Experiment 4 were also represented in the design of Experiment 1. The only difference was that the task in Experiment 1 was a semantic one, lexical decision, whereas in Experiment 4 it was an episodic one, item recognition.

In the lexical decision task, a string of letters is presented to the subject, and the subject has to decide, as quickly as possible, without making errors, whether or not the presented string is a word. In a typical lexical decision task, letter strings about which decisions have to be made, are presented at a fast rate. In McKoon and Ratcliff's experiment, for instance, a new string appeared 250 ms after the subject had made the response to the previous string.

'Priming effect' is the label for the finding that the lexical decision response is faster to the nth word (target) in the test series if the $n - 1$th word (priming word) is meaningfully related to the nth word. Two kinds of priming effects can be distinguished, direct and indirect. In direct priming, the priming word is identical with the target word; in indirect priming, the priming word is not identical but related to the target in some other systematic fashion, for instance, associatively (Meyer and Schvaneveldt 1976). For McKoon and Ratcliff priming effects were indirect.

The three experimental conditions shared by Experiments 1 and 4, in addition to the control condition, were defined in terms of the relation between the priming and target words: (a) associated both episodically and semantically, (b) associated episodically, and (c) associated semantically. Semantic association was defined in terms of normative semantic free-associations (e.g. *green*–GRASS); episodic associations in terms of the study of a pair of words in the first phase of the experiment, with the priming word constituting the A member of the pair and the target the B member (e.g. *city*–GRASS learned as a pair in the first phase, and *city* serving as the priming word and GRASS as the target word in the second phase). In the condition in which both episodic and semantic associations were present, a normatively associated pair of words, such as *green*–GRASS, was studied by the subject in the first phase of the experiment.

In both Experiments 1 and 4, subjects first studied pairs of words, both pre-experimentally associated and not, and in the immediately following second stage made lexical decisions (Experiment 1) or Yes/No recognition decisions (Experiment 4) about single words presented at a rapid rate.

Table 5.4 summarizes the outcomes of the relevant comparisons. Mean reaction times of correct decisions are shown for three priming conditions for both the semantic and the episodic tasks. These data show that the manipulation of priming conditions had no effect on the lexical decision

Table 5.4
Response latencies (s) in McKoon and Ratcliff (1979)

| Task | Relation of priming word to target | | |
	Episodic and semantic	Episodic	Semantic
Semantic			
Lexical decision	0.53	0.54	0.53
Episodic			
Recognition	0.57	0.62	0.74

task, but a sizable effect on the episodic-recognition task. This pattern is similar to the 'fanning' data reported by Shoben *et al.* (1978); it can be regarded as evidence in support of the episodic/semantic distinction.

Jacoby and Dallas experiment

A third series of experiments relevant in the present context has been reported by Jacoby and Dallas (1981). Although their experiments were not explicitly designed to test the episodic/semantic distinction, they do conform to the method of experimental dissociation, and therefore can serve as a source of pertinent evidence.

Jacoby and Dallas described six experiments in all. In every one, the effect of one or more experimental variables on subjects' performance in two different tasks was studied. Jacoby and Dallas referred to the two tasks as recognition memory and perceptual recognition. I will refer to them here as episodic recognition and perceptual identification, in order to minimize possible confusions that the occurrence of the term 'recognition' in both phrases might cause.

I will briefly summarize Jacoby and Dallas' first experiment. Some, but not all, experiments in the series produced results similar to those in the first experiment.

The experiment was patterned after the Craik paradigm (Craik 1973; Craik and Tulving 1975). It consisted of two successive parts. In the first, subjects were shown 60 words, one at a time, about which they answered different questions. Some questions were designed to induce the subject to pay attention to the visual appearance of the word ('Is the word typed in capital letters?'), some to the sound of the word ('Does the word rhyme with *teach*?'), and some to the meaning of the word ('Does the word refer to a form of communication?'). Half of the questions in each of the three encoding categories elicited 'Yes' answers, the other half 'No' answers.

In the second phase of the experiment, subjects were given either the episodic-recognition test or the perceptual identification test. For the former, the 60 previously seen words were mixed with 20 new words, each was presented individually, and the subject had to say whether or not he had seen the word in the study phase. In the perceptual identification test, the same 60 'old' and 20 'new' words were flashed on a video-screen, one at a time, for a duration of 35 ms, and the subjects had to say what the word was.

Table 5.5
Response probabilities in Jacoby and Dallas (1981, Exp. 1)

Task	First-phase encoding condition		
	Appearance	Sound	Meaning
Semantic			
Identification	0.80	0.81	0.82
Episodic			
Recognition	0.50	0.63	0.86

The results of the experiment are summarized in Table 5.5, in the form of percentages of correct responses to the words that the subjects saw in the study phase. The data show that the probability of episodic recognition increased systemically from the graphemic through the acoustic to the semantic encoding condition, and that the effect of the type of encoding was greater for the words in the 'Yes' encoding categories than in the 'No' categories. This pattern of data is typical of the Craik paradigm, replicated many times in the literature. The proportion of correct responses in the perceptual identification task, however, varied neither with the encoding condition nor with the 'Yes'/'No' categories.

The pattern of results is very similar to the 'fanning' data from the Shoben *et al.* experiment and the results of the McKoon and Ratcliff studies: it reveals a strong dissociation of performance on episodic and semantic tasks, and thus provides evidence in support of the distinction of episodic and semantic memory as functionally different systems.

Kihlstrom experiment

Different experimental conditions in experiments demonstrating dissociations between episodic and semantic tasks can be brought about not only by manipulation of the learning materials, as was done in the Shoben *et al.*, McKoon and Ratcliff, and Jacoby and Dallas experiments, but also by creating differences in brain states. Some of these differences occur naturally, as a result of disease or normal development; others can be created in the laboratory through administration of psychoactive drugs, hypnosis, and other like means. The relation of such brain states to performance in episodic and semantic memory tasks can be assessed and the logic of experimental dissociation used in evaluating the implications of the outcome of the experiment for the episodic/semantic distinction.

Consider as an illustration an experiment by Kihlstrom (1980, Exp. 1).

Four groups of university students, representing different levels of hypnotic susceptibility, were hypnotized, and, while under hypnosis, learned a list of 16 common words by the method of multitrial free recall. When the subjects had reached the criterion of two perfect recall trials in succession, they were administered an amnesia suggestion: they were told that when they awakened from hypnosis, they would not remember having learned any words while in the hypnotic state. They were further told that upon a particular signal from the experimenter, however, they would regain the knowledge not only of the fact that they had learned the list but they would also remember the words from the list.

After the subjects were awakened from hypnosis, they were first asked whether they remembered what had happened while they were hypnotized. Most subjects remembered learning the list, although seven out of ten subjects in the group of highest susceptibility did not. All subjects were then asked to try to recall the words that they had learned; the seven subjects were informed by the experimenter that they in fact had learned a list. The number of words recalled represented a measure of performance on the episodic task of free recall.

A measure of semantic-memory performance was obtained in the next stage of the experiment. All subjects were administered a semantic free-association test. The stimulus words in the test were words that were highly likely to elicit the learned list words as their primary associates. In addition, other stimulus words were used in this test whose normative, primary or other, associates did not include words from the studied list. Subjects were instructed to give three responses to each stimulus word. (Kihlstrom gave two additional memory tests to his subjects, but the results from these two tests are less relevant to our present purposes.)

The results of the experiment are summarized in Table 5.6. Free association and free recall proportions are shown for three groups of subjects; the performance of the subjects in the medium- and low-hypnotizability groups did not vary greatly, and the data from these groups were combined. The free-association scores represent the probability that the subjects gave as their first response the normative primary associate of each

Table 5.6
Response probabilities in Kihlstrom (1980)

Task	Hypnotizability of subjects		
	Very high	High	Medium and Low
Semantic			
Free association	0.61	0.50	0.53
Episodic			
Free recall	0.01	0.47	0.86

stimulus word, that is, a response identical with one of the studied list words. (These data would not be changed materially if all three responses given by subjects were taken into account.)

The data in Table 5.6 show a striking dissociation between performance on the semantic and episodic tasks. Whereas the semantic free-association probabilities are approximately the same across the three groups, free-recall probabilities varied systematically with hypnotizability. The subjects in the 'very high' group recalled virtually nothing, whereas the subjects in the 'medium' and 'low' groups recalled 86 per cent of the previously learned words.

Kihlstrom had assigned his subjects to the four groups on the basis of their scores on the Stanford Hypnotic Susceptibility Scale, Form C. Systematic differences in the free-recall scores across the groups provided internal validation of differences in subjects between the groups: post-hypnotic amnesia varied directly with hypnotic susceptibility. The fact that semantic free-association performance was unrelated to hypnotic susceptibility indicates that post-hypnotic amnesia entailed subjects' memory for the word-events that had occurred during the study phase, and not access to the nominally identical words in semantic memory, or suppression, deliberate or otherwise, of corresponding responses.

The results of Kihlstrom's experiment thus provide evidence in support of the episodic/semantic distinction.

Brain states

The next experiment we shall briefly consider comes under the heading of brain states, in that it entailed measurement of brain activity of subjects engaged in either an episodic or a semantic memory task. This interesting experiment, reported by Wood *et al.* (1980), had several purposes, one of which was to obtain evidence relevant to the episodic/semantic distinction. The evidence was obtained by taking measurements of regional cerebral blood flow.

Changes in the blood flow in different cerebral regions are assumed to reflect changes in the pattern of neural activity in the cerebral cortex, mainly in superficial cortical structures (Ingvar 1979). Blood flow in conscious, non-anesthetized patients can be determined by means of recording the arrival and subsequent clearance of small concentrations of radioactive material by radiation detectors placed at the side of the patient's head. The recorded impulses from a number of detectors surrounding the patient's head are fed into, and processed by, a computer that computes the rate of blood flow in different regions.

The method used by Wood *et al.* was simple but ingenious. Fourteen volunteer patients from a hospital, free from neurological defects, served as subjects. Each subject went through two sessions. The recording of blood flow in the first session provided a baseline measurement for each patient. Patients inhaled low concentrations of xenon-133, a radioactive isotope, for a period of one minute. Then, while the subject was sitting with his eyes closed and with extraneous auditory input attenuated by headphones, clearance of the isotope in eight cortical regions was recorded over a period of ten minutes. Following this recording, all patients were presented with 40 common words through the headphones. Each word was presented twice, and the patients were instructed to listen to each word carefully and to repeat the word after hearing it.

The second blood-flow measurement trial was staged after the presentation of the list. The same inhalation and recording procedure was followed. On this trial, the subjects were divided into two groups, a recognition-memory group, and a semantic-classification group. Both groups were presented with a second list of 80 words, consisting of the 40 words heard in the previous list and 40 new ones. The subjects in the recognition-memory group were told to lift their left index finger every time they heard a word that had occurred in the previously presented list: these subjects engaged in an episodic-memory task. The subjects in the semantic-classification group were told to lift their left index finger every time they heard a word representing a concrete object that would fit into a room: these subjects engaged in a semantic-memory task. The test list of 80 words contained approximately 40 words to which such a positive classification response would be given by a typical subject. Thus, both groups were treated alike in every way except one: they went through the same blood-flow measurement procedure, they heard the same list of 40 words at study and the same list of 80 words at test, and they had to communicate the results of their mental activity to the experimenter through the same physical response. The only difference between the groups had to do with the nature of their mental activity, episodic versus semantic.

The question that Wood *et al.* posed concerned differential activity of different brain centers in the two tasks. The suggestion that the episodic/semantic distinction might have anatomical validity had earlier been made by Kinsbourne and Wood (1975). They speculated that episodic memory, which is selectively impaired in amnesia, might be particularly dependent on subcortical activity, whereas semantic memory, which is selectively impaired in aphasia and agnosia, might be relatively more dependent upon cortical activity. If so, blood-flow measures in different cortical regions might differ in mental activity involving one or the other system.

The results of the Wood *et al.* experiment revealed statistically significant differences in blood flow in the left hemisphere for the episodic and semantic groups. In addition, significant negative correlations were found between accuracy of performance and blood flow in the occipital and temporal-occipital regions of the left hemisphere for the subjects in the episodic-recognition group but not for the subjects in the semantic-classification group.

Wood *et al.* concluded that, 'The results are considered to support an anatomical basis for the distinction between episodic and semantic memory and to suggest that occipital flow may diminish with accurate memory performance because of an upstream demand of blood in the medial temporal lobe' (p. 113). Wood *et al.* also pointed out that alternative interpretations of their findings cannot be excluded. For instance, it might be possible that the differences they observed are attributable to differences in the level of difficulty of the two tasks, rather than to their episodic/semantic characterization. Future research will be necessary to evaluate the role that factors other than episodic and semantic processing play in determining the differences in observed patterns of regional cerebral blood flow. For the time being, however, the results of the Wood *et al.* experiment can be regarded as favorable to the hypothesis of the distinction between episodic and semantic memory.

Pathological dissociations

Pathological dissociations supporting the episodic/semantic distinction have been discussed elsewhere (Schacter and Tulving 1982). Here I shall just mention a few examples of relevant evidence.

One set of data that could be interpreted as representing a pathological dissociation between episodic- and semantic-memory tasks is represented by the Warrington–Weiskrantz effect (1974, Exp. 1) that I mentioned earlier (p. 30). Warrington and Weiskrantz compared the performance of four amnesic patients with that of four control subjects. Both groups studied lists of 16 common words; performance was tested in two different tasks.

One task was a standard Yes/No recognition task: 'old' words together with 'new' words were presented one at a time, and the subject had to say whether or not he had seen it in the studied list. The other task was referred to by Warrington and Weiskrantz as 'cued recall', but I will use the label of 'word-fragment completion' for it in order to minimize the possibility of confusion with the widely used term 'cued recall' in episodic-memory experiments. In the word-fragment completion task, the subjects were presented with the first three letters of each studied word and asked to complete each fragment with a word from the studied list. Since 'retention' of the studied list by both methods was assessed ten minutes after the study of the list, the amnesic patients frequently did not remember having studied a list at all, and the instructions to complete the fragments with words from the studied list, therefore, did not make sense to them. In these cases, the experimenters asked the subjects to complete the fragments with any meaningful familiar English word that fitted it.

Table 5.7
Response probabilities in Warrington and Weiskrantz (1974, Exp. 1)

Task	Patient group	
	Amnesics	Controls
Semantic:		
Word completion	0.34	0.25
Episodic:		
Recognition	0.28	0.72

Note: Adopted from Fig. 1 in Warrington and Weiskrantz (1974)

The word fragments used by Warrington and Weiskrantz were selected in such a manner that each fit at least ten common words in the dictionary. The fact that both patient groups performed at a level higher than what might have been expected by chance implies that the performance was facilitated by the encounter with the words in the study list. In what sense, then, should we classify the word-fragment completion task as one tapping semantic memory? We have a complication here. On the one hand, the task is semantic in that it can be performed in the absence of any particular episodic learning experience. Indeed, the amnesic patients, who denied having any recollection of the learning experience, managed to do as well on the task as the control patients, all of whom clearly did remember the learning of the study list. On the other hand, performance on this 'semantic' task was clearly influenced by the learning episode, and approximately to the same extent in both groups.

We could think of the performance of Warrington and Weiskrantz's patients in the word-fragment completion task in terms of subjects' use of episodic information in a nominally semantic task, in keeping with the idea I mentioned earlier (p. 77). This hypothesis implies that such use is possible even when the circumstances surrounding the acquisition of the information are not accessible to conscious awareness. The situation is well known from everyday life: people do remember all sorts of things from their personal experiences without remembering the episodes in which the information was acquired. Nevertheless, the relation between such episodic information without awareness of the episode, on the one hand, and information in the semantic system needs to be discussed more fully. I shall do this in the next chapter.

More recent evidence reported by Warrington and Weiskrantz also, and less ambiguously, points to a dissociation between episodic and semantic tasks when amnesic patients are compared with control patients (Warrington and Weiskrantz 1982, Exp. 1). This evidence was provided by the performance of the two groups of patients on four semantic-memory tasks: (a) word-fragment completion in the absence of any learning episode, (b) classification of words into conceptual categories, (c) a semantic restricted-association task, and (d) naming an instance of a given conceptual category. Subjects were given two trials in each task, separated by a five-minute interval; in a given task, stimulus words and questions were the same on both trials. Latencies of subjects' verbal responses were recorded and constituted the data of interest.

The overall pattern of results revealed relatively little difference between the performance of amnesic and non-amnesic patients. Response latencies on the first trial on all four tasks were roughly comparable, both groups showed about the same amount of improvement (reduction in latencies) from the first to the second trial. Since the absence of differences in these semantic-memory tasks contrast sharply with sizable differences between amnesics and non-amnesics on many episodic-memory tasks, Warrington and Weiskrantz's findings can be regarded as providing a picture of dissociation.

Dissociations of episodic- and semantic-memory performances are found in many clinical descriptions of the amnesic syndrome. I shall briefly mention two pieces of anecdotal evidence. One concerns anterograde amnesia, the other retrograde amnesia.

The first case is described by Claparède (1911). While interviewing a 47-year-old woman suffering from Korsakoff's disease, Claparède jabbed her hand with a pin hidden between his fingers. A few minutes later the patient no longer remembered the event. Yet, when Claparède again reached out for her hand, she pulled it back 'in a reflex fashion, not knowing why'. When Claparède asked her for a reason, she said, 'Doesn't one have the right to withdraw her hand?' And when Claparède insisted, she said, 'Is there perhaps a pin hidden in your hand?' When Claparède inquired why she would suspect him of hiding a pin in his hand, or wanting to jab her, she responded that, 'That was an idea that went through my mind', adding that, 'Sometimes pins are hidden in people's hands' (Claparède 1911, pp. 69–70).

Claparède's patient showed no memory for the pinprick episode, but nevertheless acted as if she had picked up some 'knowledge of the world' from the episode. The separation between two kinds of knowledge exhibited by the amnesic patient represents a particularly extreme case of a relatively normal phenomenon of memory: people retain knowledge that they have acquired on a particular occasion long after they have forgotten the episode itself.

The second anecdote is part of the description of the case of a patient who, two years after recovering from a long and difficult bout with tuberculous meningitis, still was densely amnesic for all events that had taken place in his life six months before and four months after the onset of his illness (Williams and Smith 1954). Shortly before his illness, the patient, as a soldier in the army, had taken a clerk's training course together with a number of other soldiers. When he was shown a group photograph that had been taken in the course, he could produce the name of every man in the photograph, but he remembered nothing about the occasion on which the photograph was taken, nor why or how he knew the men who appeared in it. Like Claparède's patient, he had no knowledge of the source of his knowledge.

Finally, under the heading of pathological dissociations, I should briefly mention an experiment with a single patient who temporarily suffered from 'functional' amnesia: severe loss of memory in the absence of any known physical damage to the brain. The experiment is described in greater detail elsewhere (Schacter, Wang, Tulving, and Freedman 1982).

A young man of 21 years of age, reported himself to a hospital in Toronto, complaining that he did not know who he was. He did not know his name or address, and had great difficulty remembering anything from his past. While the patient was in the amnesic state, we gave him two simple tests, one directed at episodic, the other at semantic knowledge, and prepared to give comparable tests after his amnesia lifted, expected on the basis of the course of development of functional amnesias. The episodic test consisted of presenting the patient with single cue words and instructing him to think of personal experiences of which the cues reminded him. The semantic-memory test consisted of showing to the patient photographs of well-known people (Albert, Butters, and Levin 1979) and asking him to identify the people, either with or without additional cues.

Since the patient's amnesia in fact did clear up in a few days, and since we did give comparable versions of the two tests to him in his recovered state, the design of the experiment can be described as a 2×2, two states (amnesia versus normal) crossed with two tasks (episodic and semantic).

The patient's performance on the famous faces test was similar on the two occasions: he identified or recognized the names of 15 of the 24 people in his amnesic state, and was correct on 16 of the other set of 24 after his recovery. His performance on the episodic task, however, was both quantitatively and qualitatively different before and after his recovery. In the first session, only a very small proportion (14 per cent) of the remembered episodes dated from the period before the onset of amnesia, most of them from a single 'island' of memory from his past. After the recovery, in the second session, a large proportion of remembered episodes (92 per cent) originated from the period that had preceded the onset of the amnesia.

Again, dissociation between episodic and semantic memory is demonstrated: severe difficulty of remembering personal episodes from a long period co-existed with the preservation of knowledge about the world acquired during the same period. Although it would be imprudent to draw strong general conclusions from an experiment with a single subject, the pattern of results from the experiment agrees well with the clinical characterizations of functional amnesia.

Evaluation of evidence

This completes our short survey of the evidence that can be regarded as relevant to the episodic/semantic distinction. I argued that the evidence based on simple transfer and transfer comparison rules cannot be interpreted unambiguously and that, therefore, its relevance to the distinction at the present time is somewhat uncertain. Evidence demonstrating dissociations between episodic and semantic tasks, on the other hand, can be interpreted in a more straightforward fashion: it is in better agreement with the hypothesis of the distinction than the idea of a unitary memory.

Although the number of studies providing the relevant evidence was small, they did exhibit considerable variety of method. Data were collected in both laboratory experiments and clinical settings, and from normal subjects, hypnotized subjects, brain-damaged patients, as well as functional amnesia patients. Dependent variables included both accuracy and reaction time. A number of different tasks represented semantic memory: sentence verification, lexical decision, tachistoscopic identification, word-fragment completion, free association, naming of category instances, production of opposites; in episodic-memory tasks, recall and recognition were measured.

The hypothesis of a functional distinction between episodic- and semantic-memory systems provides an economical explanation of the finding of the same pattern of performance—dissociation of tasks—in the face of a great deal of situational diversity. We assume that the manipulated variables affected performance on episodic and semantic tasks differently, because the tasks tapped different memory systems. In the absence of such an overall explanation, a large number of different, unique explanations would have to be provided for the results of each experiment. Note that the hypothesis of the episodic/semantic distinction in no way 'predicts' the outcomes of experiments demonstrating dissociations, nor does it 'explain' them in the usual sense of the term. The hypothesis removes the necessity for the explanation of the observed dissociations. If episodic and semantic memory tasks are mediated by different functional systems, why should we expect that a given independent variable has the same effect on both? Only if a phenomenon departs from what we find intelligible, or from what we expect in terms of our understanding of the world, does it require explanation (Toulmin 1961).

Would it be equally meaningful to interpret the observed dissociations by assuming that they reflect different informational requirements of different tasks within a unitary memory system? Consider, for instance, the Jacoby and Dallas (1980) finding that encoding operations at study affect episodic recognition but not semantic identification of target words. What is wrong with assuming that informational changes in the (unitary) memory system brought about by the encoding operations, although relevant to recognition, were irrelevant for the words' perceptual identification? And could we not repeat the same line of reasoning for each of the dissociations that we considered, and do so in the future for all other dissociations that might be reported? We could, but the procedure would not offer much intellectual satisfaction. We would end up with as many explanations as we have patterns of data. To provide a general answer to the question as to why performance on certain tasks is not affected by certain changes in the informational contents of the (unitary) memory system, we might have to assume that certain kinds of tasks, call them semantic-memory tasks if you will, exist that are unaffected by certain kinds of informational changes in the system. This 'solution' is not altogether different from the hypothesis of a functionally separate semantic-memory system; the class of 'semantic tasks' helps to make general sense of many different patterns of data in the same way that the concept of 'semantic-memory system' does for theories assuming the distinction. In the final analysis, whether one prefers an explanation couched in terms of a distinctive class of tasks or a distinctive memory system is a matter of intellectual taste and scientific style. As long as we are limited to psychological methods, the issue cannot be decided on empirical grounds.

In some ways the most intriguing, and potentially most significant, data were those reported by Wood *et al.* (1980). If their findings of different cerebral blood-flow patterns associated with mental activity involving episodic and semantic memories turn out to be replicable and could be extended to other tasks, and other methods of measuring neurophysiological processes, and if alternative explanations of the observed differences could be precluded, the case for the distinction would be greatly strengthened. The hypothesis that episodic and semantic memory are functionally distinct would appear in a different light if it were known that different brain centers are involved in mediating the two kinds of memory activity.

More convincing than dissociations between episodic and semantic tasks might be observations of global changes in one system without corresponding changes in the other. For instance, if it were possible to temporarily suppress all or most of the operations of the episodic system without affecting the information-processing capability of the semantic system, the reality of the separate existence of the system would be enhanced. Clinical descriptions of patients suffering from amnesia associated with hysteria, fugues, or multiple personalities (Hilgard 1977; Nemiah 1979) are suggestive in this respect. Under these conditions, people may experience complete loss of personal identity together with dense amnesia for their past lives without showing similar impairment for their knowledge of the world. Like post-hypnotic amnesia (Kihlstrom and Evans 1979; Kihlstrom 1980) the 'dissociative amnesias' (Nemiah 1979) are characterized by lack of access to episodic or autobiographical memories; the patient's language skills and general knowledge of the world usually show little loss.

If we assume that the person's 'me-ness', his personal identity, is the ultimate 'control element' (Estes 1972, 1976b) that subsumes all the information in episodic memory and that must be 'activated' before personalized knowledge can be remembered, conditions under which the person loses his personal identity would be expected to lead to the suppression or inactivation of the whole episodic-memory system. Unfortunately, clinical descriptions of amnesia associated with hysteria, fugues, and multiple personalities do not contain sufficient evidence to permit us to assess the extent to which episodic memory is and semantic memory is not affected. Only one systematic comparison of episodic and semantic knowledge during and after a period of functional amnesia has been reported in the literature (Schacter *et al.* 1982). Although the data supported the hypothesis that episodic memory is selectively impaired in functional amnesia, the scope of relevant evidence was extremely limited. Future research undoubtedly will help to fill the existing gap.

The potential importance of studies in which the functioning of episodic and semantic systems is compared under conditions when one of the systems is globally inactivated—or its operations globally facilitated—cannot be overemphasized. Demonstrations of dissociations of episodic and semantic tasks of a large variety, in many different situations, certainly will help, and the overall impact of such studies, particularly when coupled with relevant physiological and neuroanatomical evidence, may turn out to be decisive enough to settle the issue. But since we are talking about the hypothesis of a distinction between two memory *systems*, observations resulting from experimental manipulations or naturally occurring interventions affecting the whole system would be especially critical.

The present verdict in favor of the distinction does not mean, of course, that the problem is hereby settled. An issue as complex as the one with which we are concerned is unlikely to be resolved on the basis of the results of a handful of experiments and clinical observations. The debate will undoubtedly continue, and more evidence will be generated that bears on the issue. The consensus that eventually will emerge is going to be shaped by the outcome of a large number of systematic studies, empirical observations, evaluation of the evidence, and rational thought. In the process, the original question, too, is likely to be changed; it is not just the relation between episodic and semantic systems that is going to be studied but also the relation of these two systems on the one hand to other memory systems on the other.

6
Extensions and contrasts

The issue of the nature of the relation between episodic and semantic memory is not settled. The proposition that they represent functionally distinct systems, therefore, is to be regarded as a hypothesis. But we can adopt two different attitudes towards the hypothesis. We can be sceptical about its validity, and concentrate our efforts on the attempts to prove it wrong. Alternatively, we can think of the hypothesis as describing a state of affairs for which there already exists good supportive evidence but which, owing to the complex nature of the overall problem, requires further thought and study. This latter attitude would encourage us to keep an open mind about the possibility that the hypothesis is wrong, but, at the same time, also recommend that we concentrate on the identification of differences and similarities of the two systems, as well as start thinking about possible extensions of the distinction.

In this chapter, we shall discuss a problem for the distinction that has emerged from some of the same experiments that provided supportive evidence for it. I shall describe the problem—it takes the form of priming effects—and will then adopt the attitude that it points to the need for an extension of the taxonomy of memory of which episodic and semantic systems are a part. I shall also offer some tentative and speculative observations about such possible extensions. In the final part of the chapter, I shall contrast the episodic/semantic distinction with a rather similar suggestion made in animal research by David Olton and his associates (e.g., Olton et al. 1979; Olton and Papas 1979).

Priming effects

'Priming' is a concept that was first used in the context of associative verbal processes (Cofer 1960). It is defined as 'a change in antecedent conditions which is specifically designed to increase the probability of a particular response being given to a particular stimulus' (Cramer 1968, p. 82). In direct priming, the antecedent conditions include the presentation of the to-be-primed response 'itself' before the critical test, whereas in indirect priming, the priming words are associatively related to the to-be-primed response.

More recently, 'priming' has been used in a much wider sense. It is a general term that refers to the facilitative effect of performing one task on the subsequent performance of the same or similar task; the term is sometimes also used to describe the underlying processes responsible for the effect. The tasks in question usually involve processing of lexical or semantic information; priming effects—facilitation of performance—are measured either in terms of response latencies or proportion of correct responses. Priming and positive transfer are closely related concepts, although 'priming' is typically used in situations in which small discrete units of to-be-processed material are specifically identified and responses to them separately measured.

Priming effects were observed in several studies that we discussed in Chapter 5. Thus, for instance, the positive transfer effects observed by Anderson and Ross (1980) could equally well be labelled priming effects. In the Mckoon and Ratcliff (1979) experiments, priming effects constituted the dependent variable of interest. And the explanation of the results of the Herrmann and Harwood (1980) study entailed a reference to priming effects. There are other priming effects, however, that we should discuss now.

Let us begin with Jacoby and Dallas (1981). The reader will remember that Jacoby and Dallas obtained results demonstrating a strong dissociation of episodic and semantic tasks: episodic recognition was, and semantic identification was not, related to the type of encoding operations performed on the target words in the first phase of the experiment. But Jacoby and Dallas also observed a priming effect: the probability of semantic identification was higher for words that had appeared in the first phase of the experiment (0.81) than for words that the subjects saw for the first time during the second phase (0.65).

The overall pattern of Jacoby and Dallas's data, therefore, can be described by saying that it manifests a dissociation between episodic and semantic tasks accompanied by a priming effect in the semantic task. We will meet exactly the same pattern in several other studies.

An experiment similar to the one done by Jacoby and Dallas was described more than ten years earlier by Winnick and Daniel (1970, Exp. 2). In the first phase of the experiment, subjects produced single-word responses to three different types of stimulus displays: printed words, pictures, or definitions of words. In the second phase, subjects tried to recall all the words they had produced in the first phase, and in the third, tachistoscopic identification thresholds were measured for both the words produced in the first phase as well as comparable 'new' words.

Winnick and Daniel, like Jacoby and Dallas, found what we now can label a dissociation of episodic and semantic tasks, as well as a priming effect in the semantic task. The proportions of words recalled were 71 per cent for the words elicited by printed words, 89 per cent elicited by pictures, and 94 per cent elicited by definitions. Tachistoscopic duration thresholds (in ms) were 49.1 for printed words, 59.3 for picture names, 61.0 for defined words, and 61.9 for new control words. Winnick and Daniel pointed out that since the strong response availability, indexed by probability of free recall, did not lower tachistoscopic thresholds, the findings are 'interpretable only as a kind of perceptual sensitization' (p. 80).

Winnick and Daniel's results have been recently replicated by Morton (1979) who did a series of experiments exploring the effect of various kinds of perceptual displays on subsequent tachistoscopic identification of single words.

Priming effects were also observed in the McKoon and Ratcliff (1979) experiments whose results were summarized in Table 5.4, p. 88. McKoon and Ratcliff measured (episodic) recognition and (semantic) lexical-decision latencies for target words preceded by priming words related to the target words episodically, semantically, or both. They found that the relation between the priming and target word affected recognition but not lexical decisions; they also found an overall priming effect. In their Experiment 1, the latency of the lexical decision for target words preceded by associated priming words averaged 0.53 s, whereas for target words preceded by unrelated words from the previously seen study list, the mean decision latency was 0.58 s, and for target words preceded by previously unseen words, 0.62 s.

McKoon and Ratcliff's data thus show that an earlier (episodic) experience facilitates a subsequent (semantic) decision involving components of the episodic experience. This overall pattern is very similar to the pattern of Jacoby and Dallas' findings: dissociation between episodic and semantic tasks accompanied by a priming effect in the semantic task. The similarity of the two patterns of data is underscored by the differences in the semantic tasks used in the two experiments. In Jacoby and Dallas's experiments , the semantic task was tachistoscopic identification of words, with probability of correct response as the dependent variable; in McKoon and Ratcliff's experiments, the semantic task involved lexical decisions, with reaction time as the dependent variable.

Another experiment demonstrating priming effects was Kihlstrom's (1980). The reader may remember that Kihlstrom hypnotized his subjects, had them learn a list of words followed by post-hypnotic amnesia suggestions, and then tested the subjects in the waking state. Subjects were given both an episodic recall task and a semantic word-association task. The striking dissociation between the performances on the two tasks was summarized in Table 5.6, (p. 90). The stimulus words used in the free-association task were of two kinds: those likely to elicit the 'old' words encountered by the subjects in the previously learned list, and those designed to elicit comparable 'new' words not seen before. The normative probabilities of the two categories of words as responses to stimuli were equal. Kihlstrom's data, however, showed that the probability of an 'old' word occurring as the first free-associate response was 0.54; the comparable figure for the 'new' words was 0.45. When all three responses made by the subjects to each stimulus were taken into account, the two figures became 0.67 and 0.57, respectively. The difference between the proportions of 'old' and 'new' responses defines the priming effect. It was small but statistically reliable. Moreover, its magnitude was approximately the same for the groups of subjects differing in hypnotic susceptibility.

Kihlstrom's findings fit into the by now familiar pattern: dissociation of episodic and semantic tasks combined with priming effects. It adds to the generality of the data from Jacoby and Dallas, and the McKoon and Ratcliff studies, and contributes a new dimension to the pattern of data: the demonstration that the magnitude of the priming effect is not correlated with performance on the episodic task. This latter finding was made possible by Kihlstrom's design, in which measures of (episodic) recall and (semantic) priming were available for each of the four groups of subjects that represented different levels of the independent variable of hypnotic susceptibility.

The overall pattern of data obtained by Kihlstrom was very similar to that reported by Williamsen, Johnson, and Erikson (1965) in their seminal experiment on post-hypnotic amnesia. Williamsen *et al.*, too, found a dissociation between episodic tasks (free recall and recognition) and semantic tasks (free association and identification of fragmented words), although, of course, they did not use these terms. In addition, they found priming effects, comparable in magnitude to Kihlstrom's, in their free-association task, and very much larger priming effects in their word-fragment identification task. In the latter, with the data averaged over three groups of subjects (high hypnotic susceptibility, low susceptibility, and controls), the probability of correct identification of 'old' words was 0.62, whereas that of 'new' words was 0.18. As in Kihlstrom's experiment, there was no relation between priming effects, on the one hand, and episodic recall and recognition, on the other.

Another set of relevant data comes from a study by Warrington and Weiskrantz (1982, Exp. 1). Warrington and Weiskrantz compared the performance of amnesic patients and control subjects on four semantic-memory tasks. These tasks included word-fragment completion, categorical classification, restricted associations, and naming of instances of categories. Two trials, separated by a five-minute interval, were given to all subjects on all tasks. The dependent variable was response latency.

Warrington and Weiskrantz found that both their amnesic and control patients responded faster on the second than on the first trial. The reduction in latency was approximately the same for both groups. This pattern of results resembles the finding from Kihlstrom's and Williamsen and his colleagues' experiments in which (temporary) amnesia was produced experimentally through hypnotic suggestions. In all these experiments, amnesic patients whose episodic-memory performance was severely impaired demonstrated performances in semantic tasks, and priming effects in these tasks, that were rather similar to those of people with unimpaired episodic memories.

The last set of data relevant to the present discussion come from an experiment by Tulving, Schacter, and Stark (1982). In this experiment, subjects were given two tasks: an episodic recognition task and a semantic word-fragment completion task. In the latter, subjects had to convert graphemic word fragments, such as A _ _ A _ _ I N, _ E _ D _ L _ M, and _ H _ O _ E M, into English words by filling in the missing letters indicated by the dashes. The subjects first saw a long list of words on a single trial, presented at the rate of five seconds per word. Subsequently they were tested for both recognition and fragment completion of study-list words as well as new words on two separate test occasions, one an hour after study, the other seven days later. Each test word was seen by each subject twice, once for episodic recognition judgment, and once, in its fragmented form, for word completion. The two tasks were given, for different sets of words, in both orders.

Three findings were of interest. First, the word-fragment completion task showed sizable priming effects. Probability of word completion was 0.31 for new words, those previously not encountered in the experiment, 0.46 for the words seen in the study list, 0.54 for the words seen in the preceding episodic recognition test, and 0.65 for the words that the subjects had encountered both in the study list and in the episodic recognition test. Second, although episodic recognition showed a typical decrement over the seven-day retention interval, the primed word-fragment completion performance did not: the probability with which subjects successfully completed the fragments was practically the same seven days later as it had been on the day of the study. Third, and perhaps most important, at the level of individual test words, primed word-fragment completion performance was uncorrelated with episodic recognition: Priming effects were essentially as large for the words identified as 'new' as they were for words identified as 'old' in the immediately preceding recognition test. This stochastic independence was observed both in the one-hour and seven-day tests, and for both the study-list words and the new words (distractor items in the recognition test).

The second finding, pertaining to the time course of retention of information tapped by the two tasks, is illustrated in Figure 6.1. The recognition score in the figure was arrived at by subtracting the false alarm rate from the hit rate, whereas the fragment completion scores are defined in terms of percentage of correct completions. The pattern of data shown in Figure 6.1 is the same that we saw in a number of experiments described in Chapter 5: They reflect a clear dissociation of performance in the episodic and semantic tasks.

The dissociation does not logically imply stochastic independence between recognition and fragment completion: It would be quite possible

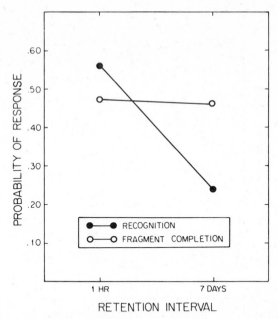

Fig. 6.1 Time course of retention of recognition and fragment-completion over seven days. (From Tulving, Schacter, and Stark, 1982.)

to obtain a pattern of the kind shown in Figure 6.1 under conditions where, at the level of individual test items, performances on the two tasks are correlated. The finding of stochastic independence between recognition and fragment completion, therefore, constitutes additional independent evidence in support of the functional distinction between episodic and semantic memory.

Priming: Episodic? Semantic? Procedural?

The experiments we have just discussed have produced the same general pattern of results: (a) an experimentally-manipulated variable affects subjects' performance on the episodic task, (b) it has no effect on the performance on the semantic task, but (c) the exposure of the material to the subjects in a study episode facilitates subsequent processing of the material in the semantic task. This pattern can be graphically described as shown in Figure 6.2. The pattern is quite general: it is found with different kinds of episodic and semantic tasks, with different types of manipulated experimental variables, with both response latencies and response accuracy as dependent variables, and in situations involving both direct and indirect priming.

The dissociation between performances on episodic and semantic tasks

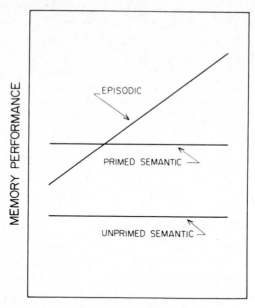

INDEPENDENT VARIABLE

Fig. 6.2 A schematic pattern of data showing the effect of a manipulated variable in an episodic task, no effect of the same variable in a semantic task, and the priming effect, independent of the manipulated variable, in the semantic task.

supports the episodic/semantic distinction. But what are we to make of the priming effects observed in the same experiments in which the dissociations have been demonstrated? How do the priming effects fit into the episodic/semantic distinction?

In keeping with the overall orientation of this book, I am here, too, assuming that one and the same general pattern of data, observed under a variety of conditions, reflects the same underlying processes or principles. The assumption may well be wrong: We really know very little about priming effects to be highly confident about any statements we make about them at this time. As we find out more about variables, conditions, and factors affecting priming and transfer in memory and learning experiments, including those observed in semantic-memory tasks, the world of priming phenomena may turn out to be as rich and complex as that of all cognition. Our present discussion of priming effects, therefore, should be regarded primarily as serving the purpose of raising questions that have to be addressed in future research. The assumption that the interesting pattern of data of the kind shown in Fig. 6.2, revealed in a number of experiments, represents one and the same phenomenon constitutes a convenient starting point for such research. It will be abandoned or revised, if experimental facts dictate such action.

The interpretation of priming effects in the experiments we have considered, as well as in others, is hampered by the paucity of information we have about them. Although interest in priming is clearly on the increase, relevant empirical evidence is still scarce. No theories of priming have been proposed. Theoretical speculations concerning priming have been concerned with matters such as the 'locus' of the effect in the sequence of separately identifiable, or postulated, stages (e.g., Lachman *et al.* 1974; Meyer, Schvaneveldt, and Ruddy 1974; Scarborough *et al.* 1977, 1979), the underlying mechanisms (e.g. Meyer and Schvaneveldt 1976; Collins and Loftus 1975), and the extent to which they are mediated by automatic versus deliberate processes (e.g. Neely 1977; Posner 1978, pp. 102–11). There is little in this work that is directly relevant to the question I am raising here: how does priming relate to the episodic/semantic distinction?

Since priming effects in semantic-memory tasks have their origin in a study episode, someone might be tempted to argue that they reflect some kind of transfer of episodic information to semantic memory. The reader may recall that Anderson and Ross (1980) interpreted the practice and transfer effects they observed in a semantic judgment task along these lines (pp. 79–82). It would be difficult to defend such an argument in light of the stochastic independence between semantic-memory performance and priming, on the one hand, and episodic recognition judgments, on the other, observed in the Tulving *et al.* (1982) experiment. These results, at least in the situation studied, make it rather clear that whatever it is that might be 'transferred' from an episodic encounter to the subsequent fragment-completion task does not seem to be the same kind of information or process that is involved in remembering events. Conversely, remembering events, as revealed in recognition judgments, seems to be unaffected by whatever information or process underlies the episodically induced facilitation of performance on the semantic task.

Although the generalizability of the conclusions from the Tulving *et al.* (1982) experiment is as yet unknown, since no comparable data have been reported by others, it may be worth noting that Jacoby and Witherspoon (1982) have reported similar stochastic independence between episodic recognition and tachistoscopic identification of words, in an extension of the kind of experiment described by Jacoby and Dallas (1981) that we discussed earlier (pp. 88–9). Thus it seems that the observed independence of priming effects from episodic memory is not limited to a single experimental paradigm. Furthermore, the fact that priming effects have been shown to be uncorrelated with episodic-memory performance in other situations (e.g. Kihlstrom 1980; Williamsen *et al.* 1965), also strengthens the conclusion that seems appropriate in light of the available data: priming effects are mediated by, and reflect the operations of, a system other than episodic memory.

The conclusion that priming is not an episodic-memory phenomenon, like others in our speculative discussion of the issue, should be regarded as tentative. Among other things, it should not be interpreted as ruling out the possibility that in some situations apparent priming effects reflect a particular kind of use of, or a particularly ready form of access to, certain aspects of episodic information. I mentioned such a possibility earlier (p. 77). The present conclusion is to the effect that there seems to be more to priming than just the transfer or some other form of ready use of episodic information

Let us next consider the hypothesis that priming effects reflect changes in the semantic system. If so, what kinds of changes? Is priming a consequence of transfer of some new information into the semantic system, that is, does it reflect changes in the *informational contents* of semantic memory? If yes, how should we think about the changed informational contents? If no, what other kind of changes? These are not easy questions to answer, partly because we have no good methods of distinguishing between the effects of changes in informational contents from the effects of changes in accessibility to, or retrievability of, unchanged contents.

Consider, for instance, Morton's (1970) logogen model. Logogen is a unit in the mental lexicon that is activated when the person sees, hears, writes, speaks, or otherwise 'processes' the dictionary unit that corresponds to it. Priming effects could be interpreted as reflecting the lowered threshold of excitability of a logogen after its activation by the priming stimulus. Similarly, in Atkinson and Juola's (1974) theory, presentation of a word for study is assumed to result in the encoding of the word in a form that increases the 'familiarity' value of the corresponding node in the lexical store. The 'familiarity' is represented by a 'reverberatory activity that dissipates over time' (Atkinson and Juola 1974, p. 250). Direct priming effects, in this theory, could reflect the enhanced familiarity value of the previously activated node. Indirect priming, on the other hand, could be explained in terms of the concept of spreading activation in the semantic network, as envisaged, for instance, in Collins and Loftus's (1975) theory. But do these hypothesized events in the system—continued excitation of the logogen, enhanced familiarity value of the node, and spreading activation—represent changes in informational contents or changes in the facility with which the information can be used in particular tasks?

The answer to this question is influenced by two important facts about priming. The first such fact is that direct priming effects can persist over long periods of time. Jacoby and Dallas (1981) picked up priming effects 24 hours after a single, brief presentation of target words, Tulving *et al.* (1982) observed no reduction in priming effects in the word-fragment completion task over an interval of seven days, and Kolers (1976) has reported data showing priming effects extending over an interval in excess of 12 months. In Kolers's experiment, students read typographically inverted text and were tested over a year later for the reading speed of the previously read pages of inverted typography as well as new pages. A statistically reliable albeit small advantage for the previously read pages was found.

These long-lived priming effects may be difficult to reconcile with the assumption that priming reflects the continued and slowly fading excitation of the logogen or activation of the lexical node. If the after-excitation subsides so gradually, the logogens or lexical-memory representations of at least the frequently used words would have to be in a continual state of heightened readiness that might be expected to be difficult to enhance any further, ruling out demonstrations of priming effects with high-frequency words. This seems an unlikely possibility. The other possible assumption, that priming effects reflect changes in the informational contents of the semantic-memory system, as envisaged, for instance, in Landauer's (1975) multicopy storage and random access theory, does not seem to fit the data much better: why should one single additional 'copy' of a lexical unit, stored in the system 24 hours or seven days earlier, make much difference in the use of the information that is presumably duplicated in hundreds or thousands of other identical copies?

The other relevant fact has to do with the absence, or at least severe attenuation, of cross-modality priming effects. Jacoby and Dallas (1981, Exp. 6) exposed potential target words either visually or auditorily, and then tested subjects' ability to identify them in the visual tachistoscopic task. Sizable priming effects were obtained within the visual modality but not across the two modalities. Similar absence of cross-modality priming effects has been reported by Morton (1979). Winnick and Daniel's (1970, Exp. 2) tachistoscopic thresholds can also be interpreted as demonstrating within-modality but not cross-modality priming.

The long-lived priming effects that do not cross modality boundaries do not provide much encouragement for the hypothesis that priming is a phenomenon of semantic memory. Why should whatever information it is that supports priming, that has reached the system through one sensory modality, be usable over a long interval of time without any degradation, and yet be largely useless in a situation in which the information to be processed is carried by a stimulus in another modality? Further research will undoubtedly illuminate the matter, but for the time being we should keep an open mind about priming in semantic-memory tasks as a phenomenon of semantic memory.

If priming is neither an episodic-memory nor a semantic-memory phenomenon, what is it? One possible hypothesis is that priming reflects an improvement in the facility with which cognitive operations are carried out, that is, that priming is a phenomenon of procedural memory. We know that even highly overlearned cognitive skills such as those involved in reading printed material or comprehension of spoken language, can be improved with practice. These practice effects, like the transfer effects in verbal learning (e.g. Postman 1971), may be general, holding for a whole class of materials, or specific, applying to particular individual units only. Striking improvements in information-processing abilities have been described by Kolers 1976, 1979), Neisser and his associates (Neisser, Novick, and Lazar 1963; Spelke, Hirst, and Neisser 1976; Hirst, Spelke, Reaves, Caharack, and Neisser 1980), Peterson (1969), as well as others, and many other examples of the 'ubiquitous law of practice' (Newell and Rosenbloom 1981) can be found in the literature on perceptual learning (e.g. Gibson 1969). Thus, various kinds of priming effects, too, may represent similar manifestations of improvement in skills with which information is processed in tasks in which priming effects are observed.

The hypothesis that priming effects—or at least some forms of it (Broadbent and Broadbent 1980)—are mediated by the procedural-memory system is similar to the hypothesis that they reflect the enhanced accessibility or retrievability of semantic (or permanent-memory) information: both assume facilitation in the use of otherwise unchanged information. They differ, however, in that the procedural-memory hypothesis assumes that the modification lies in the way the system carries out one or more operations, the 'how' of the process, whereas the enhanced-accessibility hypothesis attributes priming effects to the changed states of the to-be-retrieved information, the 'what' of the conditions. The procedural-memory system has wider scope than semantic memory; it can, and does, operate in situations in which neither the initiation nor the goal of the activity depends on the organism's knowledge of language or any other symbol system; and it may represent a phylogenetically older system than either of the two propositional-memory systems, episodic and semantic (Squire 1982).

At the present time the idea that priming effects in semantic-memory tasks reflect changes in procedural memory seems to be somewhat more attractive than the idea that they reflect changes in semantic memory. Among other things, it helps us to understand the numerous demonstrations of acquisition and improvement in perceptual-motor and cognitive skills by amnesic patients who have great difficulties acquiring any new semantic knowledge. Relevant evidence has been summarized by Baddeley (1981), Schacter and Tulving (1982), Squire (1982), and Weiskrantz and Warrington (1979). A particularly striking demonstration has been reported by Cohen and Squire (1980). They presented their densely amnesic patients with sets of words printed in inverted typography of the kind used by Kolers (1975, 1976) in his well-known series of experiments. Patients were asked to 'decipher' each word in the set and read it out loud. Some words appeared only once in the series, whereas others were repeated. Cohen and Squire found that not only did the amnesic subjects become progressively faster on the task, their learning improved at the same rate as that of the non-amnesic control subjects. Moreover, amnesics read the repeated words faster than they read words seen for the first time, despite the fact that their recognition memory for the words they had encountered in the task was grossly impaired in relation to that of the controls. Cohen and Squire interpreted their data as showing that the amnesic subjects' procedural knowledge—knowing how—was intact, implying a functional separation between procedural and propositional memory systems.

One problem with the interpretation of priming effects in semantic tasks as improvement in cognitive skills, or modifications of procedural memory, has to do with the nature of some of the tasks that have been used in priming experiments. Consider, for instance, the word-fragment completion task used in the Tulving *et al.* (1982) experiment. Each of the word fragments we used (A_ _A_ _IN, _E_D_L_M, _H_ O_EM, and the like) uniquely specified a single word in English (ASSASSIN, PENDULUM, THEOREM) that was well known to the subject before the experiment. As we saw in the description of the results of the experiment (pp. 104–5), the subjects in the experiment were capable of successfully completing the words approximately 30 per cent of the time in the absence of any priming. It seems natural to think of this level of performance as reflecting the joint effects of the lexical information about the target words and the information provided by the graphemic fragment. Since it is very easy to improve the subjects' performance on this task, in the absence of any priming, by simply providing them with more complete fragments of target words, it is tempting to think that the major difficulty in the task is produced by the inadequacy of the selection information provided by the fragment cues, rather than the absence or low level of development of appropriate cognitive skills.

If priming effects are to be thought about in terms of skills, the skills involved are highly item-specific. Lyn Turner and I have done an experiment, which has not been published, whose results showed that there is no general improvement in the facility with which subjects can complete graphemic word fragments. In the experiment, subjects were tested in four successive sessions, at one-week intervals, with word fragments corresponding both to words previously encountered in the experiment and words not encountered. Subjects did no better with 'new' words in the fourth session than they had done in the first. In this respect, the word-fragment completion task is different from a task such as Kolers' task of reading inverted typography: Cohen and Squire (1980), as we have seen, found that both their control subjects and amnesic patients showed improvement in performance with practice in reading not just previously seen words but also new ones.

For these reasons, then, it is not entirely clear that we should think of priming effects in semantic-memory tasks as manifestations of changes in procedural knowledge. The hypothesis is attractive, as I mentioned, but the picture is far from being clear.

It is probably too early to start thinking of priming effects as reflecting the operation of a system other than episodic, semantic, or procedural memory, but the hypothesis is at least worth mentioning. As we gain more empirical evidence pertaining to priming effects, and as our theoretical thinking becomes sharper, we will be in a better position to evaluate this hypothesis along with others. Among these other hypotheses may also be one that sees the relation between priming effects and something called 'free radicals', to be discussed next.

If we think of priming effects of the kind that we have been discussing here as a manifestation of a new—to the scientists, that is—memory system, we could also contemplate the hypothesis that it falls somewhere between procedural memory and propositional (episodic and semantic) memory. It is like procedural memory in that the person need not be consciously aware of the product of cognitive operations involved in the acquisition of skills or knowledge and that sheer repetition may be the most important determinant of such acquisition. It differs from procedural memory, and is more like propositional memory, in that the knowledge acquired, retained, and used by the system can be highly specific and precise in the same way in which propositional knowledge can be, that is, capable of reflecting extremely fine discriminations about the state of the world. We could further speculate that a memory system of this kind may have played a more important role in cognitive functioning of people in the distant past, before episodic and semantic memory systems in the form in which they exist today were fully developed, and that we pick up evidence of the remnants of the system under highly specialized laboratory conditions called priming experiments. It would be interesting to test Jaynes's (1976) bi-cameral men in both episodic-memory and priming experiments. Would we find that they rely on the priming system to accomplish what their modern counterparts do with the aid of episodic memory?

Free radicals

Let us now turn to another potential problem for the episodic/semantic distinction: the hypothesized existence of what Daniel Schacter and I (Schacter and Tulving 1982) have referred to as free fragments. I will call these free fragments 'free radicals', to minimize possible confusion among different sorts of fragments, for instance those used in the Tulving *et al.* (1982) experiment. The term 'radical' is used in the sense of 'a root or fundamental part of something'. In the present discussion, radicals are rudimentary units of remembered experiences. Free radicals are radicals that have become detached from episodic memory but have not, or not yet, been attached to any structure in semantic memory.

Like free radicals of the chemical world, and those in biological systems (Pryor 1970), that are highly reactive and unstable, and cannot be isolated by ordinary methods, free radicals of the mind can be observed only under special conditions. The most suggestive source of evidence for the existence of free radicals is provided by observations on amnesic patients. A clinical anecdote will provide the flavor of what Schacter and I have in mind when we talk about free fragments, or free radicals. It comes from the description by Claparède of the same amnesic patient whom we met earlier (p. 95):

> When one told her a little story, read to her various items from a newspaper, three minutes later she remembered nothing, not even the fact that someone had read to her; but with certain questions one could elicit in a reflex fashion some of the details of those items. But when she found these details in her consciousness, she did not recognize them as memories but believed them to be something that 'went through her mind' by chance, an idea she had 'without knowing why', a product of her imagination of the moment, or even the result of reflection (1951, p. 69).

The patient had no recollection of the episode of having listened to someone read to her, even only a few minutes afterwards. But she remembered something of what she had heard: some of the details of the material could be 'elicited in a reflex fashion'. Since the patient herself did not recognize these details as having been derived from her own past experience, and since she described them to be something that 'went through her mind' or ideas she had 'without knowing why', it would be difficult for us to classify them as a part of her episodic memory.

We all know many things that we have learned on particular occasions without remembering those occasions, and in that sense we are all like Claparède's patient: we suffer from 'source amnesia' (Evans and Thorn 1966). But there are two important differences. First, she forgot the source of the information she had received in a few minutes; we can retain it for days, months, and years. Second, when we retrieve information from which episodic knowledge has been stripped, we are still very much aware of how it is related to many other things that we know about the world: a normal person cannot think of a single bit of semantic knowledge that is not a part of the larger structure. Moreover, we do not think of semantic knowledge of which we are aware at a particular time as something that 'just goes through our mind', or as ideas that we have 'without knowing why'.

The clinical literature on amnesia is replete with case descriptions containing references to free radicals. The patient described by Williams and Smith (1954), whom I mentioned earlier (p. 95–6) provides one illustration. The reader will remember that this patient knew the names of all the people in a group photograph, but did not know how or why he knew these people, or what the group was. In this case, each face–name pair represents a free radical: The name-part of the fragment of knowledge can be elicited by the face-part, but neither the eliciting stimulus (face) nor the elicited idea (name) is related to anything else in the patient's episodic and semantic knowledge.

A clinical case reminiscent of Williams and Smith's patient was described by Luria (1976). Luria's patient suffered from a severe Korsakoff's syndrome but was capable nevertheless of learning a set of 10 paired-associates consisting of pictures as stimulus terms and words, unrelated to the pictures, as response terms. After only two presentations of the list, the patient could make the correct word-response to the picture-stimulus. Retention of this learning was perfect even a week later. But in sharp contrast with the patient's ability to make appropriate responses to appropriate stimuli was his complete inability to state in words anything about the learning episode, even immediately after the episode itself. When Luria asked, 'What were we just doing together?' the patient responded with irrelevant associations, or with descriptions of activities dating from several days previously (Luria 1976, pp. 284–5). The patient had no perceptual, motor, or speech disturbances, he could exhibit evidence of the contents of an earlier learning episode, but even immediately after such an episode could not produce a verbal description of it. The contents of the episode—individual pairs of associations—had become functionally separated from the episodic system. It is a reasonable conjecture that the associations had not become a part of the patient's semantic-memory system, either.

Detachment of bits of learned memories from their episodic settings is regarded by many students of amnesia as a general characteristic of the amnesic syndrome. Jaspers, in his classic *Allgemeine Psychopathologie*, summarized many observations on the patients suffering from Korsakoff's disease as follows: 'Korsakoffs' perception is normal, but they cannot fix memories; the few memories which do become fixed remain as "isolated fragments' '' (quoted by Fraisse 1963, p. 164).

Yet another illustration of the kind of 'source amnesia' (Evans and Thorn 1966)—very rapid forgetting of the setting but retention of a fragment of information learned in it—is provided by a patient who became amnesic after closed-head injury (Schacter and Tulving 1982). The patient was taught little-known real facts about the world which he did not know before (e.g. What is the most popular brand of cigarettes in the world?) Later, he was tested for his knowledge of these facts. His performance showed that he had retained a number of the facts he had learned earlier in the same session, but he was not aware of the source of his knowledge. In response to the question of how he knew that, for instance, the world's most popular brand of cigarettes is Marlboro, he gave a confabulated answer: 'I must have read it somewhere'.

It is possible that the bits of knowledge that this patient learned and retained, even if not part of his episodic memory, represented at least temporary additions to his semantic memory. Since there is no relevant evidence, we cannot reject this possibility. But it is quite conceivable that the newly-acquired knowledge of the patient existed only in the form of free radicals. This hypothesis would be strengthened if it could be shown that, unlike other parts of his semantic memory, the newly-acquired knowledge can be elicited by an extremely limited set of retrieval cues, and perhaps only in a particular context.

In the cases we have briefly reviewed, the patients' fragmentary knowledge is clearly derived from particular episodes. The memory for the event as such is lost, but fragments of its factual contents remain. Claparède's patient did not recognize the details of experiences elicited 'in a reflex fashion' as memories, thinking them to be simply something that 'went through her mind' or ideas that she had 'without knowing why', but she was quite aware that these ideas were clearly hers. If our hypothesis is correct and the free radicals are really free, a part of neither episodic nor semantic structures, yet capable of elicitation by stimulus events and queries, we can say that they do seem to enjoy a sort of an independent 'existence' of their own.

The Warrington–Weiskrantz (1974, 1978) effect, which we discussed earlier (p. 93) as an example of pathological dissociation between episodic and semantic memory, can also be interpreted with the aid of the concept of free radicals. We could assume that the study of target words by amnesic subjects leads to the creation of corresponding free radicals detached from the episodic experience, analogously to the scattered ideas floating through the mind of Claparède's patient, or the face–name combinations of Williams and Smith's patient. When presented with a copy of a target item in the episodic recognition test and asked whether he remembers having seen it in the study list, the amnesic patient may fail, not only because he may not remember having studied the list, but also because he does not remember the particular word: the free radicals have become detached from the cognitive representation of the study episode, or else they cannot be contacted through the (non-existent) engram of the episode. When the patient, however, is confronted with a fragment of one of the target words, and asked to find a word from his subjective lexicon that fits it, he can do so, because of the ready accessibility of the free radical through its graphemic components.

This interpretation is quite similar to that offered by Warrington and Weiskrantz (1982) to account for the dissociation between episodic recognition and word-fragment completion performance in amnesic patients. They argue that amnesia represents a functional disconnection between two memory systems, a 'cognitive mediational' and a semantic-memory system. Amnesic patients can learn and retain information that does not require cognitive mediation. In the word-fragment completion task the normal subject need not know, and the amnesic patient usually does not know, that the response he is making to the fragment is related to, or facilitated by (primed by) an earlier episode, in which the same response was made.

Another experimental finding concerning the amnesic syndrome that might be amenable to an explanation in terms of free radicals has been described by Winocur and Weiskrantz (1976) and Warrington and Weiskrantz (1978). Amnesic subjects have no difficulty learning rule-governed paired-associate lists, but do experience difficulty learning a second list related to the first in the A–B, A–C paradigm. We could assume that learning of related pairs creates a number of free radicals consisting of both members of each pair, of the kind exhibited by Williams and Smith's patient. Patients may have difficulty recognizing these pairs as having been encountered on a particular occasion, but they can make the appropriate response if the other part is given as the eliciting stimulus. If we further assume that free radicals, as cognitive units detached from integrated mental structures, are more vulnerable to interference than are well-structured units, patients' difficulty of learning new free radicals including the same components might become understandable.

Free radicals in normal remembering.

Are free radicals only a manifestation of pathological memories, or do they exist in normal memory, too? The question concerns the existence of symbolically expressible knowledge whose episodic source is unknown to the person and which, at the same time, is not part of the semantic structures. It is quite possible that free radicals in normal memory are so short-lived and fleeting that they are difficult if not impossible to detect. But we can point to certain normal-memory phenomena in which larger structures act analogously to free radicals.

Remembered intentions are in some sense similar in status to free radicals. You may know, for instance, that you should take your car in for regular service, if not tomorrow then soon, without having any idea about the particular occasion on which that intention was formed. In this sense, the intention has become detached from your episodic-memory system. But the remembered intention does not seem to constitute a part of the semantic system, either, at least not a permanent part, since people usually do not recover intentions by 'searching' their semantic memories. Moreover, at least the casual impression is that the intention is 'forgotten' the moment the intended action or plan is carried out. We know relatively little about memory for intentions—or whether intentions are 'remembered' at all—and on closer study it may turn out that there is no sharp distinction between memory for intentions and memory for other kinds of things, situations, and events. But we may also find that intentions for unique actions formulated at one point in time and not rehearsed, nor repeated time after time, share certain functional properties with free radicals.

Another possible candidate for free radicals in normal memory may be represented by jokes. Jokes seem to enjoy some sort of an autonomous existence of their own. Frequently their episodic source is lost very rapidly, yet few of them are recoverable from semantic memory when instructions are given in terms of, 'Tell me a joke, any joke'. Nor do we typically think of jokes when we are asked to 'Tell everything you know' about people in particular categories (e.g. professors, psychiatrists, mothers-in-law, newlyweds, etc.), even if we do know jokes about them. Jokes seem to have in common with free radicals the feature of extremely restricted 'access routes': remembering of jokes seems to be a sort of a state-dependent retrieval phenomenon. The 'activation' of a joke occurs when certain key words or ideas are given as retrieval cues in an appropriate, mirthful state. Be it as it may, the hypothesis that jokes are comparable to free radicals would be strengthened if it was found that retrieval of both jokes and free radicals were especially strikingly dependent on the emotional (Bower 1981) or pharmacological (Eich 1980) state.

Can we think of some of the priming effects that we considered earlier in the chapter as reflecting the existence of free radicals? I do not know, because the matter has neither been thought about nor investigated from this point of view. We need to find out much more than we know about the conditions under which priming effects occur and do not occur, as well as their characteristics. Superficial similarities between certain kinds of priming effects and manifestations of amnesic phenomena that can be thought of as representing free radicals are not difficult to detect, but their deeper significance constitutes an open problem.

The evidence for free radicals in the amnesia literature is only suggestive; in descriptions of normal memory it is completely lacking. Nevertheless, it may be useful to pursue the hypothesis that they exist, and to try to identify some of their functional properties. The potential usefulness of the hypothesis of free radicals is threefold.

First, the notion of free radicals provides a possible extension of the episodic/semantic distinction. The hypothesis holds that free radicals represent contents of episodes that have been detached from them and have not (yet) been attached to the (permanent) semantic-memory system. The original construction of free radicals, as that of all other contents of episodes, may be greatly influenced by semantic memory; in that sense free radicals represent new products of the semantic system. The hypothesis is that these new products have been assimilated neither into the episodic nor the semantic system.

Second, the hypothesis of free radicals allows us to describe certain phenomena of amnesia without the necessity of allocating them to one or the other of the two systems. Thus, in response to the query of, 'What kind of knowledge is a patient's knowledge of an "idea that goes through her mind"?' we need not say 'episodic', 'semantic', or 'both'. We can say that these and other similar kinds of bits of conscious awareness belong to a separate category of free radicals.

Third, the hypothesized existence of free radicals may turn out to be relevant to the important but largely unexplored problem of acquisition of semantic knowledge (Brown 1975; Kintsch 1974; Nelson and Brown 1978). How are knowledge structures that characterize semantic memory constructed? If we think of the mind as a model of the external world (Craik 1943), we can assume that the world provides the blueprint for such construction. But what are the elementary building blocks? We could speculate that they are something like the free radicals: apprehended recurrent regularities of the knowable world and internalized by the developing individual in his interaction with the physical and social environment. These recurrent regularities become differentiated and detached from episodic experiences, acquire an independent status of their own, and, under normal conditions, coalesce into superordinate constructions that define semantic memory and model the world.

A similar hypothesis has been articulated in a more detailed and sophisticated fashion by Ehrlich (1979). He conceptualizes semantic memory as a system of 'free elements', emphasizing the fact that our knowledge of the world consists of actual, optional, possible, and impossible semantic structures.

The reader will have realized by now that the whole notion of free radicals, as briefly discussed here, is highly speculative. If it has any value, it may lie in raising questions and suggesting problems for future research, rather than in providing any firm explanation of some of the puzzles that arise from the distinction between episodic and semantic memory. When thinking about free radicals, we should keep in mind Woozley's (1949) advice that applies to the attempts to evaluate all kinds of hypotheses: We should approach the matter with considerable suspicion, 'because it is only too easy to invent a solution to a problem and yet to persuade oneself and others that one had not invented, but discovered it' (p. 76).

Working memory and reference memory

In this final section of the chapter, we will briefly consider an interesting parallel to the episodic/semantic disctintion. It has been proposed by Olton and his associates. Working with animals, they have obtained evidence that points to the existence of two types of memory: working and reference memory (e.g. Honig 1978; Olton, Becker, and Handelmann 1979, 1980; Olton and Papas 1979).

Olton's distinction is specified in terms of two types of procedure, or tasks. In a working-memory component of a test procedure, the animal must remember information specific to a particular trial in order to perform correctly on that trial, whereas in a reference-memory component of a test procedure, the animal can respond perfectly on the basis of acquired and retained information common to all test trials. For instance, in the delayed-matching-to-sample task, a stimulus is presented to the animal for inspection, and then, after a delay interval, the same 'old' and a 'new' stimulus are presented, and the animal is reinforced for choosing the 'old' one. This task involves both reference memory and working memory components. Reference memory is involved in the animal's knowledge that responding is positively reinforced in the presence of certain discriminative stimuli, and not reinforced in the absence of the same, or in the knowledge that a particular response will initiate a new trial. Working memory is involved in the knowledge of the particular stimulus presented on a particular trial, a stimulus that requires a particular response.

Olton and his associates have operationally defined the two types of memory in terms of the experimental animals' performance on the radial-arm maze task (e.g. Olton, Becker, and Handelmann 1979; Olton and Papas 1979). In a radial-arm maze, a number of arms extend from a centre platform, like spokes on a wheel. A piece of food is placed at the end of each 'baited' arm; no food is present on the 'unbaited' arms. A food-deprived rat, starting from the centre platform, is allowed to explore the arms of the maze, and to eat the food encountered. The optimal strategy for the rat is to enter each 'baited' arm once and only once (that is, not return to any baited arms) during each test, and to completely avoid the unbaited arms. To distinguish between working memory and reference memory in this task, a number of successive tests are given to experimental animals. On each test , the set of baited and unbaited arms is the same, thus making it possible for the animal to learn the distinction between those arms where food is likely to be found and those arms on which it is never found. The probability of choosing any baited arm provides a measure of the performance on the reference-memory component, since the stimuli guiding the choice are constant throughout the experiment. The probability of choosing a baited arm that has not been entered previously on a given trial, given a choice of an arm within the baited set, on the other hand, provides a measure of the working-memory component of the performance on the task, since this probability reflects the animal's memory of the previous events on the test.

The logic used by Olton and his associates in obtaining evidence for the two components of memory is the same as that used by human memory researchers in their attempts to demonstrate the functional separation of episodic- and semantic-memory systems. Performance on the two components of the radial-arm maze task is examined as a function of surgical lesions to the hippocampus. A typical experiment involves a pre-operative and post-operative comparison of performance. In such an experiment (e.g. Olton and Papas 1979), normal animals are first trained on the radial-arm maze task with fixed sets of baited and unbaited arms. When they reach a high level of performance on the working-memory (seldom enter those baited arms again that already have been explored) and reference-memory (seldom enter the unbaited arms at all) components, they undergo operations in which the fimbria fornix is bilaterally destroyed. Post-operative testing shows that reference-memory performance is initially impaired, but it recovers over successive test trials and reaches the pre-operative level. Working-memory performance, on the other hand, is no better than chance and shows no signs of recovering in the course of testing. Thus, destruction of the external connections of the hippocampus produces a permanent impairment in the working-memory component but not in the reference-memory component. This dissociation can be taken as evidence, if not for two different types of memory, then at least for two different types of memory components in this task.

The working/reference memory distinction parallels the episodic/semantic distinction in that working memory reflects the organism's knowledge of particular events temporally organized in the organism's own (recent) past, whereas reference memory has to do with the organism's knowledge of the world that, within limits, is independent of time. Moreover, the stimulus-response associations mediated by working memory are flexible, that is, the 'correct' response to a particular stimulus is not always the same, but rather varies from occasion to occasion, whereas the stimulus-response associations in the reference-memory tasks are more permanent. This situation is analogous to the distinction between, say, a recognition-memory and a lexical-decision task involving strings of letters: in the former, whether the subject classifies a test item as 'old' or 'new' depends on whether or not the item occurred in the study list, whereas its classification as a word or a non-word is independent of the item's occurrence or non-occurrence in a particular experimental study list. The third parallel between working/reference and episodic/semantic distinctions concerns interference: like episodic memory, working memory is relatively vulnerable to interference, whereas reference memory, like semantic memory, is less affected by it.

It remains to be seen how close the parallel between episodic/semantic and working/reference memories turns out to be. But it is clear that research with animals on the problems of memory taxonomy will provide an important supplement to that with humans. Although animal research cannot replace human research, it does possess certain unique advantages, for instance, the possibility of surgical intervention in the functioning of memory systems. If the 'final proof' of the separate existence of different memory systems lies in the observations of global effects of the functioning of different systems, then animal research may well play a decisive role in the eventual solution of the problem.

Part II
General Abstract Processing System

7
Conceptual framework

Remembering of past events is an exceedingly familiar experience to all. Everyone knows what it means to witness an event, or do something, now, and to remember it later. Thus, the study of episodic memory, like the study of many things in psychology as well as in other sciences, is concerned with phenomena of which we have a great deal of knowledge before we launch into their objective and systematic analysis. Such a state of affairs places certain constraints on our enterprise.

Rememberers' and psychologists' memory

At the outset of the study of episodic memory it is useful to distinguish between two views of remembering. One is that of the person who does the remembering—I shall refer to him henceforth as 'the rememberer'—and the other of the person who studies remembering by observing the rememberer in situations in which remembering occurs—I shall refer to him as 'the psychologist'. The rememberer's memory is phenomenal, the psychologist's is objective; an important task of the science of memory is to relate the two.

The psychologist, in private life, is also a rememberer; before he begins his scientific study of memory he knows as much about it as the rememberer does. Whether this private knowledge is useful to him in his halting dialogue with Nature about the object of his study is not known. My suspicion is that the psychologist's intimate familiarity with his own mind is more of a hindrance than a help.

The task of science is to 'penetrate beyond the immediate and visible to the unseen' (Holton and Brush 1973, p 31), or, as I might say in the security of this typeface, to apprehend the world of lathomena that lies behind the world of phenomena. ('Lathomenon' is a new word coined by Professor Jaan Puhvel of UCLA, from λαθεῖν 'to lie hidden, to be unnoticed'; it means, 'that which has remained unrevealed, which has stayed hidden'.) In this task, empirical observation and power of imagination play equally important roles. It is the exercise of the latter that has probably suffered because of the psychologist's private knowledge of memory: when he tries to decipher Nature's answers to the questions posed in experiments, he tends to be distracted by his introspective awareness of how memory works. Most great conceptual breakthroughs in scientists' understanding of the world have been non-transparent; by accepting or favoring ideas that are sensible because of our personal experience we may complicate the task of penetrating the world of lathomena.

For the rememberer, to remember a previous occurrence of some sort means to become aware of it again, to 'have' a particular mental experience that is immediately recognized as 'a memory'. The rememberer usually has no difficulty describing his experience. It is not unlike a perception, or a thought, or a dream; yet it is easily distinguished from these other kinds of awareness. A remembered experience has definite 'contents', and the rememberer feels the contents to be familiar in a way in which perceived objects and situations or those dreamt about are not. The particular state of consciousness that characterizes the experience of remembering includes the rememberer's belief that the memory is a more or less true replica of the original event, even if only a fragmented and hazy one, as well as the belief that the event is a part of his own past. Remembering, for the rememberer, is mental time travel, a sort of reliving of something that happened in the past.

For the contemporary psychologist studying memory, remembering is a sequence of cognitive processes that begins with the rememberer's perception of an event and ends with the making of a response representing recall or recognition of a specified aspect of the original occurrence. The psychologist has no immediate access to the rememberer's experience. Its phenomenal reality, the subjective feeling of veridicality and the pastness of the experience, are matters of which the psychologist can have no direct evidence. The psychologist can classify the responses that the rememberer makes in the test of retention of the event as 'correct' or 'incorrect', or perhaps as somehow systematically related to correct responses, but this classification is performed independently of the state of the rememberer's mind. Remembering, for the psychologist, is correlation between the present response and an earlier stimulus event.

To illustrate the two views of remembering, let us compare how a perspicacious rememberer and a group of equally perspicacious psychologists have described it. First, the rememberer's view:

> Suppose that once and only once, I smelled a tuberose in a certain room where it grew in a pot, and gave a very grateful perfume. Next day I relate what I saw and smelled. When I attend as carefully as I can to what passes in my mind in this case, it appears evident, that the very thing I saw yesterday, and the fragrance I smelled, are now the immediate objects of my mind when I remember it. Further, I can imagine this pot and flower transported to the room where I now sit, and yielding the same perfume. . . . I am conscious of a difference in kind between sensation and memory, and between both and imagination. I find this also, that the sensation compels my belief of the present existence of the smell, and memory my belief of its past existence. There is a smell, is the immediate testimony of sense; there was a smell is the immediate testimony of memory. If you ask me, why I believe that the smell exists? I can give no other reason, nor shall ever be able to give any other, than that I smell it. If you ask, why I believe that it existed yesterday; I can give no other reason but that I remember it (Reid 1970, pp. 25–6, originally published 1764).

Now listen to three contemporary psychologists who could be talking about Reid's tuberose, although they are not. They are describing the operation of episodic memory in a situation in which a person observes an incoming stimulus and subsequently recognizes it as one previously seen:

> In our scheme, semantic memory acts as a part of a pattern-recognition system whose function is to interpret incoming stimuli by means of complex analysing and encoding operations. The product of these operations is the memory trace, which forms the latest addition to episodic memory—that part of the system comprising the temporally ordered collection of all encoded episodes and events. The deeper and more elaborately a stimulus is analysed by the perceptual system, the richer and more detailed will be the episodic memory trace. At the time of the recognition test, the probe stimulus is again encoded by the pattern-recognition system and the resulting encoding is used to specify the initial trace. For recent items, retrieval information is used to select the required trace; while for remote events, the encoded probe information is used as the basis for reconstruction of the initial stimulus—this reconstructive activity is constrained and guided by information contained in the memory trace (Lockhart *et al.* 1976, p. 77).

The striking difference between these two passages does not lie in Thomas Reid's view of memory as a phenomenal experience and Lockhart *et al.*'s view of it as a set of interlocking cognitive systems. There is nothing incompatible, in principle, between mental experience as something to be explained and an abstract theoretical system that provides the explanation. The psychological science of perception is replete with parallels of this kind. What is striking is that in the description by Lockhart's *et al.* there is *nothing* that corresponds to Thomas Reid's phenomenal experience of the tuberose and its smell. The description seems to apply better to computers and to Jaynes's (1976) bicameral men than to conscious human rememberers.

The missing experience

The absence of phenomenal experience, or concepts corresponding to it, characterizes just about every conceptual account of memory that we have had in experimental psychology, although paradoxically it is particularly true of current cognitive theories of memory. I could provide a very long list of contemporary experimenters and theorists who have talked about all sorts of things that pertain to memory but not about the conscious experience of remembering. The list would include most of my own writings. It looks almost as if there was something basically incompatible between human cognition as seen by contemporary cognitive psychology and the human experience that characterizes one of the most advanced forms of cognition, episodic memory. Why?

Why have our psychological theories of memory had so little to say about the mental experience of remembering, the subjective feelings of veridicality and awareness of pastness of remembered events, and the relation of the experiences, feelings, and awareness to overt memory performance? Philosophers have dealt with these issues, guided by their own rules of the game. The rememberer's view of remembering constitutes the starting point for their analysis. They have raised questions about different forms of memory, modes of remembering, trustworthiness and veridicality of memories, the feeling and concept of pastness in remembering, memory beliefs and memory claims, the relation between personal identity and memory, and the like (e.g. Furlong 1951; Grice 1941; Malcolm 1942; Shoemaker 1959; Smith 1966; Von Leyden 1961). But cognitive psychologists have not. We do not even have a term to express what I have referred to as '(conscious) experience of remembering'. This means that if anyone decided to make a systematic survey of what experimental or cognitive psychologists have said about conscious experience of remembering, he would be frustrated at the outset, because he would not know what key words are that he would have to use in the search.

One possible reason for the absence of concepts corresponding to experience of remembering lies in the fact that it is *possible* to study learning and memory without any reference to conscious awareness of the learner or rememberer. Although for the rememberer the veridicality of a memory is given as part of the awareness of the memory, the psychologist can judge the veridicality of the memory for an event by comparing the 'input' with the 'output'. Such an objective method, indeed, could be regarded as not just the preferred method but the only one: the rememberer's subjective feelings of veridicality of his memories may be, and frequently are, wrong. The correlation between input and output provides us with true facts about the functioning of the system, and we can build our science on these facts; we certainly would not want to build it on the 'wrong' facts, would we? Similarly, the psychologist can arrive at the conclusion that the present response is derived from an earlier occurrence by virtue of an objective comparison of input and output; whether or not the rememberer feels the 'pastness' of the remembered event to be in intimate part of the experience as such is irrelevant to the correlation of the input and output.

It may be worth remarking parenthetically at this point that some of the concepts that the psychologist may find crucial in describing 'his' memory may be as irrelevant to the rememberer as the rememberer's experience is irrelevant to the psychologist's theorizing. For instance, the psychologist distinguishes sharply between recall and recognition as two different types of retrieval. But the rememberer does not 'recall' or 'recognize' his mental experience of remembering a past event, he simply 'has' the experience. The experience is immediately given to him when certain conditions are fulfilled. He may 'recognize' some components of his memory image as familiar, or as belonging to the experienced whole, and he may 'recall' their names, but the experience itself is neither recognized nor recalled. Or, consider another example: to the psychologist, the rememberer's performance entails both memory and decision processes. To the rememberer, however, decision processes in most remembering situations have no more phenomenal reality than they do in perceiving space as three-dimensional. If you were asked to remember what you did immediately before you picked up and started reading this book, and you come up with a phenomenally real recollective experience, where are the 'decisions' in that remembering?

Another possible reason for the discrepancy between the rememberer's and the psychologists' memory is that the discrepancy represents the result of a deliberate decision on the part of the memory theorists: they have contemplated the advisability of including concepts such as experience of remembering, subjective veridicality, and awareness of pastness of remembered events in theoretical accounts of remembering, but they have concluded that it would not add significantly to our understanding of memory, or perhaps would even complicate matters unnecessarily. It has sometimes been said that psychologists have already overloaded the memory systems of their subjects with all sorts of unnecessary parts and questionable components (Underwood 1972). To add yet another component would complicate matters even further, particularly if it is not clear how the addition would help our understanding of memory.

I rather doubt that this is the reason. Chances are that if memory theorists had entertained any such thoughts we would have heard about it, in one way or another. I think it is more likely that the issue somehow has managed to escape the attention of psychological memory theorists. If so, we are still left the question of 'why'?

Is it because the rememberer's mental experience of remembering, and his awareness of subjective veridicality and pastness, being private events, cannot be observed? Probably not. Science, and its precursors—natural philosophy and metaphysics—throughout the ages have consisted of attempts to identify the hidden 'causes' through their observable 'effects'. Memory theories, too, have asserted the existence of entities that are no more directly observable than the rememberer's awareness of past events. Memory traces, acquired associations, and other kinds of neural, mental, or conceptual residues of the original experiences have always played a prominent if not a central part in theoretical accounts of memory. For the rememberer, his own mental experience of 'reliving' a previous experience is very much more real than the hypothetical 'memory trace'; for the psychologist, the rememberer's subjective experience should be no *less* real than the memory trace.

Has the mental experience of remembering been neglected because it is an unreliable part of remembering, sometimes occurring and sometimes not? If so, and if it is possible for a person to have 'imageless memories', or utilize stored information about a past experience without being consciously aware of it, then the inclusion of a concept corresponding to rec-ollective experience would not add anything to our understanding of remembering, and it could make it more difficult. We would have to explain how it is possible for a person to benefit from past experience either with or without conscious awareness of the experience.

But even if there are two kinds of remembering, with and without con-scious awareness—or a continuum of experiences from compellingly and strikingly clear to ephemerally fleeting and vague—this is not a good rea-son for completely neglecting instances where the experience of remem-bering is phenomenally real to the rememberer.

Yet another reason for the benign neglect of the rememberer's subjec-tive experience by psychologists may lie in the historical traditions. Ebbing-haus (1885), who started it all, thought of memory very much from the point of view of the rememberer. On the first few pages of his monograph he talked about 'mental states' that 'once present in consciousness return to it', and defined remembering as the recognition of the returned mental state 'as one that has already been experienced' (p. 2). Elsewhere in his book, too, he talked about 'return to consciousness' of 'ideas committed to memory' (p. 19). Yet his own major contribution to the experimental study of memory, measurement of memory that until his time had not been measurable, shifted his and his successors' attention from the phenomenal experience to objectively quantified performance. Studying memory became synonymous with the measurement of the capacity of the system under various experimental conditions; understanding of the system was thought to be predicated on the knowledge of *how well* and *accurately* rememberers could reproduce some studied material. Moreover, in the kind of situation that Ebbinghaus studied—well-learned or overlearned series of nonsense syllables—it is an almost self-evident truth that the suc-cess in reproduction of the series depends on how well it has been impressed on the learner's mind. Thus, there exists an excellent corre-spondence between the learner's mental awareness of the material learned and his reproduction of it. In this situation, talking about the mental experience of the rememberer separately from his overt behavior would be highly redundant and any concept corresponding to the mental aware-ness superfluous.

The conclusion about the high degree of correlation between the mental state of the learner and his performance may not have been made explic-itly, but it may have been adopted implicitly by students of verbal learning as a part of the orienting attitudes guiding their thinking and research. And when information-processing language and ideas gave rise to the study of memory, the implicit assumption was taken over along with other similar ones.

The final answer to the question of why cognitive psychology of mem-ory has neglected subjective experience of remembering—the answer I find most plausible—is this: the question can meaningfully arise only in the study of episodic memory; it has not been raised, because cognitive psychology has not yet begun such study. Experiments done in the past *can* be interpreted as episodic- rather than semantic-memory experiments —I did so in my 1972 essay—but they were not designed as a part of a grand plan to understand how people remember personal experiences. From the large majority of the experiments done during the era when memory was memory and not memories, we have learned as much, or as little, about semantic memory as we learned about episodic memory. Had Ebbinghaus, or someone like him, clearly articulated the difference between remembering past episodes and knowledge of their symbolic contents, the history of verbal learning and memory might have been quite different.

Imagine that this conjecture is true, and that experimental psychologists of any persuasion have done relatively little work that is of *direct relevance* to the study and understanding of episodic memory. And imagine that we now wish to start doing such work. How would we go about it? Where should we begin?

A good place to begin is with a broad perspective on how we might want to think about episodic memory and its study.

A general abstract processing system of episodic memory

The rest of this chapter, together with the two following chapters, will describe a conceptual framework for the study and understanding of episodic memory. The framework is intended to serve several purpose. First, it provides a reasonably coherent and internally consistent set of ideas, concepts, and hypotheses that help us to relate the diverse manifestations of episodic memory to one another and to perceive their commonalities and differences. Second, it helps us to identify the focus and thrust of research questions and their theoretical interpretation in an overall scheme. Third, it allows us to classify theories of episodic memory in terms of the components of the framework to which the theories pertain. Fourth, it helps us to set priorities for research, and to evaluate the importance of problems investigated. Finally, the framework attempts to make explicit the relation between the rememberers' and the psychologists' memories: it helps us to see how the recollective experience of rememberers fits into the psychologists' view of remembering as an information-processing system.

The framework is not a theory, at least not in the ordinary sense of the word. Its purpose is not to explain, let alone 'predict', any specific phenomena. It represents an overall structure within which explanations of various elements of remembering and their interactions can be, and perhaps must be, sought. It is logically compatible with a large variety of specific models of precisely articulated empirical facts and relations.

Most of the components (elements) of the framework represent ideas that enjoy wide currency among students of memory today. They have grown out of the work of several generations of psychologists. Although a few of them are somewhat more idiosyncratic—having been suggested by, and in some instances representing speculative extensions of, the work that I and my students have done—none of them is original. Every single idea in the description of the framework can be traced to identical or similar ideas in the past or more recent literature. Although the thoughts that I will express here have much in common with what I and my co-workers have said in earlier papers (e.g. Tulving 1972; Tulving and Thomson 1973; Watkins and Tulving 1975; Tulving and Watkins 1975; Watkins, Ho, and Tulving 1976; Tulving 1976, 1979b; Flexser and Tulving 1978; Schacter and Tulving 1981, 1982). I do not wish to claim that the framework is 'my' or 'our' framework, a 'superior' alternative to someone else's framework. With the exception of the element of recollective experience, and perhaps the distinction between ecphory and conversion as separate sub-processes of retrieval, the framework represents what I take to be common knowledge in cognitive psychology today. The only reason for describing it in some detail lies in the fact that this common knowledge has not quite been expressed in the form in which I will discuss it.

In order to make it possible to refer to the present set of ideas with a unitary label, and to differentiate it from other comparable sets of ideas that have emanated from many places over the years under different authorships, including those originating in Toronto, I propose to refer to the framework described here as a General Abstract Processing System of Episodic Memory.

The term, 'General Abstract Processing System', is only slightly strained, attributable to my inability to resist the temptation of adopting an expression whose acronym would reflect our current state of knowledge about memory. Over the years, as I have studied memory, I have become more and more impressed by the complexity of the subject matter, the difficulty of its understanding, and our ignorance about it. I have also been struck with the relative absence of statements like 'I (or we) do not know' or 'It is not yet known how . . . ' in the literature, even in (the many) cases where such statements would clearly approximate the truth better than whatever utterances take their place. I have sometimes wondered whether we might not be better off if, instead of playing the game of 'our words are better than your words' (McGeoch and Irion 1952, p. 44), we would every now and then confess that 'my ignorance regarding X is more profound than yours'. Perhaps GAPS will help us remember that we really know very little about remembering.

The framework is *general* in the sense of 'lacking in constraint'. It applies to remembering of events of all sorts; it is not limited to particular kinds of to-be-remembered experiences. Although the ideas that constitute the framework have been shaped by the evidence from laboratory experiments employing simple verbal stimulus events, GAPS is meant to be sufficiently general to describe remembering of more complex events outside the laboratory as well.

The framework is *abstract* in the sense that the specific nature of its components is left unspecified. For the purposes that GAPS is intended to serve, it does not matter, for instance, whether the episodic information stored is conceptualized in terms of associative networks (e.g. James 1890; Anderson and Bower 1972), images (e.g. Locke 1690; Shiffrin and Atkinson 1969), propositions (e.g. Clifford 1890; Kintsch 1972), or some other form. In keeping with the currently popular idea (Estes 1959; Bower 1967; Underwood 1969; Wickens 1970) I will assume that stored engrams are collections of more elementary characteristics, features, or attributes, but I will make minimal assumptions about the nature of these characteristics.

The abstract nature of GAPS similarly means that no strong assumptions are made about specific characteristics of processes such as encoding and ecphory (retrieval). With respect to ecphory, for instance, I will assume that it entails an interaction between retrieval information (cue) and stored information (engram), but since no one yet knows the nature of this interaction, the least misleading way of describing it is to call it 'abstract'. Although many specific mechanisms of retrieval have been described in the literature, all of them are metaphorical only (Roediger 1980), and no one has yet discovered a method for verifying their nature by purely psychological techniques.

Third, GAPS is a *processing* system inasmuch as important components of it have to do with activity and function rather than structure of memory. The underlying assumption is that what a person remembers, or how well, depends not as much on what the memory system is like than on how it works. Although, as we will see presently, it is convenient to think of phenomena of remembering as manifestations of both the informational 'contents' of the system and the processes operating on it, the tools available to psychologists seem better suited for providing some understanding of remembering as an activity than of memory as an entity.

It is possible to argue that one of the failings of the now 'classical' (that is, early) information-processing view of memory, ironic as it may seem, had to do with its preoccupation with the structure of the memory system. All the elaborate floorplans of the edifice of memory, showing the paths along which information flowed from and to its various resting places, characterizing the 'boxes' models of memory so effectively criticized by Craik and Lockhart (1972), helped to convey the impression of mind as a machine. It was a machine that converted entities of one sort (stimuli, sensory energy, input information) into those of a different sort (responses, perceptual information, output information) according to the laws and principles whose nature and interrelations it may have been psychologists' business to discover but which were determined largely by the structure of the machine.

The conception of the mind as an information-processing machine, or device, may have made the psychological study of the mind respectable, by putting us squarely on the same side with more mature and established sciences. It may have also given us a useful basic analogy that provided inspiration for many interesting questions. What kind of a machine or device is the mind? What are its components? How do different components differ from one another? How are they related to one another? What is the overall structure of the machine?

Yet the analogy did not turn out to be useful, and it did not take psychologists too long to realize it. In changing the emphasis from structure to function, students of memory recapitulated a small part of the history of science, compressing it into a much shorter time. Although a purely mechanistic conception of the universe was popular with Renaissance thinkers, much of the modern science has rejected the idea that the universe is a machine, and replaced it largely with a view of the universe, and its parts, as evolution. It has even been argued that the machine analogy has been replaced with the analogy of history (Collingwood 1945).

We may not be able to do away completely with all concepts that smack of structure when we think about the mind, or its manifestations such as remembering. Even if we wanted to, as some do (e.g. Watkins 1981), we could not graciously talk about memory solely in terms of action sequences, or processes such as perceiving, encoding, retrieving, and thinking, or processes such as copying, comparing, discriminating, and selecting. But we could, and in what follows I will, adopt the orientation in which mental activity plays a central role and in which constructs implying stationary states—such as 'engram' and 'recollective experience'—serve simply as labels for dispositions, or processes held in abeyance, or as indicants that some processes have been completed and others have not yet begun.

The conceptual framework is a *system* in the sense of an ordered and reasonably comprehensive collection of interacting components whose assemblage constitutes an integrated whole. The system is quite complex but nowhere nearly as complex as we have reasons to believe is the episodic-memory system that the framework represents. The complexity of the system resides partly in the multiple determination of changes in the system as a result of many parallel and interacting processes, and partly in the diversity of operations that can bring about a given objective or accomplish a particular goal.

Thinking of episodic memory, an aspect of the mind, as a system also helps us to circumvent a persisting problem that has plagued theories of memory for a long time. It has to do with the necessity of postulating homunculus-like agents in our explanations of how memory works. Unlike physiologists, who have found ways of making organisms engage in biological processes such as respiration, digestion, and reproduction without having to postulate any agents responsible for such 'processing', psychologists can not yet talk about remembering and its sub-processes without introducing homunculus-like entities that do things or supervise happenings in whatever place it is that remembering occurs.

Sometimes, indeed, we even permit the rememberer himself to poke around in his own memory store, doing the job that at other times we entrust to homunculi or internal executives. Consider, as an illustration, the following excerpt from a volume that contains one of the most enlightened theoretical discussions of episodic memory:.

'Suppose a subject in a free-recall experiment is faced with the task of memorizing a list of words. It is assumed that as the words are presented the subject traces out a path from one word to the next through his memory net, leaving tags as he moves along that will enable him to retrace this path upon retrieval, thus implicitly locating list members along this path' (Kintsch 1974, p. 74). It almost sounds like Hansel and Gretel dropping bread crumbs along their path in the forest.

We must hold the influential William James at least partly responsible for encouraging students of memory to confuse the phenomena to be explained with the explanation of the phenomena. The reader will recall that he had people search through their memories for a forgotten idea just as they rummage their house for a lost object. 'In both cases we visit what seems to us the probable *neighborhood* of that which we miss. We turn over the things under which, or within which, or alongside of which, it may possibly be; and if it lies near them, it soon comes to view' (James 1890, p. 654).

Given the greater sophistication of, and greater information-processing requirements imposed on, modern minds, it is not surprising that the task accomplished less than a hundred years ago by a single searcher now requires co-ordinated efforts on the part of different homunculi with special skills. Thus we have homunculi called 'liguistic parser', 'perceptual parser', 'language generator', as well as 'the executive' (Anderson and Bower 1973). All these homunculi are very clever. For instance , linguistic parsers can do many things that people who carry them in their heads cannot: construct a probe tree to represent a query, produce a meaningful description of what is in the auditory or visual buffer, and handle symbolic systems such as formal logic (pp. 138–40). An even cleverer homunculus is the executive. 'It has at its disposal powerful problem-solving and inferential capacities which can be used in deciding how to direct the information processing' (p. 138). Among other things the executive 'can reflect upon its own opinions and form spontaneous propositions of its own' (p. 140).

Comparing William James's searcher rummaging the house for a lost object and Anderson and Bower's team of homunculi and what they can do, I am somewhat embarrassed about my earlier statement that we have not made much conceptual progress in understanding the human mind. Is it possible that I was mistaken, after all?

We are in a quandary. On the one hand, we should not rely too much on homunculus-like concepts that provide colorful metaphors for the workings of the mind without explaining or illuminating anything. On the other hand, we find that it is awkward to describe the workings of a highly complex system or systems of which we are largely ignorant by relying exclusively on the passive voice. If nothing else, it becomes tiresome to talk about information being received, the input being encoded, the engrams being formed, contents of a memory location being retrieved, and so on. This is where the term 'system' comes in handy: we can fill voids in our thinking and avoid the passive voice by attributing homunculus-like freedom of activity to the system as such. For instance, we say that 'the system can produce a certain output after but not before a certain input' (Tulving and Watkins 1975, p. 272), or that 'the system never retrieves anything "incorrectly" '(Tulving 1976, p. 65). Although it does not change anything materially, it does provide for a more natural—in the sense of less jarring—language. The statement that the system 'does' something can be taken as equivalent to the statement that the system is engaged in a particular activity or is in a particular mode of operation.

Having endowed the system with powers that in other theoretical accounts have sometimes been reserved for remembering persons, homunculi, or executive subroutines, we may wish to extend the usefulness of the concept of 'system' even further, by thinking of the system as the 'place' in which the abstract processes that we talk about occur. Thus, we could say that memory processes occur 'in the memory system' without having to worry about the implications of the statement for spatial metaphors of memory (Roediger 1980).

Circumlocutions of this kind, of course, do not diminish our ignorance about the real 'locus' of memory processes in the brain, but they appear more respectable than expressions.to the effect that memory processes take place in the 'head' or in the 'mind'. (In this connection it may be worth mentioning that we already know, or at least have reasons to suspect, where some of the homunculi reside in the head. According to Anderson and Bower (1973, p. 138), 'The linguistic parser may be localized in the left cerebral hemisphere and the perceptual parser may be in the right hemisphere'.) But even if the processes of interest are purely 'abstract', it is sometimes convenient to think of some place of the universe in which they take place. If it were really important to defend ourselves against the charges of reifying mental processes and allocating them to locations, we could always say that when we talk about remembering taking place 'in' the memory system, we simply reaffirm the importance of interaction among mental activities that constitute remembering.

Elements of episodic memory

The basic unit of the conceptual analysis of episodic memory is what I will refer to as an 'act of remembering': an act that begins with an event that is perceived by the rememberer and ends either with recollective experience, the rememberer's private awareness of the event on a subsequent occasion, or with memory performance, the overt expression of the recollective experience. Episodic memory is that aspect of the mind, or the brain, that makes the successful completion of individual acts of remembering possible.

The conceptual framework for studying episodic memory, the General Abstract Processing System, can be described in terms of the components and structure of the (temporally extended) single act of remembering. A schematic summary of this structure is depicted in Fig. 7.1, under the title of 'Elements of episodic memory'. It consists of thirteen conceptual elements, organized in three groups which in the figure appear in vertical configurations. The three groups of elements are referred to as observable entities (or simply, observables), hypothetical processes (or simply, processes), and hypothetical states (or simply, states). Each element is connected to one or two other elements by arrows. Each arrow represents a relation that could be called 'influences', 'has an effect on', or 'brings about'. Thus, the cognitive environment and the original event have an effect on encoding that brings about an original engram. The original engram, together with an interpolated event, have an effect on recoding

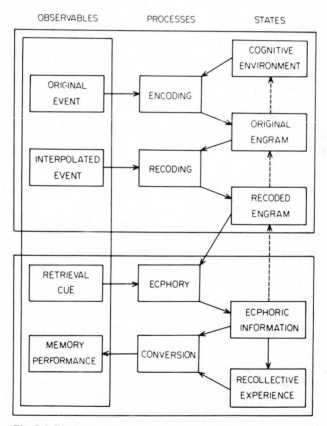

Fig. 7.1 Elements of episodic memory and their relations.

that brings about a recoded engram. The recoded engram and the retrieval cue jointly influence the process of ecphory that brings about the state of ecphoric information. The state of ecphoric information influences the rememberer's recollective experience of the event, and has an effect on conversion of information that influences the observable memory performance.

The broken arrows in the scheme represent relations of the designated sort that will not affect the outcome of a given act of remembering but may influence the outcome of a subsequent one. Thus, for instance, the construction of an (original) engram may change the cognitive environment in which the encoding of a subsequent original event takes place and hence exert an effect on it. Similarly , ecphoric information of one act of remembering may bring about a change in the recoded engram that initially influenced its formation; the recoded engram may then influence the next act of ecphory which in turn changes the ecphoric information, in the manner of a progressive feedback loop.

The scheme shown in Fig. 7.1 is not a diagram that depicts the flow of information through the organism (e.g. Broadbent 1963), although it bears a certain resemblance to it. Nor, obviously, is it an architectural floor plan that shows the components of the structure of episodic memory. Rather, it represents a structured decomposition of the total process of remembering a particular event, depicting the components, both observable and hypothetical, and relations among them, that must be included in a complete analysis of the process. From the perspective of GAPS, the thirteen elements of the system constitute obligatory concepts for theoretical analysis of episodic memory: they must all be taken into account if we want to understand remembering.

Not all of the thirteen elements have always been used in theoretical accounts of episodic memory. A long succession of theories throughout the short history of the science of memory shows that it is quite possible to ignore some, and sometimes the majority, of the elements shown in Fig. 7.1. Thus, for instance, the hypothetical processes and states could be ignored altogether, and remembering of events described and explained in terms of only the four observables listed in the left-hand column of Fig. 7.1 Whether or not this sort of 'black box' approach is more or less successful, or desirable, than approaches that postulate the existence of processes and states is a judgment whose popularity waxes and wanes with the times. At the present it is a rather unpopular attitude, and few serious students of memory advocate it.

A somewhat more popular approach is one that tries to make do with, or at least strongly emphasizes, the processes. The important concepts in the pure processing approach are encoding and retrieval, or their various equivalents under different labels, with recoding usually playing a subsidiary role. The early version of the highly influential levels-of-processing approach (Craik and Lockhart 1972) illustrates such a relatively 'pure' process orientation to the study of episodic memory.

Another possible approach takes the form of emphasis on the hypothetical state elements. For instance, Gestalt psychology was much more concerned with internal states than with either the external events or processes. The nature and properties of associations, mental structures, and autonomous changes in memory traces towards ideal figure constituted the main topics of interest about memory to Gestalt theorists (e.g. Asch 1969; Koffka 1935; Köhler 1941).

Other 'stripped down' versions of the structure have been of a 'hybrid' variety, mixing elements of different types. One of the simplest, and historically the oldest, schemes consists of two observables connected with one hypothetical element: the original event, the engram (memory trace, association), and memory performance. Here, the properties of the original event determine the properties of the engram which in turn determines memory performance, that is, how well the original event can be reproduced.

A somewhat more elaborate scheme consists of two observables, two processes, and one state, as follows: original event→encoding→ engram→retrieval→memory performance. In this kind of scheme, it is usually assumed that, because of the intervening encoding process, the engram need not represent a faithful copy of the original event, and that, furthermore, exactly how much or what of the engram can be 'reproduced' depends on the characteristics of the retrieval process. This is a relatively sophisticated scheme inasmuch as discrepancies between the original perception and later remembering can be attributed to the selectivity and bias of both the encoding and retrieval processes.

The structure depicted in Fig. 7.1 is highly schematic as well as incomplete. Other factors, not shown in the structure, could be introduced into a more complete description; undoubtedly this will happen in the future. For instance, the component of the system that is labelled 'cognitive environment' does not only influence the encoding of the original event, but also recoding, ecphory, and utilization of ecphoric information. Moreover, it can be analyzed into more elementary components that can be manipulated and varied independently of one another.

Although the structure of an act of remembering depicted in Fig. 7.1 is highly schematic, the cumulative effect of the happenings at various stages in the process implies a high degree of complexity of determination of the outcome of the act. Recollective experience of an event is multiply determined or influenced by the characteristics of the original event, the cognitive environment in which it was perceived, the nature of its encoding, the recoding of the original engram by virtue of related interpolated events, as well as by the characteristics of the retrieval cue and the process of ecphory operating on the recoded engram.

If anyone despairs of the complexity inherent in a scheme such as just described, in which a large number of determinants, singly and in interaction, converge on an outcome , and in which the 'error', or 'noise', or 'unreliability' of the information transmitted from the original event to recollective experience or memory performance grows exponentially through the various stages, they might want to take comfort in the knowledge that complexity, like beauty, is in the beholder's eye. Considering the complexity of the subject matter that we wish to study , I find that the complexity inherent in the scheme is rather mild in comparison with the complexity of much simpler domains, such as a *single sentence*, subjected to psycholinguistic (Miller and Johnson-Laird 1976, p. 326) or neo-associationistic (Anderson and Bower 1973, p. 182) analysis, as illustrated in Fig. 7.2 and 7.3.

Because of the multiple determination of characteristics of individual components in the structure, and their cascading effect on components 'downstream' in the system, the interpretation of observed relations between recollective experience and memory performance on the one hand and various manipulated conditions and independent variables on the other hand is not easy. However, because of the unidirectionality of the dependency relations among the components of the system, the possibility of arriving at empirically justifiable conclusions is not entirely precluded. The logic that relates the effects of intervention at different points in the overall scheme to the observed outcome of the act of remembering can be summarized as follows: changes in memory performance associated with changes in one of the components of the system can be attributed

$$MAN(x) \,\&\, GREATER(VERT(DISTANCE(earth, TOP(Mike)))),$$
$$NORM(VERT(DISTANCE(earth, TOP(x)))))),$$

Fig. 7.2 Decomposition of the proposition 'Mike is tall'. (From Miller and Johnson-Laird 1976, p. 182.)

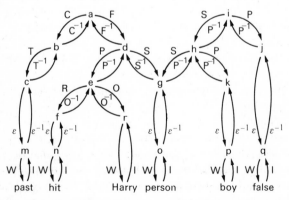

Fig. 7.3 Representation of the proposition 'It was not a boy who hit Harry'. (From Anderson and Bower 1973, p. 182.)

only to the components that follow the manipulated component in the structure. Thus, for instance, if memory performance changes as a function of changes in the retrieval cue, the effect is logically 'localized' to ecphory, ecphoric information, or conversion of the latter, or some combination of these components; the effect cannot be attributed to any of the earlier stages, such as the original or the recoded engram. Although this statement may not seem to be particularly profound, it does explicitly deny the hypothesis—possibly tempting to some theorists—that a retrieval cue 'directed at' a particular event changes the engram of that event. Retrieval-induced recoding is perfectly possibie, but is must occur through the ecphoric information.

Mental processes as events

The total process of remembering an event, from its original perception to recollective experience, or its expression in behavior, necessarily is extended in time. Its component processes, however, need not be. Indeed, we should do well to consider encoding, recoding, and ecphory as more-or-less instantaneous changes in state rather than activities enduring in time. Thus, although I have labelled four elements in Fig. 7.1 as processes, some of these 'processes' are not like the process of remembering of which they are a part.

Miller and Johnson-Laird (1976, p. 443 ff.) distinguish between two types of action verbs: those that refer to processes and those that refer to events. Processes endure in time, whereas events are 'instantaneous' processes. For instance, travelling is a process, whereas reaching is an event. We can say that a person travels for such-and-such a length of time, but a similar statement about reaching is not normally acceptable. When we extend the distinction between process- and event-like actions to terms denoting mental activity, we would classify encoding as an *event* rather than a *process*. An act of encoding is like the act of reaching a destination: at one moment in time the event is not encoded, at another it is, denoting a change in state.

A number of theories of (episodic) memory have been concerned with the nature of the 'mechanism' of encoding, as well as the 'mechanism' of retrieval, and these mechanisms may well be described in terms of processes extended in time. These process-activities may include terms such as 'analyze', 'compare', 'sample', and others like it. All of these denote activities more akin to 'travelling' than to 'reaching', and in this respect they differ from the 'instantaneous' process of encoding.

Another term, closely related to 'encoding', and frequently substituted for it, without substantive changes, is 'perceiving'. Perceiving, too, is an *event-like* action without extended duration, simply serving to indicate that a change in state has occurred: object X was not perceived before, but it is perceived now. We do not normally say that a person 'kept perceiving' an object, or that 'she perceived it for over ten seconds'. We can say, however, that she 'observed, listened, watched, or (simply) saw or heard X for *n* seconds', denoting activities extended in time. Observing, listening, watching, seeing, and hearing do not denote changes in state, whereas perceiving does.

Whether we interpret the verbs referring to mental activities as Miller and Johnson-Laird's process-verbs or event-verbs is more than an idle exercise in semantic analysis. To the extent that terms such as 'encoding' and 'ecphory' ('retrieval') represent important theoretical constructs, their interpretation as processes or events will affect our theoretical thinking about problems. Consider as an illustration the concept of retrieval. If one theorist thinks of it as a process extended in time, whereas another conceptualizes it as a term denoting a change in state, the two may engage in a futile debate about retrieval that they are unlikely to resolve, as long as the different premises concerning the contrast between processes and events are not made explicit.

I have always thought of retrieval as an event-like mental activity. Retrieval is something that occurs when certain conditions are fulfilled, such as the availability of appropriate trace information and the presence of a relevant retrieval cue. When retrieval occurs, it has empirically identifiable consequences, such as increased probability that the event can be recalled on a subsequent occasion. In addition to the *conditions* and *consequences* of retrieval, however, it is also possible to raise questions about the *processes* of retrieval, as was done by Richard Semon in the first decade of this century (Schacter *et al.*, 1978), and as is being done by many contemporary theorists, *but only if* one assumes that retrieving is a process-like activity.

My approach to problems of retrieval has sometimes been criticized as not including a specification of the retrieval 'mechanism'. I plead guilty as charged. I could argue that it is difficult to specify the 'mechanism' of an activity that denotes only a change in state. It would be like asking for stipulation of the 'nature of the process' of 'reaching' in Miller and Johnson-Laird's analysis. But this argument is not convincing: If other theorists can talk about 'mechanisms' of retrieval, why can not I?

I must admit that I have had peculiar difficulties appreciating the importance of concern with the anthropomorphic nature of internal processes that so many students of memory like to put into the rememberers' minds. The major problem is the absence of rules of the game that tell us what is permissible and what is not. Given that there are no rules—at least I have never seen them discussed—it is possible to contemplate an infinitely long list of human activities that constitute the 'mechanism' of event-processes such as encoding and retrieval.

Underwood once complained about psychologists overloading rememberers' memories: 'Memories now have attributes, organization, and structure; there are storage systems, retrieval systems, and control systems. We have iconic, echoic, primary, secondary, and short-, medium-, and long-term memories. There are addresses, readout rules, and holding mechanisms; memories may be available but not accessible (or is it the other way?). Our memories are filled with T-stacks, implicit associational responses, natural-language mediators, images, multiple traces, tags, kernel sentences, markers, relational rules, verbal loops, and one-buns' (Underwood 1972, p. 1).

That was ten years ago. We can do much better now. I have culled the following list of internal mental activities from the literature, that is, internal processes, various combinations of which make up the 'mechanisms' of encoding and retrieval. The list contains the following items: accepting, activating, adding, analyzing, anticipating, arousing, attenuating, categorizing, choosing, communicating, comparing, comprehending, computing, consolidating, copying, deciding, desiring, discriminating, distracting, eliciting, estimating, examining, extinguishing, filtering, going, generating, inhibiting, interfering, interpreting, locating, looking, marking, matching, mismatching, operating, organizing, pigeon-holing, placing, reaching, recovering, rehearsing, rejecting, replacing, requesting, retrieving, scanning, searching, selecting, sending, sorting, supplementing, suppressing, switching, tagging, transferring, transforming, understanding, and using.

The real list is undoubtedly longer, I did not try very hard. I also must apologize to all the authors whose terms and ideas I have borrowed here without acknowledgement; it would have been a bit unwieldy to provide all the references.

If the specification of retrieval 'mechanisms', or any other kind of 'mechanisms', in terms of these or similar component processes helps us to understand retrieval, then, of course, we should do so. But when we do, it would be most helpful to be told how we can go about evaluating or assessing the necessity or perhaps even indispensability of the postulated processes. How do we reject one 'mechanism' in favor of another one?

If, as I suspect, experimental outcomes and other empirical observations are insensitive to the *nature* of the postulated processes and their concatenations, the 'mechanisms', then their inclusion in specific theories concerned with one or more of the components of the conceptual framework of the kind depicted in Fig. 6.1 could not be regarded as an important contribution to knowledge, or as a step to such a contribution. It is my impression that no experiments have yet been done whose findings cast serious doubt on any particular 'mechanism' of retrieval that has been described in the literature.

As I mentioned earlier, the schema depicted in Fig. 7.1 is not meant to be complete. The complexity of human memory, or even a small part thereof, such as episodic memory, cannot quite be captured by a few words and arrows on a single page. But we must begin somewhere, and the thirteen concepts and their interrelations that comprise the general framework provide a convenient point from which to do so. In the next two chapters we shall discuss the thirteen components of the framework in somewhat greater detail.

8
Elements of encoding

The elements of the General Abstract Processing System can be classified into two categories, elements of encoding and elements of retrieval. The encoding part of an act of remembering begins with the perception of an event and ends with the formation of a recoded engram; the retrieval portion begins with the perception of a retrieval cue and ends with the recollective experience of the event or conversion of ecphoric (retrieved) information. In this chapter we consider the elements of the encoding process.

Original events

The world may be a booming, buzzing confusion for an infant, as William James said, but it certainly is not so for an adult. Indeed, usually it is strikingly orderly. Although we can discriminate contors and surfaces, shapes and colors, we normally do not 'see' them. Instead, we perceive the world around us as filled with stationary or moving objects or groups of objects. Elementary units of perception of space in which we live are objects that 'fill' the space.

As with space, so it is with time: our experiences in the fourth dimension are as orderly as they are in the other three. The basic units of perceived time are events. When you ask a person what he or she did the day before, you will get a description in terms of succession of events. Many events in daily life are part of what we call routine, some are exceptional, some occur infrequently, and some are unexpected. None, however, upsets the perceived temporal order of our experiences in time. People may not always be aware of the succession of their experiences as events, anymore than they are aware of the grammatical categories of the words they utter in conversation, but if asked to do so, they can identify events in the flow of their personal happenings as they can identify grammatical categories.

Like most other components of human experience, events are not easy to define. For our present purposes we accept the dictionary definition of an event as something that occurs in a certain place at a particular time. Thus, one characteristic of an event is that it has a beginning and an end in time, although sometimes the beginning and end are so close to one another that we think of the event as 'instantaneous'. Second, an event always occurs in a particular location, or setting. The relation between the setting and the event is of some importance to the analysis of episodic memory; we will take it up shortly. Events can vary greatly in complexity: there is a huge difference between perceiving an event consisting of a small inhomogeneity in an otherwise completely homogeneous field and an event such as visiting Rio during the carnival. Events are temporally related to one another: one event precedes or follows another, is simultaneous with it, or overlaps another partially. Events are also embedded within other events, in an extensive arrangement in which an individual's life represents the highest-order event. Events can always be described in terms of some action, frequently, but not always, exhibited by one or more actors. The rememberer may be a witness to an event, or a participant in it, or both.

The term 'episode' as used in this volume may be regarded as a close synonym of 'event', although 'episode' usually carries with it the connotation of an event that occurs in an ongoing series of events. But since we hardly ever deal with events that are not part of some ongoing series, almost all events in which we are interested are also episodes.

Settings and focal elements

Logical and psychological analysis yields a number of components and features of events and episodes that can be used for describing and classifying them, and for determining their similarities and differences (e.g. Rumelhart, *et al.* 1972; Jenkins, Wald, and Pittenger 1978). For our present purposes, however, we need to be concerned only with the distinction between the setting and the focal element (or elements) of an event. The terms have been adopted from Hollingworth (1913, pp. 532–533). The setting refers to the time and place in which the event occurs, together with the personal significance of the time and place for the rememberer. The focal element refers to a salient happening within the setting; the equivalent of a perceived figure against the background of the setting.

Imagine that you are visiting a faraway city called Krungthep and there, at the famous Wat Pho temple, which houses the huge and famous Reclining Buddha, you meet your friend Elizabeth. The place and time constitute part of the setting, your own reason for being there (for instance, sightseeing on a holiday) defines the 'personal significance' of the setting, and your (unexpected) seeing and talking to Elizabeth is the focal element of the event. Note that the event is defined in terms of *both* the focal element *and* the setting, the event is not 'seeing and talking to Elizabeth'. We can, of course, say that an event occurred in a particular setting, identifying 'event' with 'focal element', if we wish to avoid using the slightly strained expression of 'focal element', but we must always remember that events never take place in a vacuum, and that the setting is always one of the defining features of an event.

To appreciate the importance of settings and focal elements as defining features of events, consider two more imaginary events. First, in exactly the same place, at exactly the same time, and under exactly the same circumstances, you meet another friend, Patricia. Although the setting is the same, the two events are clearly different because their focal elements are different. Second, instead of (unexpectedly)meeting Elizabeth at Wat Pho, you (unexpectedly) meet her as you get off the chairlift at Heavenly Valley. Although the focal element here is the same as before, unexpectedly meeting a particular person, the settings are different, and thus we would classify the events as different.

Events are always unique, they never repeat themselves. But the differences between events, like differences between other things in the universe, can vary over a wide range, from highly similar to highly dissimilar. Similarity of events plays an important role in recoding, to be discussed presently.

Miniature events in the laboratory

Only a smattering of data exists in the literature on remembering complex events. These events include visits to the hospital (Cannell 1977) or the psychological laboratory (Baddeley, Lewis, and Nimmo-Smith 1978), victimization in a crime (Garofalo and Hindelang 1977), daily happenings (Linton 1979), simulated automobile accidents (Loftus 1975), or walks (Jenkins *et al.* 1978), and goal-directed behavior in daily life (Lichtenstein and Brewer 1980).

An overwhelmingly large proportion of the memory literature has been concerned with remembering miniature events in the laboratory: a familiar word appears in a list (e.g. Waugh 1963) or is shown and 'acted out', (Gardiner and Watkins 1979), a concept is generated by thought (Erdelyi, Buschke, and Finkelstein 1977; McFarland, Frey, and Rhodes 1980; Johnson and Raye 1981), a picture is seen (Potter 1976), a sentence is heard (Moeser 1979), or a short story is comprehended (Mandler and Johnson 1977), and a shorter or longer time later, the experienced event, or a part thereof, is recollected.

These mini-events are different from the events in everyday life in many ways. They are simpler, and they last for a much shorter time than most events outside the laboratory. They are less predictable than larger events in daily life. They are less meaningful, in the sense that there is no rational reason, from the rememberer's point of view, why a particular event should occur when it does. Mini-events in the laboratory do not fit into the expected flow of experiences in the real world. A very large majority of people manage to live to a ripe old age without ever having had the fun and challenge of participating in a memory experiment. Finally, there is little transfer value for experiencing and remembering the mini-events of a psychological memory experiment: people do not go home after having served in an experiment much wiser than they came in. In this sense the mini-events of the laboratory are unlike many life experiences that do contain useful lessons for the future.

Because of these obvious differences between the materials used in laboratory experiments, as well as some other reasons, it has become fashionable in certain circles, in recent years, to criticize and sometimes even condemn laboratory experiments in memory as 'artificial' and therefore of little relevance to memory in the real world. Some of the critics doubt that we can make any progress in understanding the human mind by studying 'pure' memory, as a separate mental function that has been artificially isolated from other mental functions with which it in reality is closely interrelated. Others criticize the sterile exercises give to rememberers in experiments in the form of meaningless tasks under carefully controlled conditions. The correct way of finding out the truth about memory, the argument goes, is to study remembering in natural everyday situations in which people adjust to, manipulate, and interact with their physical and social environment, and in which they *use* memory in going about their daily tasks and solving the many, smaller or larger, problems confronting them in their natural habitat.

The critics are right when they say that some of the research that has been done and some that is being done today is unlikely to be useful or of permanent value in our quest for the understanding of the human mind. They are also right when they point to the need of studying memory under conditions other than those that have figured prominently in traditional experiments. But they are wrong if they assume that they know the only right way of studying memory, or if they think that careful control over the conditions under which people remember things makes the situation 'artificial' and therefore irrelevant.

The history of science has convincingly demonstrated that there is no single way of finding the 'truth'. Nor is it usually possible to say in advance, without trying, what method or approach will succeed and which will fail. Many fundamental discoveries of lasting importance have been made under 'artificial' conditions, under circumstances not duplicated in the real world. And many problems that originate in real life have been solved under 'artifical' conditions in the laboratory. For instance, Louis Pasteur, one of the greatest biologists who ever lived, made many basic discoveries in the course of solving problems that had arisen in the real world. These problems included the nature of fermentation, silkworm disease, anthrax, and rabies. All of them arose in the real world, constituting sources of suffering, anguish, and financial loss in huge proportions. Yet Pasteur solved them in the laboratory. He was often ridiculed for his methods; what was perceived to be his naiveté of trying to gain an understanding of real-life problems in a faraway laboratory was derided by many. He succeeded, not only because of his own genius, but also because he relied on the methods of science that could be more effectively applied under carefully controlled conditions than 'out in the field'. (For a fascinating story of Louis Pasteur's life, see Vallery-Radot (1923).)

Events in the laboratory and events outside it that people remember do have a number of things in common. They can be attended to and apprehended. They have temporal duration, and people have usually no difficulty deciding when one event ends and another one begins. They can be described verbally as well as in other ways, and they can be frequently designated with distinctive labels. They can be analyzed into smaller elements. They vary in characteristics such as meaningfulness, vividness, complexity, and they may vary in their predictability.

Because the mini-events and real events have many characteristics in common, we can assume that understanding of how the mini-events are remembered provides us with some understanding of how real events are, too. There are also undoubtedly many differences in the remembering and memorability of mini-events and real events, as there are differences in remembering and memorability of different kinds of mini-events in the laboratory, or different kinds of real events in the world outside. In our search for understanding of episodic memory we will want to know how to make sense of those differences. But I know of no compelling reasons why the general principles that apply to remembering of mini-events in the laboratory should be greatly different from those governing the remembering of real-life experiences. Rememberers do not leave their brains and minds behind, or switch them off, when they enter the memory laboratory.

Words and word-events

The most widely used materials in episodic-memory experiments have consisted of words and sets of words. A few comments about words and word-events, therefore, may be appropriate.

Words to the memory researcher are what fruit flies are to the geneticist: a convenient medium through which the phenomena and processes of interest can be explored and elucidated. Although language as a means of communication plays an exceedingly important role in human affairs, and although many things that people remember are verbal in nature, words are of no more intrinsic interest to the student of memory than *Drosophila* are to a scientist probing the mechanisms of heredity. Other bits and pieces of perceptible reality might serve almost as well, nevertheless words do have certain properties that render them uniquely suitable for studying memory.

A word has well-defined bounderies, it can be presented as a single item, separately from others, or as a member of a smaller or larger grouping. Its occurrence represents a discrete event that can be accurately dated in time and located in space. either in physical terms (clocks, calendars, and geographical coordinates, if anyone cares) or in relation to other temporal events that occur within the perceptual reach of the individual. The rememberer can readily perceive the word-event, and the psychologist can satisfy himself that the rememberer has indeed done so. One word-event can be readily discriminated from others, since there are thousands of words in a literate person's repertoire, or lexical memory. Even when words are presented in rapid succession, each is clearly indentified and uniquely labelled, both by the rememberer and by the psychologist. Words have useful properties: they have meanings and semantic senses; they can be presented either visually or auditorily, or both; their mode of presentation within a given modality can also be varied, by using different type-scripts, speakers' voices, spatial locations, and the like; for bilingual speakers and polyglots they come in different languages. Furthermore, words can be grouped in a variety of systematically describable ways: conceptual categories, acoustic or orthographic similarity groups, semantically associated pairs, as well as phrases, sentences, and larger linguistically meaningful units.

Although many experiments in which words have been used as to-be-remembered materials have been concerned with rememberers' memory for the name of the word-event, the many properties of word-events that can be identified, varied, and manipulated have also made it possible to study rememberers'· recollection of other aspects of word-events, things such as their appearance, sound, and significance (e.g. Nelson 1979), their temporal coding (e.g. Underwood 1977), and the collection in which they occurred (e.g. Winograd 1968).

Factual contents of events

I mentioned earlier (p. 129) that few laboratory experiments in memory and verbal learning have ever been done for the express purpose of studying how people remember events. In my 1972 essay I suggested that most of the work that had been done should be classified as concerned with episodic memory, because it had to do with rememberers' knowledge of what they had learned on a particular occasion rather than with changes in their knowledge of the world. But most of the 'episodic-memory' experiments have been of a rather peculiar kind. They have been mostly concerned with rememberers' learning, retaining, and retrieving upon appropriate instructions their knowledge of the *contents* of previously experienced events, rather than their knowledge of events as such.

According to our definition, an event consists of both a focal element and a setting. If we wanted to know whether you remembered the event of unexpectedly meeting your friend Elizabeth at Wat Pho, we should phrase our question to you in such a manner that you could describe the whole event, its setting and the focal element. We might say, 'Tell us all about your trip to Thailand', or 'Did anything interesting happen to you on your trip?', or perhaps even, 'You did not see Elizabeth by any chance at Wat Pho, did you?'. Most likely you will respond affirmatively to the last question and it is at least possible that you will not mention the meeting in response to the first question. Whether or not you remember the event depends not only on the information stored about it in memory but also on the question asked, the retrieval cue. It is also possible, of course, for people to have incomplete recollections of events. Many years later, for instance, you may remember visiting the Wat Pho temple, but not the unexpected meeting; similarly, you might remember that you once met Elizabeth in a rather unlikely place, but not what that place was. In any case, however, the pyschologist's interest centers on the rememberer's recollection of the whole event: what components and aspects can be recollected and in what form.

In principle it is possible to raise similar questions about word-event memory experiments. A word (focal element) appears in a particular situation (the setting) and the critical question has to do with the rememberer's recollective experience of the whole thing.

Students of memory have not done such experiments. The rememberer's knowledge and memory of the setting is always taken for granted, and the 'test' is directed at the focal-element part of the event. This is so even in experiments on recognition memory. When the subject in a recognition-memory experiment is shown a copy of an item studied previously, the question is not whether the item 'retrieves' or reminds him of the setting in which he saw it earlier. There is no need for a test item to evoke the recollection of the setting of the original event: the subject remembers the setting quite well. Rather, the question is, does he remember the event of seeing another item like the one before him now in that earlier setting.

It is quite possible for a person not to remember the setting of an event but remember the focal element. You may hear someone tell a joke, and sometime later remember the joke but not remember from whom or where you heard it. When the loss of the recollection for the setting is exceptionally rapid, as can happen for people with brain damage, or people under hypnosis (e.g. Evans and Thorn 1966), the phenomenon is referred to as source amnesia. When the same phenomenon occurs naturally in daily life, we could think of it as a consequence of transfer of the factual contents of the event to the semantic system.

In an earlier attempt to deal with problems created by findings that people under certain conditions can utilize information acquired in an episode without remembering the episode itself, Daniel Schacter and I discussed the need for a distinction 'between memory for the *factual content* and autobiographical memory for the episode itself' (Schacter and Tulving 1982, pp. 43–4). What we had in mind in that formulation were experiments with both normal people and amnesic patients, in which the people demonstrated retention and utilizability of symbolic information acquired during a learning episode without remembering the episode itself. But the 'autobiographical memory for the episode itself' in that formulation is vague: what is 'the episode itself'? I am suggesting here that the memory 'for the episode itself' is the memory for the setting of the event.

The 'factual content', or the 'semantic contents' (Schacter and Tulving 1981, p. 25) 'is a term that should be distinguished from 'focal element', and reserved as a designation for the symbolic, usually verbal, substance of the focal element. Thus, in a particular setting (a memory experiment) the focal element may consist of hearing an utterance, or seeing a three-word phrase. If the three words are, say, in English, and if the rememberer comprehends English, we can refer to the linguistic message in the utterance as the factual content of the event. If the rememberer does not comprehend English, the event defined by the same setting and the same focal element has no factual content. Whether or not the factual content of an episode is transferred into semantic memory depends upon conditions that we do not yet understand. But we suspect that the conditions transcend the mere occurrence of an utterance, even a novel one, in a particular episode.

Cognitive environment

One of William James's many contributions to the budding science of psychology was his proof of what he called 'the general law of perception': *'Whilst part of what we perceive comes through our senses from the object before us, another part* (and it may be the larger part) *always comes out of our own mind*, (James 1890, Vol. 2, p. 103).

There has not been a psychologist or philosopher alive in the last one hundred years who has seriously doubted the veracity of this law. Words used to express it, of course, change from time to time and from person to person. Some eighty years after James, Gordon Bower put it as follows: 'Most psychologists today agree that responses of the organism to stimulation are mediated by that organism's cognitive state, which provides a context for and an interpretation of the stimulus as it makes contact with the record of his past experiences' (Bower 1972*b*, p. 85).

Other terms that have been used to refer to the process by which a part of the perception 'comes out of our own minds', or by which the organism's cognitive state provides a context for the stimulus, include apperception, popularized by Herbart, and a number of 'perfect synonyms' of the Herbartian term, according to James (1890, Vol. 2, p. 107)—psychic reaction, interpretation, conception, assimilation, elaboration, psychostatical conditions, and simply 'thought', as well as terms such as experiential context, attitude complexes, sentiments, and psychic tension-systems, which Eich (1977) has culled from various sources. Various sorts of sets, determining tendencies, perceptual readinesses, and peripheral consciousnesses could probably also be added to the list, together with mood states (Isen, Shalker, Clark, and Karp 1978; Bower 1981), and 'drug-altered states of mind, or brain' (Eich 1977, p. 143).

The point of all of these concepts, and the ideas that they refer to, is that the mental residue of the perception of an event, what is stored about it in memory, depends not only on the event as such and its characteristics, but also on a large number of permanent and temporary characteristics of the memory system. In an earlier paper I used the term 'cognitive environment' (Tulving and Thomson 1971, p. 123) to refer to the factors other than the event that influence its encoding. Cognitive environment was meant to be equivalent to what McGeoch (1942, p. 501) referred to as the 'context of the individual's symbolic or ideational events'. I thought a different term was preferable to McGeoch's, because 'context' had been used in too many different senses and hence its usefulness as a designation of a particular idea seemed to be preempted.

Each event is perceived and encoded in a particular cognitive environment. There are many ways of manipulating and influencing the rememberers' cognitive environment and to demonstrate the effect of such variations on their recollection and memory performance. The most popular methods for doing so in experimental psychology have been concerned with transfer and proactive effects, both positive and negative. The so-called 'release from proactive inhibition' effect (Wickens 1970, 1972) provides a clear illustration of the effects of a particular change in the cognitive environment on retention of material over short intervals of time; Underwood (1957) has marshalled relevant evidence of the same kind for 24-hour retention.

Other effective ways of changing the cognitive environment are illustrated by experiments in which the external environment is manipulated at study and retrieval (e.g. Godden and Baddeley 1975; Smith *et al.* 1978), as well as experiments involving changes in the rememberers' mood state (Bower 1981), or drug state (Birnbaum and Parker 1977; Eich 1980; Weingartner and Faillace 1971).

Sometimes writers have used an expression like 'an event occurring in a context'. The 'context' here can refer either to what I suggest we designate by the term 'setting', as discussed earlier, or to what might be more appropriately referred to as the cognitive environment. The term 'context' can be quite ambiguous (Wickelgren 1977) and is best reserved as a designation of particular manipulations rather than used as a generic term. For instance, one word in a pair of words can be thought of as a 'context' for the other (e.g. Light and Carter-Sobell 1970; Thomson 1972), but two different word lists learned in different rooms and at different times are also said to be learned in different contexts (e.g. Smith *et al.* 1978).

Encoding

The concept of encoding is one of the success stories of recent memory research. Only three decades ago the idea was virtually unknown. In the important book by McGeoch and Irion (1952), which provided a more or less complete listing and discussion of the determinants of retention known at that time, there was nothing comparable to encoding. Only twenty years later, however, a whole volume was published to review the accomplishments of cognitive psychologists whose theorizing had relied heavily on the concept of encoding (Melton and Martin 1972). The editors of the volume even thought that in the then current excitement of discovery and theoretical speculations they could detect the 'symptoms of a Kuhnian "paradigm shift" within the science of human learning and memory, with the structure and function of coding processes as the focus of the new paradigm' (Melton and Martin 1972, p. xi). In the same volume, Bower called encoding 'the truly central concept in modern theories of memory' (1972*b*, p. 85).

I have my doubts about the Kuhnian paradigm shift—I do not think that cognitive psychology has as yet reached the stage of a Kuhnian paradigm. But the great popularity of the concept of encoding, and its immense relevance to the study of memory, cannot be gainsaid. Part of the popularity undoubtedly derives from the many senses in which the term can be used. Already in 1972 Bower voiced his suspicion that the high frequency of occurrence of the term in the literature of memory may be partly accounted for by the fact that it is used in many different senses; 'It would take a practicing semanticist forty days hard labor to disentangle all its senses and their commonality of reference' (1972*b*, p. 85). By now the job probably could not be done in forty days.

Encoding is the process that converts an event into an engram. This preliminary definition of the concept relates encoding to the perceived event on the one hand and engram on the other. The characteristics of engrams of experienced events are determined not only by the characteristics of the events, they also depend on how the events are encoded.

Most of the time the rememberer is not aware of the encoding process, and could not verbalize anything about its characteristics on a particular occasion. Yet we must assume that encoding is a necessary condition for remembering, and that it always occurs when information about a perceived event is stored in memory. We must also assume that encoding plays as important a role in determining remembering in real life as it does in the laboratory, although the evidence for the central role of encoding so far has come exclusively from laboratory experiments, most of them involving verbal materials.

Encoding paradigm

In the historical development of the concept of encoding it is possible to detect two stages. The earlier one was characterized by concern with deviations from some normal or standard activity involved in learning or memorization; the later stage, accepted by most students of memory today, no more distinguishes between 'normal' remembering activity and deviations from it.

Let us consider an early experiment as an illustration of the encoding paradigm typifying the first stage. The experiment was done by Postman,

Adams, and Phillips (1955). Subjects were shown a list of 30 adjectives either under intentional or incidental learning conditions. The intentional learners were simply told to try to remember the adjectives as well as they could, whereas the incidental learners were asked to make judgments about frequency of occurrence of the adjectives in the language, but they were not told anything about the impending memory test.

The recall of the studied adjectives was tested under three different conditions: (a) free recall, (b) words associated with studied list adjectives presented as extralist retrieval cues, and (c) words semantically unrelated to the list adjectives presented as retrieval cues. Thus, two kinds of learning activity—intentional learning and frequency judgments—were combined with three test conditions to produce six experimental conditions. The experiment represents an early example of what I later on will refer to as an encoding/retrieval experiment, a type that has played an important role in the study of the interaction between encoding and retrieval as determinants of remembering.

The results of the experiment are shown in Table 8.1. The table shows the mean number of words recalled out of a maximum of 30 in each of the six experimental conditions. We see that free recall was higher for intentional than incidental learners, although the two learning conditions did not differ when retention was tested with cues. For both intentional and incidental learners, the presence of associated cues facilitated recall in relation to free recall, whereas the presence of unrelated cues reduced the level of performance.

Table 8.1

Probabilities of recall in an experiment by Postman, Adams, and Phillips (1955, Exp. 2)

| Learning condition | Retrieval condition | | |
	Free recall	Associative cues	Unrelated cues
Intentional	0.42	0.59	0.24
Incidental	0.31	0.60	0.25

These results are interesting in several respects. For our present purposes we simply note that the learners' mental activity while contemplating the material makes a difference in its subsequent recallability. If we regard the intentional learning condition as standard, we could describe the observed difference in free recall as indicative of the 'interfering' effect of making frequency judgments about presented words. (We could also say, as did Postman *et al.* (1955), that the effects of both incidental and intentional learning can only be stipulated with respect to the method of measurement, and that, therefore, the interference explanation does not apply to cued recall.) Other experiments, too, have demonstrated that when subjects are 'distracted' from the study of presented material through the requirement that they do something else at the same time that the material is presented to them, recall suffers (e.g. Eagle and Ortof 1967; Murdock 1965).

Other experiments have been done in which the subsidiary activity of the learner *facilitates* retention performance when it is compared with that observed under the 'standard' conditions. Thus, for instance, Earhard (1967*a*,*b*) showed that when subjects were told to pay attention to the initial letters of the words they were trying to learn, their recall performance improved, and Bower (1972*a*) has described several experiments in which subjects instructed to use visual imagery in encoding of the to-be-remembered material outperformed subjects working under conventional intentional learning instructions.

The early approach to the study of encoding processes entailed comparisons of intentional and incidental learning. In incidental learning, subjects' instructions did not prepare them for the kind of the test that followed their exposure to the materials: either no instructions at all were given or the instructions that were explicitly provided did not specify the aspects of the task that in fact were tested. Postman (1964), in his well known discussion of the literature on incidental and intentional learning, pointed out that it is not intention as such that determines the difference between the two conditions, but rather the nature of internal processes that are instigated by learning instructions and orienting tasks. Postman described these processes in terms of differential cue-producing responses, or responses elicited by the stimuli. Now, some twenty years later, we would probably be more comfortable with some other terminology, but despite the differences in language, the basic idea has remained the same: some unobservable processes, correlated with instructions to the subjects and the subsequent mental activity, determine the extent to which the studied material is retained.

More recent research on encoding processes has moved away from the consideration of the intentional learning conditions as representing some basic reference level, and frequently has entailed a comparison of different learning conditions in which intentional learning is not included. The basic paradigm is one in which conditions such as the nature of to-be-remembered material, abilities and previous experience of the learners, amount of study time, length of the retention interval, and other 'classic' variables of the sort dealt with by McGeoch and Irion (1952) are held constant, and the learners' mental activity while inspecting the to-be-remembered material is manipulated. A large variety of methods and techniques has been used in these manipulations. Subjects have been asked to cross out vowels in visually presented words, copy the words, or judge how well a word belongs to a particular category (Tresselt and Mayzner 1960); they have been asked to generate rhymes or synonyms to words whose memory is later on tested (de Schonen 1968), they have judged the presence of certain letters or the pleasantness of words (Hyde and Jenkins 1969); they have answered questions about the appearance, sound, and meaning of words (Craik 1973); they have classified words into categories (Frase and Kammann 1974; Schulman 1974; Bock 1976); they have followed instructions to make up mental images of words (Bower 1972a; Paivio and Csapo 1973); rehearsed the words in their own mind (Craik and Watkins 1973; Woodward, Bjork, and Jongeward 1973) or in imagined voices (Geiselman and Glenny 1977; Geiselman and Bjork 1980); made up meaningful sentences of the presented words (Bellezza, Richards, and Geiselman 1976), answered questions about relations between to-be-remembered words and conceptual categories (Klein and Saltz 1976; Mathews 1977; Johnson-Laird et al. 1978; McClelland, Rawles, and Sinclair 1981); and judged the descriptive belongingness of adjectives to people they know better or worse (Keenan and Baillet 1980), and other such things. The ingenuity of experimenters has known few bounds in creating variations in learners' mental activities that define encoding operations. All these variations have been shown to be related to memory performance.

Effects of encoding

The effects of encoding operations in many experiments have turned out to be surprisingly large. Surprisingly, because effects of similar magnitude through the manipulation of other variables frequently require massive intervention of one kind or another: many trials of study versus a single one, retention intervals measured in days versus those measured in minutes, and the like. Given that these variables are held constant, the differential consequences of different encoding operations occupying only a few seconds during study might be expected to be rather circumscribed. Moreover, the way any particular event or object is encoded is greatly influenced by habitual ways of perceiving and classifying things, involving skills and knowledge learned over a lifetime. Because of the existence of these habitual modes of perceiving and encoding the world around us, experimental manipulations designed to affect the nature of encoding processes in particular situations can only be expected to be partially successful. It is generally conceded that the experimenter can influence or bias the encoding to some extent but never control it completely (e.g. Postman, Thompkins, and Gray 1978; Nelson 1979). Yet, despite these restrictions, large effects have been observed.

As a single illustration, consider an experiment done by Mathews (1977). Mathews described three experiments, all rather similar. I will briefly mention here his Experiment 3.

The basic unit of the material that subjects had to remember in Mathews' experiment was a triplet of words. Two members of the triplet, the to-be-remembered words, were semantically related, representing instances of a common conceptual category (e.g. LION and WHALE). The third member of the triplet was a single word or a short phrase designating a category. The experimental manipulation involved the nature of the relation of the designated category and the two to-be-remembered words. There were three conditions. In one, both to-be-remembered words were members of the designated category (e.g. *mammal*), in the second, only one of the two words was (e.g. *part of a circus*), and in the third, neither of them was (e.g. *metal*). At the time of study, subjects made a decision about each triplet in terms of the number of to-be-remembered words related to the category: both of them, only one, or neither. Thus, LION and WHALE would receive the 'both' response when related to the category of *mammals*, response of 'only one' when related to the category of *part of a circus*, and 'neither' in relation to the category of *metal*. Moreover, half the subjects were given instructions about an impending memory test before making the judgments, whereas the other half of the subjects were not. Those subjects given the warning instructions were told that at the time of the test they would be presented with any one of the words of the triplet as a cue for the recall of the other two.

Recall results showed no difference between incidental and intentional learning conditions. With the data pooled over this variable, large differences were observed in the recall of one of the to-be-remembered words cued with the other in the three experimental conditions. The recall proportions were 0.10 for the 'neither' judgment, 0.45 for the 'one only' judgment, and 0.68 for the 'both' judgment. These are large differences. In some of the experiments reported by Craik and Tulving (1975), differences in free recall or recognition of a similar magnitude were reported, but it is important to note that in the Craik and Tulving experiments, different experimental conditions entailed encoding of different *types* (graphemic, acoustic, and semantic), whereas in Mathews' experiment the striking differences were observed across three different *semantic encoding* conditions: in each of the three experimental conditions the subjects had to consider the meaning of each word.

Mathews had designed his experiment in such a way that the nominal identity of cue and target words was held constant across the three experimental conditions. There are other experiments in the literature in which the effects of various encoding operations on *cued recall* have been reported (e.g. Craik and Tulving 1975, Exp. 7; Fisher and Craik 1977; Moscovitch and Craik 1976). But in all these experiments the nominal identity of retrieval cues and hence their pre-experimental relations with the target items have varied with encoding conditions. In these experiments, therefore, the interpretation of the results in terms of pre-experimental properties of cues and their semantic relations to target words cannot be ruled out. In Mathews' experiment they can.

Mathews' experiment neatly illustrates the encoding paradigm: across three encoding conditions, (a) the nominal identity of cues and targets constituting a to-be-remembered unit was held constant, (b)the pre-experimental, semantic-memory relation between the cue and the target was held constant, and (c) the physical facts of the co-occurrence of the cue and the target at the time of study were held constant. In addition to semantic relatedness and episodic contiguity relation of the cue and target that were the same in all experimental conditions, learning instructions, study time, frequency of presentation, recency of occurrence, and the type of retention tests were also all the same. The differences only in mental activity accompanying the inspection of each triplet, lasting less than four seconds per triplet, produced large differences in recall.

Explanations of encoding

A number of different explanations of the differential effectiveness of encoding operations have been offered, beginning with the seminal paper by Craik and Lockhart (1972) in which the differences were attributed to differences in the depth of encoding. This appealingly simple account of encoding differences was soon abandoned, and other hypotheses and theories advanced (e.g. Jenkins 1974*a*, *b*; Postman 1975*b*; Postman *et al.* 1978; Craik and Tulving 1975; Lockhart *et al.* 1976; Anderson 1976; Anderson and Reder 1979; Eysenck 1979; Nelson 1979; as well as others). Most of the explanations have represented attempts to understand encoding differences in terms of a single factor, or a single concept. Terms such as meaning, meaningfulness, integration, interactiveness, elaboration, differentiation, attunement, breadth of encoding, spread of encoding, uniqueness, distinctiveness, and a number of others, have been pressed into service as explanatory devices. As yet, however, no convincing explanations that apply to a reasonably large proportion of demonstrated phenomena of encoding have been produced.

The theoretical efforts directed at encoding have recently shifted to the domain of semantic encoding operations. Differences in memorability resulting from different kinds of semantic encoding rule out a number of possible explanations of phenomena involving comparison of *types* of encoding, structural, acoustic, semantic, and so on. Relevant research has also come into focus on one of the deficiencies of the original formulation of the levels-of-processing approach to the study of memory (Craik and Lockhart 1972), namely the apparent circularity in defining the depth of processing in terms of observed memory performance, a deficiency discussed by a number of critics (Nelson 1977; Baddeley 1978; Eysenck 1978). Several experiments have shown that the number of uncorrelated semantic decisions made about to-be-remembered words is correlated with memory performance, thus suggesting an independent, and independently manipulable, index of 'depth of processing' (Klein and Saltz 1976;

Johnson-Laird *et al.* 1978; McClelland *et al.* 1981). In the meantime, progress is also being made in coming to grips with the problem of specifying levels across types of encoding (Parkin 1979).

Two predictions can be made for the future of theories of encoding. First, explanations of encoding are unlikely to be much less complicated than explanations of episodic remembering as a whole. Second, no explanation of encoding is likely to succeed unless it takes into account other components of the process of remembering, especially retrieval processes. Some of the theoretical accounts of encoding that have been offered do so (e.g. Lockhart *et al.* 1976; Craik and Jacoby 1979; Eysenck 1979; Nelson 1979), whereas some others do not (e.g. Anderson 1976; Anderson and Reder 1979; Craik and Tulving 1975; Postman *et al.* 1978).

Engram

We usually do not think of Ebbinghaus as a person who was greatly concerned with the hidden world of remembering, the kinds of processes and states that we are discussing as elements of our General Abstract Processing System. But he was. Although he devoted his talents to a scientific development of those aspects of memory that had been neglected up to his time, he was very much aware that the observed phenomena of memory reflected the internal workings of the mind.

He began his classic book with the following words:

> Mental states of every kind—sensations, feelings, and ideas—which were at one time present in consciousness and then have disappeared from it, have not with their disappearance absolutely ceased to exist. Although the inwardly-turned look may no longer be able to find them, nevertheless they have not been utterly destroyed and annulled, but in a certain manner they continue to exist, stored up, so to speak, in the memory. We cannot, of course, directly observe their present existence, but it is revealed by the effects which come to our knowledge with a certainty like that with which we infer the existence of the stars below the horizon (Ebbinghaus 1885, p. 1).

What were these effects that provided certain knowledge of stored-up mental states? There was essentially just one: the fact of remembering. When we recognize a recalled 'image' as something that we formerly experienced, Ebbinghaus argued, 'it would be absurd to suppose that our will has created it anew and, as it were, out of nothing; it must have been present somehow or somewhere' (pp. 1–2).

Unlike Ebbinghaus, William James did not like the idea of 'stored up' mental states of which we are unconscious. Yet his disagreement with Ebbinghaus lay only in words and not in the concept. Like many of his predecessors, he analyzed the 'complete exercise of the phenomenon of memory' into 'two things': the *retention* of the remembered fact, and its *reminiscence* (recollection, reproduction, or recall). He said that the proof of retention is the fact that recall actually takes place. But he also said that retention 'is no mysterious storing up of an "idea" in an unconscious state. It is not a fact of the mental order at all. It is a purely physical phenomenon, a morphological feature, the presence of these "paths", namely in the finest recesses of the brain's tissue' (Vol. 1, p. 655).

Neither Ebbinghaus nor James gave a special name to the stored up unconscious idea or the liability to recall. But many other people have. Although many different terms have been used, the most popular of them has been 'memory trace'. In what follows I, too, will be talking a great deal about memory traces. But because the term carries undesirable connotations to some students of memory, I will use it interchangeably with the term 'engram'.

Some students of memory associate the concept of memory trace with some sort of 'fixed, lifeless object' that resides in the mind, or in the brain, and with a theory of memory according to which remembering consists of partial or complete reactivation of these otherwise lifeless objects. Neisser (1967) labelled this idea 'reappearance hypothesis', and convincingly argued for its inadequacy. Fights against picture-theories or copy-theories of remembering, however, are not new. They go back at least as far as Thomas Reid (1710–1796).

I think that altogether too much fuss is sometimes made about problems such as whether memory traces are 'lifeless' or dynamic, fixed or mutable, permanent or transient, and whether they really exist or whether they are simply figments of the imagination of memory theorists. Memory traces may not quite exist in the same way in which Ebbinghaus' stars below the horizon did, but they certainly exist in the sense that they are responsible for observable effects that could not occur in their absence. To deny such existence is an affectation that does not substitute for originality of thought.

Engram is the product of encoding, one of the necessary conditions for recollection of the experienced event. We can also think of the engram of an event as the difference between the state of the memory system before and after the encoding of the event. This is a very broad definition that conveys the intended meaning of the term without asking the listener to make any theoretical commitments. As such, it is reminiscent of the definition of the soul by Jean Fernel (a well-known French physician and savant of the sixteenth century) in terms of the comparison of the organism 'just before and just after death' (Hall 1969, p. 194).

Within the General Abstract Processing System, however, engram, like other hypothetical concepts, is defined in terms of its position in the overall scheme of things and in terms of its relations to other elements in the system.

The term 'engram' was introduced by Richard Semon (1904) to represent the enduring changes brought about by the energetic effect of stimuli in the organism. His own definition was as follows:

> When an organism has been temporarily stimulated and has passed, after the cessation of the stimulus, into the condition of 'secondary indifference', it can be shown that such organism . . . has been permanently affected. This I call the engraphic action of a stimulus, because a permanent record has been written or engraved on the irritable substance. I use the word engram to denote this permanent change wrought by a stimulus (1921, p. 24).

The nature of the changes constituting engrams were not known to Semon. (They are not known to us, either.) The functional significance of engrams, according to Semon, lay in their ability of being reactivated by stimuli weaker than the original one, by only part of the original stimuli, or by qualitatively different ones.

For a brief summary of Semon's theory of memory, the reader is referred to Schacter *et al.* (1978). A more complete account of Semon's interesting life and tragic end, his remarkably modern and far-sighted vision of the nature of memory, and the reasons why his name is so little known to contemporary students, can be found in Schacter (1982).

The term 'engram' became known is psychological circles through the work of Karl Lashley. Every introductory student of psychology today is expected to know that despite determined efforts Lashley failed to find the engram (Lashley 1950).

In the General Abstract Processing System, engrams possess functional properties rather than structural ones. Structural properties of memory traces imply their conceptualization as entities that can at least be imagined to exist independently of their function; functional properties, on the other hand, can be identified and described without postulating any such independent existence. In a review of some of the methods that psychologists have used in attempts to describe memory traces, Gordon Bower and I (Tulving and Bower 1974) rejected the idea of memory traces as parts of the 'structure' of memory, and suggested that psychological descriptions of memory traces should be given not in terms of what the memory traces *are* but rather in terms of what they *do*. The implications of this position were expressed as follows:

> Once we adopt the attitude toward memory traces as a component of mental activity, it becomes immediately clear that memory traces do not do anything by themselves. They only act in combination with other processes. We do not yet know what all the other relevant processes are, but we have a fair idea that some of them are in an important way involved in retrieval, and utilization of stored information. Since memory traces do not possess independent existence and only manifest themselves in combination with retrieval processes, the interrelation between stored information and conditions of retrieval cannot be ignored by anyone interested in the format and characteristics of memory traces (Tulving and Bower 1974, pp. 293–4).

Engrams, too, must be specified in terms of both their antecedent conditions—particular events particularly encoded in particular cognitive
environments—and their consequent conditions, including the circumstances surrounding their subsequent retrieval.

Whether we think of engrams as information stored about past events,
as a record of operations, attunements, or dispositions, or even as pictures,
images, copies, propositions, analogue representations, feature bundles,
or as particularly marked parts of associative networks, makes relatively
little difference to our understanding of how memory works, although it
may influence the thinking of individual students of memory, the kinds of
questions they pose and the kinds of data they collect. No techniques exist
as yet for determining that one set of words is better than another, or that
some ways of talking about the nature of engrams are incorrect or even
preposterous. Although sometimes a great deal of heat is generated in the
debates directed at the issue of the nature of representations, and although
sometimes useful ideas may emerge from these debates, the issue is
unlikely to be settled by psychological means.

Psychologists interested in memory sometimes have a difficult time
remembering that all theories and models in psychology as in many other
sciences are 'as if' ideas, and that concepts other than those that represent
names for the physically observable entities refer to components of hypothetical analogues of the system we wish to understand. Time after time,
when reading a theoretical explanation of some phenomenon of the human
mind, I find myself deeply puzzled about the intentions of the theorist: when
he is explaining something, that is, going beyond a description of the phenomenon in particular or general terms, is he talking about his model or
about what the model is supposed to represent? I realize, of course, that
explanations mean different things to different people, as do terms such as
'theory', 'model', and 'understanding', and that it is difficult to change people's minds on these matters once they have been made up. It also seems
that many practicing psychologists are not always very keen on trying to
clarify issues through an examination of the philosophical underpinnings of
conflicting positions. More than once have I been told by some anonymous
referee that he is not interested in my version of 'elementary philosophy of
science', and that he would rather see the journal space devoted to 'real science' (my phrase, of course, as well as the quotation marks).

Engrams as feature bundles

I am partial to the idea that the engram of an event is a bundle of features,
or a collection of some other kind of more primitive element. This idea,
that can be traced back at least to the work of Estes (e.g. Estes 1959) and
adopted for theoretical analysis of problems of memory by theorists such
as Bower (1967, 1972*b*), Underwood (1969), and Wickens (1970) helps us
to talk about, and in some sense even understand, phenomena of memory
that could not have been equally gracefully handled in other languages,

for instances, the language of associations and associative networks. Thinking of engrams in terms of feature bundles provides a basis for specifying similarity relations among events, their engrams, and recollective experiences, it makes it possible to imagine a finely graded variation of objects, situations, and events that can be perceived and remembered, it helps us to understand how variations in encoding operations are correlated with variations in engrams, it suggests a basis for ecphory (retrieval), and it poses many problems that would be difficult to think of otherwise.

My preference for the feature-language rather than some other comparable language is just that, a preference; it is by no means an essential part of the GAPS framework. Other thinkers, for equally good or bad reasons, may find it more convenient to think theoretical thoughts that fit better into some other pre-theoretical model. In most cases statements in one kind of language can be readily translated into another, as we know from practical experience, and as has been demonstrated formally (Hollan 1975). The powerful influence that the language we use seems to exert on our thought processes, a personal although not necessarily unshared observation I mentioned earlier (p. 19), may operate at the level of intuition rather than logic, affect rather than cognition.

Although the feature-language has many attractions, it does entail problems. We have no idea about the number and identity of features that the human mind or its memory system has at its disposal for the purpose of construction of engrams, bundles of retrieval information, collections of ecphoric information, and the like. A currently accepted assumption holds that the features of the mind correspond to discriminable differences in our perceptual environment and to the categories and the concepts that the language we use imposes on the world. But no one has yet prepared a list of mental features, nor rules or methods for determining their characteristics.

Other problems exist in connection with the feature-language. Thus, we have no idea about the 'glue' that keeps features of an engram together, or what happens when some of them are 'lost' or otherwise changed. If a feature has been 'lost', can it be 'grafted' back on to the rest of the bundle, or is the change of individual features of an engram irreversible? Is it possible to recall an event reasonably faithfully even if its engram has lost some features? Are the features that define an engram equally important, or do some carry greater weight in determining its nature?

The fact that the features of an engram do not necessarily correspond to the features of the original event even when the event can be accurately reproduced can be demonstrated in the following thought experiment. If you give a person a list of words in a perceptual display, he can equally well select from the list a word that, say, represents the name of a musical instrument (HARPSICHORD) or a word whose fifth letter is 'S' (HARPSICHORD). If you ask the person to store the same list of words in memory, and then ask him to 'select' from the stored list a word meaning a musical instrument, he can do it very much better than he can select the word whose fifth letter is 'S', despite the fact that one of the features of the reproduced word HARPSICHORD is the letter 'S' in the fifth position. Some of the features of the original event are not stored, or they are stored in a manner different from their presence in the perceptual object. A larger graphemic fragment of the word, of course, may be as effective, or even more effective, a retrieval cue than the semantic cue *musical instrument*.

A puzzling phenomenon in relation to the idea of engrams as feature bundles lies in people's inability to recall any features of unrecallable words. If you present to a person a list of familiar words, ask him to study each word carefully, and then give a liberal amount of time for free recall of the words, he will recall some words but not others. When you are satisfied that the subject's further efforts at recall are unlikely to yield much more fruit, you ask him to recall features of those words that he has not yet recalled. You tell him that although he may not be able to recall any more complete words, he may have some partial information about the unrecalled words, information derived from the study of the list but incomplete in the sense that it does not quite enable him to produce an intact word. These features might include things such as the conceptual category to which the word belongs, its affective connotations, descriptions of its graphemic and orthographic features, initial letter or letters, some idea about the sound of the word, and so on. The subject is encouraged to report any or all such incomplete but list-based information.

The results of such a test are straightforward: subjects cannot produce any relevant partial information. Indeed, many of them find the request frustrating and unreasonable. Sometimes a subject may come up with a response, a partial description of a word. Before you accept it as evidence against the result I have just described, it is necessary to evaluate its validity. This can be done in several ways. One method consists of giving the subject's response to a panel of judges, together with the list of unrecalled target words and a comparable list of distractors of the same general type, words that did not occur in the study list, and asking the panel to select one of the words from the test set on the basis of the information provided by the subject. Only if the selection of the correct words is above the chance level is it appropriate to conclude that a partial response represents information derived from the study list. When such checks on the validity of partial responses, recall of features of unrecalled words, are done, the outcome shows the original conclusion to be correct: people cannot produce features of unrecalled words. The question is, why not?

The puzzle is relevant to our conceptualization of words as feature bundles. Certain phenomena involving retention and forgetting of word-events can be accounted for in terms of changes in the composition of different traces of stored words. Underwood (1969), among others, for example, has suggested that attributes may be forgotten at different rates, thus implying that the composition of memory traces may change qualitatively over time. It is conceivable, then, that at some point in time an originally 'complete' memory trace, which could support the overt act of recall of the event, has lost some of its attributes and that what is left is an incomplete trace, containing some of the original attributes but not others. But if so, why has the rememberer no access to the features of the incomplete memory trace?

Subjects' inability to recall features of unrecalled words seems to stand in curious contrast both to the well-known tip of the tongue phenomenon (Brown and McNeill 1966) as well as the phenomenon of 'false recognition' (Underwood 1965; Anisfield and Knapp 1968), both of which have been explained in terms of the availability in the memory store of features of 'incomplete' words. The discrepancy may therefore constitute just a problem for future research, and need not completely shake our faith in the usefulness of the idea of engrams as feature bundles. But, at the same time, further thought about the concept of features would not seem to be entirely misplaced, either.

The mind's eye—the encoding system—can fixate any object, or any event, in many different ways, somewhat like an observer can perceive an object from many different vantage points. The physical features of the object do not change as the observer changes its vantage point. But what the observer directly sees differs, sometimes greatly, depending upon the point of view. Yet, the observer's *knowledge* of the perceived object need not change equally drastically: parts hidden from view, or distorted, can be added or rectified in the model that the mind constructs of that part of the world that the object under scrutiny represents. Both the perceived perspective and the constructed object become part of the stored engram, together with the knowledge of which part was what. Particular encodings of to-be-remembered events may be thought of analogously to the notion of vantage-point perception of objects.

One of the most important advantages of the feature-language lies in the fact that it allows us to think about engrams of different events as *qualitatively* different. Two engrams are similar to, or different from, each other to the extent that they possess shared and distinctive features, in keeping with the theoretical analysis of Tversky (1977).

Engrams as such do not differ from each other in terms of 'strength'. For a long time students of memory have assigned this property to memory traces, associations, and representations called by other names, but the usage has always been metaphorical: in all strength-theories of memory, strength of traces has been measured in terms of certain quantifiable characteristics of memory performance. In the General Abstract Processing System, characteristics of memory performance do not depend on the engram, but on the interaction between the engram and various retrieval factors, especially the cue. Therefore, according to GAPS, endowing memory traces with 'strength' makes little sense. It only creates the problem of explaining why sometimes 'strong' traces yield poor memory performance and 'weak' traces support excellent recollection. We will be discussing experimental evidence demonstrating such states of affairs in the third section of the book. Within the present framework, one of the problems for memory theories is to relate qualitative differences of engrams to different quantitative degrees of memory performance. We will discuss some ideas relevant to this problem also in the third section of the book.

Recoding, interpolated events, and recoded traces

One of the most pervasive facts about episodic memory has to do with changes, over time, in recollective experience and memory performance pertaining to a given event. Recollective experience of the event now is different from what it was before; these differences show up as increments or decrements in memory performance. Although some of the changes can be attributed to changes in retrieval factors, others come about because of changes in engrams.

Mutability is one of the distinctive characteristics of engrams of events: Functional properties of engrams change over time. *Recoding* is the generic name of all the processes and operations that take place after the encoding of the original event and that bring about changes in the engram.

A great deal of experimental and theoretical work has been devoted to the study of recoding. This work appears under headings such as repetition effects (e.g. Peterson, Saltzman, Hillner, and Land 1962; Melton 1967, 1970; Glanzer and Duarte 1971), rehearsal (Rundus 1971; Woodward *et al.* 1973), retroactive effects (e.g. Barnes and Underwood 1959; Postman, Keppel, and Stark 1965), retrieval-induced recoding (e.g. Allen, Mahler, and Estes 1969; Darley and Murdock 1971; Bartlett and Tulving 1974; Bjork 1975; Bartlett 1977), 'mental contiguity' (Glanzer 1969; Wallace 1970), diffusion of trace elements (Shepard 1961; Shepard and Chang 1963), cue overload (Earhard 1977; Watkins and Watkins 1975), information integration (Bransford and Franks 1971; Loftus 1975; Loftus, Miller, and Burns 1978; Pezdek 1977), 'incrementing' (Raaijmakers and Shiffrin 1981), among others.

Recoding paradigm

The basic paradigm necessary to demonstrate recoding effects is schematically depicted in Table 8.2. It requires the participation of three *identical* rememberers Rememberers A and B encode the original event, whereas C does not. Subsequently rememberers A and C encode an interpolated event, while B does not. Then all three rememberers recollect the original event. Recoding is said to have occurred to the extent that the recollection of the original event by rememberers A and B differs, and to the extent that this difference is not reflected in the 'recollection' of the original event by rememberer C. Rememberers A and B define the classical retroaction paradigm; rememberer C is added to the recoding paradigm to enable the psychologists to attribute the difference in the recollections of A and B to the change of the original event by the interpolated event rather than to the fact that the interpolated event was witnessed by rememberer A but not B. In many cases the control condition represented by rememberer C is only an imaginary part of the experiment, since the assumption can safely be made that rememberer C, not having been exposed to the original event, could not recollect it at all. In other cases, however, actual inclusion of rememberer C in the paradigm is necessary.

The difference in the memory performance of rememberers A and B in this paradigm is interpreted as reflecting qualitative differences in (recoded) engrams, on the assumption that other conditions affecting the performance are held constant. As in other episodic-memory situations, the basic question of interest is always about *what* the rememberers remember when their recollection of the original event is assessed. In most laboratory experiments, however, the differences in qualitative character-istics of recollective experiences are converted into quantitative observa-tions: the performance of rememberer A can be shown to be higher or lower than that of rememberer B. Thus, in quantitative terms, the effect of recoding of the engram may facilitate or inhibit the recollection of the original events, or enhance or reduce the performance measured in some other way.

Improvement in retention of an original event over time has sometimes been observed in situations in which the interpolated events are held con-stant but the rememberer's drug state is changed (e.g. Parker, Morihisa, Wyatt, Schwartz, Weingartner, and Stillman 1981). This phenomenon, which has been interpreted as 'consolidation' of memory traces, should be distinguished from the kinds of recoding effects we are discussing here. Similarly, the classical 'reminiscence' effects, showing that recall of some earlier learned material is higher after a longer retention interval than after

Table 8.2
Recoding paradigm

Rememberer (condition)	Original event	Interpolated event	Recollection of the original event
A	Yes	Yes	Yes
B	Yes	No	Yes
C	No	Yes	Yes

a shorter one, probably cannot be classified under the category of recoding, since the activities of the rememberer responsible for the effect cannot be identified. I will reserve 'recoding' as a label for the effects to which the recoding paradigm shown in Table 8.2 either applies or could be imagined to apply.

Similarity of interpolated events

It is generally known that an 'interpolated' event can bring about recoding of an extant engram only if its encoding is similar to the engram. The functional properties of many engrams are unchanged as a result of all sorts of mental activity, since the ongoing processing does not have the requisite similarity relations to them. The experimental and theoretical difficulty lies in assessing the similarity of interpolated events and their encoding to engrams as they exist at the time of the interpolated activity. Within limited domains, we have been reasonably successful in working out some general principles governing the relation between the similarity of original and interpolatrd materials on the one hand and manifestations of recoding on the other (e.g. Osgood 1949; McGovern 1964; Postman 1971). But few empirical or theoretical generalizations about the role of similarity in recoding have emerged in other situations. In interpreting outcomes of individual experiments, experimenters rely on their intuition in assessing the similarity relations between interpolated events and original ones.

One problem in working out the similarity relations in recoding lies in the fact that it is the *encodings* of events whose similarity governs the effect that the stored form of one can have on that of the other. And, as we know, any object or event can be encoded in many different ways. A large number of experimental demonstrations exist in the literature showing the effect of the similarity of the interpolated material to the original material on recall of the original material. But it is also possible to show differences in retroaction under conditions where the relation of the interpolated material to the original material is held constant, but the *encoding* of the interpolated material is manipulated. For instance, Wood (1970, Exp. 2) had subjects study 50 words in one list, and then either study another list or sort the second list words into the same categories that had been used in List 1 or different categories. Recall of the first-list words ranged from 24 per cent for the same-category sorting group to 58 per cent for the study group. Many other experiments also exist whose results point to the important role that encoding processes play in determining similarity relations between memory traces.

Repetition effects

A special and interesting case of recoding is found in situations in which events are 'repeated'. Strictly speaking, as I have argued earlier, events are always unique and therefore, by definition, do not repeat themselves.

But when we are dealing with simple events, such as occurrences of familiar words in a to-be-remembered list, we can think of the repetition of a given word in a list as a repeated event. In other situations, the relation between any two events is that of a certain degree of similarity rather than identity.

When in an otherwise heterogeneous list a to-be-remembered item occurs twice, its probability of recall is higher than that of an item presented just once. We assume that when the item occurs for the second time, an engram is formed of that event as of any other events, and that, in addition, the original trace may be recoded. The observed memory performance reflects both the properties of the recoded trace of the first event and the properties of the engram of the second event.

Two other possible interpretations of the enhanced recall of a repeated events are less likely. First, the idea that the second presentation of the item 'strengthens' the existing trace is difficult to reconcile with the fact that subjects usually know that an item has been presented twice. The other possibility, that the occurrence of the second event produces a separate and independent engram is difficult to reconcile with the fact that under certain conditions the probability of recall of the unit presented twice is more than twice as high as a unit presented once (e.g. Mathews and Tulving 1973, Exps. 2 and 3).

Another reason for assuming that an item's repetition in a list brings about recoding of the engram of the same item's first presentation has to do with the fact that similar recoding processes are suggested by observations in a situation in which the 'repetition' of an item involves the presentation of an item highly similar to the first one. For instance, in an unpublished MA thesis done at the University of Toronto by Karalyn Friedman in 1966, subjects saw, on a single trial, lists of 22 common words. In some of the lists two associatively related words would occur, words such as BOY and GIRL, or DAY and NIGHT. For instance, in one list the word BOY would appear in the sixth serial position and the word GIRL in the twelfth position. In a comparable control list the word BOY would occur in serial position 6, but the word GIRL would be absent altogether. The probability of free recall of single critical words (e.g. BOY) was 0.34, and the probability of recall of the critical words (e.g. BOY) recorded by virtue of the subsequent occurrence of a related word (e.g. GIRL) was 0.60. We can assume that at the time of the presentation of the word GIRL the subject 'thought back' to the earlier presentation of the word BOY, and that, as a result, the engram of BOY was recorded (cf. Glanzer 1969; Wallace 1970; Jacoby 1974).

Recoding of an event as a result of the later occurrence of a related event, like all encoding or recoding effects, should not be thought of in terms of 'strengthening' of the original memory trace. Whether recoding is brought about by 'repeated' events or related events, the functional properties of the recoded trace depend on both the characteristics of the interpolated event and the particulars of its own encoding.

Elizabeth Loftus, in a systematic series of experiments, has demonstrated striking recoding effects in situations in which the to-be-remembered events are much more complex than single words in experimental lists (e.g. Loftus 1975, 1977; Loftus *et al.* 1978; Loftus and Palmer 1974). In these experiments, subjects witness a simulated automobile accident presented on slides and then are asked questions about what they have seen. Some of the questions are designed to imply the presence of objects not actually seen in the original series of slides. Subsequent memory tests show that subjects frequently 'remember' things implied by the questions as a part of their original experience.

Loftus has interpreted these kinds of findings to suggest that 'information to which a witness is exposed after an event, whether that information is consistent or misleading, is integrated into the witness' memory of the event' (Loftus *et al.* 1978, p. 19). In other words, the interpretation is that the memory trace of the original event has been recoded as a consequence of the question about it.

Recoding of the engram implies that it is changed, and after the change has taken place some of the information in the original engram is no more available. Some theorists might want to argue that engrams, once formed, are never changed, and that recoding phenomena imply the existence of additional memory traces, resulting from the interpolated events, and the utilization of information from those traces.

A strong implication of the recoding process as envisaged in GAPS as well as by Loftus is that, depending upon the nature of the modification of the original engram, utilization of certain information originally contained in it should not be possible after recoding has taken place. To prove the recoding hypothesis wrong, therefore, all that is necessary is to show that all originally stored information is still functionally intact after recoding has taken place. Attempts to put the hypothesis to test will undoubtedly be forth-coming.

The elements of GAPS that make up the encoding process 'end' with the formation of an engram or, optionally, its modification through recoding. A recoded engram may exist in its latent form in the system for a long time before it participates in the second main process that constitutes an act of remembering, that of retrieval. All of us carry with us a myriad of latent engrams, and many of them, indeed, will never be actualized. Many others, however, will. This happens when the right retrieval cue 'happens to come along'. We shall turn our attention to the retrieval process next.

9
Elements of retrieval

Engrams are dispositions, potentialities, processes held in abeyance. Tens of thousands of them exist in an individual's episodic-memory system without having any effect whatsoever on ongoing mental activity. They become effective only under special conditions that are collectively called 'retrieval'. In this chapter we discuss the elements of the retrieval process.

For retrieval to occur, two necessary conditions must be met. First, the system must be in what I will refer to as the 'retrieval mode', and second, an appropriate retrieval cue must be present that sets off the process. In GAPS, the obligatory elements of the retrieval process consist of ecphory, ecphoric information, recollective experience, conversion of ecphoric information, and memory performance. For the rememberer the process of retrieval results in recollective experience, feedback from behavior supported by ecphoric information, or both. For the psychologist, the process ends with the rememberer's description of recollective experience, memory performance, or both.

Retrieval mode

We know next to nothing about retrieval mode, other than that it constitutes a necessary condition for retrieval. The important role that it plays in retrieval is given to us in casual observation. We look around us at objects and events in our environment, we participate in conversations, read books and newspapers, see a great variety of things on television, and in general are bombarded with information almost continually. Nevertheless, few things that we perceive make us think of previous happenings in our own lives: people have marvellous capacities for remembering their past, but they usually spend very little time in reminiscing. Moreover, many stimuli that could potentially serve as reminders or cues, even if prominently displayed to a person, have no such effect on him. Walk up to a person—preferably someone you know—and say, 'a long journey', and see what happens. Chances are that he will just look at you as if you were in need of help. Or show a person you know a picture of a mutual friend, without comment, and watch his reaction. He may say something like, 'Why, this is Benjamin, why are you showing it to me?'.

Neither the phrase nor the picture brings back any memories to the subject in your informal experiment. Yet, all you need to do to convert these stimuli into effective retrieval cues is to tell the person that you want him to think of a particular event in his life that the phrase or picture of the friend reminds him of. He would have no difficulty whatsoever in thinking of many happenings from the past that are prompted by the cue. Research shows that even single words can be effective retrieval cues to personal episodes, eliciting them in a few seconds (e.g. Crovitz and Schiffman 1974; Robinson 1976). Adding the requirement that the remembered episode should be a happy one or a sad one does not make the rememberer's task much more difficult (e.g. Lloyd and Lishman 1975; Teasdale and Fogarty 1979).

If retrieval mode is such an important determinant of retrieval, and if no retrieval occurs unless the system is appropriately set for treating stimulus events as cues to stored episodes, why has it escaped the notice of experimenters and theorists? Probably the main reason has to do with the fact that we as rememberers cannot detect—perceive or feel—the difference between the retrieval mode and the encoding mode of the memory system. When something that happens to us—an event we witness, an anecdote we hear, an odor we smell, or whatnot—reminds us of a personal episode, we do not feel that we are in a different state than we are when similar happenings have no cueing effect. Whenever a stimulus becomes a retrieval cue, we attribute its effect to its own characteristics, since we have no awareness of the 'retrieval mode'. Another reason for the neglect of retrieval mode may have to do with the fact that it is so easy to institute in all situations in which psychologists are studying memory. Experimental instructions always have the effect of placing the memory system in the retrieval mode. It is difficult to study something of which we are not aware, and how can we become aware of something that is always present?

Ebbinghaus launched his epoch-making study of memory from a solid philosophical base that was accepted by just about everyone at his time. This base included a distinction that divided recollective experiences into those that resulted from deliberate attempts on the part of the individual to remember a past event, and those that were forced upon him through causes other than his own desire. This distinction between voluntary and involuntary remembering was like the distinction between voluntary and involuntary attention. 'We can call back into consciousness by an exertion of the will directed to this purpose the seemingly lost states . . . that is, we can reproduce them *voluntarily*', Ebbinghaus said, and contrasted it with the remembering of the other kind: 'Often, even after years, mental states once present in consciousness return to it with apparent spontaneity and without any act of the will; that is, they are reproduced *involuntarily* (Ebbinghaus 1885, pp. 1–2).

By the time Ebbinghaus had finished his work, the associative basis for the study of memory was firmly established and there was no more need to postulate any role for the 'will'. In the learned series of nonsense syllables, recall of each individual syllable took place in response to others acting as stimuli: 'Each member of the series has a definite tendency on its own return to consciousness to bring back others with it' (p. 117). Ebbinghaus over-looked the role of 'will' in the associative elicitation of learned syllables, because in his experiments, with himself as the sole well-trained and highly motivated subject, the 'will' was always present. And it was present in all experiments to come.

What kind of a state is the retrieval mode? Is it cognitive? Affective? Con-ative? Is it the same as the 'determining tendency' of the Würzburg school? Is it the same as Ebbinghaus 'will'?

I do not know the answers to these questions, nor, I suspect, does anyone else. But the study of retrieval mode, and its similarities to and differences from the encoding mode of the cognitive system, seem like a promising and timely research enterprise. Since we know so little about it at this time, how-ever, it does not figure as an identifiable element in the retrieval system as envisioned in GAPS.

Retrieval cues

A retrieval cue can be thought of as the especially salient or significant part of retrieval information, those aspects of the individual's physical and cognitive environment that initiate and influence the process of retrieval. In daily life, retrieval cues are presented to the rememberer—or the rememberer notices their presence—in the ongoing interaction with the environment. In laboratory experiments, the presence and nature of retrieval cues is manipulated, directly or indirectly, by the experimenter.

We can also think of retrieval cues as descriptions of descriptions. First, we assume that 'experience is the formation of a description' which, or part of which, is retained (Bregman 1977, p. 271), and then we think of retrieval cue as 'the formation of a description of the information sought' (Norman and Bobrow 1979, p. 109). Putting the two thoughts together, we end up with retrieval cue as the present description of a past descrip-tion. This definition covers particularly well instances of retrieval where the cue assumes a symbolic form—a word, a phrase, a question, a spoken hint, or a symbolic 'test analogue' (Raaijmakers and Shiffrin 1981, p. 125) of the engram. It could also be metaphorically extended to situations in which the cue cannot be expressed in language or some other symbol system.

Although recall has sometimes been said to be either stimulated or not (Bilodeau, Fox, and Blick 1963), cued or non-cued (Tulving and Pearl-stone 1966), or prompted or unprompted (Bahrick 1969), these contrasts refer to methodological distinctions that only describe experimental treat-ments in particular experiments. From the point of view of theory, and until such time that someone produces evidence to the contrary, we should assume that all retrieval is always cued (e.g. Jones 1979; Tulving and Madigan 1970; Tulving 1976; Watkins 1979). An important research prob-lem is the identification of the nature of 'invisible' cues (Tulving and

Watkins 1975; Eich 1980) in situations in which no cues seem to be present.

Although it has not been done, it may turn out to be useful or even necessary to distinguish between cues to episodes and cues to the factual content of episodes. Very little evidence is available on cueing of episodes in the literature of cognitive psychology (e.g. Crovitz and Schiffman 1974; Lloyd and Lishman 1975; Robinson 1976; Teasdale and Fogarty 1979), although a good deal of survey research has been concerned with people's memory for particular personal experiences. Thus, for instance, survey researchers have been interested in the population statistics on things such as hospitalization (e.g. Cannell 1977) and victimization in crime (e.g. Garofalo and Hindelang 1977). When a person is asked, 'Have you recently stayed in a hospital?' or 'Have you, or has any member of your family, been mugged recently?' the question is about the occurrence of an episode, rather than, or in addition to, its focal element or factual contents. In an overwhelming majority of experiments reported in the literature of cognitive psychology, as we have already seen (p. 148), the rememberer's awareness of the episode is taken for granted before cues are presented for the retrieval of its factual contents.

What is the difference between 'stimuli' or 'stimulus items' of the classical verbal learning literature and 'cues' in the contemporary study of memory in experimental psychology? The question is not easy to answer, because the concept of 'stimulus' in verbal learning was never systematically discussed; at least I am not aware of such discussion, nor would I know where to look for it. Experimenters were interested in problems such as stimulus familiarization, stimulus selection, and sometimes questions were asked about 'the' stimulus in a particular verbal learning task, but more often than not, this work was primarily empirical in nature. Questions that have been asked under the banner of 'retrieval cues', concerning problems such as effectiveness of cues, specificity of cues, and theoretical implications of successive cueing—some of the matters discussed in this book—were not raised in the classical verbal learning literature.

Copy cues

In some ways, of course, 'retrieval cue' is simply a synonym for 'stimulus' or 'stimulus item'. For instance, whether we talk about retrieval cues or stimulus terms in standard paired-associate tasks is immaterial. In this situation, Bartlett's observation that 'psychologists seem to like a fairly frequent change of terminology, even when they do not greatly change their working notions' (Bartlett 1967, p. 631) would seem to both explain the switch from stimuli to cues and evaluate the significance of the switch. In other situations, however, there may be more to the switch than just semantic variation.

Consider, for instance, copy cues or identity cues (Tulving and Thomson 1973; Watkins and Tulving 1975; Watkins 1979). A copy cue is one that is physically identical with the focal element of the to-be-remembered event, although its meaning can be extended to situations in which the differences between the target items and their copy cues vary in form but not substance. Although the concepts of identity, form, and substance can be sticky ones, defining and identifying copy cues entails no great difficulties in simple laboratory experiments in which the to-be-remembered items are words, pictures, and the like.

The idea of copy cues fits in naturally into the theoretical framework in which the effectiveness of the cue depends on its similarity or 'informational overlap' with the to-be-remembered event. The copy cues represents one extreme on the continuum of similarity. One characteristic of the recognition-memory task is that the retrieval cues provided to the rememberer are copy cues. But copy cues, or identity cues, can also be used in recall tasks: a word is presented to the rememberer as the cue and the correct response consists in writing down a word identical with the cue (e.g. Tulving and Watkins 1973; Tulving 1974b). Recall to identity cues may sound like a trivial and easy task, but in fact it is not. In two experiments I described in my 1974 paper, rememberers did better with cues that were associated to the target words than with cues that were identical with them (Tulving 1974).

Would it have been possible to think of copy stimuli or identity stimuli during the heyday of verbal learning research? If so, what would it have meant to give the subject a learning task in which stimuli and responses were the same? Again, all we know is that no experiments were ever done in which stimuli and responses were identical, therefore we can only speculate about the answers to the questions. My own impression is that learning of pairs of words in which stimuli were identical with responses would not have been regarded as a very interesting idea by verbal-learning theorists; I can even imagine that some of them might have thought of it as nonsense. If the reader does not share my sentiments, he may wish to think about the meaning of the concept of copy stimuli or copy responses in animal learning from which verbal learning theorists derived much of their theoretical ideas. What would it have meant to do a learning experiment with animals in which stimuli and responses were identical?

A staunch believer of the hypothesis that 'retrieval cue' is nothing more than a new-fangled label for the old respectable 'stimulus'—a person who thinks that people talking the cue language constitute living proof of Bartlett's theory of psychologists' use of language—might wish to argue that copy stimuli or identity stimuli did exist in the deeds and thoughts of verbal learning theorists, namely in recognition tests, where they were called 'old' test items. But this would not be a strong argument, for the following reasons. First, recognition tests were not very popular with verbal-learning theorists who spoke the stimulus-response language, probably because recognition memory did not fit in too well into the accepted theoretical framework. After all, at the time of study the subject makes the (implicit) 'new' response to an item, whereas at the time of test the correct response is 'old'. What is the response then that the learner has retained? Second, whenever recognition tests were done, they served as a measurement operation, as a means of telling the experimenter something about what the subject had learned and retained. Retention tests simply provided one of the possible measures of associative strength (e.g. Postman 1963*a*; Bahrick 1965). Third, students of verbal learning simply did not think of old test items as stimuli in the same sense, for instance, in which the stimulus-term of a learned pair in the paired-associative task was regarded as the stimulus. It was this very basic attitude that lay at the root of the generation/recognition theories of recall about which I will have much more to say in Chapter 11.

I proposed that retrieval cues are present and play an important role in recognition tests as they do in recall tests in a short paper published in 1968. The title of the paper was, 'When is recall higher than recognition?' (Tulving 1968*b*). The answer I arrived at, on the basis of experimental evidence, was that 'recall is higher than recognition whenever retrieval cues present at the recall test are more effective in providing access to stored information than are retrieval cues present at the recognition test' (Tulving 1968*b*, p. 54). The idea of *cues* in recognition was at variance with the then-prevailing thought and must have been difficult to accept for many theorists. The presence of retrieval cues implied a retrieval process, and the prevalent view at the time was that there was no such thing, recognition was 'automatic'. Fully seven years later, in a theoretical debate concerning recognition failure of recallable words, Light, Kimble, and Pellegrino (1975) did not accept the copy cue in recognition as a cue. (I shall have more to say about this is Chapter 13). Light *et al.* were criticizing our experiments in which we had presented learners with A–B pairs of words for study, and then tested them both for recall of B words (with A words as cues) and recognition of B words (with B words as cues). They described our situation, however, in the following words: 'In the Tulving and Thomson experiments, the cues for cued recall were those used at input, but the cues available for recognition were not present at input' (Light *et al.* 1975, p. 32). The disagreement here seemed to go beyond mere terminological issues. One interpretation of the curious comment by Light *et al.* is that, for unstated theoretical reasons, cues cannot be nominally identical with the to-be-remembered items.

Cue effectiveness

Another issue that has emerged as a consequence of the introduction of the concept of retrieval cues (Tulving and Pearlstone 1966) has to do with their effectiveness. What makes a retrieval cue effective in bringing about the actualization of an engram? Or, let us put the issue more generally: what must be the relation between the cue and the engram for the system to produce a particular recollective experience? We will discuss this issue in the next section of the chapter. Let us here only briefly consider possible parallel questions phrased in stimulus-response language.

The question of what makes a particular stimulus effective in eliciting a particular response in verbal learning tasks was never raised in this form. The reasons probably were that the answer to the question was obvious: a stimulus, A, becomes effective in eliciting a response, B, as a result of the acquisition of an association between them; A and B become associated when they occur together, the strength of the association being influenced by such variables as frequency, recency, meaningfulness of the connection, learners' intentions, and the like.

In the next chapter I will describe some phenomena that, I think, would have been difficult to accommodate within the associative framework and the stimulus-response language. The phenomena have to do with the effectiveness of such retrieval cues as the initial letter of a word, or a physical description of the word (e.g. 'a long word' for NOTWITHSTANDING). Should *a* be expected to be an effective eliciting stimulus for the to-be-remembered word ARMY? Since the 'stimulus' here has always 'occurred together' with the word ARMY, it might be expected to be an effective stimulus. If it is not, why not? And under what conditions would it become an effective cue?

To anticipate the answers to these questions, and to offer one distinction between stimuli and retrieval cues: an effective retrieval cue is a product of the rememberer's mental activity both at the time of the formation of the engram and the time of attempted retrieval. Depending upon these activities, one and the same stimulus item may have widely different cueing functions.

Ecphory

Ecphory is the (hypothetical) event-process that converts the relevant information in the retrieval environment and the (original or recoded) engram into ecphoric information. Like most other elements in the world of lathomena of episodic memory—the unobservable elements of GAPS—ecphory is the name of the relation between certain other elements in the system. The term 'ecphory', like the term 'engram', was invented by Richard Semon (1904). I am using it here for reasons very similar to those for which Semon found it necessary to create the term three-quarters of a century ago.

Semon needed a term that referred to the activation of a latent engram, its change into an active state, a state in which the rememberer would be conscious of it. There was no such term in existence at that time. Students of memory talked about associations as responsible for remembering, but for Semon 'association' was a term that described relations that existed between ideas and idea complexes. Semon thought it was important to distinguish between dispositions and a process through which the dispositions were actualized. The etymological root of 'ecphory' is the Greek word εκφορσσ—'to be made known'. Now, owing to Semon, the *Oxford English Dictionary* defines ecphory as 'the evocation of a disposition from a latent to a manifest state'.

Although I am adopting Semon's term, I am using it in a somewhat different sense, as indicated earlier: ecphory refers to the conversion of information from two sources, the engram and the retrieval cue, into another form, ecphoric information.

Although Semon's 'engram' represented a successful addition to the psychological vocabulary, thanks greatly to Lashley's use of the term, his second major concept, 'ecphory', was studiously ignored by generations of memory theorists who came after him. Psychologists working within the associative framework and verbal-learning theorists felt no need for a special process of activation of associations and hence had no use for the term; memory theorists speaking the information-processing language adopted the term 'retrieval' to serve the function that ecphory had served for Semon.

Stephen Madigan and I (Tulving and Madigan 1970) once made a half-hearted attempt to introduce the term ecphory to contemporary students of memory. We suggested the name 'ecphoric processes' for the field of memory and verbal learning. We also defined 'ecphory' in a footnote. But we suspected, justifiably as it turned out, that other workers would not take kindly to the term: human nature does not change a great deal in seventy-five years. Six years later I tried it again in a somewhat more determined fashion (Tulving 1976). This time I had a good reason for trying to revive the term 'ecphory': the alternative term 'retrieval' had been adopted by certain theorists for their own special purposes, and I needed another term for mine. At that time I defined ecphory as 'the process by which information stored in a specific memory trace is utilized by the system to produce conscious memory of certain aspects of the original event' (Tulving 1976, p. 40). That definition is very similar to the one I am proposing here. With a few notable exceptions (e.g. LeCocq and Tiberghien 1981) the rest of the world of memory still does not want to have anything to do with the term. Perhaps it is one of the symptoms of the generalized resistance to retrieval processes as a legitimate part of the study of memory that has characterized theoretical thinking through long periods in the short history of experimental study of memory.

Ecphory is not retrieval

It is only one of the elements in the process of retrieval. The other important process of retrieval is conversion. It is necessary to distinguish between ecphory and conversion not only because one precedes and the other one follows the state of ecphoric information, and the rememberer's recollective experience, but also because it helps us to deal with the fundamental theoretical problem of the relation between recall and recognition. As we shall see in Chapter 14, one important distinction between recall and recognition has to do with the process of ecphory, and another with the process of conversion. The difficulties that theorists have had in agreeing on the relation between recall and recognition may be partly attributable to the non-analytic treatment of the overall process of retrieval.

When I talk about retrieval here, I have in mind the second of two main stages of an act of remembering, as defined by its constituent elements discussed in this chapter. Other people have used retrieval to mean different things. Indeed, the problem with the term is that it is gradually losing its communicative value, because of its liberal use by many people for many different purposes. It was originally mentioned by Sir William Hamilton (1859) as a synonym for recall, and then, a hundred years later, given a truly useful definition by Melton (1963) who said that retrieval is utilization of stored information. Less than twenty years later, and depending upon who uses the term and when, it may mean (a) recall (b) recall, or recognition, or both, (c) thinking of a learned item without necessarily saying it, (d) the first of two stages of the recall process in which the second stage is decision (e.g. Kintsch 1968), (e) the second of the two-stage process of recognition in which the first stage is the familiarity decision (e.g. Mandler, Pearlstone, and Koopmans 1969; Mandler 1980), (f) the process by which a verbally expressed proposition is judged to be true, the so-called 'fact retrieval' (e.g. Anderson and Bower 1973), (g) naming of words belonging to a particular category (Indow 1980), (h) access to a location in the memory store in which some 'desired' information is stored (e.g. Bobrow 1975), and a number of others.

Although these different senses of 'retrieval' are characterized by a family resemblance, and thereby define a category (Rosch and Mervis 1975), their diversity is sufficiently rich to make it difficult to comprehend the meaning of any particular token of the type without special research. The situation is not altogether different from an imaginary textbook of anatomy in which all parts of the body below the knees are referred to by their common category label, 'foot-part'. We can perhaps add a rider to Bartlett's observation about psychologists' penchant for a fairly frequent change of terminology: psychologists seem to like a fairly steady expansion of the domain of their favorite terms, even when it reduces their ability to communicate with each other.

I am making these observations simply by way of commentary. I know perfectly well that they will have no effect whatsoever on the behavior of practicing researchers. Most other students of memory seem to be much more comfortable with the terminological state of affairs in our field than I am. I remember raising the question about terminology at one of the Arrowhead conferences. These conferences, held annually at the University of California Conference Center at Lake Arrowhead in the 1960s and 1970s, and attended by a small group of active practitioners in the field of ecphoric processes, afforded an excellent opportunity to talk not only about the latest 'hot' data from the participants' laboratories, but also about the general state of the art in the field. On one occasion I proposed that we discuss, and perhaps try to do something about, the terminological confusion that seemed to characterize certain parts of the field. I did not even get to first base. One of my friends and colleagues, in a firm but patient voice, explained to me that America was not the kind of a place that I came from, it was a free country, everybody could do what they wanted and use language the way they wanted, and he certainly was not going to join in any scheme of depriving people of their basic freedom. I apologized, and promised never to mention the matter again in his presence.

Ecphory is not retrieval in any of the senses in which 'retrieval' has been used in the literature. This means that ecphory is not recall or recognition, it is not the first stage of the two-stage theory of recall, or the second stage of the two-stage theory of recognition; it is not a search for a desired datum in the memory store, access to a particular location, or activation of a part of an associative network. It is the process by which retrieval information is brought into interaction with stored information, and in that sense it is compatible with some but not with other specific senses in which the term 'retrieval' has been used.

Theories of retrieval

A large number of theories of retrieval have recently appeared in the literature, a welcome change from the state of affairs in the field of memory between 1885 and 1970. A partial list of these theories includes Anderson and Bower (1972, 1974); Atkinson, Herrmann, and Wescourt (1974); Jones (1976, 1980); LeCocq and Tiberghien (1981); Murdock (1979); Murdock and Anderson (1975); Norman and Bobrow (1979); Raaijmakers and Shiffrin (1980, 1981); Ratcliff and Murdock (1976); Ratcliff (1978); and Shiffrin (1970). These theories deal with different aspects of the retrieval process, a fair number are concerned with retrieval processes in recognition (an especially striking change in attitudes); they vary in scope, in degree of specificity or generality with respect to tasks, and also in overall objectives. They all, however, share two features that may be worth attention. First, they are all concerned with memory performance; none includes the rememberer's recollective experience, or an equivalent notion, as an important component. Second, they all assume that memory performance depends on the kind and amount of information that has been stored. I shall have a little more to say about recollective experience later on in this chapter. I shall consider the second common feature of all the theories here.

A long tradition in the study of memory has held that what a person remembers about an event depends on what information has been stored about it and is still available at the time when retrieval of the event is attempted. Depending upon the dominant theoretical thoughts of the time and the idiosyncratic preferences of individual theorists, the basic ideas have been phrased in a variety of ways, but their essence has been the same. Whether these ideas have been expressed in terms of notions such as search through the memory store for the desired information, redintegration, activation of marked nodes and pathways in an associative network, or matching of retrieval information to stored information, what the rememberer remembers depends on the properties of the residue of the original experience. The instructions for the recall of the experience, together with the cue presented at the time of the retention 'test' serve an activating or energizing function: they convert a potentiality into actual behavior. The instructions and cues have no effect on what memory performance is like, they only bring it about. They are like a starter's pistol that signals to the runners to start the race, without having any effect on its course or outcome.

As an illustration, consider the following excerpt from a recent influential work on human memory. (The reader is already familiar with this part of the theory; I mentioned it briefly on page 133.) A part of the retrieval mechanism called the 'parser' receives and interprets the query directed at the system. This query is held in the working memory 'while HAM attempts to match it to a corresponding structure in long-term memory. The best-matching long-term memory structure is generated as the output' (Anderson and Bower 1973, p. 140).

Anderson and Bower's is a sophisticated model: the retrieval cue has a complex structure, and it is matched to an even more complex structure of the engram. But it is an 'activation' theory of retrieval in that what is 'generated as the output' is a *part of the engram*. The retrieval cue (query) only provides the information of what part it is that is to be recalled, it contributes nothing else to the product of ecphory. Similar examples abound in the literature. In search theories, too, what the rememberer remembers, or what his memory performance is like, depends on what has been stored, and what is found by the retrieval mechanism, or what is selected from what is found. The output from the memory system is influenced by the properties of the retrieval cue or question to the extent that these properties determine what parts of the engram are actualized; but retrieval information as such does not appear as a component of what is retrieved.

I do not have a theory of retrieval in the sense of the specification of a more or less complex retrieval 'mechanism'. The reader may remember my earlier comments about 'mechanisms' (p. 240). For the time being at least I am quite happy to regard the problem of the mechanism of ecphory as an unknown, and to contemplate the possibility that this lack of knowledge is not going to greatly hamper our efforts to understand memory. But speculation about the general nature of ecphory is unavoidable. The role that retrieval information plays in the process figures prominently in the speculation.

Complementary function of retrieval information in ecphory

Let us assume that insofar as the activation and selection theories of retrieval ignore the active contribution that retrieval information makes to the product of ecphory, they are wrong. And let us contemplate a somewhat different hypothesis according to which the rememberer's recollective experience derives its 'contents', its informational ingredients, not only from the engram in episodic memory but also from the retrieval cue as interpreted by the semantic system and the general cognitive environment in which retrieval occurs. On this view of remembering as trace/cue interaction, recollective experience and measured aspects of memory performance do not provide evidence about the properties of information stored about the event, but rather evidence about the joint (synergistic) effects of *both* the stored information and the retrieval information. Retrieval information does not determine what features or components of the engram are sampled or selected, it *complements* the information in the engram, in some as yet unidentified sense it 'adds' to whatever information from the engram enters into the ecphoric interaction.

In the sense just suggested, ecphory differs from retrieval even in its broadest definition as utilization of stored information. Ecphory is like retrieval in that it involves utilization of stored information, but it is also more than that: it also involves utilization of information in the retrieval cue *and* the retrieval environment.

The idea of ecphory as a synergistic process that *combines* information from two sources, the engram and the cue, is very similar to the ideas about the nature of remembering advocated by Bartlett (1932), Neisser (1967), Bransford and Franks (1971), as well as by some others. According to these ideas, remembering is not an activation of something that exists in the form of a latent disposition, whether this activation is complete or partial, nor is it like locating an object at an unknown location and then deciding that it is the one needed. Rather, it is a *constructive* activity that uses components from episodic memory (the engram) as well as semantic memory (the cue) and that results in a mental experience that the rememberer subjectively identifies as remembering an event. Ecphory is a *re*-constructive activity only in the sense that the rememberer feels the ecphorized event to belong to the past, and in the sense that sometimes psychologists think like rememberers; from the point of view of theory there is nothing *re*-constructive about it.

The way in which episodic memory (the engram) and semantic memory (the retrieval cue) jointly contribute to the process of remembering may be thought of as analogous to the manner in which heredity and environment jointly influence the development of an organism's characteristics and behavior. Different characteristics vary in the extent to which they are affected by variations in the environment. At one extreme, for instance, the blood group to which an individual belongs is determined by the genes only, at the other extreme are the many learned behaviors and skills as well as attitudes and values that are probably largely determined by environmental factors. In remembering, too, the relative contributions of trace information and retrieval information may vary over a wide range. In the general case, however, both factors are important, and what the individual remembers is determined by the interaction between them. We can assume that in many cases the attempt to understand recollection in terms of encoding processes and the stored episodic information alone is analogous to trying to understand the development of organisms in terms of hereditary factors alone. The enterprise can be quite successful with respect to some characteristics, but it fails miserably in regard to others.

Some anecdotal evidence may be brought to bear upon the proposition that recollective experience and the attendant memory performances may reflect properties of retrieval information as much as they 'reproduce' the stored episodic information. For instance, memory distortions, rememberers' 'remembering' things that did not occur, could be attributed to the constructive role of retrieval information. Because of the overpowering influence of the view of remembering as reproduction or reconstruction, however, few experiments have been done to investigate the possibility that the function of retrieval information is more than, or other than, activation of the memory trace or parts thereof. All known phenomena that can be regarded as supporting the hypothesis of the complementary function of retrieval information in ecphory as construction can also be interpreted in other ways. Critical evidence does not as yet exist. It would have to be derived from experiments especially designed for the purpose.

A notable exception to activation or selection theories of retrieval has been proposed by Kintsch (1974). In Kintsch's theory the retrieval information complements the stored information at the time of retrieval. In set-theoretic terms, if X represents the elements of retrieval information, and Y the elements of stored information, what I here refer to as ecphory can be expressed as follows: 'Some set of elements X may be matched with another set Y if most of the elements of X are also members of Y. Pattern completion makes available the union of the two sets, $X \cup Y$. Biased selection of elements from this completed set may then occur, or the members of this set may be used for further matching operations' (Kintsch 1974, p. 81). In activation and selection theories of retrieval, the product of retrieval would be represented by the intersect of sets X and Y, $X \cap Y$.

The experimental work that comes closest to providing relevant evidence for the complementary function of retrieval information in ecphory has been done by Loftus and her colleagues in experiments I mentioned briefly (p. 168) in connection with our discussion on recoding (Loftus and Palmer 1974; Loftus 1975, 1977; Loftus *et al.* 1978; Loftus and Loftus

1980). The reader remembers that in these experiments the subjects 'witness' an automobile accident and are then asked both relevant and misleading questions about what they have seen. The questions function as retrieval cues, and the recoding of the originally stored information, suggested by the results of the experiments, represents retrieval-induced recoding. The complementary function of retrieval information in Loftus's experiments thus is suggested by the subjects' 'remembering' non-existent or changed features of the originally witnessed event. Alternative explanations of the results of Loftus's experiments are still possible, however. Further refinements of the design of the experiments should go a long way towards eliminating these other interpretations, if the basic hypothesis is correct. Thus, for instance, measurement of the properties of recoded engrams in terms of the trace-reduction method (Tulving and Watkins 1975) may provide useful additional evidence.

The concepts of ecphory and recoding are closely related, and for some purposes indistinguishable. This point was one of the major theoretical contributions of Richard Semon (Schacter *et al.* 1978; Schacter 1982). Recoding implies ecphory, and ecphory implies recoding. The main reason for distinguishing between the two concepts at all lies in the products of the two processes: recoding operations may well take place without the rememberer's having any recollective experience of it, whereas ecphory usually results in a mental state of which the rememberer is aware in some way.

Ecphoric information

Ecphoric information is the product of the process of ecphory; it determines the particulars of recollective experience and provides the input into the conversion process. According to activation and selection theories of retrieval, ecphoric information represents a subset of the information available in the engram; according to the hypothesis of ecphory as construction, it represents a product of retrieval information and relevant episodic information.

Whether we think of ecphory as activation, selection, or construction, ecphoric information is similar to both the stored episodic information and the (semantic) retrieval information, although the similarity relations may vary, and sometimes vary greatly, depending upon the particular situation. We can conceptualize these similarity relations in terms of features that ecphoric information shares with the engram and the retrieval cue, but as ecphoric information represents only a hypothetical entity in the GAPS framework, these similarity relations can never be directly measured.

What a person remembers of an event depends directly on the quantity and quality of relevant ecphoric information. Ecphoric information is never 'right' or 'wrong', it simply is what it is at any given time: a state of the system determined by a number of other components of the system. The fact that ecphoric information is only similar to but not identical with the original engram, and the fact that the similarity may vary over a wide range, provide the basis for (a) veridical remembering, as determined by the psychologist, using his own criteria, (b) distortions of memory, where the individual 'remembers' something that in fact did not happen, or 'remembers' a component of a remembered event incorrectly, and (c) forgetting, a change in 'veridical' remembering over time, as a result of recoding of the engram and possibly changed (semantic) interpretation of the retrieval cue.

According to the structure of GAPS, the immediate co-determinants of the characteristics of a particular assembly of ecphoric information include (a) the original or recoded engram, (b) the retrieval cue, or more generally, the retrieval information, and (c) the process of ecphory. Variations in any one of these three co-determinants can affect the composition of ecphoric information.

By far the largest amount of relevant, albeit indirect, evidence concerning variations in the quantity and quality of ecphoric information has been derived from experiments in which characteristics of engrams have been manipulated and corresponding changes in memory performance observed. A smaller number of studies are now on record that have explored the effects of retrieval information on ecphoric information, with episodic trace information held constant. (Some of this work has been reviewed by Tulving and Thomson (1973), Tulving (1976), Nelson (1979), and Craik (1981).) Almost no evidence, however, exists on the effect of the process of ecphory on ecphoric information, under conditions where both retrieval information and trace information are held constant. According to GAPS, it should be possible to show these effects in a fashion analogous to the effects shown by different encoding operations.

Jacoby and Craik (1979) as well as Craik (1981) have discussed the parallels between encoding and retrieval operations at somewhat greater length. Craik, for instance, points out that 'just as encoding processes can be described as varying in modality, depth, and extensiveness, so retrieval processes can also be described, although fewer studies have focused on retrieval operations up to the present time' (Craik 1981, p. 395). He mentioned two experiments (Hasher and Griffin 1978; Tulving 1981) to illustrate the effects of different ecphoric processes applied to the same encoding material. But since, in both cases, forms of ecphoric processes were confounded with types of retrieval cue, these examples do not quite meet the logical requirement for demonstrating the effect of the process of ecphory with retrieval information and stored episodic information held constant. Experimental investigation of the effect of the process of ecphory on ecphoric information constitutes one of the problems for future research.

Ecphoric information is largely a task-free component of the retrieval process in GAPS: the rememberer's task does not affect the actual composition of ecphoric information as it does the way in which it is used, that is, converted into some other form. The task may influence the particulars of ecphoric information to the extent that it affects the process of ecphory, but given the constraints on ecphory by engrams and retrieval cues, the variations in ecphoric information attributable to the tasks are unlikely to be large. On the other hand, larger differences in the measured aspects of memory performance may be observed in different tasks even when the ecphoric information is held constant. The relation between ecphoric information and memory tasks will be discussed at somewhat greater length in Chapter 14.

Ecphoric information can also serve as retrieval information: it can be brought to bear upon the trace information—activating it, matching it, or interacting with it in the constructive mode—very much in the same way as any other kind of retrieval information. The product of ecphory involving ecphoric information as one source of input into the process is a new and different assembly of retrieval information. The recursive operation can be repeated *ad libitum* until some stop-rule is invoked. The recursive ecphoric process of this sort was described in some detail by Semon (1921), as well as by a number of contemporary theorists (e.g. Kintsch 1974; Lockhart *et al.* 1976; Raaijmakers and Shiffrin 1981).

GAPS as described in this book entails what we might call a 'snapshot view' of episodic memory: we are concerned with the conditions, including various 'instantaneous' processes, that bring about a timeless state, or a slice of experience frozen in time which we identify as 'remembering'. The recursive operation of the process of ecphory, feeding upon the (changing) ecphoric information, and combining it with the 'fixed' stored episodic information, produces many snapshots whose orderly succession can create the illusion of the flow of past time.

Recollective experience

The act of remembering that begins with the perception and encoding of an event ends with recollective experience of the event: at time T_2 the individual is aware of a mental state that he feels or interprets as remembering something that happened at a previous time T_1. For the rememberer, the impalpable but highly familiar awareness is the essence of memory: take the awareness away and the term 'memory' becomes meaningless.

In theories of episodic memory, recollective experience should be the ultimate object of interest, the central aspect of remembering that is to be explained and understood. The what, how, and why of those aspects of the mind that we think of as remembering, in the final analysis, applies to the mental stuff on which the expression 'I remember' is predicated. Yet, as we have already heard, psychologists have successfully evaded problems entailed in recollective experience, and have gone about studying memory without mentioning it. If you wanted to find out what contemporary students of memory have to say about recollective experience, under what term would you try to locate the relevant material through the subject indexes of books, or what key words would you be looking for in the titles and abstracts of papers? You would find many references to recall, recognition, judgements of recency and frequency, and, of course, retrieval, but these terms refer to overt behavior of the rememberer, characterize different memory tasks, or represent hypothetical components of theories of memory and memory processing. You might think that recollective experience is related to, say, recall, recognition, or retrieval, and no one would dispute such a claim, but the fact remains that theories of retrieval are silent on recollective experience.

In GAPS, recollective experience refers to the rememberer's awareness of ecphoric information. This awareness may be clear and precise, but it can also be vague and fuzzy. In either case, however, it is open to introspection.

I am assuming that not all of any particular pattern of ecphoric information is involved in recollective experience: the rememberer need not be consciously aware of all the products of ecphory. But this is pure speculation, since we have almost no evidence to go on. The problem of the relation between ecphoric information and recollective experience is central to the definition of episodic memory. It may turn out that we should define episodic memory solely in terms of recollective experience. But in the absence of relevant evidence, and in the presence of a conjectured possibility that rememberers may have available knowledge from particular episodes even though they are not aware of it introspectively, we think of the ecphoric information that gives rise to recollective experience as a subset of total ecphoric information.

It is not easy to talk about ecphoric information. The observation recently made by Kolers and Smythe (1979) that 'perhaps the most difficult problem facing the cognitive psychologists is to find a satisfactory way to describe experience', (p. 165) applies as much to the subjective experience of remembering as to any other kind. The fact that there is no satisfactory name for what I am here referring to as 'recollective experience' highlights the difficulty.

Two terms that have most frequently been used in descriptions of the mental experience of remembering are 'memory image' and 'consciousness': when a person remembers a past event, he has a memory image of it and he is consciously aware of its being a mental replay of what happened once before. Thus, for instance, if you think about what you did immediately before you picked up this book and starting looking at it or reading it, you are likely to be conscious or aware of one or more memory images that you recognize as representing your recent personal past.

Memory images and consciousness

'Memory image' could serve as an acceptable synonym for 'recollective experience'. We can think of both memory images and recollective experiences as varying in sharpness and clarity, as well as in richness of detail. We know from Sir Francis Galton's early work that some individuals do not have any imagery, or at least they claim that they do not. They are likely however, to have something corresponding to recollective experience when they 'think about' past events.

It is not without interest in the present connection to observe that little mention has been made of episodic memory in the currently flourishing literature on mental imagery, even when the imagery-work or thinking about it has been done by theorists with known interests in, and contributions to, the study of episodic memory (e.g. Anderson 1978; Kolers and Smythe 1979; Kosslyn 1976; Neisser 1972; Paivio 1976, 1977; Shepard 1975, 1978; Simon 1972).Almost invariably, the images of the contemporary theories of imagery reside in, or come from, what in the episodic/semantic distinction of memories would be regarded as the semantic part. This state of affairs represents yet another symptom of experimental psychologists' lack of interest in the rememberers' mental experiences.

The concept of 'consciousness' is closely related to imagery, for obvious reasons. People are always conscious of their images, as they are conscious of their perceptions and observations, thoughts and dreams, and recollective experiences. In the literature on memory, the concept has been most frequently used in descriptions of primary or short-term memory (e.g. Atkinson and Shiffrin 1971; Craik and Jacoby 1975; Shallice 1972). The general idea is that the rememberer, consciously aware of the input into his (primary-memory) system, has a lingering awareness of this input even after the cessation of the physical stimuli. Consciousness is also involved in various 'operations on' the contents of primary memory.

Much less has been said about consciousness in theoretical discussions of 'long-term' episodic memory. For instance, in none of the theories of retrieval, some of which I listed on page 178, can we find constructs that correspond to recollective experience.

Psychologists writing on problems of consciousness are no more interested in episodic memory than students of episodic memory are interested in consciousness. Analogously with the situation characterizing the study of images, discussions of consciousness typically have little or nothing to say about episodic remembering (e.g. Mandler 1975; Natsoulas 1970, 1978; Posner and Warren 1972; Shallice 1972, 1978). A notable exception to the general trend is provided by G. Underwood, who has explicitly discussed the distinction between 'conscious' and 'unconscious' memories, that is, memories of which we are or are not aware, the difference being attributable to the level of activation of a given memory at a particular instant (G. Underwood 1979).

'Conscious memory', like 'memory image', could serve as a substitute term for recollective experience. One difficulty with the term 'consciousness' has to do with its many meanings. Natsoulas (1978) has distinguished seven different senses in which the term can be used. Unfortunately, none of the seven exclusively fits the kind of consciousness that people have of their past experiences when they remember them. Consciousness$_2$, Consciousness$_3$, and Consciousness$_4$ in Natsoulas' classification all seem to be related to awareness in episodic remembering, although the matter may be debatable, because decisions of the kind I have just made are based largely on intuition.

Pastness and veridicality

The relation between recollective experience of an event and the original event as perceived is one of similarity. The degree and nature of this similarity in any given situation is determined by a large number of variables and processes that we have discussed under the headings of various elements in GAPS. The immediate determinant of recollective experience is ecphoric information, but since the latter is multiply determined by the nature of the original event, its encoding, many possible recodings, as well as retrieval cues and the ecphoric process, recollective experience does not always faithfully reflect the properties of the originally perceived event. In addition to the designated elements in the structure of GAPS, there are other conditions that affect ecphoric information and hence recollective experience: motives, interests, feeling states, biochemical (hormone, drug) states, alertness, fatigue, and so on. Although a good deal of remembering is more or less veridical, a good deal of it is not. We cannot, therefore, safely infer from a rememberer's recollective experience that a remembered event actually occurred, or that its characteristics were as described by the rememberer. Like a person's perceptual experience of the present environment, recollective experience of past events can at best be only an incomplete and stylized model of the apprehended reality.

The feeling that the present recollective experience refers to a past event, and the feeling that the experience is veridical, that is, that it represents the past event faithfully, are given as an integral part of the subjective experience of remembering. These feelings cannot be based on any mental comparison of the recollective experience and the original event, since in most situations rememberers have no independent or objective evidence of what the original events were like. We are forced to the conclusion, therefore, that the subjective feelings of pastness and veridicality of memory must be provided by intrinsic properties of ecphoric information. A reasonable assumption is that the 'intensity' of the feeling of past-ness is directly correlated with the relative contribution that the stored *episodic* information makes to the ecphoric information.

On the other hand, no equally plausible hypotheses can be offered concerning the ecphoric-information correlates of the subjective feeling of veridicality of recollective experience. No experimental evidence exists on conditions and variables related to feelings of pastness and veridicality. Although it would be possible to argue that confidence judgments in recognition-memory experiments provide a measure of subjective veridicality, the fact that usually confidence judgments correlate positively with objective measures of veridicality may have discouraged experimenters and theorists from raising questions about the nature of the relation between subjective and objective veridicality, and conditions and variables related to this relation. Although in many experiments, evidence of the discrepancy between subjective veridicality and objective veridicality are noted—in the form of intrusions in recall and false positives and misses in recognition—most of the time these discrepancies are simply regarded as 'errors'. The fact that both the nature of these 'errors' and their frequency or probability varies with all kinds of independent variables is taken for granted as a commonplace, and usually not much theoretical attention is paid to these variations. Exceptions to this general attitude are only seldom found in the literature. A notable one takes the form of research on 'false recognition' (e.g. Underwood 1965; Anisfeld and Knapp 1968) and on 'trace diffusion (Shepard 1961).

As mentioned earlier, recollective experience may not always be verbalizable. The concept of recollective experience applies to all of the ecphoric information of which the rememberer is aware in one form or another, regardless of whether he can translate this awareness into language.

Experimental evidence most closely related to the proposition that unverbalizable recollective experience is sometimes available to the rememberer is provided by experiments on feeling of knowing. The results of a number of experiments, originated by Hart (1965) and recently reviewed by Schacter (1981), show that people can make reasonably accurate predictions about recognizability of specific items that they cannot recall. The item-specific feeling-of-knowing accuracy implicates the existence of information of which the rememberer is aware, but which he cannot convert into the name of the otherwise familiar to-be-remembered item.

The concept of recollective experience, and the role that it plays in the study of episodic memory, is highly relevant to several fundamental issues. One of these has to do with the distinction between recall and recognition. I mentioned earlier in the book (p. 126) that recollective experience cannot be identified with either recall or recognition. How do we, then, think about the differences between recall and recognition? We will take up this problem in the next section of the chapter. Another issue has to do with the distinction between memory and decision processes in signal-detection analyses of recognition memory. This matter, too, is discussed in the next section.

Before we conclude our consideration of recollective experience, a personal comment is in order. When I talk about experimental psychologists' lack of concern for recollective experience, my comments apply as much to my own work as to that of others. Every now and then I have mentioned terms such as 'consciousness' (e.g. Tulving and Thomson 1973) or 'conscious memory' (e.g. Tulving 1976), and my own awareness of the rememberers' awareness may have influenced my thinking about episodic memory indirectly, but I have done nothing about recollective experience explicitly. Thus, with respect to 'consciousness' in remembering, just about the only thing we can do right now is to divide memory students into two categories, those who mention it in their work and those who do not. Is it possible that in the not-too-distant future, the two categories consist of those who have done relevant research and those who have not?

Conversion and memory performance

Frequently the act of remembering a particular episode ends with a recollective experience. The rememberer 'just thinks about' the experience and does not express it in any overt fashion. At other times, recollective experience, or ecphoric information of which the rememberer is not directly aware, is converted into behavior. Such conversion, however, is not an obligatory part of the process of remembering, as are components such as encoding and ecphory.

Conversion of ecphoric information outside the laboratory is shaped by situational demands. It must occur if we wish to study remembering. The only way to find out what the rememberer remembers, or what his recollective experience is like, is through the rememberer's description of the recollective experience or its use in ongoing activity, in his interaction with the physical or social environment, in solving problems, and in other kinds of 'transfer'.

Conversion of ecphoric information and recollective experience into some other form completes the process of remembering an event. People tell each other about their experiences in the form of narratives, or they respond to questions asked by others about remembered episodes. Some of the questions may be open-ended, with essentially unlimited number of alternative responses, whereas others may require the respondent to make a choice among a few alternatives. There are also questions that the respondent can answer by a simple Yes or No. In other situations, the rememberer does not convert his recollective experience into verbal descriptions. but rather into some other form. The foresight of taking an umbrella before beginning a trip may be based on the memory of a previous trip that also began on a sunny day and ended in a torrential down-pour at the destination. The decision not to vote for the politician representing one's favorite party may be based on the memory that the party broke its election promises the last time. And one may refrain from following a 'hot tip' at the racetrack or on the stock market when one remembers losing money on three previous occasions when similar 'hot tips' were received. Anticipating future happenings, making choices, and refraining from doing certain things are all ways, along with many others, in which ecphoric information is used, or converted.

The form of conversion of ecphoric information is more precisely stipulated in laboratory experiments than in real life, but the general principles governing conversions are very much the same. In recall tasks, the remem-berer provides a stylized description of his recollective experience by producing the names of to-be-remembered items or other aspects of the original events. In recognition tests, he chooses one out of a number of alternative test items, or responds Yes or No to a given test item. In other laboratory tasks, utilization of ecphoric information and conversion of recollective experience entails other kinds of cognitive activity. For instance, subjects may be asked to answer questions about frequency of items, recency, temporal separation of events, modality of presentation of to-be-remembered items, and the like. According to the requirements of the task and the availability of ecphoric information, the individual either succeeds or fails in producing answers to the questions asked. And depending upon the relation between what the rememberer produces and what the psychologist knows about the original event, the psychologist classifies the answer given as either correct or incorrect.

Although the success of episodic memory performance depends on the availability of appropriate ecphoric information, it also depends on appropriate utilization of knowledge from semantic memory. In many laboratory tasks, conversion of ecphoric information entails complex manipulation and processing of the information. Sometimes, for instance, subjects may be asked to make inferences on the basis of information derivable from one or more episodes; whether or not they succeed depends on factors other than mere 'access' to the relevant ecphoric information (e.g. Moeser 1976). Sometimes people can be asked to 'recall' the name of an event that did not originally occur; they can do so, if they know the range of possible alternatives and if they remember the events that did occur (e.g. Buschke 1963). Sometimes subjects are instructed to recall only part of some stored information; they meet the demands of the task by retrieving all the contents of the relevant episode and then selecting only some of it for conversion, in a post-retrieval operation (e.g. Roediger and Tulving 1979).

The process of ecphory is 'automatic' in the sense that once the system is in the retrieval mode and the retrieval cue and the engram are given, the rememberer has little control over the product of the ecphoric process.

Conversion, on the other hand, is largely an optional process. Just because an engram has been ecphorized, it need not be converted into any other form.

Recognition and recall

The distinction between ecphory and conversion as two separate components of retrieval helps us to think about recognition and recall as two basic memory tasks. They differ with respect to (a) retrieval cues provided, and (b) memory performance required. The differences between retrieval cues lead to differences in ecphoric information; the differences in performance requirements lead to further differences in conversion of the ecphoric information. Thus, comparisons of recognition and recall are hampered by the confounding of ecphoric and conversion processes in the two tasks. Potentially useful empirical evidence may be provided by situations in which the confounding is eliminated. We will discuss the problem at greater length in Chapter 14.

In several papers in the past, I and my colleagues have argued that recognition and recall are more similar to one another than many other theorists are willing to concede. These arguments have changed over time, in reaction to available experimental evidence and momentary theoretical concerns. Thus, for instance, in 1971 we argued that 'recognition memory is no exception to the general principle that successful utilization of stored mnemonic information, in whatever retrieval task, depends on both availability and accessibility of that information' (Tulving and Thomson 1971, pp. 123–4). If we identify availability with the engram, and accessibility with the retrieval cue, the statement is a forerunner of the suggestion made here that it is ecphoric information that is used in memory tasks, or converted into overt performance, and that many different kinds of retrieval cues, including copy cues, could enter into interaction with stored information to produce ephoric information. In that sense, the 'processes of recall and recognition' are very similar.

In another paper, Michael Watkins and I discussed the continuity between recall and recognition. We suggested that 'retrieval' in both recall and recognition is 'essentially the same, a joint product of the information stored in the past and that in the immediate environment' (Tulving and Watkins 1973, p. 739). As in the Tulving and Thomson (1971) paper, the continuity hypothesis has to do with what I am here explicitly referring to as ecphory. But, since in neither of the two papers a distinction between ecphory and conversion was made, our argument was probably less clear than it could have been.

A few years later, I dealt with the problem of recognition and recall at greater length (Tulving 1976).On that occasion I suggested that we give up the question of whether recall and recognition are similar or different, and instead ask, in what sense they are different and in what sense similar. In that paper, too, I explicitly introduced conscious memory into the sequence of hypothetical processes constituting an act of remembering, and made it precede the 'output decision' in the sequence of processing stages. My over-all conclusion was summarized in the following words: 'Recall and recognition are different inasmuch as the retrieval information that is present at the time of recall is different from that at the time of recognition. They are the same inasmuch as in'both cases ecphory is a consequence of appropriate combining of trace information with retrieval information' (p. 67). Judging by the reaction to that paper I am afraid that my arguments still did not make much sense to many people, again probably because of my failure of explic-itly separating the 'pre-conscious' process of ecphory from the 'post-con-scious' process of conversion or utilization of ecphoric information. I failed to make the distinction for the simple reason that it had not yet occurred to me in 1976, or at the time when I wrote that paper. Its articulation here, and in Chapter 14, should at least make my own position clearer, even if it will not result in the conversion of many discontinuity theorists to the continuity point of view.

Memory and decision

The elements of the retrieval process in GAPS that I am calling 'ecphoric information' and 'conversion', and the relation between them, are in a cer-tain sense related to what have been called 'memory' and 'decision', and the relation between them, in signal-detection analyses of memory (e.g. Lockhart and Murdock 1970; Murdock 1974). Every student of memory knows that the probability with which the subject responds to an old test item as 'old' depends not only on the 'strength' of the item but also on the decision criteria that the subject has adopted in translating the 'feeling of familiarity' evoked by the item into one of the prescribed response cate-gories. The theory of signal detection provides one method of assessing the separate contributions of the memory component and the decision criterion to recognition performance.

The parallel between signal-detection analyses of recognition memory and retrieval processes of GAPS is easy to see: in recognition-memory tasks, 'decision processes intervene between memory and response' (Murdock 1974, p. 8); in GAPS, conversion processes intervene between ecphoric information and overtly observable memory performance.

But there are also differences. GAPS, as a general framework for research in episodic memory, has wider scope than the signal-detection analogy of recognition memory; the latter, however, is embodied in a spe-cific mathematical model that provides a precise prescription for a quan-titative analysis of the data. Yet another difference has to do with the comparison between 'memory' on which the decision system operates, and the 'ecphoric information' that provides the input into the conversion proc-ess. In signal-detection analyses of recognition memory, the 'memory' component is usually specified in terms of some attribute of the stored information, or the memory trace—strength, familiarity, evidence, num-ber of contextual elements, and the like. Retrieval cues play no role in signal-detection analyses other than that of pointing to the stored item, or the engram, about which the decision is to be made. In GAPS, as we have seen, conversion processes operate on ecphoric information which is regarded as a product of retrieval information and the stored episodic information. In other words, what is missing in most signal-detection analyses of recognition memory is the process identified in GAPS as 'ecphory'. The extent to which this omission matters, if it does, is a matter that could be evaluated with the help of appropriate experiments.

The 'memory' on which decision processes operate in signal-detection analyses could readily be identified with the recollective experience of GAPS: the rememberer is presumably quite aware of the retrieved information that has to be converted into an overt response, even if most signal-detection analyses of recognition memory have not explicitly referred to the rememberer's conscious state. The picture is somewhat less clear for generation/recognition theories of retrieval (Kintsch 1974; Watkins and Gardiner 1979). In these theories, too, two stages are postulated that bear a certain resemblance to the ecphoric process and conversion process in GAPS: (a) the generation of possible response alternatives or response candidates, and (b) recognition-decision as to the acceptability of each generated alternative. Since the generation stage is guided by available retrieval cues, we might think of it as comparable to ecphory; as the recognition-decision is an operation performed on the product of ecphory, we might liken it to conversion.

There are two differences between generation/recognition models and the corresponding parts of GAPS. First, in typical generation/recognition theories the generation stage is conceptualized as something that provides 'access to' the memory trace, or the stored episodic information; recognition decision is made about the trace. Thus, the operations of the first stage, if successful, produce the same outcome as does the presentation of an 'old' test item in recognition memory: access to the stored information. In the terminology of GAPS, the successful first stage of the generation/recognition theories would create a situation in which the (recoded) engram can provide 'input' into the conversion process. In GAPS, the conversion process operates on ecphoric information, that is, on the product of retrieval information and the *recoded* engram. A generation/recognition theory whose first stage produces a retrieval cue that is combined with stored information, to produce ecphoric information, rather than a 'copy' of the to-be-remembered item, would be quite compatible with GAPS.

The second problem has to do with the uncertainty as to the presence of a conscious state of remembering (recollective experience) in the sequence of hypothetical events according to generation/recognition theories. Published accounts of the theories provide no guidance on this matter: we do not know whether, and if so, where, conscious awareness enters the picture. On an earlier occasion (Tulving 1976) I thought that both the generation and decision stages of generation/recognition theories would run their course before the product is entered into consciousness. I did so because I could not quite imagine how the subject in a cued-recall experiment would explicitly think of and consciously reject all kinds of incorrect alternatives before encountering the correct one. Most people report that when they are 'searching for' an item from a previously studied list, their 'mind is blank' until suddenly the right item 'pops into it'. If my interpretation was wrong (cf. LeCocq and Tiberghien 1981), and the decision-stage of the generation/recognition theory represents a conscious operation, the problem of the rememberer's mind being 'blank' during 'search' must be confronted.

Part III:
Synergistic ecphory

10

From organization to encoding/retrieval interactions

The General Abstract Processing System as a framework for studying episodic memory is not a theory. It is a collection of pretheoretical ideas that, at some level of abstraction, match all phenomena of episodic memory. Like a paradigm in a mature science (Kuhn 1962), pretheoretical ideas in a developing science, such as the science of memory, restrict the range of problems that are selected for study, determine the significance of facts, provide guidelines to the activities in which the practitioners engage, and dictate the way facts are matched to theory or how theories are articulated. Problem-solving activities of the kind characteristic of mature sciences can also be undertaken in a developing science, under the guidance of pretheoretical ideas accepted by a smaller or larger group of active researchers. Like a paradigm does, pretheoretical ideas force nature, or that part of it that is of interest to a group of scientists, into a preconceived and partially established mold.

When I first read Kuhn I was impressed by the striking similarity between his characterization of pre-paradigmatic sciences and that part of psychology which I knew best. He seemed to have had the psychology of memory and verbal learning in mind in developing his thesis. Like developing sciences, we, too, were blessed with a number of competing schools and sub-schools. These schools had something in common, but their similarity was primarily a family resemblance alone. Each school emphasized phenomena that its theorists could handle, and ignored those that did not fit in. Practitioners in different schools could not take for granted a common body of belief. As a consequence, each writer was forced to build his field anew from its foundations, almost every time he started writing an article or a book. In the absence of the paradigm, all facts that could possibly pertain to the development of the field seemed equally relevant. Research itself was characterized by gathering of facts in a somewhat random fashion, with major constraints on the selection of problems provided by data already on hand, or by problems on which other people had worked. We spent a lot of intellectual energy on trying to relate observed facts to those that for a long time had remained too complex to be integrated into any theory. We overlooked facts that later turned out to be important. When confronted with one and the same phenomenon, we interpreted it in different ways.

Before reading Kuhn, I had not thought about the stage of the development of the fascinating enterprise of which I was a part. The realization that everything we were doing was essentially nothing more than the search for our first paradigm came as a thunderbolt.

Others have argued that we in fact do possess paradigms. Lachman, Lachman, and Butterfield (1979), for instance, have suggested that the problem has not been the absence of a paradigm, but the simultaneous existence of a number of different paradigms in psychology and parts of it. They propose that cognitive psychology is now strongly identified with what they call the 'information-processing paradigm' (p. 34). I do not agree with this assessment. There are many 'competing' schools and sub-schools in the science of memory, all of which may speak the information-processing language, but which otherwise differ as much from as they agree with each other. Some of the apparent differences may be semantic only. Like workers in other creative enterprises, we always strive for originality of thought or, failing that, at least of expression. But why should we have all this richness of expression if we all shared a common paradigm?

The pretheoretical ideas that constitute GAPS restrict the domain of episodic memory and describe legitimate problems in a definite manner. Episodic memory is concerned with remembering events, not with acquisition, retention, and use of other kinds of knowledge. Engrams of events are determined by what the events are, how they are encoded, and the cognitive environment in which the encoding takes place. Engrams initially established are frequently recoded by subsequent related and similar events. The question of central interest in episodic memory has to do with *what* the rememberer remembers, the contents of his recollective experience. These contents are determined by ecphoric information, a joint product of retrieval information and that stored in the form of the (recoded) engram of the event. Conversion of ecphoric information into recollective experience, or into overt behavior, can take many different forms; it is influenced by the nature of the rememberer's 'task'.

These pretheoretical ideas apply to remembering of all kinds of different events, by all kinds of different rememberers. Variations in the nature of to-be-remembered events or characteristics of rememberers may affect the outcome of any particular act of remembering, but the restrictions stipulated by the structure of GAPS always apply. Problems, facts, and theories of memory can be categorized as 'episodic' to the extent that they fit into the framework of pretheoretical ideas of GAPS.

In my 1972 essay, I suggested that most of the research in verbal learning and memory that had been done since Ebbinghaus had been concerned with episodic memory. I thought that a large majority of typical experiments entailed tasks in which the subjects had to remember 'what particular perceptual event occurred in what temporal (sometimes also spatial) relation to other events' (p. 402) On logical grounds, and at that time, the thought was not entirely indefensible. In light of the definition of episodic memory in terms of GAPS, however, the 1972 claim could not be justified.

The interest of experimental psychologists in phenomena of memory has waxed and waned throughout the short history of their discipline. Differences between the pretheoretical framework implicit in, say, the comprehensive treatment of the literature by McGeoch and Irion (1952) and that made explicit in GAPS in the present volume are much more striking than their similarities. In the first full volume of the *Journal of Verbal Learning and Verbal Behavior* (1962–1963), it is difficult to find a single article reporting an experiment that could be readily classified as having to do with episodic memory. Certainly there is not a single article that anyone would do as an attempt to explore a problem implicitly or explicitly entailed in GAPS. And even in the current literature, a good deal of research is directed at neither episodic nor semantic memory. Instead, it is motivated by previous research that did not acknowledge the distinction.

In this chapter I briefly review my own past research, and that of my students and associates, in the course of which I was converted into thinking about episodic memory in the way I do now. The account is personal, one-sided, and undoubtedly biased. Like any other historian, I have selected and interpreted past facts in light of their significance from the perspective of the present. Some of my early work may now seem to have been pointing to something like GAPS as its distant goal; in reality, of course, the development of a general framework for the study of episodic memory existed no more in my imagination than in anyone else's. But the fact that the early work was not totally unrelated to the current state of affairs as exemplified in GAPS, provides some justification for the historical excursion.

Subjective units and intratrial retention

My interest in human memory had its beginnings in a thought that occurred to me early in 1956 when, as a graduate student at Harvard, I took a seminar in information theory from George Miller and Edwin Newman. The thought was that information-theoretic measures could be useful for quantitatively determining the orderliness or organization of response sequences in free-recall learning. I had never taken any courses in verbal learning, and thus I had no way of knowing at the time whether the application of information theory to free recall might have any theoretical meaning or significance. Nevertheless, when, a year later, I found myself a brand-new lecturer in the psychology department at the University of Toronto, I decided to try out the idea. The result was the development of a method for measuring the amount of sequential constraint in subjects' recall responses over successive trials in free recall. I called this sequential constraint 'subjective organization' (Tulving 1962a).

In a number of simple experiments, I found that the degree of subjective organization was correlated with the amount of material recalled, both across subjects and across trials. Borrowing an idea that Miller (1956*a*,*b*) had suggested for immediate recall, I interpreted the observed correlation between subjective organization and trial-by-trial recall as evidence for the development of higher-order units of material in the course of learning. The increasing size of these units could then be thought to represent the mechanism by which the subject could overcome the limitations of his immediate memory and learn a long list of words (Tulving 1964).

Why was the learner's immediate recall limited? Why would a typical learner recall only five or six words out of a list of sixteen on the first trial? No generally agreed-upon answer to these questions existed at that time. Some theorists regarded the limitation of immediate memory as a basic given, others accounted for it in terms of incomplete formation of associations. The controversy between all-or-none versus incremental learning (Rock 1957; Estes 1960; Postman 1963*b*; Underwood and Keppel 1962) was relevant to the question. According to the incremental view, the strength of associations, or response strength, of only some items reached a level above the evocation threshold after a single trial of study. According to the all-or-none formulation, only some words were learned on the first trial.

Both the incremental and all-or-none theories were, however, inconsistent with the simple fact that a single item could always be recalled by the learner immediately after its exposure. Why is the associative or response strength always above the evocation threshold for the single item, or why are single items always learned, whereas the same items in larger collections are not? It seemed more logical to assume that all words are always learned when they are presented, and that the limited first-trial recall reflects intratrial forgetting of the learned items (Tulving 1964).

How were we to interpret intratrial forgetting? I thought the best idea was one offered by Miller, Galanter, and Pribram (1960) who had suggested that the main difficulty in many recall tasks lies in retrieval of stored information rather than in storage as such. Similarly, Feigenbaum (1961) had constructed an information-processing model of memory in which forgetting occurred not because information in storage was destroyed, but because learned material became 'inaccessible' in the growing association network. Intratrial forgetting, too, could be thought of as reflecting inaccessibility of learned members of the list. The idea was attractive, because it also suggested that the utility of the development of subjective higher-order units lay in the enhanced accessibility of items organized into a unit. This line of reasoning permitted me to speculate that, 'The functional significance of the development of (subjective) units lies in the increased accessibility of individual items constituting a unit. An item can be retrieved on its own merits, or through other items in its higher-order (subjective) unit' (Tulving 1964, p. 234).

Availability and accessibility of information

At this juncture, one of the obvious things to do was to test the ideas that (a) intratrial forgetting reflects inaccessibility of otherwise intact memory traces, and (b) organization of list-words into higher-order units increases the words' accessibility. Zena Pearlstone, my research assistant at the time, helped me to do a large experiment designed with these ideas in mind (Tulving and Pearlstone 1966).

The design of the experiment had two objectives. First, we wanted to create conditions under which our subjects would organize individual list words into higher-order units, and second, we wanted to manipulate the accessibility of information about the 'stored' words while holding constant the storage conditions.

We accomplished the first objective by using lists of categorized words, and presenting words from the same category together in the list, accompanied by the name of the category. It seemed like a reasonable assumption that under these conditions most subjects would adopt the organization inherent in the list, and that the different categories and their presented instances would constitute higher-order units similar to those assumed to evolve over trials in free-recall learning. The second objective was accomplished by having a large group of subjects learn the same list under the same instructions and conditions, and then testing half of the group with and the other half without category names as retrieval cues. The difference in the level of performance under the cued and non-cued conditions would provide evidence that some information was available in the memory store that was not accessible under the free-recall (non-cued recall) conditions.

There was nothing particularly original about the Tulving and Pearlstone experiment. Categorized lists had been used before (e.g. Bousfield 1953; Cohen 1963; Mathews 1954) and comparisons between what we called cued and non-cued recall were not novel either (e.g. Postman et al. 1955; Fox, Blick, and Bilodeau 1964). Problems of accessibility of stored material had been investigated by Williams (1953), and the role that cues play in memory had been discussed by William James (Jones 1978b). We just rearranged and combined some of the previously used procedures and terms.

Although, in light of the speculations in my 1964 paper, the Tulving and Pearlstone experiment was a logical next step, I might not have taken the step if it had not been for a minor incident. One day early in 1963 in my memory seminar I made what I thought was a casual comment about people 'remembering' many things that they could not in fact recall. A student in the seminar challenged me on the point, wanting to know what kind of experimental evidence existed to support this claim. He wanted to accept neither anecdotal evidence nor the results of a thought experiment I offered. Since I could not think of anything relevant in the experimental literature, I made up a simple test during the break in the seminar to persuade the sceptical student and his friends in the group that some of the learned words in a list that were not recallable under the free-recall conditions could be elicited by appropriate cues. The successful demonstration prompted me to set up a more systematic demonstration along the same lines.

In the experiment, we crossed lists of three different lengths (12, 24, or 48 words) with three different sizes of categories in lists (1, 2, or 4 words per category) to create nine different conditions of 'storage'. The lists in different storage conditions were presented for study on a single trial. Half the subjects studying particular list were then tested twice in succession with category names as cues, whereas the other half received first a non-cued test and then a cued test. A total of 948 high-school students participated as subjects.

The experiment yielded four findings we thought interesting. First, cued recall was higher than non-cued recall in all nine storage conditions, with the magnitude of the difference varying systematically with both list length and category size. The smallest difference between cued and non-cued recall proportions was found for lists of 12 words with four words per category (0.83 versus 0.78), and the largest for 48-word lists with 1 item per category (0.74 versus 0.32). The second finding of interest was that the presentation of category names as retrieval cues affected only the number of categories represented in the subjects' recall and had no effect at all on the proportion of words recalled within the recalled categories. With the data pooled over the lists with two and four items per category, the proportions of categories recalled were 0.94 and 0.69 for the cued and non-cued conditions, respectively. On the other hand, the proportion of words recalled within categories was an identical 0.89 for both cued and non-cued conditions in lists with two items per category and 0.71 and 0.72 for lists with four items per category.

The third finding was that, for lists of 24 and 48 words, the number of categories recalled varied directly with list length, but the proportions of words recalled from within recalled categories of a certain size was invariant. With the data pooled over both cueing conditions and lists with two or four items per category, the mean proportion of words recalled within the recalled categories was an identical 0.77 for both 24-word and 48-word lists.

The fourth finding was that the category and within-category recall measures 'behaved' much better than the overall measures of numbers or proportions of words recalled. At all levels of list length, and for both cued and non-cued recall conditions, the proportion of categories recalled was an increasing function, and the proportion of words recalled within recalled categories was a decreasing function, of category size, whereas no systematic relation existed between the proportion of words recalled and category size.

All of these findings could have been pursued in future research, and all of them, except the fourth, indeed were. In the context of our present discussion, however, the important finding was the first: superiority of cued over non-cued recall. The finding itself is hardly surprising; it could have been derived as a result of armchair thought. Moreover, as I mentioned earlier, it had been demonstrated by others. Why, then, was it interesting?

What was interesting about the finding that cued recall is higher than non-cued were the implications for theory. There were three such implications, all closely related: (a) recall depends both on the conditions of storage and on the conditions of retrieval; (b) failure of recall of a studied item does not permit the inference that information about the studied item is not available in the memory store; and (c) with the availability of stored information held constant, successful recall varies as a function of the number and appropriateness of retrieval cues. The first two implications represented straightforward conclusions from our data, the third one required a small stretch of the imagination.

We used the term 'availability' to refer to the hypothetical presence of information in the memory store, resulting from the act of studying the word. That part of the available information that could be recalled was said to be 'accessible'. Availability can be thought to be determined by all the conditions under which the to-be-remembered material is studied— conditions such as the type of material, list length, amount of study time, different learning strategies used by the learners, and so on—whereas accessibility, we thought, is jointly determined by availability and by the conditions prevailing at the time of recall. Availability is specified in terms of conditions of study, independently of conditions of recall, and it can never be measured; accessibility, on the other hand, depends not only on availability but also on conditions of recall, and it can be measured.

Although we did not know, in a situation such as the Tulving and Pearlstone experiment, what information was available as the result of study of a particular list, we knew, by experimental design, that the available information was identical for the subjects in the cued and non-cued recall groups. The differences between the groups, therefore, could be attributed entirely to differences in the retrieval conditions. Since in our experiment, as well as in hundreds of others, evidence had been obtained about the importance of study conditions determining what the subject could recall, and since now the importance of retrieval conditions was also demonstrated, it logically followed that recall depends both on the conditions of storage and the conditions of retrieval, and that inferences about what has been stored cannot be made on the basis of what can be recalled in a particular situation.

Now no student of memory has any reason to doubt these statements, and many may even find them trite, but at the time when we published the paper the situation was less clear. There were around several theories, concerned with the distinction between short- and long-term memory, that implicitly seemed to assume that there was no access problem in memory. These theories (e.g. Atkinson and Shiffrin 1965; Waugh and Norman 1965), variations on what Murdock (1967) called 'modal models' of short-term memory, represented a great improvement over the classical associative learning theories, in that they could readily account for the fact that subjects could always learn and immediately recall any single item, or an association between two simple items. As I mentioned before, this fact, although not acknowledged as such, was a distinct embarrassment for both the incremental and all-or-none theories of learning. But the modal models possessed a different inherent weakness: they identified availability with accessibility. Failure of recall of an item from the long-term store, after the item had been studied and therefore entered into the short-term store, was interpreted as indicating the failure of transfer of that item from the short-term to the long-term store. What the modal models ignored was the possibility that information about an item was available in the long-term store even if it was not accessible under the retrieval conditions of a particular experiment: accessibility always implies availability, but lack of accessibility does not imply lack of availability.

Although the lessons and conclusions we drew from our experiment were based on a single study, I had no reason to believe that they would not apply more generally, holding in a wide variety of memory situations and tasks. Certainly it was difficult to imagine any kind of a memory experiment, or a memory situation in real life, in which the three conclusions mentioned earlier (p. 203) would not hold, especially as they could have been readily generated as general principles in the absence of any specific experimental findings.

An important personal lesson I learned in connection with the Tulving and Pearlstone experiment was a discovery about the attitudes of experimental psychologists towards analysis of variance. Our experiment was reasonably tightly controlled, and we had large samples of subjects in each of our 18 experimental groups. One would expect that under these conditions the results are reasonably stable, and indeed they were. To test the stability of our data, I used the simple method of randomly splitting each of the experimental groups into two, calculating the mean recall scores for each group separately, and then computing an intraclass correlation coefficient between the 18 pairs of means. This coefficient turned out to be 0.997, indicating that the pattern of results obtained with one set of 18 samples of subjects rather accurately predicted the pattern of results obtained with a different set of 18 samples of subjects. When I submitted the paper for publication I thought that this single statistic would be sufficient to assure the reader that we were dealing with reasonably stable data. The editor of the journal was willing to accept my rather 'unusual' way of handling the data quantitatively, but he pointed out that some of the readers might be unhappy if I did not provide information about the outcomes of standard statistical tests. As an author wanting to get his paper accepted I was, of course, in no position to argue with the editor, and therefore I dutifully cranked out and reported the results of a three-way analysis of variance.

Why these intense feelings about analysis of variance? Are we slaves of habit, living examples of the functional autonomy of methods, victims of early imprinting, or what? I do not know a single fact or finding in our science contributing significantly to advancement of our understanding of what we are trying to understand, that was in any way dependent upon the value of F, d.f., SE, or even p. Certainly it is the responsibility of each individual investigator to make sure that the facts he reports are reliable and replicable, but there is only one way to find out about replicability, namely to replicate the experiment. Significance testing is a poor substitute for it.

Lest the reader misunderstand me, let me hasten to add that I have nothing against analysis of variance as a potentially useful tool in some situations. But I do have misgivings about its automatic and often mindless use that characterizes a great deal of psychological research. Even articles in a relatively enlightened journal such as the *Journal of Verbal Learning and Verbal Behavior* are still too cluttered with numerical values of F-ratios.

Effectiveness of retrieval cues

The Tulving and Pearlstone experiment had demonstrated that not all of the information available in the memory store was accessible under free-recall conditions: with stored information held constant, presentation of category names as retrieval cues led to an increase in recall. But what about cued recall? Would all of the available information be accessible in the presence of category-name cues? We had no relevant evidence from our experiment, but on purely logical grounds it seemed probable that category names did not provide access to all of the potentially available information. It was easy to imagine that some other cues might be effective where category names had failed, and that, in general, the level of recall would be found to be a function not only of conditions of storage but also of the number and type of retrieval cues. What were these other kinds of possibly effective cues?

Although it seems peculiar to me now, at the time I did not think of what I later called 'copy cues' as 'legitimate' cues. Everybody knew, of course, that recognition is easier than recall, and that fact alone could have been regarded as evidence for the proposition that availability of information always exceeds its accessibility. But neither others nor I reasoned that way at that time. At the time of the writing of the Tulving and Pearlstone paper I thought that, 'Unaided recall requires the (subject) to reproduce the whole item, while in recognition the correct item is given to the (subject) and his task is to decide whether or not it occurred in the list. To distinguish between availability and accessibility of information that is sufficient for *reproduction* of a given item, comparisons between recognition and recall are only partly relevant and other methods must be used' (Tulving and Pearlstone 1966, p. 382). My preoccupation with 'reproduction', as a bit of overt behavior, and my inability to think of recall and recognition as two somewhat different modes of expression of knowledge about learned word-events, must have reflected the then dominant *Zeitgeist*. At any rate, the insight that recall and recognition, as studied in memory experiments, are more similar than different was still in the future.

The fact that category names helped learners to recall words in the Tulving and Pearlstone experiment seemed hardly surprising. Not only were the category names and corresponding study-list words associated pre-experimentally, but their appearance together in the list would also provide an opportunity for strengthening the association. Cued recall, therefore, could have been thought to represent a simple case of activation of either the pre-experimental or the experimentally established associations. In the non-cued recall situation, on the other hand, the subjects would have to rely only on contextual associations between study-list words and the general situation, and these would be expected to be weaker than the specific associations between presented category names and words.

Thus, from the point of view of the standard associative theory of recall, there were no puzzles in the Tulving and Pearlstone data, and no particular reasons for raising questions about effectiveness of retrieval cues. The newer information-processing views, as I already mentioned, had little to say about associative phenomena, and hence nothing much to offer on the question of effectiveness of cues.

But there was a fly in the ointment. Underwood, Runquist, and Schulz (1959) had done an experiment in which they compared free recall of response members of a paired-associate list with paired-associate recall. This comparison, formally at least, was rather similar to the Tulving and Pearlstone comparison between non-cued and cued recall. Yet the results obtained by Underwood *et al.* were the opposite of ours: their subjects did considerably better in free recall than in the paired-associate recall. Why the difference?

The major difference seemed to lie in the kinds of materials used. The paired associates used by Underwood *et al.* consisted of nonsense syllables as stimulus members and adjectives as response members. The strength of pre-experimental associations for these materials was essentially zero. It looked, therefore, as if pre-experimental associations played an important role in determining the outcome of our experiment.

I was not particularly interested in trying to resolve the discrepancy between the results obtained by Underwood *et al.* and our own results, because, with the materials that we had used, our findings made perfect sense to me. Yet the fact that formally similar experiments could give such discrepant results suggested that the 'obvious' explanation of our results in terms of associations between cues and target words need not hold generally, or at least would have to be treated with some scepticism. The question about the conditions under which retrieval cues become effective, in the sense of facilitating recall over and above the level observed under free-recall conditions, therefore, appeared worth pursuing.

We did a number of small 'quick and dirty' experiments, under relatively casual conditions in the classroom, trying out the effectiveness of various kinds of cues. We quickly found out that pre-experimental associations between cues and to-be-recalled list words sometimes did, and sometimes did not, result in the superiority of cued over non-cued recall. It seemed that some other factor besides the pre-experimental associative strength between cues and target words was also relevant.

In one type of experiment, for instance, we would present a homograph, together with a category name related to one of its meanings, as one of the many items in a to-be-remembered list. Then, at the time of recall, we would provide the category name related to the other meaning of the homograph as a retrieval cue. For instance, the to-be-recalled word might be BRIDGE, and it might be labelled as 'highway construction' at the time of study. At the time of recall, we would give the cue *social game*. Or, we might present the word VIOLET with the category name 'color' at the time of study, and then test the subject with the cue *flower* at the time of recall. or vice versa.

With only a few such homographic target words embedded in an otherwise standard list, the results were nothing short of spectacular: when the cues were switched, hardly any subjects ever were capable of recalling the target word.

The results of switching cues from study to recall for homographic target words were striking. But how general was the phenomenon? When I raised the question about the effectiveness of retrieval cues, I was looking for some kind of a simple 'general law'. It was not at all clear that playing games with homographs provided much insight into any general law. 'Violet' as the name of a color, and 'violet' as the name of a flower may have the same spelling and pronunciation, and in that sense the two are the 'same' word. But if the switching-cue effect is caused by the differences in the meaning of what is stored and what the cue 'points to' at the time of retrieval, then the results are easy to understand and of limited significance. To extend the generality of the results, we tried other experiments in which we looked at the effectiveness of kinds of cues that had little to do with the meaning of the to-be-remembered words.

During the days when I was interested in free recall, I had done an experiment in which I compared free recall with alphabetic recall (Tulving 1962*b*). In the alphabetic condition, the subjects were encouraged to look at each presented word and to think of it in terms of its initial letter, and then, at the time of recall, organize the output in alphabetical sequence. The results showed that the alphabetic strategy was very effective, producing a very much faster rate of learning than that observed with free recall. At the time, I interpreted these data in terms of changes in organization. This interpretation was wrong. Marcia Earhard, in her Ph.D. dissertation at Toronto (Earhard 1967*b*), showed that although the consistent sequencing of words in alphabetic recall had a small facilitative effect, by far the larger source of facilitation lay in the cueing power of the initial letters of to-be-remembered list words.

In another experiment, Earhard (1969) looked at the effects of switching the subjects from free recall to alphabetic recall at various points in the course of trial-by-trial practice. Subjects would learn a 22-word list under free-recall conditions for a number of trials, and would then be told to start recalling the words alphabetically. The results of the experiment were extremely clear: as the subjects were switched from standard free-recall practice to alphabetic recall, their retention performance suffered, the extent of the reduction being positively correlated with the stage of practice. That is, the longer the subjects had been studying the list of 22 words, and the better they 'knew' the words in the list, the greater was the *impairment* in recall when they had to use cues different from those, whatever they were, that they had been using before.

These results were reminiscent of the results we had obtained with switching the meaning-cues for homographic target words. The initial letter of the to-be-remembered word, which can be shown to be a very effective cue, is quite ineffective under certain conditions. The fact that the letter-cue had nothing to do with the meaning of the word suggested that the 'inhibiting' effects observed with switched-meaning cues for homographic target words seemed to represent a particular instance of a more general 'law'.

One of my many unpublished experiments dates from the early days of the study of effectiveness of retrieval cues. The experiment is almost certainly unique in that all of its 18 subjects are holders of Ph.D. degrees in psychology, professors in a number of illustrious universities in the United States and Canada. It is also unique in that I personally tested all the subjects.

The experiment consisted of two stages. In the first, the subject would be asked to call out the months of the year as rapidly as possible, and I would time them. All of the subjects in this situation named the months in their natural order, requiring anywhere from four to six seconds for doing so, depending upon the flexibility of the tongue. In the second stage, they would be given instructions to do it again, as quickly as possible, without making any mistakes, not backtracking when mistakes were made, but this time the task was to recall the names of the months of the year *in alphabetical order*. The fastest time shown by my clever subjects for getting through from April to September was 55 seconds, and the mean was approximately two minutes. More important, not a single subject could proceed through the twelve names without making any mistakes.

The purpose of this demonstration is similar to that of experiments with switched cues and homographic target words: to illustrate that some ways of retrieving stored information are more effective than others, and that for a given retrieval cue to be effective it must have a special relation to the target item at which it is directed.

Other kinds of graphemic fragments of words could also be shown to behave like initial letters. For instance, in one of our small experiments, we used descriptive phrases, such as *double letter in the middle* as retrieval cues. We found them to be very effective for the recall of to-be-remembered words such as SUMMER, or COTTON, *but only if* that same phrase had accompanied the to-be-remembered word at the time of study. The same cue was quite ineffective in situations where it had not been present with the to-be-remembered word in the input list. Similarly, a cue such as *a long word* would be an effective cue for words such as NOTWITHSTANDING, or THERMOMETER, but again only if the to-be-remembered words were designated in this fashion at the time of study. If they were not, the cues did not help the subject to recall them.

After all these little experiments, explanation of cueing effects in terms of pre-experimentally established associations seemed no longer tenable. A subject knows long before appearing for the experiment that BRIDGE is a *social game*, that the word ARMY begins with an *A*, that SUMMER has a *double letter in the middle*, and that NOTWITHSTANDING is *a long word*. In some sense, then, we could say that *A* is associated with ARMY, *B* with BARRACKS, *long word* with NOTWITHSTANDING, and so on. Nevertheless, these 'associations' did not help the subject at all when they were 'activated' at the time of the presentation of the retrieval cues unless the subjects had been 'reminded' of these common facts at the time of study.

What was happening? In a purely perceptual task, no person would have any difficult in identifying and selecting the word SUMMER from a long list if he is asked to select the words with a *double letter in the middle*. He would simply scan the list, one word at a time, and pick out the one that satisfies the description. But when the list is stored in memory, the situation changes. Whether or not the description is now an effective cue depends on how the word was studied. If the subject studied SUMMER as a word with a *double letter in the middle*, the description, presented as a retrieval cue, was effective; if not, it was not. It was as if one had to store the cue with the to-be-remembered word for the cue to be effective, even if in some other sense, and on the basis of a large number of encounters with the word, the subject *knew* the relation between the cue and the target word.

By the time we had finished all these 'quick and dirty' experiments— this was about the time that the Tulving and Pearlstone article had worked itself through the pipeline and had appeared in print—I strongly suspected that the effectiveness of retrieval cues in some way was critically dependent upon certain (directly unobservable) processes occurring at the time of study. Homographic to-be-remembered words provided a particularly clear illustration of the point, but the same principles seemed to be governing cued recall of words that were not homographic by any stretch of the imagination, in situations where the retrieval cues had nothing to do with the meaning of the to-be-remembered word, and under conditions where the cues and the to-be-remembered words were systematically related, in the sense that any person could have picked out the word specified by the cue from the perceptual display of the study list.

What was the process, occurring at the time of study, that was responsible for converting a potentially effective cue into a really effective one? And was it possible that the effectiveness of category names as retrieval cues in the Tulving and Pearlstone experiment, too, was dependent upon the same critical study process? Were the category names effective simply because the subject had, in fact, studied the list members as instances of designated categories, analogously to the subject studying the word SUM-MER as one that has a *double letter in the middle*? But if so, what role did the previously established relatedness, or association, between the category name and its various instances play? Was the critical study process something like the 'strengthening' of an existing association? But if so, in what sense could one 'strengthen', in a second or two, an 'association', such as that between *musical instrument* and VIOLIN, or *A* and ARMY, that must have been in an overlearned state already before the experiment? Was it really possible that the learner's preexperimentally acquired knowledge of words, their appearances in print, their pronunciation, and their meaning, as well as their associative and other semantic relations to other words, influenced how the words were stored, and that the cues were effective only if they were in some sense part of what had been stored? The questions implied exciting possibilities. The more I pored over the data from our pilot studies, and the more I thought about the issue, the more unavoidable the conclusion seemed to become: effectiveness of retrieval cues depends directly on how the to-be-remembered word is stored, and only indirectly on the pre-experimentally established relations between the cue and the to-be-remembered word. The problem now was, how to communicate the message to the rest of the world.

'If and only if . . . '

Our pilot studies in which we had explored the effectiveness of different kinds of cues were not publishable. They were lacking in all the niceties and controls on which editorial referees are so keen. In order to convince others of the critical importance of storing the cue information with the to-be-remembered words it seemed necessary to conduct an experiment more acceptable to others.

Ideally, the experiment would be designed in such a fashion that people who might initially have different ideas about cue effectiveness would have minimal objections to the conclusions. For the sake of continuity with the previous literature, graphemic components of words as retrieval cues should be avoided, since potential critics might argue that whatever we found would be limited to redintegrative recall, redintegration being defined as an association between a whole and one of its parts. It was also desirable that in the experiment the cues and targets would already be pre-experimentally related, thus permitting us to get reasonably good levels of recall following a single presentation of the material that would avoid possible complications, either real or imagined, resulting from practice with the material over successive trials. Finally, the to-be-remembered words should be 'normal' words rather than homographs, since many people would be sceptical about the generalizability of homograph results to other kinds of materials.

My research assistant Shirley Osler and I did an experiment to illustrate the importance of encoding conditions in determining the effectiveness of retrieval cues (Tulving and Osler 1968). It was another mammoth experiment, entailing 19 experimental conditions and the participation of 674 eighth-grade students from 10 different elementary schools in the Metropolitan Toronto area. Subjects were shown a list of 24 familiar words that they were asked to remember. Each word was presented once, for a few seconds. In different groups, each to-be-remembered word appeared (a) alone, (b) accompanied by a cue word, or (c) accompanied by two cue words. The cue words were words for which the to-be-remembered words were weak (1 per cent) normative associates. Two such cue words existed in our pool for each target word. Some examples of the two cue words and their corresponding to-be-remembered words were: *fat, leg*—MUTTON; *village, dirty*—CITY; *dark, girl*—SHORT; *body, vigor*—HEALTH; *empty, hurt*—STOMACH; *emblem, soar*—EAGLE. After the subjects had seen the study list, their recall for the target words was tested in (a) a free-recall situation, (b) the presence of a cue word, or (c) the presence of two cue words. When the subjects had studied the target words alone, all cue words that were presented at recall were extralist cues, related to the target words on pre-experimental grounds alone. When the target words had been studied in the presence of a cue word, the cue word presented at recall was either the same cue (intralist cue) or the alternative cue (extralist cue). The former was related to the target words both pre-experimentally and experimentally (we would now say, both semantically and episodically), whereas the latter was related only pre-experimentally. When the subjects had studied the target words together with both cue words, none, one, or both of the cue words were presented at recall.

The results of the experiment, expressed in terms of the mean proportions of words recalled out of 24, are summarized in Table 10.1. (Data from three of the experimental conditions have been pooled with those in three highly similar conditions, both in terms of procedure and outcome,

Table 10.1
Proportions of words recalled in the Tulving and Osler (1968) experiment

Study-list cues	Retrieval cues			
	None —	Cue A *body*	Cue B *vigor*	Cues A and B *body, vigor*
None	0.44	0.35	0.36	0.35
A: *body*	0.36	0.62	0.29	0.62
B: *vigor*	0.36	0.33	0.62	0.62
A and B: *body, vigor*	0.36	0.47	0.49	0.60

Examples of cue words fit the target word HEALTH.

hence only 16 conditions in Table 10.1.) The pattern of data can be described in a relatively straightforward manner when the percentage of words recalled in the typical free-recall condition (0.44) is taken as the reference level. In five experimental conditions, recall is clearly above that of the reference level, ranging from 0.60 to 0.62. These are the conditions in which the study-list cues are also present at retrieval. In another set of eight conditions, recall is somewhat below that of the reference level, ranging from 0.29 to 0.36. In all these conditions, the cues present at retrieval were not present at study. Finally, in the remaining two conditions, recall is slightly above that of the reference level. In these conditions one of the two study-list cues was also present at retrieval.

Although the whole experiment was designed to answer several questions, only one is of immediate relevance to us at this time: how does the effectiveness of retrieval cues depend upon whether or not they were also present at the time of study? The data in Table 10.1 provide a very clear answer to this question. We phrased it as follows: 'Specific retrieval cues facilitate recall if and only if the information about them and about their relation to the (to-be-remembered) words is stored at the same time as the information about the membership of the (to-be-remembered) words in a given list' (Tulving and Osler 1968, p. 599).

The statement sounds strong, of the sort that many cautious psychologists frown upon. In fact it was an unassailable summary of the results of the experiment; it did nothing more than describe the results of our 19-condition experiment in a condensed and general form. But I also had the results of the many small 'quick and dirty' experiments in my mind when I put our results in such a stark manner. I mentioned some of those experiments briefly in the discussion section of our paper, pointing out that several different kinds of cues had been found to facilitate recall 'if the cues are present both at input and at output' (Tulving and Osler 1968, p. 599). Because of the other findings, I also felt that our conclusion might hold generally, perhaps without any exception at all. The 'if and only if . . .' statement was meant as a signal of that private belief, although sufficient public grounds were lacking for an explicit claim for generality. Finally, I thought that it might be better to take an extreme position, and to hold it until such time that its abandonment is forced by contrary facts. Strong assertions, after all, do possess the virtue that they can be shown to be wrong much more easily, if in fact they are wrong, than weak ones. Besides, as the poet said, 'A man's reach should exceed his grasp, or what's a heaven for?'.

An empirical fact apparently contrary to the 'if and only if . . . ' conclusion had to do with the effectiveness of extralist cues, strongly related to target words on pre-experimental grounds, in facilitating recall. These facts had been demonstrated by other experimenters (e.g. Fox *et al.* 1964; Bilodeau and Blick 1965); they also accorded with common sense. We thought that certain extralist retrieval cues might be effective, because appropriate coding of to-be-remembered words 'with respect to the cue' can occur at the time of the study even when the experimenter does not attempt to manipulate the coding and is not aware of its nature. The cues may not be present explicitly at the time of study, but because of the coding process they can be assumed to be present implicitly.

We referred to this covert unobservable process as 'subjective coding', and tried to concretize the concept by referring to the possibility that the subject might 'think about' the cue word when studying a particular list word. Using an example from the experiment by Bilodeau and Blick (1965) we suggested that when the subject is studying a list word such as BULB, with a view to recalling it later on, he might 'think of it as something to do with light' (Tulving and Osler 1968, p. 600). If then the cue *light* is presented in the recall test, it is nominally an extralist cue, but it functions as an intralist cue, and is effective for the same reason that a list cue that was present at the time of study, namely, the to-be-remembered word was encoded 'with respect to it'.

One of the immediate upshots of our experiment and its general conclusion was another important lesson that I learned: never try to clarify a good abstract idea by giving a bad concrete illustration. I had obviously made a mistake in equating subjective coding with the subject's 'thinking about' a particular cue when studying a to-be-remembered word. An anonymous reviewer of our manuscript took a very dim view of it, and got rather excited about the silly nonsense of the assumption that extralist cues in experiments such as Bilodeau's were effective only because, or only when the subject 'happened to think about' the unknown cue at the time of study. The reviewer used the expression 'trivial' several times in describing what we had done, found, and concluded, and expressed serious misgivings about the publishability of the paper. The editor of the *Journal of Experimental Psychology*, David Grant, however, thought that the paper might be acceptable, if I looked over the criticisms and tried to take them into account in the revision of the

214 Organization to encoding/retrieval interactions

manuscript. He thought that perhaps we had 'problems of communication'.

Grant was certainly right; we did have problems of communication. In one sense I completely agreed with our anonymous colleague. I, too, did not want to identify 'subjective coding' with 'thinking about' an absent cue word when studying a to-be-remembered word, in order for the cue to become effective in a later test. I did not think that a learner, upon seeing a word such as BULB in a list he is trying to memorize, would mutter 'light, light, light . . .' to himself, or go through the whole associative hierarchy of response words to BULB under his breath until the next to-be-remembered word appeared. Nor did it seem reasonable to assume that the subject would have to be consciously aware of the semantic meaning and associates of the word BULB. The covert 'subjective coding' process that I had in mind as responsible for the cue word's implicit 'presence' at the time of study, as far as I was concerned, could well have been quite different from the processes underlying subvocal or muted speech, or conscious thought.

In another sense, however, I and the reviewer disagreed completely. His review left little doubt that he believed that extralist retrieval cues are effective by virtue of their pre-experimentally established associations with target words. The whole point of our paper was that that view was wrong.

Encoding specificity

After the Tulving and Osler paper had been published, we had two loose ends to worry about. First, in the absence of the knowledge about the results of our small unpublished experiments, it would have been very easy to account for the results of the Tulving and Osler experiment in a highly conventional fashion. Second, the subjective coding hypothesis was just that, a hypothesis; there was not a shred of evidence for it in the published literature. The two loose ends had to be tied up.

The conventional explanation of the Tulving and Osler results could have been that (a) extralist retrieval cues did not facilitate recall, because the pre-experimentally established associative connection between the cue and target words was weak, and (b) list cues did facilitate recall, because of the association established between the cue and target words at the time of study. The implication of such an explanation was that a strong pre-experimental association between cue and target would render the cue effective.

The 'subjective coding' hypothesis seemed amenable to experimental test. One possibility was to interfere with the hypothetical process. If it is subjective coding of a particular kind that renders certain extralist retrieval cues effective, then curtailment of the process by the expedient of inducing the subject to encode the to-be-remembered item in a different manner, would convert an effective cue into an ineffective one.

Both issues were addressed in a paper that Donald Thomson and I published in 1970.

Donald Thomson arrived on the scene in the fall of 1967. He had come from Australia to do graduate work in penal psychology at the University of Toronto. When, upon arrival, he found out that no one in the Department knew what penal psychology was, he decided to look around for some other equally exciting field. When he heard that I was looking for a research assistant, he decided that verbal learning was it, and came to see me. I remember our first meeting well.

Having some misgivings about penal psychologists who wanted to do research in verbal learning, I first gave him a 'test' of his knowledge of the field. I asked him whether he knew who Underwood was. Yes, he did: Underwood was the author of a book on psychological research that he had read. Was he familiar with Postman's work? Yes, indeed; he had read a paper by Postman on perceptual defense. He had flunked the test, and if he was going to be hired, it was going to be on some other grounds. These other grounds became apparent when I talked to him about his past life. I decided that he was obviously an extremely capable person, one who would get things done. So, I hired him on the spot, and gave him a recently completed research proposal to read, telling him that he could select any one of the experiments described in it as his first research project.

He returned a few days later and informed me that he wanted to do the study that I had described as an attempt to extend the Tulving and Osler conclusions to strong extralist cues. When I asked him why he had selected that particular study, he told me that the experiment obviously would not work the way I had predicted it would, but that it nevertheless sounded like a fun thing to do. I was very impressed with my newly found research assistant. The auspicious beginning of our relationship evolved into five years of most satisfying co-operation.

Thomson and I did three experiments. They were patterned after the design used in the Tulving and Osler experiment: two or more study conditions were factorially combined with two or more retrieval conditions. The main difference had to do with the nature of pre-experimentally established relations between words serving as cues and words serving as targets. We used both 'weak' and 'strong' cues. 'Weak' cues were words which, when given as stimulus words in a free-association test, would be expected to elicit the to-be-remembered word 1 per cent of the time: 'strong' cues were words which, when used as stimulus items in a free-association test, would be expected to elicit the to-be-remembered words as their primary associates. The mean associative strength between 'strong' cues and to-be-remembered words, according to the norms, was 52 per cent. The designations 'weak' and 'strong' thus referred to the strength of the pre-experimental associative relation between the cue and the to-be-remembered word. Our experiments were designed to find out how these 'weak' and 'strong' cues worked in what we now would refer to as an episodic-memory task.

The critical experiment was the second in the series of three. The first one produced data that suggested that we had been less than completely successful in our experimental manipulation of encoding conditions, and the third one ruled out two uninteresting but logically possible interpretations of the findings of the second experiment. I will limit my present comments, therefore, to the results from our second experiment.

Two study conditions were factorially combined with three retrieval conditions; a separate group of subjects represented each of the six experimental conditions. In one study condition, to-be-remembered words were presented alone, one at a time, on a single study trial. In the other study condition, the same words were presented, each accompanied by its 'weak' cue. In one of the retrieval conditions, no specific retrieval cues were presented and subjects had to recall the target words under non-cued conditions. In the second, the 'weak' cues were presented, and in the third the 'strong' cues were presented.

The results of the experiment are summarized in Table 10.2. The proportions of words recalled in the six conditions exhibit a pattern of strong interaction between encoding and retrieval conditions.

Table 10.2
Probability of recall (Thomson and Tulving 1970, Exp. 2, List 3)

| List cue | Retrieval cues | | |
| | None | 'Weak' | 'Strong' |
	—	(*fruit*)	(*bloom*)
None	0.49	0.43	0.68
'Weak' (*fruit*)	0.30	0.82	0.23

Examples of cue words fit the target word FLOWER.

Two findings are of especial interest. First, when subjects studied a target word such as FLOWER under the single-word conditions, expecting to be tested for free recall, a 'strong' extralist cue, such as *bloom* was quite effective. Probability of recall of the target word in the presence of the 'strong' cue was higher (0.68) than it was in the absence of any specific retrieval cues (0.49). Second, the effectiveness of the 'strong' extralist cue varied drastically with the study conditions. When the target word, such as FLOWER, was presented alone in the to-be-remembered list, strong-cue recall was 0.68; when it appeared with its weak cue *fruit* and the subjects studied the pair in the expectation that *fruit* would serve as a retrieval cue for FLOWER, the probability of recall obtained in the presence of the strong extralist cue *bloom* was very low at 0.23.

This interaction between encoding and retrieval conditions, and the demonstration that the cue effectiveness of even a strong pre-experimental associate of the target word depends on what happens at the time of study, extended the generality of the Tulving and Osler findings to strongly associated cues and provided support for the 'subjective coding' hypothesis. These conclusions were based on the assumption that if a target word, such as FLOWER, is presented for study by itself, its specific encoding pattern would include reference to close pre-experimental associates such as *bloom*, thereby rendering it an effective retrieval cue. We also assumed that the presentation of a weakly associated list cue, such as *fruit*, with the to-be-remembered word at the time of study would produce a different encoded engram of the target word, and thereby eliminate the effectiveness of the otherwise strongly related extralist cue. The two assumptions seemed to fit in quite well with the data we obtained.

All veteran researchers know that the sequence of events in solving problems by experiments does not follow that described in reports of experiments. Typically, an investigator gets an idea, reflects on it in light of what he knows about the problem area, designs and conducts the experiment, analyzes the data and draws appropriate conclusions. Then, before, or in the course of, writing up the experiment for publication, he undertakes a more or less extensive literature search that may or may not yield any relevant information in addition to what he knew before doing the experiment. (It is not completely unknown for experimenters to skip this stage of research altogether. Doing so enhances the probability of making an 'original' discovery; it also increases the likelihood that the referees and editors criticize the work as being short on scholarship.)

Although the set of ideas that later became known as the generation/recognition theory of recall was clearly in the air in 1967 when we began our research, it was not yet an indelible part of many particular theories. By the time we started writing up the Thomson and Tulving paper, however, Bahrick's (1969) article had appeared in which the associative continuity hypothesis I mentioned earlier (p. 23) was implicitly incorporated into the generation/recognition theory that he proposed to account for the effectiveness of extralist cues. The generation/recognition theory, as embodied in Bahrick's paper, provided an appropriate substitute for some straw man hypothesis with which we otherwise would have been obliged to contrast our ideas. Thus it was that we discussed the results of our experiments in terms of how well they did or did not agree with the associative hypothesis on the one hand and what we called the encoding specificity hypothesis, on the other.

Only many years later did I find out that we had endowed Bahrick's hypothesis with much greater intended generality than what he himself had in mind. Bahrick has recently reminded others that his 1969 model applied only to words 'not accessible to free recall' (Bahrick 1979, p. 148). I had overlooked this limitation of the scope of the associative continuity hypothesis, or the generation/recognition theory, and in my own interest in 'general laws' of retrieval, had failed to 'distinguish between recall that is based on search and recall that is effortless and immediate' (Bahrick 1979, p. 148). I thought then, and think now, that it is profitable to look for relations that hold over a wide range of conditions. The hypothesis that the effectiveness of all cues—intralist cues, extralist cues, word-fragment cues, associatively related cues, and so on—depends on the processes occurring at the time of study was meant as a broad generalization.

It is easier to make sense of, and to describe, the implications of the results from our experiments now than it was then. We were handicapped by the lack of relevant experimental work and theoretical ideas about retrieval as well as by the absence of a suitable language in which to talk about what we thought we were doing. Our interest in the conditions responsible for effectiveness of retrieval cues had taken us quickly outside the established paradigms, to situations in which extralist cues played an important role. Questions about the effectiveness of extralist cues seemed irrelevant to serial, paired-associate, and free-recall learning situations, the three dominant paradigms at the time that provided data for both short-term and long-term memory theories. Bilodeau and his associates had done some work on recall of to-be-remembered items in response to cues that had not been explicitly present at the time of study, but he and his research group seemed more interested in conditions determining the probability of the subject making a particular response than in the probability of the subject remembering a particular study-list item. In one of the earliest explicit comparisons of cued and non-cued recall (Bilodeau *et al.* 1963), for instance, the 'major purpose of the experiment was to reveal covariation of the obtained response probabilities with probabilities of the Kent–Rosanoff words' (p. 424). Since the objectives of the experiment were 'developed in extending motor-memory methods to verbal recall' (p. 427), it is perhaps not surprising that Bilodeau's work on cued recall did not provide much theoretical inspiration for us.

Terminological problems arose in connection with attempts to contrast our own hypothesis with the associative continuity hypothesis represented by Bahrick (1969). We could say that, according to the associative continuity hypothesis, word A was an effective retrieval cue for word B, if an association existed between them. Whether the association had been formed some time before the actual situation in which A was going to be used as a cue for B, or whether it was formed at the time of study of word B in a particular list, was not supposed to matter: the important condition, a sufficient one for cue effectiveness, was the existence of the association. But the same kind of language did not seem to be adequate for talking about the hypothetical encoding process that we thought was responsible for the power of word A to remind the learner of word B's occurrence in the list. Reference to pre-experimentally and experimentally established associations were, we thought, misleading. They implied that the only important thing was the time at which the association was established, before or during the study episode, and that otherwise the 'association' was, or could have been, the same. Such a state of affairs would have been just another version of the associative continuity hypothesis; I did not think that sufficient reasons existed for subscribing to it.

Whatever the reasons—struggling with novel notions, difficulties with terminology, or something else—the explication of our position in the Thomson and Tulving (1970) paper left a good deal to be desired. Among other things, we made conflicting claims about exactly what the encoding specificity hypothesis was, and how it related to the findings of our experiments. We thereby probably confused and misled a number of readers of the paper. In trying to get our message across, we had to rely on unwieldy expressions such as, 'Retrieval of event information can only be effected by retrieval cues corresponding to a part of the total encoding pattern representing the perceptual cognitive registration of the occurrence of the event' (Thomson and Tulving 1970, p. 261). The immensely useful feature-language that I mentioned earlier (p. 160) had not yet been widely accepted, and without it we had difficulty talking about encoding specificity. A term such as 'the total encoding pattern representing the perceptual cognitive registration of the occurrence of the event' clearly reflects our desperation of not knowing how to talk about ideas that seemed much clearer before than after we tried to put them into words.

Encoding/retrieval paradigm

Both Tulving and Osler (1968) and Thomson and Tulving (1970) experiments conformed to what we might call 'encoding/retrieval paradigm'. In this paradigm, both encoding and retrieval conditions are experimentally manipulated. Subject and material variables are usually held constant, although they could be varied as additional dimensions of the basic encoding/retrieval paradigm. Since the data from experiments based on the encoding/retrieval paradigm are critical in the evaluation of ideas related to encoding specificity, I will describe and review its logic briefly here.

A schematic representation of a minimal encoding/retrieval experiment is shown in Fig. 10.1. In it, two encoding conditions, A and B, are crossed with two retrieval conditions, X and Y. Of course, elaborations on the theme are also possible.

The minimal encoding/retrieval experiment consists of two retrieval experiments and two encoding experiments, all conducted simultaneously. In a retrieval experiment, encoding conditions are held constant and retrieval conditions varied; each of the two rows in Table 10.3 represents a retrieval experiment. In an encoding experiment, retrieval conditions are held constant and encoding conditions manipulated: each of the two columns in Table 10.3 represents an encoding experiment.

An experimental situation in which *both* the encoding and the retrieval

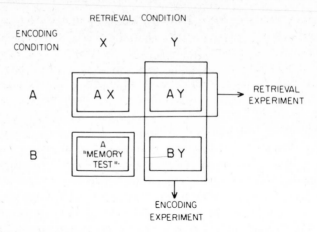

Fig. 10.1 A schematic diagram of the encoding/retrieval paradigm of episodic memory research.

conditions are held constant represents a 'memory test' in the psychometric sense. In a memory test, some fixed, prescribed material is presented to all subjects for remembering under standard and constant conditions, and memory performance of a particular type observed under equally fixed, prescribed retrieval conditions. Memory tests of various sorts can be given to different individuals, or to different groups of individuals, and individual or group differences in performance observed, and perhaps related to a set of norms based on the performance of a specified group of individuals. Memory tests are frequently given to people as a part of general assessment of their intellectual functioning or for diagnostic purposes in clinical practice; they are seldom used for the purpose of studying memory in experimental psychology.

Outcomes of single retrieval experiments, and single encoding experiments, are theoretically uninteresting, because they seldom exclude particular explanations, and seldom permit discrimination among alternative explanations. Consider, for instance, 'the retrieval experiment' represented by the three conditions in the Thomson and Tulving experiment whose outcomes are shown in the upper row in Table 10.2. The greater effectiveness of 'strong' cues than either no cues or 'weak' cues can be explained by (a) assuming that cue effectiveness depends on the strength of the pre-experimental association between the cue and the target, (b) assuming that trace-features corresponding to, or overlapping with, 'strong' cues were stored at the time of the study of the target word, whereas those corresponding to, or overlapping with, 'weak' cues were not, or (c) in several other ways.

Or consider the 'encoding experiment' whose outcomes are shown in the right-hand column in Table 10.2. The experiment shows that 'strong' cues are more effective when target items were presented alone than when they were presented with their 'weak' cues. This outcome can be explained by (a) assuming that the memory trace of the target word appearing as a member of a pair is 'weaker', perhaps by virtue of the subject's having to remember both words of the pair, than it is in a situation in which the target word appears and is studied alone, (b) assuming that features corresponding to, or overlapping with, 'strong' cues were encoded when target words appeared alone and not encoded when they appeared with their 'weak' cues, or (c) in several other ways.

The *interaction between encoding and retrieval conditions* exhibited by the data in Table 10.2 rules out many explanations that fit individual encoding and retrieval experiments into which the encoding/retrieval experiment can be decomposed. The explanation of the 'retrieval experiment', to the effect that the 'strong' cues were effective by virtue of their pre-experimental association with target words is ruled out by the results of the 'encoding experiment': The strength of the pre-experimental association was the same in both encoding conditions, yet probabilities of recall varied greatly (0.68 v. 0.23). Similarly, the explanation of the 'encoding experiment', to the effect that memory traces were weaker in the pair-wise study condition than in the single-item condition, is ruled out by the findings in the other retrieval experiment, represented by the data in the lower row, showing that the 'weak' traces were recalled quite well in the presence of corresponding 'weak' cues (probability of recall of 0.82).

The encoding specificity hypothesis does not only fit the data from both the Tulving and Osler and Thomson and Tulving experiments, it also produces no jarring contradictions when it is related to the results of our many 'quick and dirty' experiments discussed earlier (pp. 207–9). When the learners are induced to encode a certain target item in a specific manner—thinking of VIOLIN as a musical instrument, noting that NOTWITHSTANDING is a long word, being reminded that SUMMER has two consonants in the middle, or studying FLOWER as a member of the *fruit*-FLOWER pair—corresponding cues are effective, although they need not be effective in the absence of the specific encoding operations. When the learner is left to his own devices during the study of a target item presented by itself, he encodes it in terms of its meaning or other salient properties, with the result that corresponding cues again are effective reminders when presented at the time of retrieval. Finally, encoding a to-be-remembered item specifically with respect to some of its properties or in relation to some other item or items can reduce, or even eliminate, the effectiveness of a cue that may be related to the target item on pre-experimental grounds.

In the Thomson and Tulving experiments, we set out to test the encoding specificity hypothesis, and we thought we found good support for it. Before doing the experiments it would have been perfectly possible to imagine an outcome showing no essential difference in the effect of a strong extralist cue in the two encoding conditions. Had we found no reduction in the effect of a strong extralist cue when the to-be-remembered word was encoded specifically with respect to its 'weak' cue, we would have had to conclude that no evidence for the encoding specificity hypothesis had been found. We might have persisted in looking for it in other experiments, but again we can imagine outcomes providing no comfort for the hypothesis. Had that been the case, we could not have expected anyone to take the hypothesis seriously. This point is worth noting here, because in Chapter 12 we shall see that charges of circular reasoning have sometimes been levelled at the encoding specificity ideas; it is worth remembering, if we want to be clear about exactly what is being questioned when the charges are made.

11

Encoding specificity

The concept of encoding specificity originated in the course of the pursuit of the problem of effectiveness of retrieval cues. A number of experiments we had done had produced results that had led us to propose that specific retrieval cues facilitate recall if and only if the information about them and about their relation to the to-be-remembered words is stored 'at the same time' as the information about the membership of the to-be-remembered words in a given list. The 'if and only if' clause in our conclusion implied the rejection of the then widely held belief that one word could serve as an effective cue for the recall of another solely by virtue of its pre-experimentally established association. This belief had been most explicitly developed in the form of the generation/recognition model of recall (e.g. Kintsch 1968; Cofer 1969; Bahrick 1970). This model subscribed to the assumption of transsituational identity of words, conceptualized the learning of a list word in terms of the attachment of a list-tag to the word's representation in (permanent) memory, and assumed that recall was a two-stage process: gaining of access to a word's representation, followed by evaluation of the evidence about the word's membership in the list on the basis of the list-tag.

The generation/recognition models at the time said nothing about the necessity of priming, strengthening, or resuscitating of previously established associations between potential cues and their targets. Our experiments, on the other hand, had shown that some such process—specific encoding—was a necessary condition for cue effectiveness. Experimental facts thus showed that the theory was wrong; encoding specificity ideas were developed partially in an attempt to fill the void left by the rejection of the generation/recognition theory of recall. The insistence that the cue–target relation be established 'at the time' of the storage of the target item represented a denial of the sufficiency of a previously established cue/target association.

Over the years, the concept has changed. It is no more just an answer to the question concerning effectiveness of retrieval cues. It now is a theory about the relation between encoding and retrieval conditions that are necessary for the recollection of an event to occur. We could now say that recollection of an event, or a certain aspect of it, occurs if and only if properties of the trace of the event are sufficiently similar to the properties of the retrieval information. The 'if and only if' clause is still there, but it refers to the nature of the relation between the trace and the cue, rather than the particular time of the establishment of the relation. The emphasis on the time is no more necessary, since we now talk about remembering of events rather than to-be-remembered items; the temporal date of the occurrence of an event is one of the defining features of the event, and a part of its engram. We can now talk about both traces and cues, and about their relations, in terms of their constituent features; we do not have to rely anymore on awkward circumlocutions. Moreover, generation/recognition models have been thoroughly revised and brought in line with the concept of encoding specificity (e.g. Kintsch 1974); the sharp conflict between the two sets of ideas is no more.

The essence of the set of ideas known as encoding specificity lies in the emphasis on the interaction between the stored information and the retrieval information in determining the recollective experience of the rememberer. The engram of an event stored in the episodic system, and the retrieval cue, as interpreted or encoded in light of the information in the semantic system, must be compatible for remembering to occur. There are many ways of thinking about the compatibility relation—associative relatedness, matching of features, informational overlap, or whatnot—and it is possible that different kinds of compatibility relations have to be satisfied in different situations. But the relation itself is all important in the sense that if it does not exist, recollection of the event will fail. The insufficiency of the compatibility relation may come about for a number of different reasons as implied in GAPS: engrams that do not fit the given retrieval cues, retrieval cues that do not match a given engram, inadequate process of ecphory, and so on. To understand remembering of events, we must understand the nature of the interaction between engrams and cues, and the nature and conditions of the compatibility relation between them.

In its broadest form, the concept of encoding specificity holds that the cue and the trace of the to-be-remembered event must be related for the potentiality of the trace to be converted into the actuality of a remembered experience. It is difficult to imagine how such a statement could be regarded as anything but trite, or how anyone would want to argue that the statement is wrong. Would someone who wanted to deny a statement of this sort wish to claim that a psychological stimulus could actualize a dormant memory even if the two are not related? Such a claim would be absurd. And yet, as we will see in the next chapter, many theorists have expressed serious reservations about encoding specificity ideas, for a number of reasons.

Some of the problems that have arisen between the proponents and critics of the idea of encoding specificity are problems of communication. I have myself contributed to the confusion, sometimes because of inability to see things clearly, sometimes because of careless expression. Other problems undoubtedly have arisen because of the fact that we have relied heavily on word-memory experiments to provide relevant evidence on episodic memory. It is so easy to fall into the trap of an assumption such as that of transsituational identity of words, and difficult to make the necessary dis-crimination between a word as a unit of language and a word as to-be-remembered event. Had we studied episodic memory in terms of people's perception and memory of more complex real-life events, statements made under the banner of encoding specificity probably would not have been questioned or criticized by anyone. Everyone would have agreed that it is possible for a person to pay attention to or concentrate on some parts of an event and not others, and that such encoding would subsequently have an effect on what the person remembers of the event, and what questions about it he could answer and what questions he could not. That a highly familiar word could be seen from a particular viewpoint or perspective (Bobrow and Winograd 1977), or that its encoding could take the form of biasing some of its aspects, must have been a much more difficult mental feat. Even now many theorists, although willing to concede that a concept, idea, or word may be represented in the memory store in a large number of separate locations, still think of them as unitary atoms of the mind. Such is the power of traditional thought in science.

In principle, it should not matter whether we talk about remembering real events in the everyday world or miniature word-events in the psycho-logical laboratory. Encoding specificity ideas should hold for both kinds equally well. We need not do any experiments to know that questions such as, 'What did you do Sunday afternoon?', 'How do you like your new sailboat?', and 'Does the word 'capsize' remind you of any event in your past life?' might or might not remind the person to whom they are directed of one and the same personal episode. We also know that whether or not they do depends on how the episode was experienced, thought about, reacted to, or, in brief, how it was originally encoded. Laboratory exper-iments tell us similar things about mini-events. After the learner has seen a list of words, we know that instructions to recall the words, together with specific retrieval cues such as, 'a word related to winter', 'a word rhyming with plumber', or 'a word with a double-em in the middle', might or might not remind the subject of a particular word from the studied list. Whether or not they do, depends on the circumstances surrounding the encoding and recoding of the to-be-remembered word-event.

In this chapter, we discuss evidence from word-event experiments that have provided critical support for encoding specificity ideas. All the exper-iments we are to consider conform to the encoding/retrieval paradigm; they all demonstrate crossover interactions (Loftus 1978) between encod-ing and retrieval conditions. Our survey is not going to be exhaustive, but it will tell us something about the variety and diversity of situations in which recall or recognition of small units of verbal material are determined jointly by the conditions of study and conditions present at retrieval. After we have finished the survey, we shall discuss implications of encoding spec-ificity, briefly consider the relation between encoding specificity and generation/ recognition theories of recall, and then conclude the chapter by comparing encoding specificity hypothesis with the encoding specificity principle.

Experimental evidence

We will now look at the findings from fourteen experiments or parts of experiments. In all fourteen cases, the data of interest correspond to the design of the minimal encoding/retrieval experiment: two encoding conditions crossed with two retrieval conditions. In many cases in these experiments, these 2 × 2 designs constituted only parts of experiments actually conducted. In no case, however, does the omission of consideration of other parts of experiments change the conclusions that can be drawn from the parts we will consider.

The experiments can be divided into four groups, depending upon the measures of performance used: (a) free recall versus cued recall; (b) cued recall; (c) recognition; and (d) free recall. We begin with five cases in which free recall was compared with cued recall.

Free recall versus cued recall

Dong (1972, Exp. 2) did an experiment in which subjects saw a list of 50 categorized words: ten conceptual categories were represented in the list, with five words per category. Encoding conditions were manipulated by the presentation of all the words belonging to the same category together in the list, the so-called blocked condition, or by the presentation of list words in a haphazard order, the random condition. Recall of list words was tested without any specific cues (free recall) or in the presence of category names as cues (cued recall).

The results of the experiment are summarized in Table 11.1. Probabilities of recall in the four conditions of the experiment describe an interaction: free and cued recall are the same following random presentation of the words, whereas cued recall exceeds free recall following blocked presentation of the words. In Dong's experiment, effectiveness of category names as retrieval cues depended upon the conditions under which the to-be-remembered words were studied and encoded.

Table 11.1
Probabilities of recall in a part of an experiment by Dong (1972, Exp. 2)

Encoding condition	Retrieval condition	
	Free recall	Cued recall
Random	0.49	0.50
Blocked	0.53	0.69

Categorized word lists were also used in an experiment by Jacoby (1973). Jacoby led his subjects to expect different kinds of tests of the presented material, and then tested them in the expected or unexpected mode. Study lists consisted of 56 words, seven instances in each of eight different categories. Subjects saw and were tested on three different lists before the critical fourth list, the recall data from which were of primary interest. Subjects in the free-recall encoding condition of List 4 had been asked for free recall of the first three lists, subjects in the cued-recall condition had been tested with category names as retrieval cues on the first three lists. On the critical fourth list, recall was either free or cued with category names the two encoding conditions were crossed with the two retrieval conditions.

The data from Jacoby's experiment are summarized in Table 11.2. They show that free recall was little affected by test-mode expectations, whereas cued recall was: subjects recalled more list words in response to category names when they had expected such a test than when they had not.

Table 11.2
Probabilities of recall in a part of an experiment by Jacoby (1973)

Encoding condition	Retrieval condition Free recall	Cued recall
Free recall	0.38	0.54
Cued recall	0.36	0.66

The results of Dong's (1972) experiment had shown that category names were effective retrieval cues when the to-be-remembered category words were blocked in the study list, and did not facilitate recall when they were presented in a random order. Jacoby's (1973) experiment, in which the categorized words were always blocked in the study lists, qualifies Dong's results by demonstrating that one of the determinants of the effectiveness of category-name cues is the subjects' expectation of how they are going to be tested. Encoding of items presumably differs depending upon such expectations.

Roediger and Adelson (1980) did several experiments comparing free and cued recall for target words studied in the context of other words. We look here at a part of their third experiment. The target words in this experiment were homographic words, such as ADDRESS. In one encoding condition each target word was paired with another word with which it was weakly associated (e.g. *oration*—ADDRESS), in the other encoding condition target words were paired with strong normative associates (e.g. *talk*—ADDRESS). Recall was either free or cued with a strong extralist associate, a word that had not been present at study (e.g. *speech*—ADDRESS). (Here,

Table 11.3

Probabilities of recall in a part of an experiment by Roediger and Adelson
(1980, Exp. 3)

Encoding condition	Retrieval condition Free recall	Cued recall
Weak cues	0.23	0.37
Strong cues	0.12	0.43

and elsewhere in the book, I am following the custom, adopted in all previous publications of our research group, of designating target words in
capital letters and retrieval cues in italics).

The findings of Roediger and Adelson's experiment are summarized in
Table 11.3. The superiority of cued over free recall was greater following
the encoding of target words in relation to their 'strong' associates that it
was following the encoding of target words in relation to their 'weak'
associates. The data shown in Table 11.3 represent probabilities of recall
of either the cue or the target member of the study pair, or both, for
good reasons discussed by Roediger and Adelson, but the overall pattern
of the data remains unchanged when only recall of target words is considered.

The next set of data comes from an experiment reported by Baker and
Santa (1977, Exp. 2). Subjects heard a list of 24 concrete words, presented
one at a time, on a single study trial. In one encoding condition, subjects
were asked to learn the words in any way they wished, with a view towards
a subsequent memory test whose nature was not specified. In the other
encoding condition, subjects were given interactive imagery instructions.
They were to form images of groups of four successively presented words.
One retrieval condition consisted of free recall, whereas in the other strong
normative associates of target words were presented as extralist retrieval
cues.

The data from Baker and Santa's (1977) experiment are summarized in
Table 11.4. Again, interaction between encoding and retrieval conditions
is apparent: free and cued recall were equivalent following imagery encod-

Table 11.4

Probabilities of recall in an experiment by Baker and Santa (1977, Exp. 2)

Encoding condition	Retrieval condition Free recall	Cued recall
Standard	0.49	0.81
Imagery	0.73	0.74

ing, whereas cued recall was higher than free recall following 'standard' intentional learning. Putting it differently, we can say that free recall was aided considerably by imagery encoding, whereas cued recall was not. Indeed, the effectiveness of strong associates as extralist cues was slightly less following imagery encoding than following intentional learning.

The last experiment we consider in which retrieval conditions comprised free recall and cued recall was reported by Till and Walsh (1980, Exp.3). Their subjects heard simple sentences such as 'The youngster watched the program', or 'The chauffeur drove on the left side'. In one encoding condition, subjects were asked to rate the pleasantness of the situation described by each sentence, in the other they had to indicate their comprehension of the sentence by responding with an appropriate word to each presented sentence. One retrieval condition consisted of free recall, in the other extralist cues were used. The cues were single words that described plausible inferences that could have been drawn from the presented sentences. For the two sentences given as examples here, the cues would have been *television* and *England*. The subjects' task was to recall the sentences they had heard; scoring was lenient. Till and Walsh had both young and old people participate in the experiment.

Table 11.5
Probabilities of recall in a part of an experiment by Till and Walsh (1980, Exp. 3)

Encoding condition	Retrieval condition Free recall	Cued recall
Pleasantness	0.37	0.34
Comprehension	0.34	0.68

The data for the old subjects (mean age 68 years) are shown in Table 11.5 in the form of probabilities of recall of sentences. The pattern of data again describes a crossover interaction: free recall and cued recall were approximately equivalent following pleasantness ratings of sentences, whereas cued recall was higher than free recall following the comprehension task at the time of study. Another way of describing the data is to say that free recall was unaffected by the encoding conditions, whereas cued recall was higher following the comprehension task than pleasantness ratings.

This completes our short survey of experiments comparing free recall and cued recall. All five experiments we considered showed that the superiority of cued recall over free recall varied with conditions of presentation or study, and encoding of the to-be-remembered material. We consider next three experiments comparing different kinds of specific cues.

Cued recall

The first experiment we should note in this category was done by Ozier (1978). She did a total of three experiments. I have pooled the data from all three in the present summary. Subjects studied lists of 20 nouns. Each word in a list began with a different letter of the alphabet, and each word represented an instance of a different category. During the study of the list over four trials, subjects in the 'letter' encoding condition were asked to pay attention to the first letter of each presented word. They were also told that their recall for the words would be tested with initial letters as cues. In the 'category' encoding condition, subjects were asked to 'think of the category' to which the word belonged, as their recall would be tested with category names as retrieval cues. In fact, half the subjects in each encoding condition were tested with the encoded cue, whereas the other half were switched to the other type of cue. Speeded recall tests were given: subjects had only one to two seconds for recall of each target word.

The data from Ozier's (1978) experiments are summarized in Table 11.6. The pattern of data is characterized by a strong crossover interaction between encoding and retrieval conditions: initial-letter and category-name cues were approximately equally effective following the encoding of target items in the initial-letter condition, but category-name cues were more effective than initial-letter cues following the study of target words in the 'category' encoding condition. Considering the two encoding experiments of the complete design separately, we can say that initial-letter-encoding produced higher recall than category encoding when initial-letter retrieval cues were used, whereas category encoding was superior to initial-letter encoding when category names were given as cues.

Table 11.6

Probabilities of cued recall in a part of a study by Ozier (1978)

Encoding condition	Retrieval cue	
	Letter	Category
Letter	0.71	0.75
Category	0.44	0.91

Fisher and Craik (1977, Exp. 3) showed their subjects pairs of words. The right-hand member of each pair was the word that the subjects were asked to remember. The other member of the pair determined the encoding condition. In the associative condition, the other member was related to the target word in word-association norms (e.g. *sleet*—HAIL); in the rhyming condition, the two members of a pair sounded alike (e.g. *pail*—HAIL). Recall took place in the presence of extralist retrieval cues that the subjects had not seen at the time of study. The cues either rhymed with

Table 11.7
Probabilities of cued recall in a part of an experiment by Fisher and Craik
(1977, Exp. 3)

Encoding condition	Retrieval cue	
	Associate	Rhyme
Associate	0.36	0.22
Rhyme	0.16	0.18

the target word (e.g. *bale*) or were associatively related to it (e.g. *snow*).

The results of the experiment are summarized in Table 11.7. The interaction between encoding and retrieval conditions shows that associative cues were more effective than rhyming cues following associative encoding, whereas associative and rhyming cues were approximately equally effective following rhyming encoding. As in previous cases, the interaction can also be described by comparing the two encoding experiments: associative encoding leads to higher recall than rhyming encoding, provided that associative retrieval cues are given. With rhyming retrieval cues the superiority of associative over rhyming encoding conditions is minimal.

The last experiment in our sample of 'cued recall' category was reported by Masson (1979, Ept. 3). Subjects were shown simple sentences, such as 'The container held the apples', and 'The scientist observed the moon'. Encoding of sentences was manipulated through the presentation of either a 'relevant' or an 'irrelevant' pair of words with each sentence, with the instructions to the subjects to select the member of each pair that fitted the meaning of the sentence better. For the sentence 'The container held the apples' the relevant pair consisted of the words 'carry, harvest', and the irrelevant pair might have been 'anger, office'. For the sentence, 'The scientist observed the moon', the comparison pair 'astronomy, crater', was used to define the relevant encoding condition, and another pair such as 'water, play' defined the irrelevant condition. In one retrieval condition, cues were sentence subjects (e.g. *container*, and *scientist*, for the two sentences given as examples). In the other, cues consisted of words representing plausible inferences from the presented sentences (e.g. *basket*, and *telescope*, for our two sample sentences). Thus, the comparison is between inferential extralist cues and redintegrative intralist cues. Subjects' task was to recall the sentences as accurately as possible.

The results of Masson's experiment are summarized in Table 11.8. Probabilities of cued recall in the table refer to recall of the gist of the sentence. The data have been pooled over two kinds of sentences that Masson used, concrete and abstract. The pattern of data describes an interaction between encoding and retrieval conditions: inferential cue is somewhat more effective than the sentence-subject cue following relevant encoding,

Table 11.8
Probabilities of cued recall in a part of an experiment by Masson (1971, Exp. 3)

Encoding condition	Retrieval cue	
	Sentence subject	Inferential
Relevant	0.43	0.49
Irrelevant	0.33	0.22

but less effective following irrelevant encoding. Alternatively, we can say that the superiority of relevant over irrelevant encoding is manifested in a much more pronounced fashion with inferential retrieval cues than with sentence-subject cues.

Like the experiments comparing free and cued recall, the three experiments entailing comparisons of different kinds of retrieval cues we have reviewed have shown that (a) effectiveness of cues depends on encoding conditions, and (b) differences in recall attributable to encoding conditions vary with retrieval cues.

Recognition

We will now turn our attention to encoding/retrieval experiments in which retrieval was tested with copy cues, in different kinds of recognition tasks.

Consider first an experiment described by Thomson (1972). Thomson did a number of experiments of the same kind, varying only certain details, and replicated the basic pattern of data across experiments. Here we will look at his Experiment 4. In this experiment, subjects were shown either single words or pairs of words at the time of study. They were instructed to study each word shown with a view to a subsequent recognition test. Appearance of a to-be-remembered word alone or as a member of a pair defined two encoding conditions. Test conditions paralleled study conditions: 'old' words were presented either alone or as a member of a pair of test words. For the target word presented alone, the other member of the test pair was a 'new' word; for a target word that had appeared as a member of a pair in the study list, the other member of the test pair was the same word with which it had been paired at study. Words that appeared in pairs either at study or at test were associatively unrelated.

The data from Thomson's experiment are summarized in Table 11.9 that shows hit rates in the four experimental conditions. (The pattern of data is not materially changed when other measures of recognition are substituted for hit rates.) The pattern describes an interaction between encoding and retrieval conditions. We can describe it either in terms of comparing the two retrieval experiments or the two encoding experiments comprising the overall design. The important point, however, is that the effectiveness

Table 11.9
Probabilities of recognition in an experiment by Thomson (1972, Exp. 4)

Encoding condition	Retrieval condition	
	Single	Pair
Single	0.68	0.54
Pair	0.71	0.80

of a copy cue in a Yes/No recognition test in Thomson's experiment was jointly determined by both encoding and retrieval conditions.

A different kind of encoding/retrieval experiment with copy cues has been described by Morris (1978). He did two rather similar experiments, with rather similar outcomes; we will look at his second experiment. Morris embedded to-be-remembered words in sentences, and manipulated both encoding and retrieval conditions by varying the type of sentence. Congruous sentences described normatively typical situations; incongruous ones described somewhat unusual situations that could possibly occur but were unlikely to do so in real life. For the to-be-remembered word PICKLE, for instance, the congruous sentence Morris used was 'The PICKLE was served with the slaw', the incongruous one, 'The PICKLE jammed the saxophone'. At the time of the test, both 'old' and 'new' test items again were embedded either in congruous or incongruous sentences. All test sentences as such, however, were new: for instance, 'The PICKLE was on top of the sandwich', or 'The PICKLE was cut by the chain saw'. The subjects' task at the time of the test was to read the test sentence and to decide whether or not they had seen the capitalized word before, in the study list.

The data from Morris' experiment, in the form of hit rates, are summarized in Table 11.10. The important finding for our present purposes is the crossover interaction: subjects recognized study-list words more readily when the 'congruence' of their test sentences corresponded to the congruence of their study sentences than when they were different. The pattern of data is unchanged when false positive rates are taken into account.

Table 11.10
Probabilities of recognition in a part of an experiment by Morris (1978, Exp. 2)

Encoding condition	Retrieval condition	
	Congruous	Incongruous
Congruous	0.71	0.67
Incongruous	0.62	0.76

Stein (1978) did two experiments in which encoding was manipulated in terms of the Craik paradigm (Craik 1973, Exps. 4 and 5; Craik and Tulving 1975). We will consider Stein's first experiment here. To-be-remembered items, familiar words, were shown to subjects in the first, incidental study, phase of the experiment. In the encoding condition that I am referring to as 'appearance' condition, subjects were presented with words whose letters, except for one, were typed in lower case. Subjects were instructed to respond 'Yes' or 'No' to questions such as, 'Does the word have a capital I?'. Given a configuration 'knIfe', the subject's encoding decision would be affirmative; given a configuration 'KNife', the response to the same question would be negative. In the second, 'meaning', encoding condition, subjects made decisions in response to the experimenter's questions about semantic properties of the presented words. For the target word KNIFE, the question. 'Does _____ have a steel blade?' would be answered affirmatively, the question, 'Is _____ a liquid?' negatively.

The two encoding conditions were crossed with two different four-alternative forced-choice recognition-test conditions. In one, the 'appearance' test, subjects had to select the 'old' test item from a set of identical words with different appearances, for example, *kNife, knIfe, kniFe, knifE*. In the 'meaning' test, the test set consisted of four different words, and the subjects had to select the one seen previously.

Table 11.11
Probabilities of recognition in an experiment by Stein (1978, Exp. 1)

| Encoding condition | Retrieval condition | |
	Appearance	Meaning
Appearance	0.27	0.68
Meaning	0.05	0.91

The results of Stein's experiment are summarized in Table 11.11. The figures in the table represent hit rates corrected for guessing according to the standard formula. The data are pooled over two categories of target words, those associated with affirmative encoding decisions and those associated with negative decisions. The pattern of results describes a crossover interaction. On the 'appearance' test, subjects did better following appearance than following meaning encoding; on the 'meaning' recognition test, this relation was reversed.

The two recognition tests in Stein's experiment were directed at different aspects of to-be-remembered words, their appearance and their meaning. The experiment differs, in this respect, from other experiments we have discussed, in which it was always the *name* of the to-be-remembered item that had to be recalled or recognized. In a certain sense, therefore, Stein's results are less compelling as evidence in support of the encoding specificity ideas that retrieval of an event, or an aspect of an event, is determined jointly by encoding and retrieval conditions. Stein points out that his results are compatible with encoding specificity, but he also says that his study 'attempts to go beyond principles explicitly discussed in the encoding specificity framework' (Stein 1978, p. 172). It is not quite clear whether such extension of encoding specificity ideas is theoretically interesting or not. It may be, for instance, that Stein's extension of encoding specificity ideas—and similar extensions represented by the concept of transfer appropriate processing (Morris, Bransford, and Franks 1977; Bransford, Franks, Morris, and Stein 1979)—is analogous to the extension of the 'limited' encoding specificity ideas from remembering of words with single meaning to remembering homonyms. I think that subjects' inability to recognize a word such as PICKLE as an 'old' item when its sentential context is changed (Morris 1978) is theoretically more interesting than the finding that subjects have difficulty recognizing JAM when its study context of *traffic* is changed at test to *strawberry*. A larger number of explanations can be provided for context-change effects involving homonyms than can be made up for similar effects involving to-be-remembered words with a single meaning. The same may be true of encoding specificity as manifested in different aspects of retention of acquired knowledge and skills in comparison with encoding specificity revealed in recall and recognition of to-be-remembered items' names.

Before leaving this matter, I should note that the contrast between appearance and meaning in Stein's experiment should not be taken to imply that subjects in the 'meaning' condition *must* process semantic properties of target words. The only permissible inference is that they *can* do so if they wish; they can also, in principle, do perfectly well in the 'meaning' recognition test by remembering only the physical appearance of to-be-remembered items. The contrast is real, however, not only because of Stein's data, but also because it is logically impossible for subjects to rely on meaning of target words under the conditions of the 'appearance' test.

Two interesting experiments conforming to the encoding/retrieval paradigm and using recognition tests were reported by Geiselman and Glenny (1977). To-be-remembered words were presented to subjects visually. They were asked to imagine each presented word as spoken by a male or a female voice with which they were familiar. At the time of the recognition test, both 'old' and 'new' words were presented auditorily, spoken in a female or a male voice. In Experiment 1, the imagined voices at encoding were the same as the voices presenting the recognition-test items; in Experiment 2, the speakers of test items were different from those whose voices were imagined by subjects at study.

The summary of the data from Geiselman's and Glenny's Experiment 2 is presented in Table 11.12. The data reported represent hit rates in the four experimental conditions; consideration of false-positive rates does not change the pattern of the outcome. A crossover interaction was found:

Table 11.12

Probabilities of recognition in an experiment by Geiselman and Glenny
(1977)

Encoding condition	Retrieval condition Female voice	Male voice
Female voice	0.57	0.51
Male voice	0.50	0.61

copy cues presented in the voice of a speaker of the same sex as that of the imagined speaker at study were more effective retrieval cues than copy cues spoken in the voice of a person of the different sex.

The four recognition experiments conforming to the encoding/retrieval paradigm have all produced data demonstrating that the effectiveness of copy cues—'old' test items—depends jointly on both encoding and retrieval conditions. These experiments represent a useful addition to others we discussed earlier. The fact that to-be-remembered items were nominally identical under different encoding conditions, that the specific retrieval cues were nominally identical in different retrieval conditions, and particularly the fact that specific retrieval cues were nominally identical with to-be-remembered items, exclude many possible explanations that might fit data from situations in which these identity relations are absent. To the extent that we consider exclusion of explanations to be one of the main functions of empirical data (Platt 1964), the observed interactions betweeen encoding and retrieval conditions in recognition experiments are particularly valuable.

Free recall in changed environments and drug states

To round off our review of encoding/retrieval experiments, we will briefly describe two experiments that illustrate interactions between encoding and retrieval conditions in free-recall tasks. One experiment involved changes in the physical environment of rememberers, the other, their internal states.

Godden and Baddeley (1975) had their subjects study a list of 36 words either on dry land or under water. These two learning environments constituted two different encoding conditions. Retrieval conditions paralleled the encoding conditions. Half of the subjects tried to recall the list words on dry land, whereas the other half made the attempt underwater. Table 11.13 summarizes the data of the experiment. The pattern is of a striking crossover interaction: recall is better when retrieval conditions match encoding conditions and worse when the environments differ at study and at recall.

Many experiments have demonstrated state-dependent retrieval when

Table 11.13
Probabilities of free recall in an experiment by Godden and Baddeley
(1975)

Encoding condition	Retrieval condition Land	Underwater
Land	0.38	0.24
Underwater	0.23	0.32

recall of learned material has been tested in the absence of specific cues
(Eich 1980). We consider a representative experiment here. It was done
by Eich, Weingartner, Stillman, and Gillin (1975). Eich *et al.* had their
subjects study a list of 48 categorized words (four words in each of 12
categories) after smoking a cigarette either containing or not containing
active marijuana materials. Thus, the two encoding conditions in the
experiment were defined in terms of marijuana or placebo. The list was
presented for study on a single trial. Four hours later, subjects were tested
either under marijuana or placebo conditions. The two encoding conditions were crossed with the two retrieval conditions to form the typical
2 × 2 design.

Table 11.14
Probabilities of free recall in an experiment by Eich et al. (1975)

Encoding condition	Retrieval condition Placebo	Marijuana
Placebo	0.25	0.14
Marijuana	0.20	0.22

A summary of the free-recall data from the experiment is found in Table
11.14. The data describe the by now familiar crossover interaction: free
recall under placebo was superior to free recall under marijuana, but only
following the placebo encoding; following marijuana encoding, free recall
was approximately the same in both retrieval conditions. Alternatively, we
can describe the data by saying that under placebo retrieval conditions,
free recall was higher following placebo encoding than marijuana encoding; free recall under marijuana retrieval conditions was higher following
marijuana encoding than placebo encoding.

Generality of the effect
The same pattern of results, crossover interaction between encoding and
retrieval conditions, has been obtained in a large number of experiments,
under a wide variety of conditions. The to-be-remembered materials used

in these experiments included unrelated words, homographs, word pairs, categorized words, words embedded in sentences, and whole sentences. Encoding conditions were manipulated in terms of distributions of target words in study lists, test expectations, verbal context of target words, intentional learning, interactive imagery, pleasantness ratings, comprehension judgments, 'thinking about' initial letters or categories of to-be-remembered words, judgments of meaningfulness of relations between comparison words and to-be-remembered sentences, single or pairwise presentation, typicality of actions depicted by sentences, imagining voices speaking visually presented words, changing the physical environment, and changing the drug state of the rememberer. In most experiments, subjects engaged in intentional learning; in some, learning was incidental. Retrieval conditions were manipulated by asking the subjects to engage in free recall, in different kinds of recognition, or by presenting various types of retrieval cues: intralist and extralist cues, associatively related words, category names, initial letters, parts of studied sentences, and words describing plausible inferences drawn from the studied material.

The authors of all the experiments we have reviewed have provided more or less elaborate discussions of the results of their experiments. Many of them have mentioned that their data fit well with the ideas of encoding specificity, and have then gone on to provide more detailed explanations that do justice to the particular situations that their experiments represent. It would be difficult, and not necessary, for us to delve into all these explanations. The purpose of our review has been simply to demonstrate the wide variety and diversity of conditions under which interactions between encoding and retrieval conditions have been demonstrated. Such a state of affairs has considerable theoretical importance.

It presents a challenge to memory theorists to construct general theories that can account for the interactions in all their diversity. The concept of encoding specificity can be used to describe all these and other comparable interactions, but it does not provide any detailed explanations of them. A general theory that does, and does so in a convincing, reasonably direct, and parsimonious fashion, is badly needed. The construction of such a theory must be regarded as an important objective of episodic-memory research.

Denials and exclusions

The acceptance of the idea of encoding specificity, supported by the empirical facts of encoding/retrieval interactions, also has implications for theory in a more immediate and urgent sense. These implications take the form of what I call 'denials and exclusions': theoretical ideas that have been held, and still are held, by memory theorists that are incompatible with encoding specificity. One way of resolving the conflict—the one that

I favor—is to reject and abandon the ideas denied and excluded by encoding specificity. Others may have different ideas on this matter, however.

The list of ideas that are denied by encoding specificity and excluded by the findings of encoding/retrieval interactions include the following.

Items (events) of class X are easier to remember than items (events) of class Y

Statements of this sort have been made about different kinds of materials whose retention has been studied in memory experiments. For instance, meaningful words are said to be more readily remembered than meaningless words, concrete words more readily than abstract words, pictures more readily than their verbal labels, and so on. Remembering of an item obviously depends on its properties, or 'previous encodings' (Eysenck 1979), or its 'structure' (Hunt, Elliott, and Spence 1979), but it also depends on how it is encoded and under what conditions its retrieval is attempted. Therefore no absolute statements about memorability of items or events are justified.

Encoding operations of class X are more effective than encoding operations of class Y

Fergus Craik and I once made a statement that, 'Retention depends critically on the qualitative nature of the encoding operations performed—a minimal semantic analysis is more beneficial for memory than an elaborate structural analysis' (Craik and Tulving 1975, p. 291). Expressed in such absolute terms, the statement is wrong. Several writers have criticized us for making the statement (e.g. Kolers 1979; Nelson 1979) and rightly so. The encoding/retrieval interactions make it quite clear that the effectiveness of any encoding operation depends on the conditions under which retrieval is attempted. No absolute statements concerning the effectiveness of different kinds of encoding operations are justifiable.

Retrieval cues of class X are more effective than retrieval cues of class Y

This is another idea that, at first glance, seems to be absolutely true. Surely we need not doubt that strongly associated cue words are more effective in reminding the rememberer of a studied word than weakly associated words, and surely category names are more effective than whatever unidentifiable cues may be subjectively present in the free-recall test. Experimental data say otherwise: it is quite possible for a weak cue to be more effective than a strong cue (Table 10.2, p. 216) and for category cues to have no facilitating effect (Table 11.1, p. 226, also Table 19.4, p. 416, in Tulving, 1979*b*). Effectiveness of any cue with respect to a particular target event depends on the event and on the conditions of its encoding and recoding. Absolute statements about effectiveness of different types of cues are not justifiable.

Copy cues provide automatic access to the stored information

Theorists sometimes think that the 'old' test item in a recognition test is an 'ultimate retrieval cue', in the sense that if it fails, no other cue can be expected to succeed, either. But a number of experiments we reviewed produced results showing that the effectiveness of one and the same nominal copy of the to-be-remembered item, presented under identical conditions at retrieval, varied greatly in its effectiveness in bringing about the recollection of the previously witnessed event. These differences could not be attributed to differences in the 'strength' of memory traces resulting from different encoding conditions, because recognition tests given under different conditions frequently reversed the pattern of the results. Moreover, a large number of experiments exist (listed in Flexser and Tulving 1978) that have demonstrated recognition failure of words that can be recalled to other cues. There are no 'ultimate retrieval cues'. The effectiveness of any cue, including cues used in recognition tests, depends on the conditions under which the target event was encoded.

Recognition-memory performance provides a measure of trace strength

This is yet another very popular misconception that must be eradicated from our theoretical thoughts if we wish to understand episodic memory. For reasons already stated, recognition-memory tests provide no better a basis for estimating the strength of memory traces than do any other memory tests, or the application of any other type of cue. Several of our sample experiments that we reviewed clearly showed that different kinds of recognition tests may provide conflicting evidence about the 'strength' of memory traces associated with different encoding conditions. Anyone who wishes to claim that recognition-memory tests provide a valid and reliable estimate of trace strength (a) has to stipulate what kind of a memory test is to be used, and (b) rationalize this choice in light of the fact that other kinds of recognition-tests may provide conflicting evidence. These are difficult if not impossible tasks.

In this connection it may be useful to remember that there is no such thing as a 'standard' recognition-memory test. Sometimes theorists talk as if such 'standard' tests exist (e.g. Anderson and Bower 1974), but any such definition is necessarily arbitrary: there is nothing in nature that would guide and constrain our choices of 'standard' tests. Any situation in which people remember events in real life is as 'standard' as any other; any experimental situation in which the psychologist observes a rememberer retrieving information stored earlier is as arbitrary as any other.

Memory traces have strength

One good reason why recognition-memory tests, or any other type of tests, cannot be used to estimate the strength of memory traces of events is that traces do not have any strength independently of conditions under which they are actualized. This state of affairs means that any given trace has many strengths, depending upon the retrieval conditions. We can use the term 'strength' to describe outcomes of acts of retrieval. In this usage, when we say that trace A is 'stronger' than trace B, we mean that event A is more likely to be recalled under a wide variety of retrieval conditions than event B. It does not mean that the probability of retrieval of event B cannot be higher than that of event A under certain retrieval conditions. But when we use the term 'trace strength' in this manner, we must remember that we are talking about the joint effect of traces and retrieval cues and, therefore, that the term is a misnomer.

Words have fixed representations in memory

This is the assumption of transsituational identity: whenever a word is seen, heard, spoken, written, or contemplated as a to-be-remembered object in a memory experiment, the same underlying representation is either fully or partially activated. Although encoding/retrieval interactions do not rule out this possibility in the same manner as they rule out other ideas we are discussing here, they strongly suggest that the idea is wrong. I have assumed in GAPS that all events, even miniature word-events, are encoded in episodic memory in the form of separate and distinctive engrams, and this hypothesis implies many possible representations of one and the same 'item' in episodic memory. But it is also possible to entertain the hypothesis that in semantic memory, too, content words are recorded in many different forms, and that there is no necessary and direct connection between and among separate representations of one and the same lexical unit.

Success of retrieval is correlated with the completeness of reinstatement of encoding conditions at retrieval

Sometimes experimenters and theorists who have accepted the concept of encoding specificity talk about it as if it were just a restatement of the old idea that retrieval depends on the extent to which original encoding conditions have been reinstated. Sometimes people also assume that the 'optimal' retrieval operations are those that are identical with the encoding operations. Both these ideas are wrong. Donald Thomson and I discussed the relation between the idea of reinstatement and the idea of encoding specificity in our paper on recognition failure of recallable words (Tulving and Thomson 1973, pp. 365–6). Other relevant evidence is available, from both real experiments and thought experiments. For instance, after the subject has studied the to-be-remembered word SLEEP as a part of a pair of words such as *wing*—SLEEP, it is quite possible that the extralist retrieval cue *dream* is more effective in reminding the rememberer of the presence of SLEEP in the list than is the intralist cue *wing* (Bahrick 1969). If the studied pair were something like *23*—SLEEP, or *qrv*—SLEEP, then the extralist cue *dream*, or even a cue such as *weep*, is likely to be more effective than the intralist cue *23*, or *qrv*. Would not the reinstatement principle make the contrary 'prediction'? Similarly, from the point of view of the reinstatement principle, why should strongly associated extralist cues be more effective than the 'invisible' cues present in the free-recall situation? The free-recall situation, after all, resembles the study situation quite closely: no special cues present in either case. The encoding specificity principle is a general assertion that remembering of events always depends on the interaction between encoding and retrieval conditions, or compatibility between the engram and the cue *as encoded*; the reinstatement principle emphasizes the importance of the physical similarity between contents and processes at study and those at retrieval.

It is possible to distinguish between 'storage phenomena' and 'retrieval phenomena'

During the early days of research on availability and accessibility of information, and cued and non-cued recall, it was fashionable to try to identify the 'locus' of a particular effect either at the storage or the retrieval stage. The logic was that if the storage conditions were held constant, and differences in memory performance observed as a consequence of manipulation of retrieval conditions, the difference would be attributable to the retrieval stage. If manipulations of storage conditions produced differences in memory performance even under constant retrieval conditions, the effect was said to be located at the 'storage stage'.

As purely descriptive terms, storage effects and retrieval effects can still be used. As theoretical statements, however, they can no more be justified. Every phenomenon of episodic memory depends on both storage and retrieval conditions. The two interact, and thereby influence the outcome, even when one is held constant in a particular experiment. Thus, we might think of the higher cued than non-cued recall in an experiment such as Tulving and Pearlstone (1966) as representing a 'retrieval phenomenon'. But we know from many other experiments, including some we have considered in this chapter, that the effectiveness of category names as retrieval cues was derived from the encoding of the target words in a particular manner during the encoding and storage stage. In the absence of such specific encoding, category names as retrieval cues would not have produced a higher level of cued recall than non-cued recall, as suggested by the results of an experiment by Bobrow and Light described by Bower (1970).

Forgetting is a cue-dependent phenomenon

I once wrote a paper (Tulving 1974*a*) in which I argued for forgetting as a cue-dependent phenomenon. Other theorists have also assumed that once the trace of an event is laid down in the memory store, it remains available in the store, intact, if not forever then at least for a very long time, and that observed forgetting reflects only the difficulty of contacting or finding the relevant information in the store. This is a fanciful hypothesis that can never be rejected. But the reasons for our inability to reject the hypothesis are dictated by human logic rather than prescribed by the laws of nature. There is no evidence of any kind that would encourage us to believe, let alone dictate the belief, that memory traces, once established, remain unchanged. Given that we know from numerous experiments that recollection, and memory performance, always reflect joint effects of both encoding and retrieval, or engrams and cues, and that variations can be produced in both, it would be only natural to believe that forgetting, too, reflects changes in the joint effects of traces and cues. Forgetting is neither a trace-dependent not a cue-dependent phenomenon, it is always both.

Generation/recognition theory of recall

One of the most popular ideas of recent years has been the view of recall as a two-stage process, in which the first stage consists of generating suitable 'response candidates', and the second one takes the form of recognition decisions about the generated alternatives. Different versions of the generation/recognition theory have, or have had, many supporters (e.g. Anderson and Bower 1972, 1973; Bahrick 1969, 1970; Bower, Clark, Lesgold, and Winzenz 1969; Cofer 1969; Estes and DaPolito 1967; Kintsch 1968, 1970, 1974; Lachman and Tuttle 1965; Murdock 1968; Peterson 1967; Postman 1975a; Underwood 1972; among others). At the time when the encoding specificity ideas were first developed, they clashed with the then current versions of the generation/recognition theory (Tulving and Thomson 1973). Subsequently, the relation between encoding specificity and generation/recognition has been discussed at some length (e.g. Anderson and Bower 1974; Bahrick 1979; Crowder 1976; Jones 1978a, 1979; Kintsch 1974; 1978; Rabinowitz, Mandler, and Barsalou 1979; Rabinowitz, Mandler, and Patterson 1977; Tulving 1976; Watkins and Gardiner 1979). As a result of these experimental and theoretical analyses, and with the changes in both encoding specificity and generation/recognition ideas, the relation between them is different from what it was ten years ago. Although even a summary of the debate is beyond the scope of the present book, a few comments regarding current agreements and disagreements seem appropriate.

The world's first society of scientific psychology was founded on 22 February 1875, at a meeting held in London at 36 Russell Square in the private residence of a Mr Sarjeant Cox. The seven resolutions accepted at the meeting included one that named the newly founded society 'Psychological Society of Great Britain', one which stated as the object of the society 'scientific investigation of psychology in all its branches', and one that fixed the fees of membership at two guineas per annum. Mr Sarjeant Cox was elected president of the society. Within three months it had over sixty members.

During its short life—the society was dissolved in 1879 upon the death of its president—a number of meetings were held at which scientific papers were presented. Several of these dealt with the subject of memory. One of them included a statement of the generation/recognition idea in the language of the day.

(Although students of memory in the decades before disagreed on a number of issues—such as whether memory represents a unitary faculty or not, whether the mind stores all the ideas it receives or only some, and whether people have an active power over voluntarily erasing ideas from memory—they also agreed on some others. Among them was the proposition that memory is endowed with two distinctive powers: a passive one called retention, and an active one called recollection. Moreover, it was generally accepted that the power of recollection consisted of two subordinate powers: the power of recalling ideas, and the power of recognition. The two subordinate powers were assigned different roles in the service of memory, expressed in the form of the generation/recognition theory of recollection.)

At the 12 May 1875 meeting of the Psychological Society of Great Britain, George Harris, LL.D., F.S.A., gave a paper under the title of 'The Psychology of Memory'. In it he expressed the generation/recognition hypothesis as follows: 'The Recollective power is, as it were, the messenger of the mind, which employs it to search out and bring back to it those ideas which have wandered away. By its other power of Recognition the memory is able to inquire whether, and to determine that, the ideas so recalled have been previously received into the mind, and transmitted to and treasured up in memory' (*Proceedings of the Psychological Society of Great Britain*, 1875–1879, p. 66).

Harris, of course, did not invent the idea. It had been there for a long time. John Locke, as everyone knows, defined memory as the power of the mind 'to revive perceptions which it once had, with this additional perception annexed with them, that it has had them before'. Thus, what we call generation, Locke referred to as revival; the recognition stage for Locke was the 'additional perception' that the mind had had possession of the revived idea before.

Ebbinghaus (1885) described a form of generation/recognition idea on the first page of his treatise. During attempts to call back into consciousness the seemingly lost states, 'all sorts of images toward which our aim was not directed, accompany the desired images to the light of consciousness . . . among the representations is found the one which we sought, and it is immediately recognized as something formerly experienced'. Included in this statement are three ideas that have persisted in the thinking of many theorists for almost a hundred years, ideas which, if not entirely wrong, are of doubtful general validity: (a) the first stage of recollection entails the activation of *many* images, (b) among them is one that is likely to be *desired*, and (c) the desired image is *immediately* recognized.

Let us first set aside matters on which most if not all students of memory would be in perfect agreement. For instance, no one could seriously doubt that situations exist or can be created in which questions directed at memory can only be answered through the generation/recognition strategy. If you are asked to 'recall' all prime numbers between 50 and 75, or the names of all European capitals in which the first letter is the same as the last, or to produce the name of the sixth month of the year in alphabetical order, you can accomplish the task only by first generating an appropriate set of items and then identifying those specified in the instructions. The common feature of all these tasks is that, in the scheme of GAPS, the first stage of processing precedes and the second stage follows recollective experience. All these tasks can also be called simple 'problem solving' tasks. The solution of the problem does require retrieval of information from memory, but retrieval is not accomplished by the cues given as a part of the instructions. The instructions contain what Underwood (1969) referred to as discriminative attributes, properties of items that can be used for telling them apart; instructions do not provide any retrieval attributes by which the stored information could be retrieved. In terms of GAPS, ecphory is effected through some other kind of cue; once the stored information is ecphorized, individual items are accepted or rejected on the basis of the properties stipulated in the instructions.

Another item of agreement concerns the use of generation/recognition strategy in situations in which the 'desired' items are not perfectly specified, but in which the rememberer believes that he might be able to recognize it if he saw it. For instance, a person who has travelled a lot may not carry a list of countries he has visited in his episodic memory. When asked to name all such countries, however, he may be able to answer the question by internally generating the image of a map of the world, and then identifying the countries that are 'desired'. Similarly, if a person is trying to recall a list of categorized words, he may use his semantic knowledge to generate some instances of the categories and perform a recognition test on each. Whether or not such a strategy succeeds depends on a number of factors (Nelson and McEvoy 1979; Rabinowitz, Mandler, and Barsalou 1979).

Yet another matter on which it is difficult to imagine that agreement does not exist is represented by the proposition that the generation process can be used to create potentially useful *retrieval cues*. Consider the following thought experiment. A learner has studied a list of familiar words. In the subsequent free-recall test, he has produced some but not all studied words. At this point the experimenter gives the subject a retrieval cue, *yonga*. This is potentially an effective cue, but not in its given form. If the subject is told that *yonga* is an anagram of a word that may be useful for recall of some of the words that he has not yet recalled, and converts it into *agony*, he might be able to retrieve the study-list word of DESPAIR. The Donald-Norman-type retrieval query, 'In the house in which you lived three houses ago, did the front door open to the left or to the right?' is like the *yonga*-type cue in that in itself it is not effective, but it can be used to generate an effective cue that does make ecphory of the desired information possible.

All these agreements concern generation/recognition procedure as a potentially useful *strategy* of remembering. But is a strategy for retrieval a theory of retrieval? I think not. A number of problems exist for the generation/recognition idea as a theory of retrieval. I have discussed some of these elsewhere (Tulving 1976); critical analyses have also been presented by Rabinowitz, Mandler, and Barsalou (1979) and Watkins and Gardiner (1979). Some others may be worth brief mention here.

One problem concerns the nature of information that shapes the process of generation: is it episodic or semantic? The early modern versions of the theory (e.g. Bahrick 1970; Kintsch 1970) were very clear on the issue: generation of response candidates was based on semantic information, whereas recognition was based on episodic information. The idea is neat but wrong. It is easy to show that the facilitative effect of cues in recall of studied list words greatly exceeds the probability with which copies of to-be-remembered items can be generated to the cues from semantic memory. In one experiment, for instances, that Olga Watkins and I did at Toronto (Tulving 1976, pp. 52–3), subjects were given word fragments such as AS_ _ _ _IN and asked to generate the corresponding word from semantic memory. The word fragments we used allowed for only one completion; the probability that the correct completion was found by our subjects was less than 0.20. On the other hand, when the same cues were given to subjects who had studied the target words (e.g. ASSASSIN) in a list, the effectiveness of the same word fragments as cues for the recall of *words not recalled* under the free-recall conditions was very much greater, the probability of cued recall exceeding 0.70. Any generation/recognition theory that assumes that generation takes place in semantic memory would be hard put to explain this result: how can the episodic effectiveness of a retrieval cue far exceed its ability to generate a semantic copy of the target word? Postulation of multiple representations of target words in memory, only some of which are marked or tagged at the time of study, only enhances the apparent discrepancy: the probability of semantic generation is low despite the fact that the subject would get credit for 'finding' *any one* of the multiple representations, whereas episodic recall is high despite the fact that successful retrieval requires access to a particular *subset* of the total set of representations.

An obvious way out of the difficulty for generation/recognition theories would be to assume that the generation stage, like the recognition stage, is influenced by episodic information. But if so, we need to know how we are to distinguish between the two separate operations, both of which are based on episodic information, or take place in the episodic-memory system. Anderson and Bower's (1972) theory has attempted to do so, but the evidence they have adduced to support it is not convincing (Tulving 1976, pp. 50–1).

Another problem for generation/recognition theory has to do with its assumption that the product of the first stage is some sort of a 'copy' of the to-be-remembered item. The acceptance of this dubious idea has undoubtedly been encouraged by the widespread use of verbal materials in studies of memory. When to-be-remembered items are familiar words, it is possible to think of the generation process as that of producing, retrieving, or constructing internal equivalents of semantic and lexical units which then can be subjected to the recognition test. But the moment we expand the domain of our inquiry, the usefulness of the idea evaporates. Consider, for instance, situations in which the rememberer inspects a complex visual scene, studies the appearance of a stranger from a particular perspective, or hears a melody. Later, he is confronted with the same scene with some of the details changed, sees the stranger from a slightly different perspective, or hears the melody with a few notes changed. Does the successful recognition of these 'test items' mean that the nominal cue, the slightly changed version of the original, was used to produce a 'copy' of the original in the generation stage and then a recognition decision performed on this 'copy'? If the answer is negative, as it should be, then why do we imagine that generation of copies of to-be-remembered items is a necessary condition for successful retrieval in word-memory experiments? Why is it necessary to assume that the generation stage produces 'response candidates', or provides access to appropriately tagged nodes in an associative network, rather than producing potentially useful retrieval cues, a notion that seems much more acceptable to all theorists?

Finally, many versions of generation/recognition theories share a fundamental weakness with many other theories of episodic retrieval in assuming that the rememberer knows what he wants to remember before the act takes place. This is the assumption behind the concept of 'desired' information. The generation process produces both wanted and unwanted response candidates, the function of the recognition stage is to separate one from the other. It is, of course, clear that frequently the rememberer is faced with the task of retrieving an item of a particular class, and that in that sense he knows something about what he is trying to retrieve before the attempt at retrieval is made. For instance, in a word-event experiment, the task is to remember familiar words and not the previous week's experiences or names of friends and acquaintances. But such general category information only helps to restrict mental activity, it does not help the rememberer to select the 'desired' from among the 'not desired' response candidates if all of them are members of the category. Moreover, frequently a person has no particular reason to expect to retrieve any specific memory; an appropriate retrieval cue, presented under appropriate conditions, produces a particular recollective experience that is recognized as such. Do we then postulate the distinction between 'desired' and 'not desired' pieces of generated information in some situations and not in others, and construct different theories to deal with these differences? Or should we look for a general theory of retrieval that does not beg the question by assuming that the rememberer knows what kind of a memory he wants to retrieve?

What, then, can we say about the relation between encoding specificity and generation/recognition ideas at this time? First, no disagreement exists with respect to generation/recognition as a conscious *strategy* of retrieval that must be used in some situations and may be used in others. Second, there is no disagreement on the possibility that retrieval *cues* can be, and frequently are, generated by rememberers faced with the task of retrieval. Third, no disagreement exists on the reality of the *post-ecphoric decision* process on the basis of which only some retrieved information is converted into behavior.

On the other hand, certain ideas that are found in generation/recognition theories are incompatible with empirical facts or inconsistent with encoding specificity ideas. The assumption that the generation stage produces copies of to-be-remembered items on the basis of semantic information, and the idea that the products of such a generation process are accepted or rejected in terms of the rememberer's advance knowledge of what is 'desired', must be rejected.

An old idea about recognition memory, which is still found in contemporary writings having to do with the process of recognition, illustrates theories of retrieval that beg the question of retrieval. It is the idea that recognition is the reverse of the process of recall. In recall, the context in which an event took place is provided as a cue, and the rememberer's task is to retrieve the focal element. 'Recognition is, schematically, just the reverse of this process. In recognition the focal element is present, in the form of sensation, image, or feeling, and the question is whether or not this element will recall a more or less definite setting or background' (Hollingworth 1913, p. 533). An illustrative comparable statement from the present generation of students of memory is that, 'All that is required in recognition is an assessment of the appropriateness of the various associations surrounding a stored item to the association demanded by the query' (Norman 1968, p. 533).

The problem is to account for the fact that a rememberer may recognize an item as one that he has seen previously. The postulated 'mechanism' of this recognition is to assume that the subject knows what the context was in which the item was seen. For recognition to succeed, the test item must elicit the retrieval, or remind the rememberer, of the context in which it occurred earlier. Alternatively, the test must provide access to its representation in memory to which is attached information about the context of its previous occurrence. If the rememberer recognizes the context information as corresponding to the information he has about the item's context of occurrence, he recognizes the item as one previously seen in that context. In either form, the assumption is that the subject has no difficulty, or has less difficulty, recognizing the context than recognizing the item. Memory, or knowledge, of one kind of information is taken for granted in order to 'explain' retrieval of another kind of information. This is hardly a satisfying state of affairs.

Hypothesis and principle

It is useful to distinguish between encoding specificity hypothesis and encoding specificity principle. The hypothesis is a tentative statement about the relation between the properties of the memory trace of an event and the effectiveness of retrieval cues; its tenability can be evaluated empirically. The principle is the assumption that the hypothesis is true. It is not subject to empirical verification.

The encoding specificity hypothesis holds that the probability of retrieval varies directly with the compatibility of the engram and the cue, or the stored information and the retrieval information. It can be tested by manipulating the informational contents of engrams and observing the effectiveness of a cue, holding constant the engram of an event and observing the effectiveness of different cues, or doing both. Simple thought experiments provide concrete illustrations of these relations. First, we can manipulate the contents of memory traces by having a subject witness two events, A and B, and then demonstrate that retrieval cues that are systematically related to A (copies of A, similar stimuli, related stimuli, and the like) can serve as reminders of the event A but not of B. Similarly, considering only the event A, we can demonstrate that the effectiveness of different retrieval cues in reminding the learner of A depends on their similarity or degree of relatedness to A.

These examples may strike the reader as somewhat trivial, and he may wonder about the profound significance of the 'data' from the thought experiments. Such significance, however, may emerge in conjunction with the idea that retrieval always reflects the compatibility (similarity, relatedness, informational overlap) relation between traces and cues, that is, even in situations in which the relations are much less transparent than they are in our thought experiments.

We have already seen that it is possible to hold the nominal identity of the to-be-remembered item constant, and manipulate the properties of its engram by having the subject engage in different encoding operations at the time of study. For instance, we can have the learner pay particular attention to a to-be-remembered word's sound, or to its meaning, and show how acoustically similar retrieval cues are more effective than semantically similar retrieval cues in one encoding condition but not in the other (e.g. Fisher and Craik 1977). The outcome is not particularly surprising, and as we become more and more familiar with the general pattern that it represents we may be tempted to think of it as trivial, too. Nevertheless, these findings, and many other similar ones reported in the literature, remind us that the encoding specificity hypothesis is testable as well as potentially rejectable. If, for instance, it turned out that the effectiveness of extralist cues depended on the strength of the pre-experimentally established relation to target words, and that encoding the target word 'with respect to' its sound or its meaning did not make any difference, then there would be no grounds for holding that retrieval depends on the interaction between the cue and the engram of the uniquely encoded event.

Three entities are involved in the testing of the encoding specificity hypothesis: the engram of the event, retrieval cue, and the relation between them. When we test the hypothesis, we must know, or must be in a position to make reasonable assumptions about, the encoded features of engrams, as well as the 'features useful for retrieval' (Flexser and Tulving 1978) contained in or extracted from the retrieval information. The results of the observations then tell us something about the third entity, the relation between the trace and the cue.

It is not necessary, and indeed it is impossible, to know exactly what the encoded features of an engram are in order to test the hypothesis. All that is needed is knowledge concerning the *differences* between two traces. In an experiment such as Fisher and Craik's (1977), for instance, we know that, to the extent that the intended encoding operations have been effective, the traces of rhyme-encoded target words are characterized by more salient phonemic features than semantically encoded target words, and that the latter have more salient semantic features than do the former. If we then find that rhyming and semantic retrieval cues are differentially effective, we can conclude that the similarity of encoded features of engrams and features of retrieval cues determines the probability of retrieval.

It is important to note that it is seldom possible for an experimenter to completely determine the informational contents of a memory trace. At best these contents can be *influenced* or *biased* by manipulating the conditions of encoding. Many features of events are encoded even when voluntary attention is not directed at them at the time of encoding (Hunt *et al.* 1979; Nelson 1979; Ozier 1978). Similarly, it is possible that encoding operations are ineffective in biasing the encoding in the intended manner. It frequently happens, therefore, that we cannot be sure how events have been encoded even in situations in which encoding conditions have been deliberately manipulated. These kinds of complications make testing of the encoding specificity hypothesis difficult although not impossible.

When we adopt encoding specificity as a principle, we assume that the hypothesis is true and that the probability of retrieval of an event in response to a cue depends directly on the similarity or compatibility between the trace and the cue. Adoption of the principle permits us to make inferences about the informational contents of memory traces on the basis of observed effectiveness of retrieval cues. Different memory traces can be probed with one and the same cue, and inferences made about the informational contents of the traces on the basis of observed measures of cued recall. Alternatively, one and the same trace can be probed with different cues and its properties described in terms of their effectiveness. This retrieval-cueing method of describing memory traces (Tulving and Bower 1974) is particularly useful when a given trace is probed in succession with two or more different cues. Applying the logic of the so-called Reduction Method to the data obtained from the successive cueing paradigm, memory traces can be described as multidimensional structures (Tulving and Watkins 1975; Ogilvie, Tulving, Paskowitz, and Jones 1980; Watkins 1979; Watkins and Todres 1978).

When we make inferences about the encoded features of memory traces on the basis of the encoding specificity principle (e.g. Barclay, Bransford, Franks, McCarrell, and Nitsch 1974; Simon 1979; Till 1977) we rely on the same logic that has been used in other situations to describe objects that are not directly observable. The effect that a cue has on bringing about the retrieval of an event tells us something about the properties of the event in the same way in which a radar or sonar beam bouncing off an otherwise invisible object describes some of its properties for us.

The emphasis in the last sentence should be on 'some'. Like radar and sonar beams, retrieval cues provide selective information only. It is quite possible that memory traces possess properties that cannot be tapped directly through the application of certain retrieval cues, properties whose actualization is mediated through other features. Underwood's (1969) distinction between discriminative and retrieval attributes of memories describes the difference between two potentially important classes of trace features. Moreover, the method of retrieval cueing may not only fail to yield information on some of the trace features, it may also provide information about features not 'present' in the engram. Such a state of affairs may come about if, in the language of GAPS, ecphoric information, as a product of trace information and retrieval information, contains emergent properties, features not found either in the trace or the cue. Thus, although a great deal of research is needed in order to perfect the technique of identifying properties of memory traces, the basic method of retrieval cueing and its attendant logic may have some merit.

12
Criticisms of encoding specificity

The concept of encoding specificity, like many other concepts not only in psychology but in other sciences, cannot be succinctly defined or explicated in a sentence or two. And like many other concepts it derives its meaning from both experiments designed to explore phenomena that have arisen in connection with encoding specificity ideas and from theoretical speculations concerning the outcomes of these experiments. The essence of encoding specificity, however, can be summarized in terms of engrams and cues: the interaction between them, the importance of the similarity or compatibility relation between them, and their synergistic determination of the product of retrieval.

Encoding specificity ideas should be non-controversial, but interestingly enough they are not. They have been criticized by a number of people on a variety of grounds. Some have declared them to be untestable, others false; some have questioned the underlying logic, others have produced data that they have interpreted as contrary to encoding specificity; some have explained findings supportive of encoding specificity without any recourse to these ideas, others have failed to replicate them.

In this chapter I will review and discuss some of the criticisms of encoding specificity. It would not be possible to deal with them all, nor is it necessary to do so. A number of early critical observations are of historical interest only at this time. They were directed at early, somewhat jumbled versions of encoding specificity. Their force has been dissipated in the course of the modification of the concept and clarification of its nature.

Conflicting evidence

We can distinguish among four different kinds of evidence that appears to conflict with encoding specificity: (a) absence of encoding/ retrieval interactions, (b) failure to replicate data from relevant experiments, (c) demonstrations that unencoded cues are effective, and (d) demonstrations that encoded cues are ineffective. We will consider these four kinds in turn.

The critical evidence for the concept of encoding specificity, as we have seen, is provided by encoding/retrieval interactions. But what are we to make of comparable experiments that yield no evidence of such interactions? One can find many experiments in the literature whose results are not the same as those of experiments we reviewed in Chapter 11. For instance, Jacoby (1973) found that free recall was little affected, whereas cued recall was more affected by subjects' expectations as to the test mode. But in a comparable experiment, Balota and Neely (1980) found that subjects expecting a recall test did better both on free recall and recognition than people who learned the same material but were expecting a recognition test. Till and Walsh (1980) found that their old subjects did approximately equally well on free recall and cued recall following pleasantness ratings of study-list sentences, whereas cued recall was higher than free recall following a comprehension-oriented encoding task. But their young subjects showed no such interaction: their performance was higher on cued than on non-cued tasks, and higher following comprehension than pleasantness ratings. Thomson (1972) found an interaction between encoding and retrieval conditions in a recognition-memory task in four experiments; yet in the fifth experiment, in which subjects studied both single words and pairs of words, there was no interaction. Finally, Godden and Baddeley (1975) reported free-recall data showing a strong interaction between encoding and retrieval environments, on land or under water; when their subjects were tested for recognition of the learned words, the interaction vanished. I could greatly lengthen the list of these kinds of examples, but those I have mentioned here suffice to illustrate the nature of the problem. How are we to interpret these discrepant results?

There is no need whatever for the concept of encoding specificity in explanations of results showing differences in retrieval for items encoded under different conditions or tested in the presence of different kinds of cues. Nor are encoding specificity ideas needed for interpreting additive effects, or non-crossover interactions, involving encoding and retrieval conditions. It is possible, therefore, to divide memory situations into two categories, those for which encoding specificity ideas, or ideas logically equivalent to them, are indicated and those for which they are unnecessary. But anyone advocating such an approach would do a service, or at least a favor, to others if he explained or rationalized the advantages of such an approach.

There is no logical inconsistency between data showing no encoding/retrieval interactions and the concept of encoding specificity. Therefore, a parsimonious view could be adopted that retrieval is determined jointly by the (specifically encoded) engrams and appropriate retrieval cues even in situations in which encoding/retrieval interactions are not present. The advantage of this approach is that one general idea applies to all memory situations, not only a particular subset of them.

Some experiments have been reported that were designed as attempts to replicate and extend 'encoding specificity' experiments. As an illustration, consider the experiment described by Postman (1975a, Exp.1).

Postman's experiment was designed to compare the effectiveness of different types of intralist and extralist cues following the study of target words in the presence or absence of associated list-cues. The experiment had a rich design, comprising 16 experimental conditions. Several of these corresponded to the conditions in Thomson and Tulving's (1970) experiments.

Postman's data did not replicate the critical interaction found in the Thomson and Tulving experiment. Instead, they showed that a 'strong' extralist cue (e.g. *bloom*) was as effective in eliciting the corresponding target word (e.g. FLOWER) following the target word's encoding in the presence of the 'weak' cue as it was following the target word's encoding as a single item in the study list, and that in both of these two conditions strong-cue recall was considerably higher than non-cued recall. This is exactly the kind of a pattern of data that would make encoding specificity ideas superfluous: cue words that are strong pre-experimental associates of target words facilitate recall over and above the level of free recall regardless of encoding conditions. If all experiments directed at the issue yielded comparable outcomes, we could reject encoding specificity ideas forthwith.

Postman's overall conclusion regarding the discrepancy between his results and ours was that encoding specificity results are obtained only under 'narrowly circumscribed conditions' (Postman 1975a, p. 64). The narrowly circumscribed conditions, according to Postman, were those prevailing in the Thomson and Tulving experiments. They involved (a) the treatment by the subjects of their task at the time of study as one of paired-associate learning, (b) the presence of a certain amount of intra-experimental interference, (c) subjects' lack of knowledge of the associative relation between strong extralist cues and target words, and (d) use of high-frequency words as target items. In Postman's own experiment these potentially restraining influences were not present. Postman did not have his subjects study and recall practice lists before the critical list, as we had done; he also used a mixed-list design, in which only half of the target words were accompanied by cues at study, and only half of them were cued at recall. Under these conditions, Postman argued, subjects are unlikely to adopt a 'pairwise encoding' strategy for target words, as they may have done in our experiments. Nor would subjects' memory performance be adversely affected by the 'sheer novelty' of the extralist cues.

Postman's interpretation is plausible, as long as we compare only the two experiments. When we extend the domain of interest, however, problems with his interpretation become apparent. First, we saw in Chapter 10 that encoding/retrieval interactions of the kind that we observed in the Thomson and Tulving experiment have now been reported in a wide variety of situations, situations in which arguments regarding pairwise contingencies, novelty of extralist cues, and interlist interference seem much less readily applicable. It is not at all clear, for instance, how Postman's interpretation could be applied to context effects in recognition memory (e.g. Geiselman and Glenny 1977; Morris 1978; Pellegrino and Salzberg

1975; Stein 1978; Thomson 1972). Similar difficulties would obtain in inter-preting results of those experiments in which subjects studied single words (e.g. Baker and Santa 1977; Ozier 1978; Roediger and Adelson 1980). We know that extralist retrieval cues can be shown to be very effective follow-ing study of target words presented singly (e.g. Thomson and Tulving 1970; Santa and Lamwers 1974; Postman 1975a). The 'sheer novelty' of extralist cues does not seem to have any adverse effect on recall under these con-ditions, yet crossover interactions between encoding and retrieval condi-tions can be demonstrated as readily following single-item encoding as in other situations.

It is interesting to note that Postman's hypothesis concerning the role of novel cues in contributing to the outcome of an experiment such as Thomson and Tulving's does not contradict the principle of encoding specificity. Indeed, his hypothesis can be regarded as a particular statement of the prin-ciple. The claim that the effectiveness of extralist cues depends on the pres-ence or absence of pairwise contingencies at the time of the study is logically equivalent to a statement that effectiveness of cues depends on the encoding conditions of to-be-remembered items, rather than on the pre-experimental associations between cue and target words. The nature of the memory trace of the to-be-remembered word may well depend on the learner's strategy, guided by his expectations of a particular type of test, as well as by the pro-cessing of the cue and target words together; it is also possible, however, that the informational contents of the cue, or the information extracted from it by the system, does not match the trace information, thus creating a sit-uation in which the number of recall attempts is reduced, as suggested by Postman. These statements are in harmony with encoding specificity ideas.

Since evidence exists now that the critical encoding/retrieval interactions can be obtained not only under the conditions of our original experiments (Tulving and Osler 1968; Thomson and Tulving 1970) but also under a wide variety of other conditions, as indicated by the experiments we reviewed in Chapter 11, the discrepancy between the results of Postman's experiments and ours cannot be interpreted as reflecting the 'narrowly cir-cumscribed conditions' under which the critical interactions manifest them-selves. A more reasonable interpretation is that, for reasons unknown, the intended manipulation of encoding conditions did not work in Postman's experiment. The failure to demonstrate encoding/retrieval interactions in all experiments in which it is attempted is no more damaging to the concept of encoding specificity than are all other experiments in which the inter-actions might have been but in fact were not obtained.

Effective unencoded cues?

There are two fundamentally different ways of thinking about the encoding of a word-event in memory experiments. One is the 'tagging' hypothesis:

information about the word's occurrence in a particular place at a particular time is 'attached to' the word's representation in (permanent) memory. The other one is the episodic-memory hypothesis: an engram of the event is constructed in the episodic-memory system, guided by the perceptual input and related information from the semantic system. The encoding specificity hypothesis fits the episodic-memory view better than the tagging view. The engram must include features compatible with those of the retrieval cue in order for the recollection of the event to be possible, and only appropriate encoding and recoding operations can ensure that particular features are included in the engram. For these reasons, we would expect, according to the encoding specificity hypothesis, that 'unencoded cues' are ineffective, that is, that cue features not 'built into' the trace of the event cannot be useful for retrieval. Several writers have produced data and arguments claiming that, contrary to the encoding specificity hypothesis, unencoded cues are effective (e.g. Anderson and Pichert 1978; Baker and Santa 1977; Kochevar and Fox 1980; Light 1972; Marcel and Steel 1973). Let us sample the evidence and its relevance.

Light (1972) did two experiments to test predictions of the encoding specificity hypothesis. Her subjects studied common words, and were tested for retention in different kinds of tests: recognition; free recall; recognition of, and recall to, extralist cues, consisting of synonyms and homophones of target words.

Both homophones and synonym cues produced levels of recall higher than those observed under the free-recall conditions. Light argued that as these cues had not been present at the time of study and were first shown to the subjects only at retrieval, the results did not support the encoding specificity hypothesis. She interpreted her data in terms of a version of the generation/recognition theory. If it were known that relevant features of cues are not encoded as a part of the trace of the event, then the finding that the cues are nevertheless effective would be devastating for the encoding specificity hypothesis. The problem is that the constituent features of traces are not known. Given a target word such as HARE, how do we know whether its trace has features in common with the synonym cue *rabbit* or the homophone cue *hair* that Light used? Light tried to get round the problem by asking her subjects whether they had become aware of the fact that the target words were homophonic, but subjects' introspections would provide reliable evidence about the nature of encoding only if the rememberers were consciously aware of the process. We do not know it, nor does it seem a reasonable assumption. Light found, too, that although homophone cues were more effective for subjects who said that they had been aware of the nature of the list than for subjects who said they were unaware, but even for the latter group the homophone cues facilitated retrieval.

The implications of Light's data for the encoding specificity hypothesis, therefore, depend on an assumption. If we assume that the features of cues useful for retrieval were not encoded, the results deny the hypothesis; if we assume that they were, the results support the hypothesis. Making the former assumption, and accepting its implications, is tantamount to *assuming* that the encoding specificity hypothesis is wrong. On the other hand, making the latter assumption, and adopting its consequences, does not do much for the hypothesis, since the same outcome can be explained in other ways as well. Encoding experiments alone, or retrieval experiments alone, as we discussed the matter earlier (p. 220), do not provide critical evidence for the encoding specificity ideas.

Light admitted the possibility (Light 1972, pp. 261–2) that specific encoding may be necessary for the effectiveness of retrieval cues in some situations but not in others. This is the kind of thinking that we should avoid as long as it is not dictated by empirical facts. Why should we assume that the encoding specificity hypothesis is true in remembering some events but not others, if there is no logical inconsistency between the hypothesis and the data? The fact that some data can be explained without invoking encoding specificity is immaterial, as long as these data do not rule out encoding specificity. What do we gain by adopting two different explanations if a single one will do?

Let us consider another example of the effectiveness of 'unencoded cues'. The illustrative data and conclusions come from two of the three experiments reported by Baker and Santa (1977). One of these experiments was discussed earlier in the book (p. 228), and its data were summarized in Table 11.4. It demonstrated an interaction between encoding and retrieval conditions: following one type of encoding, strong normative associates of target words given as extralist cues produced a higher level of recall than that obtained in free recall, following another encoding condition there was no difference. In Baker and Santa's first experiment, one encoding condition consisted of the presentation of target words in the presence of 'weak' normative associates, whereas in the second encoding condition, the same pairs of words were embedded in sentences. The two retrieval conditions, crossed with the encoding conditions, consisted of (a) free recall, and (b) cued recall with strong extralist associates as cues. The results of the experiment showed an interaction between encoding and retrieval conditions: free recall of target words was the same in the two conditions of encoding, and the extralist cues facilitated recall, but to a larger extent in the pairwise encoding condition than in the sentence-encoding condition.

When the results of Baker and Santa's two experiments are taken together, they describe a pattern that, according to the logic of encoding/retrieval paradigm, provides strong support for encoding specificity. Baker and Santa, too, concluded that their results 'provide support for differences in cue effectiveness depending on the goodness of the initial context' (p. 312). Although one of their findings was 'consistent with the encoding-specificity interpretation' (p. 311), by and large, Baker and Santa thought, their results could not be interpreted in terms of encoding specificity. First, the finding that in several cases cued recall with extralist cues produced higher recall than that observed under conditions of free recall could not be attributed to cue inclusion at the time of encoding, because subjects did not report using the strategy of generating associates to the target words at the time of study. Second, extralist cues were found to be effective in the first experiment following encoding of target words under conditions similar to those in Thomson and Tulving's (1970) experiments, conditions under which subjects would not be expected to encode the targets with respect to strong cues. The effectiveness of extralist cues under these conditions, therefore, could not be attributed to the inclusion of relevant cue features into memory traces at the time of study.

Baker and Santa rejected the encoding specificity hypothesis on the basis of comparisons of free and cued recall; they took into account only the results of various retrieval components of their complete encoding/retrieval experiments. Rejection of the hypothesis under these conditions, as we have already seen, reduces to the acceptance of the assumption that cue inclusion had not occurred at encoding. This assumption is no more nor less valid than the assumption that cue inclusion had occurred. Arguing about conflicting assumptions does not constitute a good way of settling disputes. A better way would be to look at the whole pattern of data and provide an interpretation of the obtained encoding/retrieval interactions. By doing so, and by invoking the principle of parsimony, the encoding specificity hypothesis becomes more attractive than the idea that sometimes specific encoding is necessary and sometimes not for the effectiveness of cues.

Baker and Santa's attitude towards encoding specificity ideas exhibited in their paper seems to be curiously ambivalent. On the one hand they observe that, for instance, 'a well integrated context seriously restricts the usefulness of alternate retrieval methods' (p. 311) a statement that could well have originated in Toronto, yet they claim that 'non-encoded retrieval strategies can be highly effective in improving recall' (p. 313). There is, of course, no law that says that everything we do has to be governed by the principle of parsimony; indeed, it would not be difficult to think of situations in which the principle becomes Procrustes' bed. Therefore, if someone wishes to construct a theory of memory according to which encoding specificity holds sometimes and does not hold at others, or in some situations and not in others, we should listen to him as we listen to anyone with ideas pertinent to the object of common interest. But since we are all agreed that 'it is impossible to know how the subject is encoding the to-be-remembered words when they are presented' (Light 1972, p. 255), 'it is impossible to know precisely what is or is not encoded at time of study' (Baker and Santa 1977, p. 308), 'the mere physical presence or absence of a cue does not *guarantee* that it will or will not be encoded' (Solso 1973, p. 28), and that we can only expect to be able to influence but not determine encoding processes, as I have suggested (p. 250), it would be interesting to hear from the critics of encoding specificity ideas why some assumptions about how subjects encode material are better than others, and why we should want to reject some hypotheses and accept others on the strength of these assumptions.

Ineffective encoded cues?

The encoding specificity hypothesis does not claim that cue/target similarity or compatibility is a sufficient condition for retrieval; it claims that some such similarity or compatibility is necessary for successful ecphory. Nevertheless, when, as far as we know, other conditions necessary for retrieval are met—in experiments where the subjects are under instructions to use retrieval cues to recall material studied earlier—we would expect the encoded cues to be effective. One way of casting doubt on the encoding specificity ideas, therefore, is to show that encoded cues are ineffective. The reference paper here is one by Humphreys and Galbraith (1975).

If the reader should happen to take a look at the abstract of the Humphreys and Galbraith paper, he may wonder why I wish to deal with it under the heading of the present section. Humphreys and Galbraith say that 'strong pre-experimental associates were effective retrieval cues even when encoding conditions were not conducive to the establishment of a target-cue association' (p. 702). This surely sounds like yet another claim for the effectiveness of unencoded cues. It suggests that I should have classified Humphreys and Galbraith's experiment with those discussed in the previous section. The apparent discrepancy between Humphreys and Galbraith's own conclusion and my interpretation of their experiment as demonstrating the ineffectiveness of encoded cues represents another instance of a familiar phenomenon: one and the same set of data can be described in different ways without necessarily violating any principles of logic.

Humphreys and Galbraith were interested in examining the tenability of encoding specificity ideas in a situation in which the to-be-remembered words are presented for study in the absence of any experimentally manipulated context. Would cues encoded at the time of study be effective and those not encoded not? To answer this question, one would compare the effectiveness of two kinds of extralist cues, those that were encoded, or were more likely to be encoded, and those that were not encoded, or were less likely to be encoded, at the time of study. Humphreys and Galbraith's general idea was this. When a subject studies a word, such as CHAIR, he makes implicit associative responses to it, for instance 'table', 'sit', 'furniture', and so on. These implicit associations can be regarded as a part of the encoding of the to-be-remembered word CHAIR, when subsequently presented as retrieval cues, they should be effective by the principle of encoding specificity. Since the to-be-remembered word CHAIR is unlikely to elicit words such as 'house', 'run', 'machinery', and so on, as implicit associates, these cues should be ineffective as retrieval cues.

Humphreys and Galbraith did not make this kind of an obvious comparison. It is not clear why not. Perhaps it was too simple and straightforward. Among other things, in this experiment the nominal identity of the to-be-remembered words could have been held constant, unlike in the experiment that they actually did, in which the to-be-remembered materials were confounded with retrieval cues. This confounding makes evaluation of their results more difficult, therefore more challenging, therefore more fun.

Humphreys and Galbraith took as their starting point the existence of asymmetrical free-association pairs of words. These are pairs in which one member is frequently given as a primary associate to the second, but the second is seldom given as a primary associate to the first. Examples of such pairs are EATING and FOOD, EAGLE and BIRD, and TOBACCO and SMOKE. If we call the first member of each pair A and the second member B, we can say that there is a strong association from A to B, but only a weak association from B to A. For instance, the word SMOKE is given as a response to the stimulus word *tobacco* approximately 50 per cent of the time in the norms; the word TOBACCO, on the other hand, is hardly ever given as a response to the stimulus word *smoke*. Humphreys and Galbraith used 20 such asymmetrical pairs as a source of their to-be-remembered words and cues. For the whole set of 20 pairs, the mean normative associative strength from A to B was 39 per cent, whereas the same mean strength from B to A was less than 3 per cent.

Humphreys and Galbraith did three experiments; we shall consider only the second, which is most relevant to the critique of encoding specificity ideas. There were two different encoding conditions, defined in terms of the kind of word comprising the study list. In one condition the list consisted of the A words from the asymmetrical pairs, and in the other, of the B words. In both study conditions, the to-be-remembered words were presented one at a time, and the subjects were told to study and remember the words for a subsequent (unspecified) test. The two encoding conditions were crossed with two retrieval conditions: (a) free recall, and (b) cued recall with extralist cues. With A words as targets, the (extralist) cues were the B words; with the B words as targets, the cues were the A words. Different groups of subjects were assigned to the four experimental conditions.

If we assume, as Humphreys and Galbraith did, that implicit associative responses made to to-be-remembered words can be inferred from the free-association norms, we have the makings of a very clever experiment here.

Not only would the experiment test the validity of the encoding specificity hypothesis, but it would also contrast it with the generation/recognition theory, since the two make contrary predictions for the outcome of the experiment. Thus, we have here the potential of a rare state of affairs in our science in which rival ideas lead to sharply distinguishable predictions. According to the encoding specificity hypothesis, B words (e.g. *bird*) should be effective cues for A words as targets (e.g. EAGLE), because they are highly likely to occur as implicit associates to, and hence to be included in the traces of, A words at the time of study. On the other hand, A words (e.g. *eagle*) should be ineffective cues for B words as targets (e.g. BIRD), because of the low probability that A words are included in the traces of B words at study. The generation/recognition theory, however, makes exactly the opposite prediction. A words should be effective cues for B words as targets, because of strong pre-experimental associations that exist from A to B, thus guaranteeing a high probability of implicit generation of the target words at the time of retrieval. On the other hand, B words should be ineffective cues for A words as targets, because of the absence of a pre-experimental association from B to A, and the consequent low probability that B words would be generated, and recognized, at retrieval.

Table 12.1

Probabilities of recall in Humphreys and Galbraith's (1975) Exp. 2

Target words	Retrieval condition Free recall	Cued Recall
A	0.49	0.43
B	0.53	0.71

The results of the experiment are summarized in Table 12.1. The pattern of data describes an interaction between target words and retrieval conditions: with A words as targets, there was little difference between free and cued recall; with B words as targets, however, cued recall (0.71) was substantially higher than free recall (0.53). These data are very much what one would expect on the basis of the generation/recognition theory, and contrary to those expected on the basis of the encoding specificity hypothesis. The pattern of data, and some additional correlational analyses, led Humphreys and Galbraith to conclude that 'the presence of an association from the cue to the target is the most important determinant of the effectiveness of an extralist cue, and when such an association is present the cue can be effective even when the strength of the association from the target to the cue is near zero' (p. 709).

There is a problem here, however. The pattern of data is in keeping with the generation/recognition theory and contrary to the encoding specificity hypothesis *only if* the critical assumption about how singly presented study-list words are encoded is valid. Humphreys and Galbraith are aware of the crucial role played by the assumption. They explicitly state that their conclusion is damaging to the encoding specificity principle if it is assumed 'that the absence of a pre-experimental association from the target to the cue implies that the encoding of the target will not specify the target's relationship to the cue' (p. 709). Thus, the overall picture that emerges from the experiment is one that we have already seen: experimental data are contrary to the encoding specificity ideas, if we are willing to solve the problem of the manner in which a word is encoded by conjecture rather than experiment.

When we test experimental hypotheses by means of findings that have to be interpreted in light of critical assumptions, it matters little how reasonable or unreasonable, plausible or implausible, the assumptions seem to be on intuitive grounds. Humphreys and Galbraith's assumption may appear to be close to self-evident truth to some students of memory: why should we resist the idea that implicit associative responses made to to-be-remembered words reflect the normative data on explicit associations? The problem is that when we play the game in terms of assumptions, one can always respond to this question with another one: why *should* we imagine that the subject in a memory experiment, faced with a word among many others in a list, explicitly or implicitly, deliberately or unwittingly, overtly or covertly generates his personal associative hierarchy of the word, or a part thereof? Perhaps he does not. Indeed, the assumption does not make intuitive sense to everyone. Baker and Santa 1977, p. 311) expressed their opinion that the 'assumption that subjects normally encode with respect to high associates' is 'unlikely'.

We already know that a better method than argument is experiment. The question about the tenability of Humphreys and Galbraith's critical assumption was posed, and relevant data provided, by Ley (1977) in a simple but imaginative modification of Humphreys and Galbraith's experiment. Ley did two experiments. The first one was an exact replication of Humphreys and Galbraith's experiment. It produced a pattern of data that was very similar to that obtained by Humphreys and Galbraith, with all their conclusions confirmed. Ley's second experiment was another replication, with one crucial difference: at the time of study, the subjects were instructed to implicitly generate associations to each target word as it appeared in the list. The logic of this manipulation was straightforward. If subjects in Humphreys and Galbraith's experiments do what the critical assumption says that they do—implicitly generate many B words while studing A words, but generate few A words when studing B words—and if the observed levels of recall in different experimental conditions reflect the consequences of such encoding, then explicit instructions to implicitly generate free associations would be expected to leave the results

Table 12.2
Probabilities of recall in Ley's (1977) Exp. 2

Target words	Retrieval condition	
	Free recall	Cued recall
A	0.42	0.62
B	0.50	0.64

unchanged. Telling subjects to do something that they do anyhow should not change anything very much. If, on the other hand, instructions for implicit generation of free associations introduced processes into the situation that otherwise were absent, the outcome of the experiment would be expected to be different.

The results of Ley's Experiment 2 are presented in Table 12.2. The interaction between types of target words and retrieval conditions observed by Humphreys and Galbraith, and by Ley in his original replication, is no longer present. Under the changed conditions, cued recall is higher than free recall for both A and B words as targets.

These data could be discussed at length, but for our present purposes only two conclusions are relevant. First, it looks as if Humphreys and Galbraith's critical assumption about the nature of encoding processes in their experiment was wrong. At least it is not immediately obvious how the assumption can be reconciled with the results of Ley's two experiments. Second, the results of Ley's second experiment seem to fit the encoding specificity ideas better than the generation/recognition theory: meaningful processing of to-be-remembered words enhances the effectiveness of semantically related extralist cues, whereas large differences in the strength of pre-experimental associations between cues and targets were uncorrelated with the effectiveness of cues.

Circularity and generality

Some critics have faulted encoding specificity ideas for circularity of reasoning inherent in them (e.g. Kochevar and Fox 1980; Santa and Lamwers 1974; Solso 1974). The problem, as seen by the critics, is exemplified in the following statement; 'If a cue was effective in memory retrieval, then one could infer it was encoded; if a cue was not effective, then it was not encoded. The logic of this theorization is 'heads I win, tails you lose' and is of dubious worth in the history of psychology. We might ask how long scientists will puzzle over questions with no answers' (Solso 1974, p. 28).

It is true that we use the encoding specificity principle in making inferences about the properties of memory traces on the basis of observed effectiveness of retrieval cues. But the idea does not constitute a revolutionary departure from the methods that have been used by psychologists for a long time. The strength of habits, associations, and memory traces has been inferred from observed measures of performance throughout the history of our discipline; the logic used has been the same as the one we have relied on in applying the encoding specificity principle. If this logic entails 'circular reasoning', so be it. Until such time that someone steps forth with a non-circular' method of describing and measuring entities and constructs that are not directly observable, there is not much else we can do but rely on 'circular reasoning'.

I have sometimes been puzzled as to why encoding specificity has been singled out for special attention by students of memory who have misgivings about the usefulness of 'circular reasoning'. Inferences of the kind that we make on the basis of effectiveness of retrieval cues have been made on the basis of other techniques as well. Gordon Bower and I identified and discussed 11 different methods that have been used to describe the nature and properties of stored information (Tulving and Bower 1974). The method of retrieval cueing, incorporating the encoding specificity principle, was only one of the 11 methods. As far as I know, the other methods have not been criticized for circularity of reasoning. For instance, the method of attribute shifts, originated and extensively studied by Wickens (1970, 1972) has been thought by many to be a useful tool for studying the nature of memory traces. Wickens' logic is very much the same as that by which we relate effectiveness of retrieval cues to characteristics of stored information: if the shift of a particular dimension of the material on the critical trial results in the 'release from proactive inhibition', then that dimension is assumed to have been encoded; if not, then not. The method of attribute shifts is no more perfect than many others, including retrieval cueing, and its shortcomings have been discussed by others (e.g. Tulving and Bower 1974; Underwood 1972), but no one has questioned its usefulness because of circularity of reasoning. Why not?

I would agree with the criticism of circular reasoning if the following state of affairs were true. We ask a question; 'Why is retrieval cue X effective in retrieving the event E?'. And we answer the question in terms of assumed properties of the trace of the event: 'The cue is effective because some of its features are represented in trace T of the event'. But, we may further ask, 'How do we know that trace T contains features of cue X?'. And we answer, 'It is simple; we know, because cue X is effective in retrieving event E'. Thus, we would have to worry about circularity of reasoning, if we explained cue effectiveness by assuming certain properties of memory traces, and if, at the same time, we justified our assumption about the trace properties in terms of observed effectiveness of retrieval cues.

But we can get out of the circle by doing what already has been done in many experiments: we can manipulate properties of memory traces by varying antecedent conditions, such as the events to be remembered, or the way in which they are encoded. It is true that we can never know or determine exactly what information has been encoded into the trace, but we certainly can influence, and make informed guesses about, the encoding in a systematic manner. We have reasonably good ideas in many situations about cues that are, and cues that are not likely to be effective, depending upon our (incomplete) knowledge of the properties of the memory trace. In many cases, the observed effectiveness or lack of effectiveness of retrieval cues make good sense in terms of what we know about events, their encoding, and their compatibility with cues at the time of retrieval. In other cases, however, they do not. We either have no reasons for particular expectations, or find that our expectations are contradicted by data. It is under these conditions that we invoke the principle of encoding specificity to make sense of what we have observed. But when we do so, we do not engage in circular reasoning; we extrapolate from what is known to what is unknown.

Extrapolation is always a hazardous business, and one has to be continuously on guard for errors that one can readily commit when playing the game. But what are the alternatives to extrapolation? If we find that a particular retrieval cue is not effective when we expected it to be, or we find that a cue is effective in a situation in which we had no prior reason for believing one thing or another, what else can we do if we do not wish to rely on the encoding specificity principle? It is always very easy to come up with a particular ad hoc explanation for any given observation of this sort, but how satisfying or useful is the piling up of such *ad hoc* explanations likely to be? Do we pretend that there are no general laws that govern remembering, even at a high level of abstraction, and that we must be forever satisfied with a large number of unrelated explanations of specific phenomena?

I think that at some, as yet undetermined, level of abstraction the encoding specificity principle holds for all phenomena of episodic memory in the sense that there are no exceptions to it. It probably also holds for semantic memory; Bransford *et al.* (1979), as we saw earlier (p. 235), have extended the same idea to all learning and memory under the name of transfer appropriate processing. The general validity of the encoding specificity principle is suggested by the wide diversity of conditions under which the critical encoding/retrieval interactions have been observed, as we saw in Chapter 11. The postulated generality implies that such interactions could be demonstrated with all kinds of rememberers, to-be-remembered events, encoding operations, and retrieval information, in appropriately controlled and sufficiently sensitive experiments. This claim, of course, does not mean that every time we manipulate encoding and retrieval conditions simultaneously in an experiment we must obtain a crossover interaction; it means that the finding of such interactions is not limited to a small subset of possible memory situations.

We have already seen that some theorists have questioned the generality of encoding specificity. Postman (1975a), for instance, published a paper under the title of 'Tests of the generality of the principle of encoding specificity', and concluded in it that the phenomena of encoding specificity 'appear to have limited generality' (p. 663). Many experimental results speaking to the issue, results from the experiments we sampled in Chapter 11, were not yet known when Postman drew this conclusion, and it is possible that he would temper it now, or change it altogether. It should also be noted that if we distinguish between the generality of encoding specificity phenomena and the generality of the encoding specificity principle, Postman's conclusion is justifiable even today: many experiments have been conducted and can be conducted whose results do not represent any 'phenomena of encoding specificity'. But this fact, in and of itself, does not mean that the encoding specificity principle does not hold generally: no experiments have yet been done whose results are inconsistent with the principle. The claim for the generality of the principle is that no such experiments can ever be done.

For reasons that I will be happy to leave to sociologists or psychologists of science to figure out, we find students of memory in our midst who are not just sceptical about the possibility of finding general laws or principles that apply to the workings of the mind but who also seem to believe that the search for such generalities is not a proper task for our science. Consider the following illustrative attitudes.

Mandler (1979), discussing the encoding specificity principle, pointed out that it is not always possible to know what has been encoded, and whether or not the cues provided by the experimenter are going to be effective in a particular situation. As we have seen, comparable thoughts have been expressed by many others, and it is difficult to imagine that anyone would disagree with them. But then Mandler went on to say that, 'Because ... a definition of encoding and cueing in terms of presentation by the experimenter is inadequate, we must abandon the promised land of simple principles and return to the complexities of the human mind' (p. 305).

Similar sentiments have also been expressed by Baddeley in his evaluation of Craik and Lockhart's (1972) levels-of-processing approach to the study of memory (Baddeley 1978, 1979). He has termed the search for global principles 'unfortunate' (Baddeley 1979, p. 355), and suggested 'that the most fruitful way to extend our understanding of human memory is not to search for broader generalizations and 'principles', but is rather to develop ways of separating out and analyzing more deeply the complex underlying processes' (Baddeley 1978, p. 150).

Baddeley's, and perhaps others', reservations about the usefulness of general principles is at least partly based on the idea that they are ultimately untestable. But lack of testability does not represent sufficient grounds for the attitudes expressed. There are two things wrong with the idea. First, many perfectly respectable, and fundamentally significant, scientific ideas have been untestable, at least at the time when they were first proposed. For instance, there was no way of testing that part of Newton's first law of motion that says that every material body persists in uniform, unaccelerated motion in a straight line, if and only if it is not acted upon by an unbalanced external force. How would you have created conditions, back in the seventeenth century, where a body was moving subject to no external force? Or consider Darwin's theory of natural selection. It was a theory that guided his observations, and his selection of facts. But in what sense was it testable?

With respect to Newton's first law of motion, it may be of some interest to remind the reader that its essence was that it permitted a test for the *presence* of an unbalanced force. Such presence had to be assumed whenever it was observed that a moving body deviated from a straight line or accelerated in any way. Yet the law in itself did not help anyone to discover either the source of the force or its magnitude (Holton and Brush 1973, p. 116). In connection with Darwin's theory of selection, it may be useful to remind the reader that it was vigorously criticized by many laymen and scientists, since it did not represent the 'true Baconian' method. Some critics said that they would believe the theory if a change in species took place before their very eyes, others wanted to see all the links in the chain, yet others rejected Darwin's idea of struggle for existence on the basis of the obvious fact that peace and harmony was the rule of nature (Hardin 1961, p. 103).

The second fact overlooked by those resisting general principles in the science of memory is that an 'untestable' principle is not the same thing as a principle for which there is no empirical support. Many facts supported Newton's first law of motion, and a large number of observations made by Darwin were consistent with his theory. On a somewhat less lofty level of thought and analysis, we can also point to many findings from experiments that are in harmony with principles such as encoding specificity and levels of processing.

13
Recognition failure

Thought experiments can save a lot of time while teaching us valuable lessons. Consider, for instance, the following one. The subjects in the experiment are four large groups of literate people who have a perfect mastery of the English language, who have memorized the selected works of Sir Walter Scott, who are highly motivated to participate in the experiment, and who have essentially unlimited time for it.

The purpose of the experiment is to find out how readily a particular word can be 'retrieved' from memory. In our experiment the target word happens to be PONIARD, but the experiment could be replicated many times with different target words. 'Retrieval' of the target word takes place under different conditions in the four groups. In two groups, the task is to 'recall', in the other two to 'recognize' the target word. Subjects in one recall group are given instructions to produce all the English words they know, whereas in the other recall group their task is to produce all the words in the collected works of Sir Walter Scott. In the first recognition group, subjects are asked whether the word PONIARD is an English word, whereas in the second recognition group, they are asked whether the word PONIARD occurs anywhere in the collected works of Sir Walter Scott.

The thought experiment does not give us the numerical data of retrieval in the four conditions, but it does yield a pattern of data. And patterns, as we have seen, frequently are much more important than absolute levels of memory performance. The results of our thought experiment show that people can recognize the word PONIARD as an English word more readily than they can recall it, but they can recall it more readily than they can recognize it when the subjects have to make the judgment about the word's presence in a particular corpus. This crossover interaction between tasks and reference categories of target words is important in that it reminds us that whether recall is higher than recognition or recognition higher than recall depends on conditions: no absolute generalization is possible. If the thought experiment had been done, say, in 1875—and I know of no reason why it could not have been done then—it might have changed the history of our science, and kept successive generations of students of memory from thinking unproductive thoughts about the relation between recall and recognition.

In case the reader's intuitions do not coincide with those of other people conducting this particular thought experiment, he may wish to read a report of an experiment by Lachman and Field (1965) that is rather similar to one-half of our thought experiment, the half concerning the collected works of Sir Walter Scott. Lachman and Field's subjects learned long prose passages over and over again until they could reproduce the passages perfectly, that is, until their recall of all the words in the passages was perfect. However, when the subjects were tested for recognition of individual words from the passages, they frequently failed to identify words from the passages as such. The only problem with the Lachman and Field experiment may have been that they did not leave their subjects too much time for the making of recognition judgments (only 1.5 seconds per word) and the truly sceptical reader, therefore, is still in a position to reject the results of the experiment as 'artifactual'. In that case I recommend that he do a real experiment along the lines suggested. Perhaps teaching the subjects just one of Sir Walter Scott's short stories, say, *The Two Drovers*, and then giving them a recognition test that includes PONIARD as one of the test items. Subjects who fail to identify it as a word from the story would then be given the following passage and asked to fill in the blank: 'Harry Wakefield fell and expired with a single groan. His assassin next seized the bailiff by the collar, and offered the bloody _____ to his throat, whilst dread and surprise rendered the man incapable of defence'. With the finding that subjects who could not identify PONIARD as an 'old' word can now insert it into the blank, the fact that recall can succeed where recognition failed is demonstrated.

In this chapter we will consider experimental evidence and theoretical speculation concerning the phenomenon of recognition failure of recall-able words. Like the encoding/retrieval interactions we discussed in the last chapter, the phenomenon of recognition failure can be treated as one of the many applications of GAPS to the understanding of remembering of word-events. We can think of the fact that a person cannot recognize a studied item but can reproduce its name as a puzzle, and we can then try to solve the puzzle within the framework of GAPS. As it turns out, no such solution exists as yet, but its pursuit has enjoyed some success and has thrown new light on the workings of memory.

The phenomenon

The phenomenon of recognition failure of recallable words is revealed in two kinds of experimental findings. The first is the superiority of recall over recognition, the second, existence of items that cannot be recognized but can be recalled. The first fact necessarily entails the second, whereas the second may be true even if the first one is not (Wiseman and Tulving 1976). Because of my penchant for generality, at least in this book, we will define the phenomenon in terms of the second kind of experimental fact. Recognition failure is the phenomenon that previously studied items cannot be identified as 'old' although their names can be reproduced to other cues.

Lest there be any misunderstanding about what it means to say that an item is not recognized but the *same* item is recalled, a few words about the nature of identity are in order. The words are borrowed from Hollingworth (1928), they express thoughts that have been accepted by scientists before and after Hollingworth's time. He put the matter as follows:

> Identity is only persistence in or membership in a class. A class is a temporally extended event or series which we name. Hereafter therefore when we say the same event, the same stimulus, the same response, it must be understood that we are not implying that events have ghosts which reappear in Nature. For us 'the same event' can mean only 'another event in a given class' . . . We thus follow the convenient linguistic custom which calls two events 'the same' if they are, for a given purpose, indiscriminable, or if one can be substituted for the other without changing the practical character of the result (Hollingworth 1928, p. 80).

Scattered examples of experimental findings showing recall to be higher than recognition had been reported in the literature before the phenomenon of recognition failure became a full object of theoretical attention. Postman, Jenkins, and Postman (1948); Bahrick and Bahrick (1964); Lachman and Field (1965); and Bruce and Cofer (1967), among others, had described data showing higher levels of performance under the conditions of recall than those of recognition. Nobody made much fuss about these findings, however, presumably because they could always be explained in terms of extant knowledge. Postman *et al.* (1948), for instance, had their subjects memorize nonsense syllables and then tested them twice, once for free recall and once for forced-choice recognition. Testing was done in both of two possible orders: recall followed by recognition, and recognition followed by recall. Among other things, Postman *et al.* found that a certain proportion of to-be-remembered items that subjects could recall were not correctly identified as 'old' in the recognition test. The authors did not discuss this finding in any form, however. They may have thought that the existence of recallable but unrecognizable items in the subjects. repertoire reflected unreliability of measurement, or some other random fluctuation of the associative strength of items over time.

I became interested in comparing recall and recognition, with a view to finding out whether recall could be shown to be 'easier' than recognition under certain conditions, about the time that I was mulling over the implications of Tulving and Pearlstone's (1966) experiment, as discussed earlier (p. 201). If recall depended not only on availability of information but also on its accessibility through certain cues, it seemed natural to think of 'old' test items in recognition-memory situations as retrieval cues, serving the same role that category names had served in the cued-recall conditions in the Tulving and Pearlstone experiment. But given the wide range of effectiveness of different kinds of cues—an assumption that bordered on self-evident truth—it seemed reasonable to entertain the thought that other retrieval cues might be more effective than the 'old' test items in recognition tests. But what kinds of 'other' cues might be more effective than 'copy' cues, and under what conditions could this difference be demonstrated?

My research assistant Shirley Osler and I spent some time trying to figure out ways of experimentally demonstrating superiority of some 'other' cues over copy cues under conditions where theoretically uninteresting 'artifactual' explanations could be precluded. We had several 'brilliant' ideas that were shattered by contact with data, but after several false starts we managed to create two different situations in which we could show that recall was higher than recognition.

In one experiment, we presented to subjects lists of five-letter words, ostensibly for free recall. In fact we tested only one-half of the subjects under free-recall conditions. These subjects remembered approximately 50 per cent of the words in the list. The other half of the subjects were given, at the time of test, letter bigrams that had occurred in the study list as parts of the to-be-remembered words, mixed them up with 'new' bigrams that had not appeared in the study list, and asked subjects for the recognition of the 'old' bigrams. For instance, for the study-list words of RIVER and STEEL, the two-alternative forced-choice recognition test would include test pairs of *ve—na* and *te—so*. Subjects had 'seen' *ve* and *te*, but neither *na* nor *so* had been a part of any of the study-list words. The mean hit rate in this test was 58 per cent, only slightly better than chance. Corrected for guessing, the hit rates was 16 per cent, a figure comparing rather unfavorably with the 50 per cent in free recall. Thus, for letter bigrams embedded in meaningful words, recall could easily be shown to be higher than recognition.

In the other experiment, subjects learned a list of 48 paired words (A–B pairs) to a criterion of two perfect trials, and were then tested for the recognition of the B members of all pairs. The A and B members were common monosyllabic English words, which, when put together, formed another meaningful unit, a compound word or an idiom, for example, *tooth*—ACHE, *air*—PORT, *floor*—SHOW, *home*—SICK. Subjects took, on the average, seven trials to reach the criterion. They were then given a sheet of paper on which were printed, in alphabetical order, 96 words: 48 B members of learned pairs and 48 comparable 'new' words. They were asked to check off all the words they had just learned. They did it readily for 90 per cent of the learned words, but failed to identify 10 per cent of the old words. Although this result was not quite as striking as that in the first experiment, we thought we had succeeded in demonstrating that under certain conditions even meaningful words that could be recalled could not be recognized, under conditions where some of the 'obvious' interpretations of the findings, such as insufficient time for recognition (Lachman and Field 1965) or extreme degrees of similarity between old and new test items (Bahrick and Bahrick 1965) did not apply.

Predictions and speculations

To share our newly found secrets about human memory with the rest of the world, I was going to present a paper at the forthcoming (1967) meeting of the Psychonomic Society. Before the meeting, I sent a letter to 16 good friends and colleagues of mine, all prominent researchers in the field of verbal learning and memory. In it I said that I was planning to give a paper at the next meeting of the Society, under the title, 'When is recall higher than recognition? I said that I thought I had an answer to the question, and some data in support of it, but because I suspected that the answer might appear obvious or trivial to many people, I was writing to them to ask what kind of an answer they would give to the question in the title of my paper.

Four of my respondents explicitly mentioned the generation/recognition idea and pointed out that under the assumptions of that theory recall could *not* be higher than recognition. A number of others speculated about the possibility that the typical result—recognition easier than recall—might be reversed in situations in which targets and distractors are extremely similar to one another.

One of my friends with a good grapevine had apparently gotten wind of our first experiment—recognition of bigrams embedded in study-list words. He wrote as follows: 'It is indeed a trivial demonstration. I assume that your talk at Psychonomics will describe an experiment in which you give subjects lists of words to learn, test them for the recall of those words, and also test them for the recognition of isolated letter segments pulled from those words. Recognition for the letter segments will be bad, very bad. The problem with this demonstration is that the letter segments never got stored as segments. Hence, they cannot be recognized. You will claim that if the word was read and learned properly, then, clearly all of the parts of the word must also have been read and learned. Rubbish. However, your talk is very clearly within the proper spirit of Psychonomic Society. Everybody will yell and scream that it is trivial, you will smile and say, then why has not any one of my friends been able to think of it (by themselves), and the end result will be that you will evoke more comment, dissension, and thought than any of the other papers. And that is the way it ought to be'.

Another respondent, who had not heard about the experiment with bigrams embedded in words, nevertheless provided an answer to the question that was perfectly correct in principle. He said that one situation in which recall scores should be better than recognition scores is one 'where the thing to be recognized is not directly coded in learning'. As an example, he gave a situation in which the recall of the pattern 'MAN' would be compared with the recognition of the same pattern from among MAN, man, Man, etc. The reader may remember our brief discussion (p. 234) of an experiment by Stein (1978) that incorporated an idea very similar to the one that my respondent came up with more than ten years earlier. His example, of course, also qualifies as a situation in which the recognition distractors are 'extremely similar' to the target item, but it further includes the thought that the similarity between the target and distractors is a function of how the target was studied, or perceived, or processed when it was originally studied, a thought that was a firm part of the folklore ten years later.

Finally, one of my correspondents hit it right on the nose: 'Recall could be superior to recognition if the conditions of testing are such that the associative context (of learning) is more fully reinstated via recall than by the recognition test. This is best illustrated by a change of associated elements or organized patterns of associated elements. An example would be, say, two short bars from a Bach fugue; I may 'know' the entire piece and be able to produce (recall) it from the beginning, but yet be unable to identify the piece or the location within the piece if I am merely given two short bars of the tune and asked "Does this occur in the piece?". Such a recognition test essentially pulls a piece of the puzzle out of its context, whereas with full recall one generates a context into which the next piece fits.' This may sound like Koffka, or Köhler, or Asch, but in fact my friend is a neo-associationist, a professor at a famous university forty miles south of San Francisco. (The other two whom I directly quoted also live on the west coast. One is a co-author of a classic paper on primary memory published in 1965, the other is well known for his studies on attention, consciousness, and other manifestations of the human mind by means of the chronometric method.)

In many ways the results of my little survey were as interesting as our experimental findings. Although a few of the correspondents saw through my plan or could anticipate it, most of them did not. Since in neither of our two experiments the explanation of recall superiority over recognition would be given in terms of the high degree of similarity between targets and distractors, it seemed appropriate to conclude that the results of our two experiments may have been trivial but not obvious.

It is only fair to point out that the question I posed to my friends was implicitly misleading, at least with respect to the second of our two experiments. The idea of cueing of recall was still rather new in 1967. Consequently, it is quite possible that most of the respondents interpreted the term 'recall' in my query to mean free recall. Had I posed the question in terms of a comparison between recognition and cued recall, many of them might have been able to suggest more appropriate answers.

I wrote up a brief report of our second experiment and published it in *Psychonomic Science*. The question, 'When is recall higher than recognition?' was answered in the last sentence of the paper: 'Recall is higher than recognition whenever retrieval cues present at the recall test are more effective in providing access to stored information than are retrieval cues present at the recognition test' (Tulving 1968b, p. 54). With the wisdom of historical hindsight, it can now be regarded as the opening salvo in our battle against the idea that there are no 'retrieval processes' in recognition, or that 'access' in recognition is automatic: if we talk about cues in both recognition and recall, processes of recall and recognition may be more similar than they are in a conceptual scheme in which cues are used to generate internal copies of to-be-remembered items which serve as input to the much simpler recognition process. The statement that recall is higher than recognition whenever retrieval cues in the recall test are more effective than retrieval cues in the recognition test was only a sort of a 'framework' statement rather than an explanation. It said nothing about why, in our particular experiment, list cues may have been more effective than copy cues. In trying to cope with that problem, I drew the distinction between nominal and functional memory units that had been useful in making sense of the findings in the free-recall literature (Tulving 1968*a*), and ended up with the kind of a 'semantic interpretation' of recognition failure of recallable words: the meaning of the B member (e.g. CRAFT) in the A–B compound (e.g. *air*—CRAFT) may be different from the meaning of the B member presented alone, and to the extent that the two meanings do not coincide, recognition fails even when recall succeeds.

Our 1967/1968 demonstration of recognition failure of recallable words made no impact on the thinking of others, as far as I could tell. Many of the target words in our experiments could be thought of as homographs (e.g. PORT, BALL, GRADE, etc.). The discovery that the learner could say PORT in response to the cue *air* after having learned the pair *air*—PORT, but could not recognize PORT when it was presented alone, among other test items, made perfectly good sense. All that was necessary was the reasonable assumption that sometimes the recognition test item PORT might be interpreted by the subject in the meaning of 'sweet wine', and *that* word had not appeared in the study list. In this sense, the word that the subject was tested with was not recognized, because 'it was never stored'. When I told Walter Kintsch about these results and asked him about their implications for the generation/recognition theory, he told me that since we had done our experiment with 'funny words' the generalizability of our results was quite questionable and the implications for the generation/recognition theory weak. Thus, our data provided no conflict with theory, and the study of memory could proceed normally. It was only the data that Donald Thomson and I reported in 1973 that invalidated the then accepted version of the generation/recognition theory.

The paradigm

The procedure we used in out first serious demonstrations of recognition failure (Tulving and Thomson 1973) was rather complicated. Subsequent research, however, showed that many features included in the design of these experiments were immaterial, and that the phenomenon of recognition failure could be produced in a much simpler experimental arrangement, in what we now refer to as the recognition-failure paradigm.

The paradigm consists of three essential steps: (a) presentation of target words in the context of some other material, (b) recognition test of target words in the absence of the study-list context, and (c) recall of target words in the presence of cues related to the list-context.

Our initial experiments conformed to the paradigm, but they also included a lot of extra baggage. To illustrate let me here briefly summarize the method in our first experiment. Subjects were first given and tested on two set-establishing lists, each consisting of 24 A–B pairs, with B members of pairs designated as targets and A words representing weak normative associates of B words. The third list was the critical list that provided the experimental data of interest. It was presented on a single study trial, at the rate of one pair every three seconds. Following the study phase, subjects were given five successive tests. (a) The first test was a cued-recall test with strong extralist cues, of the kind used in the Thomson and Tulving (1970) experiments. Subjects were given 12 extralist cues, strong associates of 12 target words from the list. They were told that each of the cues was related to one of the target words they had seen in the critical list, and that their task was to write down as many targets as they could beside the appropriate cue words. The mean number of target words recalled on this test was 1.8, or 15 per cent. (b) The second test was again a cued-recall test with strong extralist associates as cues, except that this was given under special 'generate/recall' instructions. The subjects were first given brief instructions about the free-asssociation procedure. Then a new set of 12 extralist cues, corresponding to the 12 remaining target words from the list, were presented. The subjects were told to think of possible associations to each presented stimulus word, and to write down those implicitly generated associations that were the same as the to-be-remembered words from the critical study list. In this test, the subjects got 3.6 words right on the average, or 30 per cent. (c) The third test was what we would now call a 'semantic' free-association test. Subjects were given once more the 24 extralist cues, which they had already seen in the first and second test, and instructed to *write down* up to six free associations to each stimulus word. They generated, on the average, 4.4 response words to each stimulus. These responses included 74 per cent of all the target words from the critical study list. (d) Next, the subjects were asked to look over their free-association responses, and to circle all words that they recognized as target words from the critical study list. The hit rate on this test was 24 per cent. (e) The final test was a cued-recall test with the original list cues. The subjects were given the 24 A members from the A–B pairs from the critical list, and asked to write down the corresponding B members. The mean number of target words recalled on this test was 15.2, or 63 per cent.

The first two tests in the experiment replicated the findings from the Thomson and Tulving (1970) experiment, but the new important result was that cued recall of target words was higher (63 per cent) than recognition of target words (24 per cent) in the subject-generated recognition test, implying that many target words were recalled but not recognized.

It was this outcome of the experiment that defined what we called the phenomenon of recognition failure of recallable words.

The outcome was interesting for at least four reasons: (a) it constituted a natural extension of our earlier findings concerning the effectiveness of retrieval cues, (b) it provided separate estimates of generation and recognition components of the generation/recognition theory, (c) it yielded evidence for great difficulty of recognition in the paradigm, and (d) it was counter-intuitive. We will consider these four findings briefly in turn.

In the Tulving and Osler (1968) experiment, we had found that 'weak' extralist cues were ineffective if they had not been present at study; in the Thomson and Tulving (1970) experiments, strongly associated extralist cues were found to be ineffective following the encoding of target words under condition where targets words were specifically encoded with respect to different cues; the Tulving and Thomson (1973) experiment extended this latter finding to the situation in which the relation between the cue and the target word was that of nominal identity. Thus, across the three experiments, the cue/target relation progressed from weak to strong to identical, whereas the outcome remained the same, namely extremely low effectiveness of cues.

The phenomenon of recognition failure is defined by only the retrieval component of a complete encoding/retrieval experiment: holding encoding conditions constant, we are comparing performance in two retrieval conditions, recognition and list-cued recall. For the finding to provide critical support for the encoding specificity ideas, we must add, in our thoughts, the results of an encoding experiment. In this experiment we measure recognition of target words following two types of encoding—target words presented alone or in the company of 'weak' associates. We know from many experiments that recognition hit rate for a 24-word list of familiar words presented singly, even after intensive interpolated activity, is considerably higher than the hit rate of 0.24 obtained in the Tulving and Thomson (1973) experiment. With this imaginary addition of data, we do have the requisite encoding/retrieval interaction that speaks directly to the encoding specificity ideas. The encoding component of the experiment tells us that the effectiveness of a copy cue, like the effectiveness of other kinds of cues, is highly dependent upon the encoding format of the to-be-remembered word; the retrieval component of the experiment tells us that a low level of performance with copy cues following pairwise encoding of the target words cannot be attributed to the 'weakness' of the trace of the target, as another cue, the list cue, makes possible a much higher level of performance.

We did not incorporate any encoding component into the designs of our 1973 experiments, as we thought that we would not learn anything of importance from the data yielded by these additional experimental conditions.

Since strong extralist associates are quite effective as cues following the presentation of to-be-remembered items one at a time, under conditions where the subject expects a free-recall test (Thomson and Tulving 1970), or under conditions where the extralist cue is simply *added* to the cue complex present at the time of study (Bahrick 1969), it seemed clear that copy cues would also be very effective under these conditions. This is why we did only retrieval components in our 1973 experiments. In retrospect, this may have been a tactical mistake. It is easy to overlook a part of the total pattern of data even when the part is there, as we saw in the discussion of some of the criticisms of the Thomson and Tulving results (pp. 252–8). It is even easier to do so when a part of the total pattern is not there at all, existing only in the form of the results of a thought experiment, however reasonable these results might be. It turns out that a number of experimenters and theorists who have taken an interest in the recognition-failure phenomenon, and have suggested explanations for it, have been concerned only with the retrieval component of the complete design and have neglected the implications of the missing encoding components for their theorizing.

The reactions

Consider now the two stages of retrieval as envisaged by the generation/recognition theory. Our learners were capable of generating 74 per cent of targets in the 'semantic' free-association task. They recognized 24 per cent of those targets as 'old' on their self-generated recognition test. If probability of cued recall is estimated by the probability of generation and probability of recognition as argued by Bahrick (1970), we would expect a cued-recall performance with 'strong' extralist cues to be approximately 18 per cent ($0.74 \times 0.24 = 0.18$). This estimate is roughly comparable to the two levels of cued recall we observed, 15 per cent without any special instructions and 30 per cent with generate/recognize instructions. Thus, in a general sense we replicated Bahrick's (1969, 1970) results showing that the effectiveness of extralist cues corresponds roughly to the product of generation and recognition. Moreover, the level of generation of copies of targets we observed was very much what we might have expected on the basis of free-association norms. From the point of view of generation/recognition theory, therefore, the low levels of recall in response to strong extralist cues observed in both Thomson and Tulving (1970) and in our 1973 experiments were attributable only to the second stage, that of recognition.

The finding of extremely low levels of recognition in the recognition-failure paradigm was surprising, but it did not constitute any evidence against the generation/recognition theory. Indeed, the finding could have been used to explain the Thomson and Tulving (1970) results in terms of the generation/recognition theory: the strong extralist associates were relatively ineffective as cues not because the pairwise presentation of study-list items had interfered with the generating power of strong associates, but because, for whatever reasons, the level of recognition was very low.

It was the addition of a list-cued recall to the sequence of tests—an afterthought we had part-way through our first experiment (Tulving and Thomson 1973)—that provided the critical data for the rejection of the generation/recogniton theory. In that test, subjects did very much better than their low level of recognition would have permitted them to do according to the theory: if only 24 per cent of the targets, whether generated or explicitly presented, can be recognized, there is no way that subjects can do better than 24 per cent in cued recall. Yet, recall in response to list cues was 63 per cent. This meant that many target words could be recalled but not recognized, a state of affairs that was not possible according to the theory. Introduction of additional assumptions, or creation of special mechanisms, could not have gotten around recognition failure of recallable words as an experimental fact. Our results, therefore, spelled an end to the generation/recognition theory.

I mentioned earlier (p. 217) that Bahrick (1979) did not wish his theory (Bahrick 1969, 1970) to apply to retrieval of all kinds, only to retrieval by extralist cues of those words that subjects had failed to recall in the absence of extralist cues. Similar observations have been made by Kochevar and Fox (1980). According to these suggestions, retrieval of words under free-recall conditions is mediated by different processes than those operating in cued recall. The issues here are complex and as yet largely unexplored. John Gardiner and I have some data showing that recognition failure, as defined in the recognition-failure paradigm, occurs to a much smaller extent for words that are retrievable under free-recall conditions than those that are not. Whatever else the implications of this pattern of data, they do suggest that the early versions of generation/recognition theories would not apply to extralist cued recall of words not retrieved in the absence of such cues.

Kintsch (1978), too, has somewhat belatedly tried to question the relevance of our 1973 data for the generation/recognition theories as they existed at that time. He has pointed out that our findings were incompatible with the then extant generation/recognition theories only on the assumption that recall and recognition decision criteria are identical. This assumption, according to Kintsch, was made by generation/recognition theories neither explicitly nor implicitly. If one assumes that decision criteria are more stringent for recognition than they are for the recognition stage in recall, there is no conflict between data and theory.

In arguing against the generation/recognition theory on the basis of our data, it certainly did not occur to us that the theory could be rescued by an assumption such as the one made by Kintsch. We had demonstrated recognition failure not only under Yes/No but also under forced-choice recognition conditions (Tulving and Thomson 1973, Exp. 3). Even if Kintsch's idea had occurred to us, we probably would have been most dubious about its tenability, since it would have required the assumption that the recognition criterion was *higher* in the four-alternative forced-choice recognition test

than in the free-choice cued-recall test. Besides, it is very difficult to experimentally manipulate the criterion in recall, and to the extent that statements
about recall criteria can be made, they represent just inferences from the
data. Finally, apparently very few people thought at the time that recall
scores might be higher than recognition scores in situations in which recall
criteria are lower than recognition criteria. Otherwise someone might have
made a statement of this sort in the literature at the time when the phenomenon of recognition failure and its implications were furiously debated.

Quite apart from the implications of the finding of recognition failure
for the generation/recognition theory, the phenomenon clearly seemed to
be counter-intuitive. In terms of the then current knowledge and assumptions about human memory, it was very difficult to imagine why or how
a typical subject in a memory experiment, a motivated, alert, and intelligent university student, could produce the target word such as QUEEN to
its pair-mate from the study list, *lady*, but not recognize it as a studied
target word when faced with a literal copy of it. One could plausibly argue
that the bigram IV could not be recognized after studying the word RIVER,
because '*it* was not stored'. One could similarly argue that PORT (sweet
wine) would not be recognized after studying *air*–PORT, because *it*, too,
was not stored. But the same kinds of arguments somehow seemed much
less plausible when dealing with word pairs such as *cheese*—GREEN, *whistle*—BALL, *glue*—CHAIR, *grasp*—BABY, *spider*—BIRD, *deep*—SLEEP, all
pairs used in our 1973 experiments.

The counter-intuitive nature of the phenomenon may have been partially
responsible for the resistance that many students of memory displayed to
the finding and its implications, both privately and publicly. John Gardiner
spent a year as a visiting professor in Toronto in 1976–77. Although he was
not doing any research on recognition failure at that time, he became sufficiently intrigued with the phenomenon, being exposed to its discussion
almost every day, to read everything on it that had been published. He was
particularly struck with the sceptical and negative reaction to the phenomenon. Relying on information culled from seven different articles (Light et al.
1975; Martin 1975; Postman 1975a; Rabinowitz, Mandler, and Patterson
1977; Reder, Anderson, and Bjork 1974; Santa and Lamwers 1974, 1976), he
compiled what he called 'A concise digest of critical reactions to recognition failure'. It consisted of direct verbatim quotes from the papers, organized under six sub-headings: (a) the phenomenon does not exist, (b) the
phenomenon does not arise from a fair test for the existence of the phenomenon, (c) the phenomenon is a consequence of the procedure, (d) the
subjects are to blame for the phenomenon, (e) the phenomenon is severely
limited in generality, and (f) the phenomenon is trivial and irrelevant. Under
the first sub-heading, for instance, he placed quotes such as '... Tulving and
Thomson have not demonstrated recognition failure of recallable words'
under the last one were quotes such as, 'A particular item is not recognized,
but is recalled in a subsequent test. This result is hardly surprising . . . .' If Gar-

diner had compiled his list a few years later, he would have been able to add to it claims that the phenomenon is an artefact, and that it is an 'epiphenomenon'.

Scientists in all fields are familiar with the 'three-line strategy' of defence against new facts that do not fit into the existing structure. First, it is wrong; second, it may be true, but it does not mean what it seems to mean; third, it may mean what it seems to mean, but there is nothing new in it, we have known it all along. The strategy has the dual advantage of guaranteeing that undesirable facts do not survive, and that, if they do, they are not undesirable.

Occurrence and magnitude

Recognition failure has now been demonstrated in a large number of experiments. Before I mention some of them, it is useful to distinguish between the fact of occurrence of recognition failure and its magnitude. Just because a learner cannot recognize a studied word now that he can recall later on does not mean that the fact is interesting or theoretically important. If the occurrence of such events is relatively rare, it can be readily 'explained' by assuming fluctuations in the learners' attention or alertness, or some other kind of 'noise' in the system. One can even postulate some random fluctuation, 'waxing and waning', and letting the postulation serve as an explanation of the phenomenon.

These strategies do not work if the effect is large: explanations in terms of variations in attention, 'noise', unreliability of measurement, and fluctuations in trace strength become less plausible if large proportions of items not retrieved on one trial are on the next. Particularly convincing seems to be evidence showing that the overall level of memory performance increases from one test trial to the next, the phenomenon of reminiscence. If such an increase takes place under conditions where one would expect the conditions of retrieval to be less favorable on the second trial (e.g. recall) than on the first (e.g. recognition), it is particularly interesting.

The magnitude of recognition failure can be indexed by the conditional probability of recognition miss given recall, that is, by the ratio between the joint probability of recognition miss and recall, and the overall probability of recall. Thus,

$$p(\overline{Rn}|Rc) = p(\overline{Rn}, Rc)/p(Rc). \tag{13.1}$$

In eqn 13.1, $\overline{Rn}$ and Rc designate recognition misses and recall hits, respectively. This measure of recognition failure was suggested by Watkins and Tulving (1975), and it has been used in almost all recognition-failure experiments. It is a useful measure for two reasons: (a) it is intuitively meaningful, since it directly expresses the proportion of recallable words that cannot be recognized, and (b) as we shall see presently, across a

Table 13.1

Recognition/recall contingency data for the 10 subjects in Tulving and Thomson's (1973) Exp. 1 given both recognition and recall tests

| | Recall | | | |
		Yes	No	Total
	Yes	0.24	0.02	0.26
Recognition	No	0.39	0.35	0.74
	Total	0.63	0.37	

large number of experiments it is highly correlated with recognition hit rate.

As a concrete illustration of the calculation of the recognition failure measure, consider the data tabulated in Table 13.1. These are data for the 10 subjects in Tulving and Thomson's (1973) Experiment I who were given both the recognition and the recall tests. These data, pooled over the 10 subjects, show the overall proportion of words recognized, proportion of words recalled, and the proportions of words in each of the four possible response categories when individual items are scored for both recognition and recall. Table 13.1 shows that the overall level of recognition (hit rate) was 0.26, the overall level of recall 0.63, the proportion of words both recalled and recognized 0.24, the proportion of words recognized but not recalled 0.02, and so on. For the data in Table 13.1, the magnitude of recognition failure, $p(\overline{Rn}|Rc)$, is $0.39/0.63 = 0.62$. Thus, for this set of data, not only is recall higher than recognition, but a large proportion of words subjects could recall were not recognized.

Although the data of theoretical interest are those expressing recognition failure of recallable words, it is usually more convenient to work with the complement of the recognition-failure measure, the conditional probability of recognition hit given recall, $p(Rn|Rc)$. It represents the proportion of recallable words that can be recognized; for the purposes of our present discussion we can refer to it as 'recognition success'. For the data in Table 13.1, recognition success is $0.24/0.63 = 0.38$, the complement of the recognition failure measure of 0.62.

Recognition-failure function

In November 1974, Sandor Wiseman completed the last of the four experiments that were published in an article later on (Wiseman and Tulving 1976). While he was working over the data, he noticed a curiously regular relation between recognition hit rate and recognition failure as defined in eqn 13.1. Recognition failure seemed to be a linearly decreasing function of recognition hit rate. The relation appeared puzzling, since there was no particular reason to expect it. Surely, with the overall recognition level held constant, it would be possible to obtain different amounts of recognition failure, depending upon other conditions of the experiment. Or was it?

We promptly examined the data from all the other. experiments for which recognition/recall contingency tabulations were available. We found, to our considerable surprise, that the tight relation between the overall recognition hit rate and recognition failure seemed to hold generally for all the experiments for which we had data. In these experiments, overall recall and recognition levels had varied over a wide range of values, without any apparent systematic relation between the two measures across the set of experiments. Nevertheless, when we plotted recognition-failure measures obtained from individual conditions in these experiments against the overall levels of recognition in each condition, a systematic relation emerged.

About six months later we published a paper in which we reported our observations (Tulving and Wiseman 1975). We had relevant data available from 40 conditions from 12 experiments. For each of the conditions we had the data in the form of a 2×2 recognition/recall contingency table. We calculated the overall recognition hit rates and the recognition success measures for each of the 40 conditions and looked at the scatterplot of the data. The picture we saw is shown in Fig. 13.1: The data points lie in a closely circumscribed area just above the positive diagonal. These data

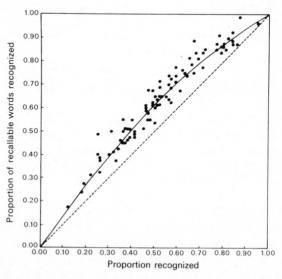

Fig. 13.1 Probability of recognition of recallable target words as a function of the probability of recognition of all target words. Each data point represents a separate experiment or a condition in an experiment.

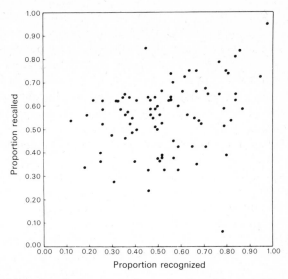

Fig. 13.2 Probability of recall of target words as a function of the probability of recognition of the same words. Each data point represents a separate experiment or a condition in an experiment.

come from experiments in which recall and recognition scores are uncorrelated, as shown in Fig. 13.2.

We fitted the data in Fig. 13.1 with a quadratic function of the form:

$$p(\text{Rn}|\text{Rc}) = p(\text{Rn}) + c[p(\text{Rn}) - p(\text{Rn})^2]. \tag{13.2}$$

This equation expresses recognition success as a function of recognition hit rate with a single constant. The equation describes the solid line that has been drawn through the data points in Fig. 13.1, with the value of the constant c set equal to 0.5 on the basis of the least-squares solution of eqn 13.2. We also calculated the product-moment correlation between the actual $p(\text{Rn}|\text{Rc})$ values of the 40 sets of data and the $p(\text{Rn}|\text{Rc})$ values predicted for each on the basis of eqn 13.2. This correlation turned out to be 0.95.

People who have had experience with 2×2 contingency tables know that they are tricky. In the case of recognition/recall contingencies, too, constraints are imposed on the relation between recognition success and recognition hits simply by virtue of the way probabilities behave in contingency tables, and not because of the way the human memory system handles recognition and recall. There are, for instance, 'forbidden' regions in the graph space depicted in Fig. 13.1 in which, depending upon overall levels of recall, no data points are possible. These facts of logic complicate the analysis and interpretation of facts of recall and recognition.

Nevertheless, when we first discovered the recognition-failure function described by eqn 13.2 and depicted in Fig. 13.1, we thought it remarkable in several ways. First, it made rather convincingly clear that the conceptualization of the relation between recall and recognition in the 'old-fashioned' generation/recognition theory is wrong. If the theory were right, then all the data points in Fig. 13.1 would be clustered parallel to the abscissa at or near the ordinate value of 1.00. Second, the data points in Fig. 13.1 are tantalizingly close to the positive diagonal, but obviously not on it. The positive diagonal represents a state of complete stochastic independence between recall and recognition within a single experimental condition, that is, within a given recognition/recall contingency table. It is described by eqn 13.2 in which the value of the constant c is zero. A state of stochastic independence between recall and recognition means that recall and recognition scores are not associated: the probability of recall of an item is independent of whether it is recognized or not, and the probability of recognition of an item is independent of whether it is recalled or not. Why the near independence of the data in Fig. 13.1, and not a complete one? And why independence at all? Surely, even if we do not accept the idea that recognition is a sub-process of recall, as postulated in the generation/recognition theory, it would be easy to think of all sorts of reasons that render traces of some items more readily retrievable than others, regardless of the nature of the cue. Or are we here witnessing yet another instance of the high degree of encoding specificity suggested by experiments demonstrating encoding/retrieval interactions?

The third remarkable aspect of the recognition-failure function had to do with the relatively small extent of the deviation of the data points from the function. This state of affairs suggested that the systematic relation between recognition success (and hence recognition failure) and overall level of recognition is independent of the many specific procedural details characterizing the 40 experimental conditions that we analyzed. These details had produced large variations in overall recall and recognition scores across the experiments and experimental conditions, but why did they not affect the relation between recognition and recognition failure? How were we to think about the largely invariant relation between recognition failure and the many conditions that greatly affected both recognition and recall?

Last but not least, the recognition-failure function seemed to be insensitive to the overall differences between recall and recognition. Figure 13.1 includes nine data points from experiments (Reder *et al.* 1974; Postman 1975*a*) in which the 'typical' result was observed: recognition was *higher* than recall. These data points are indistinguishable from others in their adherence to the function.

As new data from experiments kept coming in and obediently distributing themselves in the graph space in the immediate vicinity of the function, our faith in the orderliness of the universe increased as our puzzlement as to what it all meant deepened. At one point we had as many as nine different 'explanations' for the function, and although all made some sense, none of them made complete sense. I gave a number of talks about the recognition-failure data and the recognition-failure function at various universities and meetings, and talked to many people who had all kinds of interesting private theories about what was going on. One of the more popular ideas was that it was all some sort of an artefact. Nobody knew exactly what kind of an artefact, but the sheer orderliness of the data seemed to make this an attractive hypothesis. Psychologists seem to be distrustful of too much order in the domain of their science.

Everybody knew, of course, that if we wanted to understand the function we had to identify conditions under which data points would deviate from it, but for a long time this seemed an impossible task. It was only later that we and others were successful in establishing exceptions to the function.

Although we did not have an explanation for the function, we began making use of the function at the empirical level, in several ways. For instance, we would play the game of 'predicting' the magnitude of recognition failure from the overall level of recognition in a particular experiment or experimental condition. When someone would tell us that he had completed a recognition-failure experiment, using the standard paradigm, we would ask him to tell us what the recognition level was, and we would 'predict' on the basis of eqn 13.2 how much recognition failure he found. We were usually pretty close to the actual figure.

The recognition-failure function also helped us to 'explain' low levels of recognition failure that some experimenters had regarded as damaging to the generality of encoding specificity ideas. For instance, Postman (1975a) found low levels of proportions of items not recognized but recalled. The lowest such value, in one of his conditions, was 0.083 (Postman 1975a, Table 7). When the joint probability figure was converted into conditional probability of recognition failure given recall, it became 0.25, rather close to the figure of 0.28 'predicted' by the function. Similarly, in one of the conditions in Experiment 1 of Rabinowitz *et al.* (1977), the 'old only' condition, the observed recognition failure was 0.15. Yet, this 'rather low' figure was exactly the same as the one 'predicted' by the recognition-failure function. In fact, all the data from the seven experiments of Rabinowitz *et al.*, with a single exception, were remarkably close to the function.

The invariant nature of the recognition-failure function meant that observed values of recognition failure in particular experiments or experimental conditions varied in magnitude largely because of variations in the overall level of recognition. It did not seem to matter how or why the recognition hit rate varied; as long as it did, the recognition-failure measures varied correspondingly. This state of affairs also suggested that it was

possible to move data points up or down the function at will, by manipulating whatever variables were convenient to produce changes in the
overall recognition hit rate.

Generality

Our 1973 experiments involved a rather complicated procedure, as
described above (p. 275). It was easy to imagine why recognition failure
might occur under these conditions. For instance, the subject looking at
a copy of the target word in the recognition test might think that it looks
'familiar', but since he himself had recently produced the word in the
(semantic) free-association test, he might attribute the familiarity to the
fact of generation and for this reason be reluctant to endorse the item as
an 'old' test item from the studied list. The subject-generated recognition
tests also necessarily consisted of highly semantically similar target and
distractor words, each set having been generated in response to a common
stimulus word in the free-association task. The high degree of semantic
similarity, too, might have been responsible for low levels of recognition.
In order to test these and other similar possible interpretations of the phenomenon, we did a number of experiments, some of which we published
(e.g. Tulving 1974*b*; Watkins and Tulving 1975; Wiseman and Tulving
1975, 1976). Other researchers, too, took an interest in the phenomenon
and did a number of experiments, directed at various issues that had
emerged. As a result, we now know that recognition failure occurs under
a wide variety of experimental conditions.

Thus, we know that recognition failure occurs as readily in experiments
in which recognition is higher than recall as it does in experiments in which
recall is higher than recognition (e.g. Flexser and Tulving, 1978; Wiseman
and Tulving 1976). It occurs in situations in which no practice lists are
given to subjects before they learn the critical list (e.g. Begg 1979; Bowyer
and Humphreys 1979). It occurs as readily in an immediate test as in one
given a week after the learning (Tulving and O.C. Watkins 1977). It occurs
with different kinds of to-be-remembered word pairs presented at study:
'weak' cues and targets, as in our original experiments, 'strong' cues and
targets (e.g. Vining and Nelson 1979), and unrelated words (e.g. Begg
1979; Rabinowitz *et al.* 1977). It does not matter whether recognition-test
distractors are semantically related or unrelated to targets (e.g. Begg 1979;
Bowyer and Humphreys 1979; Postman 1975*a*; Rabinowitz *et al.* 1977).
Indeed, it is not necessary to have any distractor items at all in the recognition test for recallable words to remain unrecognized (e.g. Begg 1979;
Wallace 1978). Low-frequency words with few semantic senses (Reder *et
al.* 1974) and words that have only a single meaning in the dictionary
(Tulving and O.C. Watkins 1977) fail to be recognized even though they
can be recalled indistinguishably from high-frequency words with many

meanings. Whether subjects come to the task without any preconceptions or fully aware of what is happening, and whether they have had a great deal of practice on the recognition-failure paradigm is immaterial (e.g. Rabinowitz *et al.* 1977; Wiseman and Tulving 1975).

Extralist cues

It is not necessary that subjects be tested with the same cues that accompanied the targets at study. Norman Park and I have done an experiment in which we used extralist cues in the cued-recall phase of the recognition-failure paradigm. Since the experiment is not published, I will summarize it briefly. Subjects studied simple three-word sentences, for example, *Fish attacked* SWIMMER; *Reptile changed* APPEARANCE; *Shelter protected* ESKIMO. The inspiration for the use of these materials came from a study by R.C. Anderson, Pichert, Goetz, Schallert, Stevens, and Trollip (1976). They encouraged subjects to encode the target words in terms of particular instances of categories designated by the subject of the sentence. Thus, the three sample sentences given above are likely to be encoded in terms of *shark, chameleon,* and *igloo.* These words can then serve as extralist retrieval cues. Anderson *et al.* showed that such extralist cues are more effective than intralist cues consisting of subject-nouns of the studied sentences.

In our experiment, subjects read each sentence and rated it on a three-point scale for meaningfulness. They were instructed that their memory for the three-word phrases would subsequently be tested. They saw each sentence once. After a 25-minute interpolated activity, all subjects were given a recognition test consisting of 36 targets (the object nouns of studied sentences) together with 144 distractor words. Half the subjects were then tested with the inferential extralist cues (*shark, chameleon,* and *igloo*), whereas the other half were tested with intralist cues, consisting of subject nouns and verbs of each sentence (*fish attacked, reptile changed, shelter protected*). Subjects' task was to recall the object-noun of corresponding study-list sentences.

The results were quite similar for both extralist and intralist cue conditions. In the extralist-cue group, the recognition hit rate was 0.42, cued recall 0.53, and recognition success 0.58. The recognition-failure function 'predicts' recognition success rate of 0.54. In the intralist-cue condition, recognition was 0.46, recall 0.58, and recognition success 0.59. The predicted value for the latter figure is 0.58.

The finding of recognition failure with sentence-like study materials and extralist cues for recall shows that the phenomenon is not limited to paired-associate learning materials and paired-associate recall tests. The materials and cues used in the original recognition-failure paradigm simply provide a convenient medium for the demonstrations of effects that hold over a much wider range of conditions.

'Spectacular' and semantic results

'Spectacularly large' recognition-failure effects have been demonstrated by Watkins (1974). He gave his subjects a list of paired associates to study on a single trial. The A members of pairs were meaningless five-letter strings (such as *lique* and *spani*) and B members were equally meaningless letter bigrams (such as FY and EL). Put together, the A and B members of each pair formed a meaningful word (liquefy, spaniel). Subjects were told to study the B items but also to pay attention to the A items, because they might be helpful for remembering the B items later on. After the study of the list, the subjects were first given a recognition test on target bigrams. In the second test, subjects were given the A members of pairs as retrieval cues for the recall of target bigrams.

The results showed that the recognition hit rate, corrected for guessing, was very low at 10 per cent, whereas recall, similarly corrected for guessing, was much higher at 60 per cent. Thus, Watkins found a large advantage for cued recall, in a situation in which many target items could not be recognized but could be recalled in the presence of the list cues. I have had students in my undergraduate memory laboratory repeat Watkins's experiment to see how well the recognition-failure data fit the function. The results have shown that the fit is excellent.

Yet another experiment in which recognition failure was found and in which the data adhered to the recognition-failure function was done by Muter (1978). There was no study list, just a recognition test followed by a recall test. The target items were names of people (e.g. CLARKSON, FERGUSON, DOYLE, THOMAS, WALKER, COOPER). Subjects were presented a long list of such names and asked to circle all those that they 'recognized as a person who was famous before 1950'. Immediately after the subjects had finished this 'recognition' test, they were given recall cues in the form of brief descriptions and first names of the famous people whose surnames had appeared on the recognition-test sheet (e.g. (a) *author of the Sherlock Holmes stories: Sir Arthur Conan*, (b) *Welsh poet: Dylan*, (c) *author of 'Last of the Mohicans': James Fenimore*). Subjects recognized 29 per cent of the names, recalled 42 per cent, and showed a recognition success rate of 47 per cent, with the recognition-failure function 'predicting' 40 per cent.

Adding Muter's findings to the large number of similar findings from a variety of episodic-memory experiments, as well as Watkins' 'spectacular' results with segmented familiar words, we can conclude that much of the information in semantic memory is encoded as specifically for access as is the information in episodic memory. We may know perfectly well who Dylan Thomas is, but we may not have recorded 'THOMAS' as a 'famous person' in our semantic memory. Similarly, we know perfectly well that FY is a graphemic part of LIQUEFY (or that IV is a similar part of RIVER), yet we need not have that information stored in a manner that allows the nominal copy of it to serve as an effective retrieval cue. And, if in an episodic-memory experiment, we encode two unrelated words such as *cottage*—ROUND or *fruit*—SHEEP, as focal elements of a miniature episode, we may find that the knowledge can be retrieved more readily to one component of the whole than another.

Exceptions to the function

Although recognition-failure data have been demonstrated, and found to conform to the Tulving and Wiseman (1975) function, under a wide variety of conditions, a number of experiments have now been reported that describe exceptions. These experiments have followed the overall recognition-failure paradigm, but their results have either shown no recognition failure at all, or shown large deviations of the data points from the function.

Begg (1979) found typical recognition-failure data in three experiments, under conditions where the subjects were induced to encode the to-be-remembered material, pairs of unrelated words, 'meaningfully'. When the same materials were studied by other subjects in a 'rote' manner, however, levels of observed recognition failure were very small or, even if larger, clearly off the recognition-failure function.

Nilsson and Shaps (1981) found practically no recognition failure with categorized materials. In their experiments, subjects saw pairs consisting of category names and category instances at study, and then took successive recognition and recall tests, as in the typical recognition-failure paradigm. Category names served as retrieval cues in the cued-recall test. Similar results, although showing somewhat larger levels of recognition failure, have been obtained at Toronto by Norman Park and Pamela Auble. In both experiments, with categorized materials, levels of recognition success were considerably higher than those 'predicted' by the function.

Yet another failure to obtain typical recognition-failure data in the standard paradigm has been reported by Gardiner and Tulving (1980) in two experiments. In this study, subjects studied either word pairs consisting of abstract nouns, or pairs in which the A member was a two-digit number and the B member a familiar word. Under standard learning instructions, levels of observed recognition failure were much lower than those predicted by the function. When subjects were asked to engage in especially 'deep processing' of the study pairs, however, recognition failure increased and its levels approached those expected on the basis of the function. The general pattern of our data thus resembles that described by Begg (1979): 'normal' recognition failure with meaningful, deep processing, and exceptional findings with rote, shallow encoding.

Once we are sensitized to the possibility that exceptions to the function do occur, it is possible to have second thoughts about some of the findings that had earlier had been classified as typical, belonging to the family defining the recognition-failure function. For instance, one of the conditions in experiment 1 of Rabinowitz *et al.* (1979) was the 'old/new' condition. Unlike the 'old only' condition, in which the subjects had to check off only the 'old' words in the recognition test, in the 'old/new' condition the subjects had to make an explicit decision, 'old' or 'new', for each test item. The observed level of recognition failure was 0.02, whereas the level predicted by the function was 0.10. It is not clear exactly what is to be made of this finding. Postman (1975*a*) also had his subjects make an active decision about each word on the recognition-test sheet, circling the 'old' test items and crossing out the 'new' items; the recognition-failure levels in his experiments were predicted quite well by the function.

In Bartling and Thompson's (1977) Experiment 3, recognition failure in the 'Adjective—Adjective' condition was 0.08, much less than that predicted by the function, and in the 'Adjective—Noun' condition it was only 0.04, considerably less than expected on the basis of the function, 0.13. In both conditions the A words in the study pairs were adjectives. The lower level of recognition failure with these materials resembles the findings of the Gardiner and Tulving (1980) study.

It would be convenient if we could entertain thoughts about a common reason for all drastic deviations from the recognition-failure function. Such thoughts, however, do not seem to be entirely reasonable. At least at the present time it is difficult to imagine what the categorized materials used by Nilsson and Shaps (1980) have in common with rote, shallow processing of pairs of unrelated nouns (Begg 1979). Moreover, it is highly likely that further exceptions to the recognition-failure function will be discovered in future research. Speculations have been offered as to the reasons why recognition failure is not obtained, or why it is attenuated, under certain conditions (Begg 1979; Gardiner and Tulving 1980; Nilsson and Shaps 1980); none of them can be regarded as especially compelling or promising. The framework of GAPS tells us that the explanation for both recognition failure and exceptions to it must be sought in terms of what the to-be-remembered events are and how they are encoded, together with what retrieval information is available and how it is used, but this type of guidance does not take us very far. The search for a theory that explains not only recognition failure but also exceptions to it remains wide open.

Explanations and implications

A large number of explanations has been offered to account for the phenomenon of recognition failure. Even if we discount the early and premature attempts to make sense of the phenomenon (e.g. Reder *et al.* 1974; Santa and Lamwers 1974), and consider only those theories that were constructed in light of a more substantial body of evidence, we end up with a wealth of theoretical thought and speculation.

Associative asymmetry

Explanations of recognition failure in terms of the concept of associative asymmetry have been proposed by Bartling and Thompson (1977), Rabinowitz *et al.* (1977), and Salzberg (1976). Of the three, the most thorough discussion is provided by Rabinowitz *et al.* They think of recognition failure as 'due to' failures in backward retrieval: the B member of an A–B pair is not recognized *because* the A member of the pair cannot be retrieved when B is given as a cue. The evidence for this assertion was derived from the data of seven experiments. There were two kinds of critical data: (a) data showing changes in recognition failure consequent upon changes in overall level of recognition, and (b) data showing differences in recognition failure for words succeeding and failing in backward recall.

There are a number of problems with the theory of Rabinowitz *et al.* First, since much of the relevant evidence is correlational in nature, it is difficult to know whether recognition failure occurs *because* of failure of backward recall, or whether backward recall fails *because* of the failure of recognition of the target item that serves as a cue for the backward recall. Second, much of the evidence that Rabinowitz *et al.* offered in support of their theory consisted in demonstrations that recognition failure varied with the overall level of recognition. Rabinowitz *et al.* succeeded in moving their data points up and down the recognition-failure function through experimental operations and methods of data selection; the observed differences in recognition failure were a direct consequence of differences in recognition. For instance, the finding by Rabinowitz *et al.* that recognition failure is lower for words for which backward recall is successful than for words for which it is unsuccessful simply reflects the differences in overall levels of recognition for the two sets of data: recognition hit rate is higher for words for which backward recall is successful than for those for which it is unsuccessful. Third, it is not quite clear how the associative asymmetry analysis would apply to situations in which recognition failure is demonstrated with extralist cues as described earlier (p. 287). The Rabinowitz *et al.* theory of recognition failure seems to be predicated on the assumption that recognition failure occurs only in paired-associate learning tasks.

Thomson and I considered the associative asymmetry explanation of recognition failure in our first paper (Tulving and Thomson 1973). We pointed out that our data implied that the 'forward' association between the cue and the target word in our experiments was stronger than the 'backward' association between the target and the cue. We said that it would be 'possible to argue that the recognition failure of target words was a result of the weak association between the target and the cue' (p. 366). We also suggested that the adoption of this kind of 'explanation' of recognition failure would essentially push the problem back to that of explaining the asymmetry of the associations between list cues and target words: if we knew what causes the asymmetry of associations, we would also know what causes recognition failure.

The empirical fact of correlation between recognition failure and backward recall is true, but the theory that recognition failure is 'due to' failures in backward retrieval does not provide much insight into the phenomenon. Its main usefulness, as that of most psychological theories, may lie in new and potentially interesting experiments it suggests.

Retrieval independence

Theories of recognition failure based on the idea of associative asymmetry, as well as a number of other theoretical accounts (e.g. Kintsch 1978; Reder *et al.* 1974) have been concerned with explanations of the *occurrence* of recognition failure. The existence of the recognition-failure function, the largely invariant relation between overall recognition and recognition failure, however, has changed the nature of the problem to be explained. Instead of a single problem of what conditions or processes are responsible for recognition failure, we now have at least four closely interconnected problems: (a) what causes recognition failure? (b) why do the data points from many experiments fall into a narrowly circumscribed region in the graph space in Fig. 13.1, in close proximity to the function described by eqn 13.2? (c) how do we account for the quantitative characteristics of the recognition-failure function: why is the constant c in eqn 13.2 equal to 0.5, and not some other value? (d) how are we to account for exceptions to the function?

At the present time no theory exists that has been directed at all four questions. But a model that Arthur Flexser and I have described (Flexser and Tulving 1978) makes an attempt to come to grips with the first three. We refer to it as the Model of Retrieval Independence, after one its basic assumptions.

In the model, the memory trace of the studied event, such as an A–B pair, is conceptualized as consisting of encoded features drawn from a large pool. Different retrieval cues—be they list cues, copy cues, or extralist cues—are similarly assumed to represent encoded feature bundles. Recollection of the to-be-remembered event occurs when a sufficient number of trace features are matched by corresponding features in the retrieval cue.

In the basic model, the so-called Special Model, there are three essential assumptions: (a) in the recognition-failure paradigm, the recognition cue and the recall cue are directed at the *same* episodic trace, (b) individual traces vary in terms of how well they have been encoded, and (c) information extracted from the recognition cue is uncorrelated with that extracted from the recall cue. The three assumptions are referred to as the trace identity assumption, the goodness-of-encoding assumption, and the retrieval independence assumption. The first two account for the fact that the data points from recognition-failure experiments lie above the diagonal of stochastic independence; the retrieval independence assumption accounts for the magnitude of the deviation of the data points from the diagonal, that is, for the quantitative aspects of the shape of the recognition-failure function. In the model, stochastic independence occurs only when both trace information and retrieval information are independent; the deviation from shochastic independence comes about because of the fact that two independent retrieval cues are directed at one and the same trace. The constancy of the trace, combined with the independent variability of the two cues, produces a weak form of dependence between the two cues as exemplified by the function.

There are six parameters in the model, representing the dimensionality of the feature space, the probability that a feature is encoded as a part of the memory trace, the probabilities of a feature being encoded as a component of recognition and recall cues, and recognition and recall criteria (the minimum number of features of the memory trace that have to be matched by the cue for recollection to occur). On the assumption that features of an ensemble (the memory trace or the retrieval cue) are encoded independently of one another, mathematical expressions can be derived for the expected probabilities of recognition and recall, as well as the four joint probabilities corresponding to the four cells in a recognition/recall contingency table.

The test of the model takes the form of a large number of simulated experiments which, as a collection, exhibit the same characteristics that are possessed by real experiments: (a) large, uncorrelated variations in overall levels of recognition and recall, and (b) the largely invariant relation between overall recognition and recognition success. For each simulated experiment, the six parameters of the model are assigned values *at random*, and expected values for recognition, recall, and recognition success (or recognition failure) calculated according to the mathematical equations dictated by the structure of the model.

The results of one run of 200 simulated experiments, adopted from Flexser and Tulving (1978), are shown in Fig. 13.3 and 13.4. Figure 13.3 shows a scatterplot in which overall levels of recall are plotted against overall levels of recognition in each of the 200 model-generated experiments. This pattern corresponds to that shown in Fig. 13.1. for real experiments: essentially zero correlation between recall and recognition across experiments. Figure 13.4 shows recognition success plotted against overall level of recognition. This pattern of data corresponds to that shown in Fig. 13.2: the data points fall in a narrow region of the graph space which is adequately described by the same recognition-failure function that we had earlier fitted to the data from real experiments. This latter point is worth emphasizing. It means that model-generated data match the data

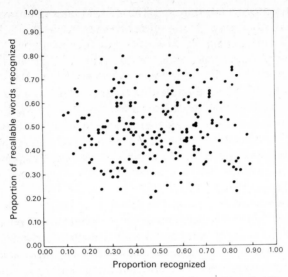

Fig. 13.3 Probability of recall of target words as a function of the probability of recognition of the same words in 200 experiments *simulated* by the Flexser-Tulving (1978) model of retrieval independence. The pattern of data is to be compared with that in Fig. 13.2.

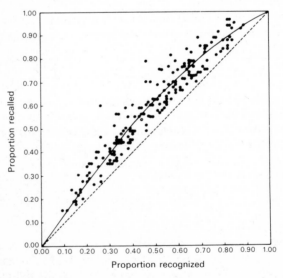

Fig. 13.4 Probability of recognition of recallable target words as a function of the probability of recognition of all target words in 200 experiments *simulated* by the Flexser-Tulving (1978) model of retrieval independence. The pattern of data is to be compared with that in Fig. 13.1

from real experiments not only qualitatively but quantitatively. When we estimated the value of c in the recognition-failure function (eqn 13.2, p. 283) for the 89 recognition-success data points in Fig. 13.1, using the method of least squares, we obtained the value of 0.51. Performing the same operation on the 200 model-generated data points in Fig. 13.4, we obtained a practically indistinguishable value of 0.47.

The close qualitative and quantitative agreement between experimental and model-generated data was achieved *without* fitting of parameters of the model. The characteristics of the model-generated data, including the recognition-failure function matching that of the real experiments, represents a logical consequence of the assumptions that the model makes about the nature of memory traces, nature of cues, and the retrieval process.

The Special Model of retrieval independence thus shows that the fact of recognition failure, the general shape of the recognition-failure function, and the value of the constant in that function in the neighbourhood of 0.5, are all natural and inevitable consequences of the relatively simple assumptions that jointly describe the structure of the model. The model tells us that *if* we conceptualize the memory trace and retrieval cues as collections of features, *if* we think that recollection occurs when a sufficient number of trace features are matched by the cue features, and *if* the encoded features (retrieval information) in the copy cue are uncorrelated with the encoded features in the recall cue, then recognition failure necessarily occurs and its magnitude is necessarily reasonably closely predicted by the recognition-failure function for which the constant c assumes a value in the neighborhood of 0.5.

It may be worthy of special note that the two sets of data depicted in Fig. 13.1 and 13.2 (and 13.3 and 13.4) are logically independent of one another: neither of the two sets implies the other. One can, for example, arbitrarily select a sub-sample of data points from Fig. 13.1 (or 13.3) in such a fashion that recall and recognition across the experiments are highly correlated, either positively or negatively, but such a selection does not change the relation between recognition and recognition success. When the recognition-failure data for such a selected sub-sample are plotted in the format of Fig. 13.2 (or 13.4), the data points will still fall close to the recognition-failure function. Thus, the concept of retrieval independence in the Flexser and Tulving model is as compatible with a state of affairs in which across experiments recall and recognition are highly correlated as it is with a situation in which the two sets of *scores* are uncorrelated.

Although the model's ability to generate two independent patterns of data that closely resemble those produced in real experiments must be regarded as rather remarkable, the correspondences are just that, correspondences. Is there any way of going beyond these 'mere agreements'? Are there any further tests of the model?

There is one, and it is important. It takes the form of what we called the General Model of recognition and recall (Flexser and Tulving 1978). It differs from the Special Model in that it replaces the critical assumption of retrieval independence with a parameter, k, which describes the degree of the relation between encoded features in the recognition cue and the recall cue. At one extreme, with $k = 0$, we have complete lack of correlation between encoded features in the two cues; at the other extreme, with $k = 1$, we have a situation where all encoded features of the recall cue are included among the encoded features of the recognition cue. Thus, the case of $k = 0$ corresponds to, or approximates, the Special Model, whereas $k = 1$ represents complete inclusion of recall-cue information in the recognition cue. When in the General Model $k = 1$, and when the recognition criterion is no higher than the recall criterion, no recognition failure for recallable words occurs: a recalled item is necessarily recognized, although items that are recognized are not necessarily recalled.

Thus, the General Model can account for many different kinds of relations between recall and recognition, from that represented in the recognition-failure function to that envisaged in the early versions of generation/recognition theories. It also makes it possible to conceive of situations in which recognition failure occurs, but its magnitude is smaller than that 'predicted' by the recognition-failure function.

The General Model provides a test of the critical assumption of retrieval independence in the Special Model. With all other features of the Special Model unchanged, relaxing of the assumption (increasing the value of k) produces results that deviate from those described by the recognition-failure function and increasingly approximate those expected on the basis of the old-fashioned generation/recognition theory.

Priming and trace loss

Humphreys and Bowyer (1980) have described a number of sets of data from recognition-failure experiments that demonstrate priming: recognition-testing of target items increases the probability of their recall in the subsequent cued-recall test. Humphreys and Bowyer argued that such priming effects introduce a degree of dependency between recall and recognition that may at least partly account for the observed recognition-failure function.

Flexser and I considered the possibility that the mild degree of dependency between recognition and recall is attributable to sequential testing (priming) effects; we concluded that they are 'negligible'. In light of the data presented by Humphreys and Bowyer it may turn out to be necessary to rethink the issue, and to examine the implications of non-negligible priming effects for theoretical explanations of recognition failure and the recognition-failure function. It is unlikely, however, that priming effects tell us the whole story about recognition failure. Priming effects seem to be real, and they may influence outcomes of experiments. But since it can be shown that *unprimed* recall can be higher than recognition (e.g. Wiseman and Tulving 1976, Exps. 1 and 2) it is obvious that recognition failure can occur, and its magnitude conform to the recognition-failure function, under conditions where priming as a causative factor is excluded.

Another potential complication for the interpretation of recognition-failure findings and their theoretical analysis has been pointed out by Begg (1979) under the label of 'trace loss'. Begg has argued, correctly, that deviations from stochastic undependence between recognition and recall can occur simply because some traces in the sample yielding relevant data are lost. These 'lost' traces, by definition, would not be accessible either in recognition or recall. The traces that are not lost may be characterized by stochastic independence between recognition and recall, but when they are 'mixed in' with 'lost' traces, contingency analyses of the kind that are used in studies of recognition failure necessarily will show some dependence between recognition and recall.

Begg (1979) did three experiments to support his reasoning. He found that, under 'meaningful' processing of the study material, the data conformed to the recognition-failure function, whereas under 'rote' processing, only small amounts of recognition failure occurred. He regarded the latter finding as evidence supporting the trace-loss theory of recognition failure. Unfortunately, the evidence is not too compelling. Levels of recall following 'rote' processing tended to be very low in Begg's experiments (as low as 0.004 in one of the conditions in Experiment 3) and it is difficult to draw reliable conclusions from such data. Moreover, one might expect that 'trace loss' occurs over longer retention intervals and that, therefore, little recognition failure following long intervals is observed. However, we have observed no drastic reduction in recognition failure in experiments in which the tests are given a week after study (Tulving and O.C. Watkins 1977) or four weeks after study (unpublished experiments done in collaboration with Ruth Donnelly).

Begg says that the central finding of his experiments was that 'measures of recall and recognition are independent after meaningful processing of items' (Begg 1979, p. 122). This statement appears to be at variance with his finding that many of the data points from his 'meaningful' processing conditions very closely conformed to the recognition-failure function (e.g. Table 2, p. 119). Begg did find independence in one of his experimental conditions ('repeated' condition in Experiment 3), but the relevance of this finding for the theoretical relation between recall and recognition is somewhat problematic, since target items were presented twice, each time under different encoding conditions. It is possible, therefore, that in this situation both encoding and retrieval processes are largely uncorrelated, a situation in which stochastic independence would be expected not only by the Flexser and Tulving (1978) model but almost any other line of reasoning as well.

Begg thought that 'measured independence' is beyond the Flexser and Tulving theory (p. 122). Reliable observations of stochastic independence under conditions of the standard recognition-failure paradigm, indeed, could not be accounted for by the model. Neither Begg nor anyone else, as far as I know, however, has yet produced such data.

Implications

The existence of the recognition-failure function has certain implications that can be considered separately from theoretical speculations as to the 'causes' of the function. Perhaps the most important of them lies in the apparent near-independence of recall and recognition scores. Such a state of affairs, as we have seen, has shifted the focus of theoretical attention from the problem of occurrence of recognition failure to the problem of explaining the observed deviation of the recognition-failure scores from the state of stochastic independence. Regardless of exactly how 'independence' is defined and conceptualized, the fact that recall and recognition are either wholly or nearly independent imposes certain important constraints on theories of retrieval.

A second implication of the recognition-failure function has to do with small amounts of recognition failure. How should we interpret a finding that a rather small proportion of target items could not be recognized but could be recalled? As I noted earlier, the tendency has always been to assume that such small fluctuations in retrieval can be attributed to 'noise' or unreliability of measurement. The existence of the recognition-failure function, however, suggests that such 'explanations' are no more necessary or appropriate for small amounts of recognition failure that fit the function than they are for large amounts 'predicted' by it.

Third, recognition failure represents only a sub-class of a much larger class of phenomena showing that a target item that cannot be retrieved now may become retrievable later, in the absence of any further study. Such 'reminiscence' effects can be demonstrated under conditions where the nominal retrieval information on the two occasions is the same (e.g. Brown 1923; Raffel 1934; Estes 1960; Buschke 1974; Tulving 1967; Madigan 1976; Wallace 1978) as well as under conditions where the retrieval information is changed (e.g. Arbuckle and Katz 1976; Tulving and Pearlstone 1966; Tulving and Psotka 1971; Tulving and Watkins 1975; Wallace 1978). Hypermnesia (Erdelyi and Becker 1974; Hoppe and Dahl 1978) and improvement in recall under conditions of protracted retrieval (e.g. Adams, Marshall, and Bray 1971; Roediger and Thorpe 1978) represent other sub-classes of the same general phenomenon. All these findings can be economically interpreted with the help of the encoding specificity principle: retrieval of a previously non-retrieved target occurs when more appropriate retrieval information is presented experimentally or becomes available from semantic memory through the process of subjective generation (Roediger and Thorpe 1978). It is easy to see that a cue such as *spani* provides more information than a cue such as *el* or *sh* for the retrieval of target words such as SPANIEL or SPANISH (Watkins 1974), or how a description such as *author of 'Last of the Mohicans': James Fenimore* provides more information than a description such as *Cooper* for the retrieval of the name of a famous person (Muter 1978). It is less obvious why a cue such as *glue* should provide more information than *chair* for the retrieval of a previously seen *glue*—CHAIR event (Tulving and Thomson 1973), or why a rememberer can internally generate relevant information for the retrieval of a drawing of a bicycle in 20 minutes but not in 10 (Roediger and Thorpe 1978). Yet, guided by the encoding specificity principle, we can entertain hypotheses that they do, and try to understand more about why and how.

Fourth, the fact that recognition failure is observed, and that its magnitude, relative to recognition, is approximately the same for studied materials as different as Watkins's (1974) *spani*–EL, Muter's (1978) *author of 'The Last of the Mohicans'*, and the pairs of unrelated words used by Rabinowitz *et al.* (1977), to mention a small sample, suggests that higher-order memory units based on 'associations by similarity' behave very similarly to those based on 'association by contiguity'. The suggestion is further strengthened by the finding of recognition failure with recall cues related to the studied materials by semantic inferences (the experiment with Norman Park described on page 287).

Finally, the phenomenon of recognition failure reminds us of the importance of the question, 'recognition (failure) *of what?*'. The answer is, 'recognition of an item as a *part of* an earlier event'. But do events as such exhibit 'recognition failure'? Is it possible that a person would fail to recognize an event consisting of some 70 separate 'actions' (Lichtenstein and Brewer 1980) and yet be able to recall it when more appropriate non-copy cues are previded? I do not know. It is difficult to imagine that the answer to the question is affirmative, but then, not so long ago, it probably also was difficult to imagine a similar state of affairs involving miniature word-events.

14
Recognition and recall

For a long time in the history of the study of memory, comparison of recognition and recall was straightforward, since it took place under standardized conditions. Recall was usually free recall; variations in recognition hardly ever entailed more than free- versus forced-choice. Under these standard conditions, the relation between recall and recognition could be stated precisely without much difficulty: recognition scores were usually higher than those of recall, and recognition represented an easier task.

The situation is different today. Recognition can now be shown to be higher than recall as well as lower; recognition and recall scores may be correlated positively, negatively, or not at all; in one situation, recall of one thing may require recognition of another, whereas in another situation, recognition of one thing may require recall of another; variations in certain variables may produce changes in recall but not in recognition, or changes in recognition but not in recall.

Even this partial summary of general experimental findings clearly suggests that a simple statement of the relation between recognition and recall is no more possible. Yet we need an overall framework within which more specific aspects of the relation can be analyzed and clarified. In this chapter I will describe one. It represents an elaboration of relevant components of GAPS. I will first discuss the basic similarities and differences between recognition and recall, then describe an experiment whose results forced a revision of some of my earlier ideas about recognition and recall (Tulving 1976), and then outline a simple model of retrieval that relates ecphoric information to memory performance. I shall refer to the model as the synergistic ecphory model of retrieval. An interesting feature of tne model is the postulation of a higher recall threshold than recognition threshold. I will then show how the model accounts for some of the major phenomena of recognition and recall, including recognition failure of recallable words and the findings from the critical experiment described earlier in the chapter. The chapter concludes with a brief review of the relation of the synergistic threshold model of retrieval to some other theories of recognition and recall.

Similarities and differences

In order to make the discussion of the relation between recognition and recall manageable for our present purposes, we must make certain simplifying assumptions. In what follows, we assume constancy of to-be-remembered events and all encoding and recoding conditions. Furthermore, we shall focus on recognition and recall of a particular component of the experienced event, rather than recall and recognition of all possible components and their combinations. We shall ignore the problem of 'correcting' recognition and recall scores for what is (frequently questionably) called 'guessing', as well as the role that the number and nature of distractor items play in determining the rememberer's performance on the recognition test. Finally, we assume that the same question is posed to the rememberer in both recognition and recall.

Holding constant conditions of encoding does not mean that experiments could or should not be done in which the effects of variations in encoding conditions on recognition and recall are studied. It simply means that here I do not wish to compare recall of an item encoded in one encoding situation with the recognition of a different item in another.

Focusing on recognition and recall of specified components of experienced events means that in situations where we compare recognition with some kind of cued recall, we will ignore questions concerning recognition of cues: we are concerned with recognition and recall of specified (and identical) 'target' items only.

Ignoring the number and nature of distractor items in the recognition (and cued recall) tests means that we focus here on what happens when the rememberer is confronted with a single ('old' or 'new') test item in the recognition situation. The number and nature of distractor items can have no effect on the rememberer's response to the test item under these conditions, for the simple reason that they have not yet been presented.

The question to the rememberer in the recognition test is usually some variant of, 'Was this item in the collection you saw?'; in the recall test it is some variant of, 'What was the item in the collection?'. Rememberers in experiments usually have no difficulty interpreting the 'this item' in the recognition question in light of the standard interpretation of identity that we briefly discussed earlier (p. 270), as referring to 'another item like this one', Thus, despite apparent variations in the two questions, they are both directed at a past event, and the rememberer can produce a veridical answer to the question in either case only by making use of information stored about the event. In our simplified procedure, the constant question that we would pose to the rememberer in both recognition and recall is some variant of the following: 'Does this item remind you of any item (or items) you encountered before in this experiment?'. It is the form of the answer that defines one of the differences between recognition and recall: in recall the rememberer must produce, say, the name of the target item, whereas in recognition he may answer it by just saying 'Yes' or 'No'. In either case, the rememberer's attention is focused on the relation between the present stimulus and a past event, while the theorist's thoughts can converge on the similarities and differences between recognition and recall.

The most important feature that recognition and recall have in common is that they are both processes of retrieval. If successful, they both result in the rememberer's awareness of a past event. The nature of this awareness may, and frequently does, differ, but the difference is more like that of a very clear and rather fuzzy picture of the same scene than that of a picture of a very simple and a very complex object.

In our simplified situation for comparing recall and recognition, we can characterize the differences between recognition and recall *tasks* in terms of only two independent dimensions. One has to do with the type of retrieval information available to the rememberer, the other with what in GAPS we refer to as conversion of ecphoric information into behavior. In the recognition task, the retrieval information includes copies of studied items, whereas in recall tasks non-copy cues, or no specific cues at all, are presented. As to conversion, in the recognition task the rememberer has to express his awareness of the earlier presence of the test item, whereas in the recall task he has to produce some other specified aspect of the original experience, usually the name of the studied item. Viewed within the framework of GAPS, the first dimension of the difference (cue information) entails processes occurring before the construction of ecphoric information and recollection, whereas the second (conversion) represents post-ecphoric processes.

The two dimensions of retrieval information and conversion, with two values of each, can be illustrated schematically in the form of a 2 × 2 matrix as shown in Table 14.1. Retrieval information does or does not include literal or symbolic copies of the to-be-remembered targets; conversion requires either expression of episodic familiarity with the retrieval cue or production of a stipulated identifying component of the target, such as its name. Henceforth I will refer to the production of such identifying evidence as 'identification'. As a concrete example, consider a situation in which the episodic target is the word CHAIR, and in which either the copy cue (*chair*) or some other cue (e.g. *table*) are presented either for familiarity or identification conversion.

Conventional recognition and recall tests occupy two of the four cells in the matrix. When the rememberer says that the copy cue *chair* is familiar, he is said to have recognized it; when he is given the retrieval cue *table* and he responds with the target CHAIR, he has recalled the to-be-remembered event, or identified its name. But what about the other two cells in the matrix?

When the rememberer declares a cue other than a copy cue to be familiar, he has made a 'false alarm' or a false positive response in the conventional recognition test. Memory theorists do not always agree as to how to think about such responses. In some situations, for instance, where signal-detection analyses are carried out, false positive responses are regarded as errors, they constitute the 'noise' distribution; in other situations, however, these responses represent instances of 'false recognition',

Table 14.1
Differences between recognition and recall tasks

Retrieval information	Conversion Familiarity	Name identification
Copy	Recognition	?
Non-copy	?	Recall

indicative of implicit associative responses made to the target items at the time of study (Underwood 1965) or representing evidence of constituent attributes of stored target items (Anisfeld and Knapp 1968).

The other empty cell in the matrix in Table 14.1, the cell representing the combination of copy cues and identification conversion, represents a situation in which the rememberer's task is to produce the name of the studied list item to its copy as the cue. The effect of recall cues identical with the target has been studied in a few experiments (e.g. Tulving 1974; Tulving and Watkins 1973). In one of them (Tulving and Watkins 1973) we argued for a 'continuity view' of recognition and recall: retrieval in both modes is essentially the same, a joint product of information stored in the past and that in the immediate environment. This argument, elaborated in another paper (Tulving 1976), will be clarified and revised here. An important impetus for the revision was provided by the data from an experiment that was designed to explore some of the implications of the state of affairs depicted in Table 14.1. I refer to it as the 'direct comparison' experiment of recognition and recall, and shall briefly describe it next.

The 'direct comparison' experiment

In the design of the 'direct comparison' experiment, conducted with the help of Judith Sutcliffe, all four cells of the matrix shown in Table 14.1 were represented, along with some other conditions less relevant for our present discussion. We combined four kinds of cues with two types of conversion. In addition to copy cues, there were three classes of non-copy cues: strong extralist associates of targets, rhyming words, and 'unrelated' words. In both forms of conversion, exactly the same cues, or test items, were presented to the subjects. In the familiarity conversion, the task consisted of the conventional Yes/No recognition test; in the identification conversion, subjects had to use the test words as cues for the recall of target words from the studied list.

There were two groups of subjects in the experiment, with 72 persons in each. Every subject studied a list consisting of 48 single words, presented visually on a single trial, at the rate of four seconds per word. They were instructed to look at each word carefully and try to remember it with a view to a subsequent memory test whose exact nature was not specified. Subjects in both groups studied the list under identical conditions and instructions.

Following the study of the list, all subjects took an immediate test, involving 24 of the 48 studied words as targets, and a delayed test, in which the targets were the remaining half of the list words. In each of these two tests, subjects were given cue-sheets containing 32 words. Eight of these were identical with eight target words (copy cues), eight were strong extra-experimental associates (associative cues), eight were rhyming words (rhyming cues), and eight were unrelated distractors. Subjects in both groups received identical cue-sheets. Only the retrieval instructions given to them differed.

The subjects in the Recall Group were told that the 32 words on the cue-sheet were clues that might help them to remember the words that they had studied. They were also told that the clues were of four different kinds—copies, semantic associates, rhymes, and unrelated words—but the relation of each cue to its intended target was not specified. If a clue reminded them of a target word from the study list, they were to write the word beside its clue on the sheet. If a clue did not remind them of any target word, they were to place an X on the line beside the clue. Examples of the four different kinds of clues were given to ensure that the subjects understood the instructions.

The subjects in the second group, the Recognition Group, were told to look at each word on the cue-sheet, decide whether the word had occurred in the study list, and indicate the result of the decision by writing either 'Yes' or 'No' beside each cue word. They were also told to make a three-point confidence judgment about each 'Yes' or 'No' decision. Subjects in both groups were allotted six minutes to complete the test. The delayed test was given 15 minutes after the end of the immediate test.

The main data of interest from the experiment have to do with the comparisons within each of the two *rows* in the matrix in Table 14.1: (a) familiarity judgments about copy cues *as* list words in the recognition test versus the production of list words *in response to* copy cues in the recall test; and (b) familiarity judgments about non-copy cues *as* list words in the recognition test versus the production of list words *in response to* non-copy cues in the recall test. As a general background for these comparisons, let us briefly look at the overall levels of performance in the 16 experimental conditions, summarized in Table 14.2.

Each proportion shown in Table 14.2 is based on 576 observations (72 subjects × 8 words). The data for the familiarity (recognition) task show proportion of cases in which the subjects regarded the test words as 'old', that is, cases in which they thought the test words had appeared in the study list. The data for copy cues represent 'correct' responses, from the experimenter's point of view, whereas the data for the other three types

Table 14.2

Summary of memory performance in the 'direct comparison' experiment

Retrieval information	Conversion Familiarity		Name identification	
	Immediate	Delayed	Immediate	Delayed
Copy cues	0.78	0.71	0.69	0.60
Associates	0.15	0.20	0.54	0.37
Rhymes	0.09	0.15	0.20	0.31
Unrelated lures	0.08	0.18	0.04	0.02

of cues represent false positive responses. The data for the identification (recall) task indicate proportions of cases in which any target word from the list was given in response to the cue.

Several comparisons in Table 14.2 are of interest. First, the probability that copy cues were regarded as 'old' was higher than the probability of production of the target word in response to its copy cue, 0.78 versus 0.71 in the immediate test, and 0.69 versus 0.60 in the delayed test. Second, the probability that the extralist associates were (incorrectly) regarded as study-list words increased from the immediate to the delayed test (0.15 versus 0.20), whereas the probability that study-list words were (correctly) produced to extra-list associates decreased from the immediate to the delayed test (0.54 versus 0.37). Third, rhymes of target words were much more effective as retrieval cues for the recall of list words than were unrelated distractors, but the proportions of false positive responses made to the rhymes were about the same as those to the unrelated distractors. Fourth, associates were (falsely) regarded as 'old' words more frequently than were unrelated distractors in the immediate test, but this difference was greatly reduced in the delayed test. Finally, the probability of recall of target words to associates declined from the immediate to the delayed test whereas recall to rhyming cues increased.

The total pattern of results from the experiment could be described as 'complex'. But there seem to be clear differences between familiarity (recognition) and identification (recall) tasks, the nature of the difference depending on the type of retrieval information. Of particular interest are two findings, one concerning the effects of copy cues, the other the effects of associative cues, in the two kinds of conversion. We will consider them next.

Effects of copy cues

The analysis of the effects of copy cues represents a simple extension of that summarized in Table 14.2. The results of the analysis are shown in Fig. 14.1.

Each point in Fig. 14.1 represents a set of six study-list words, selected

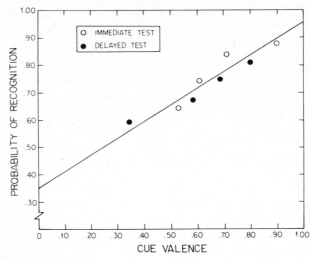

Fig. 14.1 Probability of recognition of copy cues of target words as a function of the valence of the same cues.

on a post-hoc basis, in terms of recognition and recall performance of the subjects. The six words with the highest recogniton and recall scores, with the data pooled from the 72 subjects in each of the two groups, were placed into the first subset, the next highest six words into the second subset, and so on, to the fourth subset, which represents the six words with the lowest recognition and recall scores. This method of grouping of words masks the variability in the data for individual words without destroying the nature of the relation between the two variables of interest here: recall of target words to the copy cues in the identification conversion and recognition hit rate of the same cues in the familiarity conversion.

The data from the two tests, immediate and delayed, seemed to describe a common function. The straight line drawn through the eight data points was fitted by eye. The data plotted in this form clarify the nature of the findings summarized in Table 14.2 which showed that the level of performance with copy cues was higher in the familiarity conversion (recognition) than for the identification conversion (recall). The positive slope of the function in Fig. 14.1 reflects the fact that there were systematic differences among target words with respect to their retrievability, and that these systematic differences were revealed more or less in the same way in familiarity and identification conversions.

The important finding is the positive intercept of the function in Fig. 14.1. It complements the finding of differences in mean proportions of recognized and recalled words (Table 14.1); it implies that some target words are regarded as familiar in the recognition test but their names cannot be identified and produced in response to copy cues in the recall test.

The fact that recognition-performance exceeds recall-performance under conditions where not only encoded information but retrieval information is held constant is clearly inconsistent with the episodic ecphory view of the relation between recognition and recall that I had proposed a few years ago. That view can be summarized as follows:

> Recognition and recall differ only with respect to the exact nature of the retrieval information available to the rememberer. In recognition, retrieval information is carried by a literal copy of the event or item to be remembered; in recall, the retrieval information is contained in cues other than copy cues. In other respects the process of utilization of trace information in the act of retrieval is thought to be essentially the same for recall and recognition (Tulving 1976, p. 37).

Quite apart from falsifying the earlier hypothesis, the finding seems to present a paradox: how can the learner have difficulty identifying the name of a studied word, given that he recognizes the test item, identical with the studied item, as one seen in the list? Why should a learner be able to decide that a test item is 'old', and yet fail to produce the *name* of the studied item to the same test item (copy cue) in the recall test? At least two possibilities suggest themselves.

First, it is possible that, despite the nominal identity of retrieval cues in the two tasks, subjects extracted more appropriate retrieval information from copy cues in the recognition task than in the recall task. In the terminology of GAPS, this hypothesis is to the effect that, because of differences in task requirements, the nature of the ecphoric process (p. 175) was different for the two groups of subjects in our experiment. Although such differences may have played a role in the experiment, there is little corroborating evidence for the hypothesis, and we must therefore leave it as an idea not to be overlooked.

The second possibility is a somewhat more realistic one. It is the idea that different types of conversion *require* different kinds, different amounts, or both, of ecphoric information. Specifically, identification of a particular aspect of an experienced event, such as its name, requires ecphoric information of 'higher quality' than does the judgment that the test item is 'familiar'. The exact reasons for such a state of affairs need not concern us too much at this time, although different speculations can be offered. For instance, the decision that a test item is 'old' need be based only on a general sense of familiarity; it need not involve retrieval of, or matching with, any particular memory trace (e.g. Kintsch 1970; Moeser 1977). Identification and production of the name of a stored episode, on the other hand, may be critically dependent on the match of the retrieval information with a particular trace. Be it as it may, different levels of performance, under conditions where trace and cue information are constant and only conversion requirements differ, suggest that the view of retrieval simply as a matter of informational overlap between cues and traces must be rejected or revised. Before we see how it can be done, let us consider the second important finding from the experiment.

Effects of associative cues

The second important finding has to do with responses made to the associative cues under the conditions of the two tasks. The summary of the data in Table 14.2 already showed a dissociation between the tasks when associative cues were used: (incorrect) judgment of associative cues as 'old' increased from the immediate to the delayed test, whereas the effectiveness with which the cues elicited the (correct) target words decreased. This dissociation, too, is at variance with the simple view of retrieval as a matter of informational overlap between cues and traces. According to such a view, the increasing tendency of learners, from the immediate to the delayed test, of making false positive responses to associative cues implies *increased* informational overlap between cues and traces, whereas the decreasing tendency of making correct responses to recall cues implies *decreasing* overlap. We obviously cannot be too enthusiastic about a theory that predicts that something increases and decreases at the same time. But how reliable is the finding? Perhaps there is something wrong with it. The results of another analysis speak to the issue.

Before we look at the results of the analysis, we should introduce the concept of 'cue valence'. The valence of a cue with respect to a particular aspect of an event refers to the probability with which that aspect of the event can be recalled in the presence of the cue (Tulving and Watkins 1975). The second finding of interest concerns the relation between the (false positive) responses to associative cues in the familiarity conversion (recognition) and the valence of the same cues in the identification conversion (recall). We used the same stratagem that we adopted for the analysis of copy cues: we selected subsets of cues varying in terms of their valence, computed the (false positive) recognition rate for each subset, and then examined the relation between the two measures.

The relevant data are summarized in Fig. 14.2. The abscissa of the graph represents the valence of associative cues in recall; the ordinate shows the rate of false positive responses made to the same cues in recognition. The sets of data from the immediate and delayed tests differ, inasmuch as the false positive rate is higher and valence lower in the delayed test than in the immediate test, in keeping with the summary of the data in Table 14.2, but they are similar in that they seem to describe more or less the same function. The straight line was again fitted to the data points by eye. The data are quite clear in showing a negative correlation between the two measures.

The negative correlation between the valence of associative cues and their false positive recognition rate is again clearly at variance with the hypothesis that holds retrieval to be a direct function of ecphoric infor-

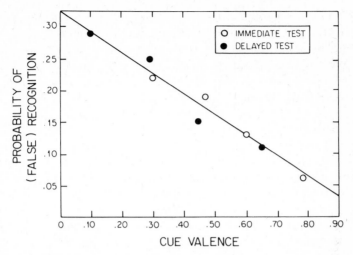

Fig. 14.2 Probability of (false) recognition of associative cues as a function of the valence of the same cues.

mation. If calling a test item 'old' in the recognition test depended on the informational overlap between cue and trace information, and if the cue valence also depended on the same kind of informational overlap, then cue valence and false positive rate should be positively correlated. Instead, what is positively correlated is cue valence and the probability with which the cues are (correctly) judged to be 'new'. How are we to interpret the negative correlation between false positive judgments and valence of associative cues?

It turns out that, again, we can make sense of the data if we assume that different conversion tasks require different kinds, amounts, or both of ecphoric information. Such an assumption implies the necessity of introducing the concept of *conversion threshold*. We will return to the problem of what to make of the negative correlation between false positive responses and valence of associative cues after discussing conversion thresholds and sketching out a model of retrieval in which conversion thresholds play a central role in relating ecphoric information to memory performance.

Conversion thresholds

Different kinds of memory performance require different kinds, amounts, or both, of ecphoric information: they have different conversion thresholds. The judgment that a test item is 'old', for instance, requires less ecphoric information, or information of 'lower quality', than does the identification, and production, of the name of a previously studied event. Given a certain ensemble of ecphoric information, a product of retrieval information and information stored in the engram of the event, some types of conversion into behavior are possible and others are not. A conversion threshold divides the total ensemble of ecphoric information into two parts: 'bundles' of ecphoric information 'above' the threshold support and make possible use of the ecphoric information for a particular purpose, whereas those 'below' the threshold do not.

Thinking about conversion thresholds is more difficult than thinking about typical psychophysical thresholds. The latter can be defined and specified in terms of absolute or relative stimulus energy or some other physical dimension, a readily measurable unidimensional quantity. Ecphoric information is neither readily measurable nor unidimensional. But we can regard conversion thresholds as analogous to psychophysical thresholds in that they map an underlying (multidimensional) continuum of ecphoric information into a binary behavioral classification: successful and unsuccessful acts of memory performance. Every task has its own characteristic conversion threshold. Here we are concerned with only two kinds of conversion—judgments of familiarity and name identification, or recognition and recall—although the general principles that apply to these two can be expected to apply more generally. It is intuitively clear that some types of memory task require ecphoric information of higher quality than others, or that some conversion thresholds are higher than others. For instance, it seems like a reasonable assumption that identification of the name, or some other detailed characteristic, of an event requires ecphoric information of higher quality ('more' of it) than does the judgment that a present test item possesses a certain degree of episodic familiarity. Since the concept of conversion threshold, defined in terms of ecphoric information, is just an unexplored idea now, we cannot say much about the possibility that conversion thresholds of different categories of tasks are arranged in some relatively invariant order, reflecting different degrees of 'difficulty' of the tasks. Relevant research and thought may illuminate the matter as it is explored. For the time being, however, I will assume that the threshold for name identification is necessarily higher than the threshold for Yes/No recognition.

An analogy with a familiar perceptual situation may be useful to illustrate the concept of conversion thresholds and their natural ordering. Recollection of an event, resulting from a particular quantity and quality of ecphoric information, is like the perceptual experience an observer has when he watches an object approaching him from a distance. At first the experience may be only that of an inhomogeneity in an otherwise homogeneous field of view: the observer detects the presence of an object without being able to say anything about its nature or properties. The awareness of this presence becomes stronger and clearer as the object approaches the observer, even if the object is still too far away for the observer to be able to tell anything about its characteristics. As the observation distance decreases, the observer can start making increasingly finer discriminations about the object. For instance, at some point the observer may become aware that the approaching object is a person, that that person walks with a limp, that the person is a man, that he wears glasses, and finally, that he has not shaved for several days, These increasingly finer judgments about what it is that is perceived require increasingly more elaborate and richer perceptual information. For any given level of perceptual awareness (e.g. recognizing the object as a person, as a man, as unshaven) the necessary information must exceed some threshold value. The threshold for a more 'difficult' discrimination is necessarily higher than the threshold of an 'easier' one. In our example, the observer who realizes that the approaching object wears glasses necessarily knows that the object is a person, whereas the awareness of the object as a person need not contain anything about the presence or absence of glasses.

We can imagine that a similar relation exists between actualized ecphoric information and the quality of recollective experience necessary for answering different questions about the retrieved event. A relatively small amount of ecphoric information may be sufficient for the learner's awareness that a test item is episodically familiar, even if the same amount is not sufficient for the determination of some of the detailed characteristics of what has been retrieved. As the qualitative richness (or quantity) of relevant ecphoric information increases, finer discriminations about it become possible.

My suggestion that recall thresholds are higher than recognition thresholds does not represent an attempt to resuscitate the classical strength-and-threshold model of recall that was used to explain the superiority of recognition over recall in the days when the comparisons were made under standardized conditions. The classical model has been rejected for excellent reasons (Anderson and Bower 1972; McCormack 1972); we also know that it is clearly incompatible with the phenomenon of recognition failure of recallable words.

The idea of a fixed order of thresholds I am proposing differs critically from the classical theory in that in the present formulation thresholds are defined with respect to *ecphoric information*, whereas in the classical theory they were defined in terms of the *strength of the memory trace*. The classical model turned out to be incompatible with certain experimental data, not because of the assumption that the recognition threshold was always lower than that of recall, but because it completely failed to take into account the critical role played by retrieval information in effecting recollection of events. When thresholds are defined in terms of ecphoric information, the conflict between theory and data disappears.

Synergistic Ecphory Model of Retrieval

We can integrate the concepts we have been discussing, particularly ecphoric information and conversion thresholds, into a simple model that helps us to understand the relation between recall and recognition, not only in terms of its particular manifestations, but also at a more general level of analysis. I refer to the model as Synergistic Ecphory Model of Retrieval. The term 'synergistic' refers to the joint effects of trace information and retrieval information in determining ecphoric information; 'ecphory' refers to the corresponding process; 'retrieval' signifies that the ideas embodied in the model extend to forms of retrieval other than just recognition and recall.

It is unfortunate that the term 'synergy' has recently become trendy; it is such a useful one for talking about phenomena of psychology. Most mental and behavioral phenomena arise out of combined, co-operative action of stimulation or information from different sources, thus we need continually to refer to various kinds of combined effects. The concept of 'synergy' has appeared in psychological theorizing from time to time, but it has not been popular. One of Hollingworth's (1928) general laws of redintegration concerned 'synergy and inhibition'. Synergy referred to a state of affairs where 'stimulating details from the same or different contexts . . . work together' (p. 83). In the case we are discussing here the 'stimulating details' take the form of trace information and retrieval information.

A version of the model of interest in the present connection—concerning the relation between recall and recognition—is shown in the form of a diagram in Fig. 14.3. It is a simple schematic description of the relations

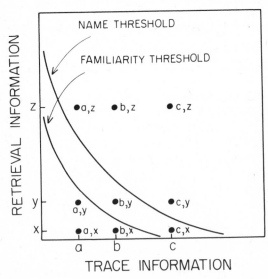

Fig.14.3 A schematic diagram of the Synergistic Ecphory Model of Retrieval. The graph space represents ecphoric information, defined as a product of trace and retrieval information.

among the relevant concepts: stored information, retrieval information, ecphoric information, familiarity threshold, and naming threshold. The horizontal axis of the coordinate system represents stored information, and the vertical axis represents retrieval information. The two-dimensional space defined by the two axes corresponds to ecphoric information. The two curved lines in the diagram represent familiarity and naming thresholds.

In order to simplify matters for the purpose of communication, let us assume that the diagram in Fig. 14.3 depicts a given event, such as the appearance of a familiar word in a particular to-be-remembered collection. Variations in trace information correspond to different engrams resulting from many different possible encodings of the event, only some of which may be realized on a particular occasion. Retrieval information corresponds to many different potentially relevant retrieval cues that may or may not be present on a particular occasion. The scale values on the two axes of the coordinate system are left unspecified, but we can think of them as representing different degrees of 'goodness' or 'richness' of trace information, or retrieval information. We could also use the term 'amount' of trace and retrieval information, provided that we always keep in mind the multidimensional nature of both engrams and cues. Thus, the 'amount' of trace information might be specified in terms of the number of encoded features, and retrieval information in terms of 'features useful for retrieval' as described in the Flexser and Tulving (1978) model. As we move from the point of origin on the graph to the right, the quality of trace information improves, it becomes larger in 'amount', or more elaborate or more distinctive; as we move up, retrieval cues become more effective, their valence increases, they become more relevant and appropriate for the event in question.

A similar schematic diagram could also be imagined as representing the episodic-memory system in general. The trace information would represent all possible encodings of all kinds of events; retrieval information would represent all possible kinds of cues and questions directed at the system; the graph space represents the universe of ecphoric information. This imaginary universe, as the real cosmic one, however, is very sparsely populated, an overwhelmingly large part of it is 'filled with a void'. But whenever and wherever a synergistic conjunction of trace and retrieval information occurs, a packet of ecphoric information is created whose properties determine the recollective experience of the beholder of the universe, and its conversion into some other form of psychological energy,

We assume that each bivariate point in the ecphoric space in Fig. 14.3, or each unique vector, corresponds to a particular bundle or packet of ecphoric information whose qualitative characteristics determine the nature of the rememberer's recollective experience as well as its conversion into various forms of behavior. The two conversion thresholds divide the total space of ecphoric information into three mutually exclusive subspaces. The region below the familiarity threshold defines ensembles of ecphoric information (combinations of trace and retrieval information) that do not give rise to the feeling of episodic familiarity aroused by the test stimulus, although they may be sufficient for other forms of conversion. The region between the familiarity and name-identification thresholds represents ecphoric information that is sufficient for making positive familiarity judgments but insufficient for naming the target event. The region above the naming threshold contains packets of ecphoric information that are sufficient for both awareness of episodic familiarity and the naming of the target event.

Since we are here concerned with the relation between recall and recognition, the version of the Synergistic Ecphory Model depicted in Fig. 14.3 shows only two conversion thresholds. In principle, a very much larger number of different conversion thresholds can be postulated, each representing a different aspect of recollection of the original event and corresponding conversion. For instance, we could postulate different recognition thresholds corresponding to different levels of confidence with which test items are judged to be 'old' or 'new'. Similarly, we could postulate different 'recall' thresholds, depending upon what features of the original to-be-remembered event are to be constructed at the time of attempted retrieval.

The diagram of the Synergistic Ecphory Model depicts the relations among the relevant concepts in only a very rough fashion. We can think of qualitative differences in trace and retrieval information being mapped onto a single scale of 'goodness' or 'effectiveness', but the scale units cannot be specified. In the same vein, the shapes of conversion thresholds are completely arbitrary, as are their distances from each other. Moreover, the diagram says nothing about the manner in which trace information and retrieval information are combined into ecphoric information.

Nevertheless, some of the features of the diagram are intended to convey certain ideas about the model; these should be briefly noted. First, the rectangular coordinates—rather than, say, oblique ones—are intended to imply that retrieval information is independent of trace information, in the sense that any bundle of retrieval information can be related to any bundle of stored information. Second, the diagram implies a trade-off between trace information and retrieval information: poor quality of trace information can be compensated for, within limits, by high quality retrieval information, and vice versa. For instance, points a,z and c,y in Fig. 14.3 represent bundles of ecphoric information that are sufficiently 'rich' to allow for the identification and production of the name of the event, although they are made up of different kinds of 'mix' between trace and retrieval information. Third, the two conversion thresholds are asymptotic with the two coordinate axes; the thresholds and the axes do not intercept. This feature of the model implies that there exist limits to the trade-off of stored information and retrieval information in the construction of ecphoric information. If stored information about an event is minimal, or absent altogether, there will be no relevant ecphoric information, or whatever there is is always below the lowest conversion threshold. A similar state of affairs characterizes the absence of appropriate retrieval information. In terms of recollective experience, this feature of the model simply says that recollection of an event cannot occur in the absence of either the trace or the appropriate retrieval information. Fourth, the model is intended to imply that quantitative measures of memory performance are reflected in the distance of bundles of ecphoric information from the corresponding conversion threshold, even though no rule for measuring the distance is given.

Although the location of each point in Fig. 14.3 completely determines the success or failure of its different possible conversions, performance measures are probabilistic: in situations in which memory performance is measured, proportion of successful conversions of a particular kind are calculated from a sample in which bundles of ecphoric information differ between and within rememberers and between and within to-be-remembered items.

Fifth, the diagram implies that situations may readily occur in which the 'amount' or 'goodness' of ecphoric information is well in excess of that needed for successful conversion of a particular kind. The point c,z in Fig. 14.3, for example, represents a situation in which there is much more relevant ecphoric information present than is needed for the production of the name of the to-be-remembered event. We could say that under these conditions recall performance (and recognition performance) is 'over-determined'. Chronic problems of over-determination lead to ceiling effects in memory experiments. When performance is over-determined, either the stored information or retrieval information, or both, can be reduced without necessarily reducing the measured memory performance. Sometimes experimental manipulation of the magnitude of such reductions may be used as an index of performance.

Finally, the placement of the naming threshold above the familiarity threshold graphically expresses the gist of our earlier discussion of this issue: it takes more, or higher quality, ecphoric information for the rememberer to construct the name of the remembered event than it does to decide that the present situation or object was encountered earlier. Identification of the name of the event entails the feeling or knowledge of the previous occurrence of the event, but the latter does not necessarily entail the former.

Explanation of recognition/recall phenomena

We are now ready to consider how several recognition/recall phenomena we have been discussing can be explained with the help of the Synergistic Ecphory Retrieval Model. Let us begin with the two findings from the 'direct comparison' experiment described earlier in this chapter.

The finding that recognition hit rate was higher than the valence of copy cues in the recall task fits well into the model; indeed, it initially suggested the need for the stipulation of different thresholds for different tasks. We can interpret the finding by assuming that in a certain proportion of cases the level (goodness, quality) of ecphoric information fell above the familiarity but below the naming threshold, making it possible for the subject to make a positive familiarity response but not possible to construct the name of the target word. Thus, the difference between the proportion of copy cues judged to be 'old' and the valence of copy cues can be attributed to the higher informational requirements of the naming task than the judgment-of-familiarity task.

Is this latter statement the same as the statement that decision criterion was higher in recall than in recognition in our experiment? I would say, no. I think it is useful to distinguish between decision criteria, which can be assumed to be manipulable by changing instructions in one and the same task and may frequently be under the remembered's own control, and conversion thresholds, which define the minimal 'amounts', or minimal levels of 'goodness', of ecphoric information that are *necessary* for the successful conversion of ecphoric information into a behavioral response. But this is to a large extent a definitional problem. If someone argued that low-confidence and high-confidence recognition decisions reflect performances on two different *kinds of task*, and that the criteria that the remembered has adopted for making these two kinds of recognition judgments are the same as conversion thresholds for the two tasks, there need not be serious disagreement.

Negative correlation

The other critical finding of the 'direct comparison' experiment consisted in the negative correlation between the valence of associative cues and their (false) recognition. Let us see how it fits into the model.

The trace information for a given target word was held constant in both recognition and cued-recall tests. Let us assume that it corresponds to that indicated by point *b* on the abscissa in the diagram in Fig. 14.3. The case in which the false recognition of the associative cue is high and its valence low corresponds to a situation in which the ecphoric information is represented by point *b,y*: the test item can be judged to be familiar, but there is not sufficient ecphoric information to permit the construction of the name of the event. The case from the other extreme of the relation depicted in Fig. 14.2, in which false recognition is low and cue valence high, corresponds to a situation in which the ecphoric information is represented by point b,z: the trace information is the same as it was before, but since the retrieval information has changed, and is assumed to be of higher quality now, the resulting ecphoric information permits the rememberer to construct the name of the event. Since the name of the event is different from the name of the retrieval cue, the rememberer can decide not to call the retrieval cue 'old' even if it looks 'familiar'. The assumption here is that the rememberer calls a test item 'old', if it looks sufficiently familiar, and if the name of the event responsible for the feeling of familiarity cannot be retrieved, or if it can be retrieved and is identical with the test item.

Let us illustrate the reasoning with a concrete example. One of the target words in our experiment was BABY. Its associative cue word *infant* had a very high valence (was a very effective cue for the recall of BABY), but it was very seldom (falsely) recognized as an 'old' word. We can interpret the finding as follows: the rememberer looks at the test word *infant*, it reminds him of the target word BABY and therefore he would 'correctly' judge that *infant* could not have been one of the target words in the study list. It may 'ring a familiar bell', but it does so because it reminds the rememberer of the different study-list word, BABY. On the other hand, in our experiment, the associative cue *small* had a very low valence with respect to the target word LARGE, yet it was frequently (falsely) recognized as an 'old' word. Here the assumption is that the test item in the recognition test again 'rings a familiar bell' but without reminding the rememberer of the study-list word LARGE. On the basis of the feeling of familiarity, and in the absence of contrary evidence about the name of the remembered event, the rememberer now is likely to make a false-positive recognition response.

Other findings

The model has no difficulty accommodating the phenomenon of recognition failure of recallable words. The situation is schematically represented in the diagram by the points b, x and b, z. Trace information is held constant at level b, and retrieval information varies in the recognition and recall test. In the recognition test, it corresponds to level x, and the resultant ecphoric information b, x is below the familiarity threshold. In the recall test with different (higher quality) cues, the retrieval information corresponds to level z, and the resultant ecphoric information b, z is above the recall threshold, making possible the production of the name of the target event.

Although we have discussed the matter before, it may be worth repeating that there is nothing paradoxical about the proposition that retrieval information contained in, or extracted from, some other cue is of 'higher quality' than that contained in the copy cue. The target word in a recognition-failure experiment is always encoded as a part of a larger event (pair of words, a sentence, or whatnot), and it can frequently be retrieved if and only if the large event is retrieved (e.g. Mandler 1980; Rabinowitz *et al.* 1977). It is not particularly surprisingly that a cue other than the copy of the nominal target more readily ecphorizes the engram of the whole event. Watkins's (1974) 'spectacular' data can be regarded as prototypical in this connection: *lique* is a more effective cue for LIQUEFY than is *fy*.

The study–test interactions involving two conditions of study, with recall and recognition tests (Anderson and Bower 1972; McCormack 1972; Tulving 1976) which provided critical data for the rejection of the classical strength-and-threshold model of recognition and recall, can be handled readily by the Synergistic Ecphory Model. For instance, points b,y, b,z, c,y, and c,z in Fig. 14.3 depict a situation in which two different study conditions have resulted in two different levels of trace information, represented by b and c, and in which the retrieval information in the recognition test is represented by z and in the recall test by y. Ecphoric bundles b,z and c,z in recognition are both above the familiarity threshold, producing no differences in the hit rate, whereas one of the ecphoric bundles in recall, b,y, is below the naming threshold, while the other one, c,y, is above it, resulting in successful recall in the latter case but not in the former.

The analysis just given for the study-test interactions in recognition and recall can be readily extended to the other kinds of encoding/retrieval interactions that we discussed in some detail in Chapter 11. In most cases the data can be fitted into the model without any difficulty; in some, some juggling of the levels of trace and retrieval information, as well as the thresholds, may be necessary, although the basic assumptions and the overall structure of the model need not be compromised in any case.

Other properties of the model

Some other properties of the simple Synergistic Ecphory Model may be worth noting. For instance, it can be used to graphically illustrate both trace-dependent and cue-dependent forgetting. Assume that the retrieval information is held constant at level y. Soon after the original event the trace information is at level c, and the resultant ecphoric information c,y is above the naming threshold. With passage of time and interpolated activities, trace information may be reduced to level b, and now the resultant ecphoric information b,y lies below the naming threshold: trace-dependent forgetting has occurred. Similarly, when we hold trace information constant, say at level b, 'forgetting' can occur when retrieval information is reduced from level z to level y: ecphoric information b,z is above and ecphoric information b,y is below the naming the threshold.

The model also implies that, because of the trade-off between trace information and retrieval information, both trace-dependent and cue-dependent forgetting can be 'reversed'. For instance, after the reduction of ecphoric information from c,y to b,y, and attendant inability of the rememberer to recall the event that he could recall earlier, increase in the relevant retrieval information (change of the ecphoric information from b, y to b, z) renders the recall of the 'forgotten' even possible again.

Straightforward illustrations of the trade-off relation between trace and cue information is provided by findings from experimental situations in which 'reversal' of forgetting is demonstrated (e.g. Tulving and Psotka 1971). Olga Watkins and I have done a number of other similar experiments. Subjects would study some material, and then be tested for different randomly selected thirds of the total material in each of three different successive tests. One test would be given immediately after the study, the second one after a longer retention interval, and the third one immediately after the second. Trace-dependent forgetting would occur from the first to the second test, and this forgetting would be 'reversed' by presenting 'higher quality' retrieval cues in the third test.

In one of our experiments, for instance—we referred to it as the 'turned-around faces' experiment—subjects saw photographs of young men. (These materials were kindly lent by Kenneth Laughery who had used them in his own experiments on face recognition (e.g. Laughery, Alexander, and Lane 1971).) A set of six full-face photographs were presented at the rate of three seconds per photograph. In the immediately following test, subjects were tested for 'recognition' of two of the six people they had seen. In this test, the faces were shown from a different angle, constituting half-profile views. An 'old' face was paired with a similar half-profile 'new' face, and the subjects had to select the person they had seem in the study-set. This sequence, of observing six faces in full frontal view and then being tested on two of them presented in half-profile view, was repeated five more times. Thus, after the sixth set of six faces, each learner had seem a total of 36 people, 12 of whom had been tested in immediate tests and 24 of whom had been held 'in reserve' for two subsequent tests. The first of these, the second overall, took place after the learners had seen and taken the immediate test for the last of the six study-sets. In this second test, 12 faces, two from each of the six study sets, were shown to the learners in half-profile view, each paired with a face previously not seen.

In the immediate test, subjects' recognition performance, corrected for guessing, was 86 per cent; in the second test it was reduced to 26 per cent. To 'reverse' the trace-dependent forgetting revealed by the reduction in performance from the first to the second test, retrieval information was 'increased' in the third set. The third test involved the remaining 12 faces, two from each of the six study-sets, but this time the faces were shown in their original full frontal view, paired with similar frontal views of previously unseen faces. The level of performance in the third test was 75 per cent,

We interpreted the data from the three tests to indicate that trace-dependent forgetting can occur, and that it can be reversed by manipulating retrieval information. Since memory performance depends on ecphoric information, and since ecphoric information consists of a 'mixture' of trace information and retrieval information, the ecphoric information required for a successful conversion of a particular kind can be varied by manipulating either the trace information or the retrieval information: smaller 'amounts' of one can be compensated for by larger 'amounts' of the other. In other experiments, we demonstrated the same kind of 'reversibility' of forgetting with different kinds of materials, familiar words, and pictures of complex scenes.

The Synergistic Ecphory Model can also be regarded as a rudimentary idea concerning the important theoretical relation between qualitative properties of memory traces and quantitatively measured memory performance. In the days when memory traces and associations were thought to differ only in 'strength', there was no problem of relating the properties of the underlying mnemonic residue to properties of observed behavior such as 'proportion correct'. But how should we think about the relation between qualitatively different memory traces (e.g. Moscovitch and Craik 1976), on the one hand, and measures of performance, such as 'proportion correct', on the other? The Synergistic Model tells us how: 'proportion correct' in an experimental condition is determined by the proportion of qualitatively different bundles of ecphoric information which lie above corresponding conversion thresholds.

Finally, it may be worth pointing out that the Synergistic Model does not entail the begging of the question concerning retrieval that I mentioned earlier (p. 5). We need not assume that the rememberer knows in advance what he is trying to retrieve, and that he recognizes the 'desired' memory-object when the retrieval (ecphoric) process discovers it. Recollective experience based on the available ecphoric information, carries its own sign of pastness; its informational contents do, or do not, suffice for answering a question, or accomplishing some other task, in the manner analogous to any other kind of information that is perceptually present.

Feeling of pastness in recollection

Given the idea that ecphoric information represents a 'mix' of trace information and retrieval information, we can speculate about one of the problems I raised earlier in the book (p. 187): what determines the feeling of 'pastness' that accompanies recollective experiences? One possible answer is suggested by the Synergistic Ecphory Model: the feeling of pastness reflects the presence of (episodic) *trace* information in the ecphoric 'mix'. In Fig. 14.3, ecphoric information represented by point *a,z* contains little trace information but a good deal of retrieval information, whereas *c,y* contains more trace information but less retrieval information. We might expect, therefore, that the recollective experience corresponding to *a,z* is tinged with a fainter flavor of pastness than the recollective experience based on *c,y*. Related to the feeling of pastness may be the extent to which the rememberer interprets a recollective experience as the memory of a personally experienced episode. We might even wish to speculate that, with other variables held constant, a systematic relation exists between (a) the angle that the direction of the vector of ecphoric information makes with the horizontal axis, and (b) the extent to which a given recollective experience is tinged with pastness and felt to be a personal memory. The continuous values that this angle can assume may correspond to the continuum (cf. Craik and Jacoby 1979) between episodic and semantic 'memories', reflecting different contributions that the two memory systems make to different acts of recollection.

Synopsis

The Synergistic Ecphory Model is not a theory of a kind that would help us to 'predict' outcomes of particular experiments; like GAPS, it is a framework within which we can interpret the findings that have been obtained. Specific theories that have greater precision and power undoubtedly can be worked out within the general model.

Although the model could be extended to other tasks, we have been concerned with recognition and recall, particularly cued recall. We have seen that the two tasks share certain processes and differ from each other with respect to some others. The most important thing they have in common is that they are both subject to the same general laws of ecphory: regardless of the particular cue, cue information is combined with trace information to construct ecphoric information that in turn determines the nature and characteristics of recollective experience and other forms of conversion. The principal, and important, difference between recognition and recall lies in their different informational requirements: more ecphoric information is needed to recall aspects of experienced events than to make recognition decisions on the basis of their felt familiarity.

My earlier contention (e.g. Tulving 1976) that recall and recognition differ only with respect to differences in the nature of retrieval information has turned out to be wrong. The rejection of the idea was aided materially by the findings from the 'direct comparison' experiment, particularly the negative correlation between the valence of associative cues and their false recognition. These findings, as well as some others, motivated the construction of the Synergistic Ecphory Model, a simple but general framework for thinking about phenomena of recognition and recall.

Other theories

The Synergistic Ecphory Model shares many ideas with other contemporary theories of recognition and recall. The view of retrieval that probably comes closest to the model, not only in its general orientation but also in its essential assumptions, is the one proposed by Lockhart, *et al.* (1976). These authors view recognition as a process, 'in which some approximation to the initial encoding of the event is reconstructed', and in which this reconstruction is 'guided and constrained by the recognition stimulus on one hand and information from the episodic trace on the other' (1976, p. 83). In the theory proposed by Lockhart *et al.*, recognition decisions can be made on the basis of what is phenomenologically experienced as a feeling of 'familiarity', even if the stimulus situation does not evoke the recognition of the '*specific* previous instance' (p. 83). Retrieval information does not simply serve to 'evoke' or 'activate' the memory trace but rather shapes the encoding of the test stimulus 'as it develops' (p. 83). Recognition is thought to be a function of the 'number of features which the presentation and test encodings have in common; other things being equal, "rich" traces will be better recognized' (p. 84).

Lockhart *et al.* similarly view recall as a reconstructive process in which the retrieval information provides the basis for the reconstruction of the original experience. 'Recall and recognition do not differ in any crucial way—they are different only in the sense that in recognition re-presentation of the stimulus provides better information from which the initial encoding can be reconstructed' (p. 85). The Synergistic Ecphory Model differs from the Lockhart *et al.* theory primarily in its formal concept of ecphoric information and explicit postulation of different conversion thresholds. Moreover, in the Synergistic Ecphory Model, only one basic 'mechanism' of retrieval is envisaged, whereas in the Lockhart *et al.* theory two different functions of cues are distinguished, 'reconstructive' and 'selective'. The process of ecphory as envisaged in GAPS and in the Synergistic Ecphory Model is more akin to the reconstructive' type of retrieval envisaged by Lockhart *et al.*; the 'selective' function of cues, in some sense, might be regarded as a post-ecphoric operation.

Thus, on the whole, the two theoretical treatments of recognition and recall are highly compatible with one another.

At one point I had a minor controversy with Craik, concerning the problem of whether 'compatibility' of trace and cue information—what I now refer to as ecphoric information—alone is sufficient to describe and understand retrieval as I argued (Tulving 1979*b*), or whether in addition to this compatibility it is also necessary to take into account the 'goodness' of encoding, as Craik and Fisher argued (Craik 1979; Fisher and Craik 1977). Our colleague, Daniel Schacter, was kind enough to point out to us that we were talking past each other and that there was no real disagreement. I was talking about the situation that existed *after* the act of retrieval was completed, in other words, taking as my starting point a particular bundle of ecphoric information. At that point, indeed, the goodness of retrieval cues and memory traces, considered separately, are immaterial; what matters is the extent to which the two have matched. Craik and Fisher, on the other hand, were talking about the situation existing *before* the beginning of what in GAPS is called the ecphoric process. At this point, a particular engram exists in the memory store, and whether or not it is going to be successfully retrieved, indeed, depends on how good, deep, distinctive, or elaborate the engram is, as does its compatibility with potential retrieval cues. The 'controversy' provided a talking point to Douglas Nelson and his colleagues (Nelson and McEvoy 1979; Nelson, Walling and McEvoy 1979), in their discussion of a series of experiments completed before the 'controversy' emerged, but otherwise it enlightened no one and did not advance our understanding by one iota. Had we had a scheme such as the Synergistic Ecphory Model then, we probably could have prevented the waste of time.

Another theory of recognition and recall with which the Synergistic Ecphory Model has a number of features in common has been proposed by Moeser (1977). She elaborated the notion of resonance as the basic recognition mechanism into a two-stage recognition process. The first stage is defined by resonance of a number of episodic traces that share features with a retrieval cue, whereas the second stage consists in retrieval of a specific trace from the resonating set. Recognition of a test item as 'old' may be based on only the first stage, resulting from the occurrence of a certain amount of resonance. It may also be brought about, however, as a consequence of retrieval of a particular episodic trace. Moeser's two stages, resonance and retrieval, may be likened to familiarity conversion and the name-identification conversion of the Synergistic Ecphory Model: in Moeser's theory, too, the second stage entails the first, whereas the first does not entail the second. The idea of a fixed ordering of different kinds of recollective experience—'feeling of familiarity' preceding, and being necessarily involved in, the naming of an event—is an important concept in both theories.

The Synergistic Ecphory Model is also similar in many ways to the theory of episodic memory proposed by Kintsch (1974). In Kintsch's theory, the nature of the interaction between episodic and semantic memory is also regarded as crucial, memory traces of episodes are conceptualized as new constructions (rather than tagging of existing structures), pattern matching and pattern completion are postulated as the basic mechanism of recognition, the existence of conversion thresholds (although not so named) proposed, and the assumption is made that the retrieval cue, encoded in terms of information in semantic memory, is matched simultaneously to all episodic traces. Kintsch's theory differs from the Synergistic Ecphory Model primarily in its assumption that the cued-recall mechanism is different depending upon 'whether or not the cue has been properly encoded together with a to-be-recalled word' (p. 90). This assumption is similar to the assumption made by Jones (1978, 1979) who also has proposed two different retrieval mechanisms, direct access and generation/retrieval. Both Kintsch's and Jones' theories are variants of the generation/recognition theory, whereas the Synergistic Ecphory Model views ecphory as a single-stage process.

Yet another theory of retrieval with which the Synergistic Ecphory Model has many features in common is that of Ratcliff (1978). Ratcliff was primarily concerned with recognition, but his theory could be readily extended to cover recall as well. Ratcliff used the metaphor of resonance to illustrate the mechanism of retrieval, allowing for variations in the amplitude of resonance with which memory traces respond to retrieval information. The amplitude of this resonance is influenced by what Ratcliff calls relatedness, the degree to which retrieval information matches the trace information. The concept of ecphoric information in the Synergistic Ecphory Model is equivalent to Ratcliff's concept of relatedness.

Ratcliff's retrieval theory is concerned with both speed and accuracy of recognition, and ingeniously accounts for the speed-accuracy trade-off. It does so by postulating two performance thresholds separating one kind of retrieval outcome from another: match boundary and non-match boundary. An 'old' response is made when the amount of evidence or relatedness exceeds the match boundary, and a 'new' response is contingent upon this evidence falling below the non-match boundary. Response latency is determined by the rate of accumulation of evidence for relatedness over time between the two boundaries.

Both Ratcliff's theory and the Synergistic Ecphory Model conceptualize stored information and retrieval information in terms of bundles of qualitatively different features; the retrieval mechanism is thought of as a feature-matching process ('comparison' in Ratcliff's theory); this process operates on a very large number of traces simultaneously; no inter-item connections or links are assumed; the output from the 'comparison' (ecphoric) process is determined by the informational overlap between cues and traces; 'new' responses in recognition result from the lack of sufficient evidence for relatedness (lack of sufficient ecphoric information); performance depends on the relation between evidence for relatedness (ecphoric information) and different performance thresholds.

Finally, it is a bit more difficult to judge how Mandler's theory of recognition (e.g. Mandler *et al.* 1969; Mandler 1980), as well as other similar dual-process theories of recognition (e.g. Atkinson and Juola 1973; Humphreys 1978; Jacoby and Dallas 1981; Tiberghien 1976) compare with the Synergistic Ecphory Model. On the one hand, the burden of memory performance in these theories is carried by what has been stored, rather than by a conjunction of stored information and retrieval information. Retrieval information in these theories plays the role of 'activating' the memory trace or providing 'access' to it, with the outcome of the attempted retrieval depending upon the probability of access and the characteristics of the 'accessed' information. The fact that there is no concept in these theories that corresponds to the central concept of ecphoric information in the Synergistic Ecphory Model characterizes the basic difference between them. On the other hand, different recognition and recall thresholds postulated in the Synergistic Ecphory Model seem to have a definite affinity to Mandler's idea that recognition consists of two separate processes, detection of familiarity and utilization of retrieval mechanisms. I am assuming that familiarity judgments are entailed in retrieval, but not vice versa, whereas in Mandler's theory the two processes are additive and separate. It is conceivable that the retrieval process underlying, say, identification of the name of the target event is independent of the process giving rise to the feeling of familiarity, contrary to the assumptions now made in the Synergistic Ecphory Model. For the time being, however, and for my immediate purposes—to seek for broad generalities in the functioning of episodic memory—an identification process that presupposes the process responsible for feelings of familiarity remains the preferred view.

References

Adams, J. A., Marshall, P. H., and Bray, N. W. (1971). *J. verb. Learn. verb. Behav.* **10**, 548–55.

Albert, M. S., Butters, N., and Levin, J. (1979). In *Alcohol intoxication and withdrawal* (ed. H. Begleiter and B. Kissen). Plenum Press, New York.

Allen, G. A., Mahler, W. A., and Estes, W. K. (1969). *J. verb. Learn. verb. Behav.* **8**, 463–70.

Altman, J. and Das, G. D. (1966). *J. comp. Neurol.* **216**, 337–89.

Anderson, J. R. (1976). *Language, memory, and thought*. Erlbaum, Hillsdale, NJ.

—— (1978). *Psychol. Rev.* **85**, 249–77.

—— and Bower, G. H. (1972). *Psychol. Rev.* **79**, 97–123.

—— —— (1973). *Human associative memory*. V. H. Winston, Washington, DC.

—— —— (1974), *Memory Cogn.* **2**, 406–12.

—— and Reder, L. M. (1979). In *Levels of processing in human memory* (ed. L. S. Cermak and F. I. M. Craik). Erlbaum, Hillsdale, NJ.

—— and Ross, B. H. (1980). *J. exp. Psychol.: Hum. Learn. Memory* **6**, 441–65.

Anderson, N. H. (1977). *Percept. Psychophys.* **21**, 201–15.

Anderson, R. C. and Pichert, J. W. (1978). *J. verb. Learn. verb. Behav.* **17**, 1–12.

—— —— Goetz, E. T., Schallert, D. L., Stevens, K. V., and Trollip, S. R. (1976). *J. verb. Learn. verb. Behav.* **15**, 667–79.

Anglin, J. M. (1977). *Word, object, and conceptual development*. W. W. Norton, New York.

Anisfeld, M. and Knapp, M. (1968). *J. exp. Psychol.* **77**, 171–9.

Arbuckle, T. Y. and Katz, W. A. (1976). *J. exp. Psychol.: Hum. Learn. Memory* **2**, 362–9.

Asch, S. E. (1969). *Am. Psychol.* **24**, 92–102.

Atkinson, R. C., Herrmann, D. J., and Wescourt, K. T. (1974). In *Theories in cognitive psychology: The Loyola Sympsium* (ed. R. L. Solso). Erlbaum, Potomac, Md.

—— and Juola, J. F. (1973). In *Attention and performance IV* (ed. S. Kornblum). Academic Press, New York.

—— —— (1974). In *Contemporary developments in mathematical psychology* (ed. D. H. Krantz, R. C. Atkinson, R. D. Luce, and P. Suppes). Freeman, San Francisco.

—— and Shiffrin, R. M. (1965). Tech. Rep. #79, Psychol. Series, Institute for Mathematical Studies in the Social Sciences. Stanford University Press.

—— —— (1968). In *The psychology of learning and motivation*, Vol. 2 (ed. K. W. Spence and J. T. Spence). Academic Press, New York.

—— —— (1971). *Scient. Am.* Aug., 82–90.

Baddeley, A. D. (1976). *The psychology of memory*. Basic Books, New York.

—— (1978). *Psychol. Rev.* **85**, 139–52.

—— (1979). In *Levels of processing in human memory* (ed. L. S. Cermak and F. I. M. Craik). Erlbaum, Hillsdale, NJ.

—— (1981). In *Human memory and amnesia* (ed. L. S. Cermak). Erlbaum, Hillsdale, NJ.

—— Lewis, V., and Nimmo-Smith, I. (1978). In *Practical aspects of memory* (ed. M. M. Gruneberg, P. E. Morris, and R. N. Sykes). Academic Press, London.

Bahrick, H. P. (1965). *Psychol. Rev.* **72**, 60–73.
—— (1969). *J. exp. Psychol.* **79**, 213–39.
—— (1970). *Psychol. Rev.* **77–1**, 215–22.
—— (1979). In *Levels of processing in human memory* (ed. L. S. Cermak and F. I. M. Craik). Erlbaum, Hillsdale, NJ.
—— and Bahrick, P.O. (1964). *Q. Jl exp. Psychol.* **16**, 318–24.
Baker, L. and Santa, J. L. (1977). *Memory Cogn.* **5**, 308–14.
Balota, D. A. and Neely, J. H. (1980). *J. exp. Psychol.: Hum. Learn. Memory* **6**, 576–87.
Barclay, J. R., Bransford, J. D., Franks, J. J., McCarrell, N. S., and Nitsch, K. (1974). *J. verb. Learn. verb. Behav.* **13**, 471–81.
Barnes, J. M. and Underwood, B. J. (1959). *J. exp. Psychol.* **58**, 97–105.
Bartlett, F. C. (1932). *Remebering: a study in experimental and social psychology.* Cambridge University Press.
—— (1967). *Encyclopedia Britannica*, Vol. 2.
Bartlett, J. C. (1977). *J. exp. Psychol.: Hum. Learn. Memory* **3**, 719–32.
—— and Tulving, E. (1974). *J. verb. Learn. verb. Behav* **13**, 297–309.
Bartling, C. A. and Thompson, C. P. (1977). *J. exp. Psychol.: Hum. Learn. Memory* **3**, 690–700.
Begg, I. (1979). *Memory Cogn.* **7**, 113–23.
Bellezza, F. S., Richards, D. L., and Geiselman, R. E. (1976). *Memory Cogn.* **4**, 415–21.
Bergson, H. (1911). *Matter and memory.* Allen & Unwin, London.
Bilodeau, E. A. and Blick, K. A. (1965). *Psychol. Rep.* 16 (Monogr. Suppl. 6).
—— Fox, P. W., and Blick, K. A. (1963). *J. verb. Learn. verb. Behav.* **2**, 422–8.
Birnbaum, I. M. and Parker, E. S. (eds.) (1977). *Alcohol and human memory.* Erlbaum, Hillsdale, NJ.
Bjork, R. A. (1975). In *Information processing and cognition* (ed. R. L. Solso). Wiley, New York.
Bobrow, D. G. (1975). In *Representation and understanding* (ed. D. G. Bobrow and A. Collins). Academic Press, New York.
—— and Winograd, T. (1977). *Cogn. Sci.* **1**, 3–46.
Bock, M. (1976). *J. verb. Learn. verb. Behav.* **15**, 183–91.
Bousfield, W. A. (1953). *J. gen. Psychol.* **49**, 229–40.
Bower, G. H. (1967). In *The psychology of learning and motivation*, Vol. 1 (ed. K. W. Spence and J. T. Spence). Academic Press, New York.
—— (1970). *Cogn. Psychol.* **1**, 18–46.
—— (1972a). In *Cognition in learning and memory* (ed. L. W. Gregg). Wiley, New York.
—— (1972b). In *Coding processes in human memory* (ed. A. W. Melton and E. Martin). Winston, Washington.
—— (1981). *Am. Psychol.* **36**, 129–48.
—— Clark, M. C., Lesgold, A. M., and Winzenz, D. (1969). *J. verb. Learn. verb. Behav.* **8**, 323–43.
Bowyer, P. A. and Humphreys, M. S. (1979). *J. exp. Psychol.: Hum. Learn. Memory* **5**, 348–59.
Bransford, J. D., Barclay, J. R., and Franks, J. J. (1972). *Cogn. Psychol.* **3**, 193–209.
—— and Franks, J. J. (1971). *Cogn. Psychol.* **2**, 331–50.
—— —— Morris, C. D., and Stein, B. S. (1979). In *Levels of processing in human memory* (ed. L. S. Cermak and F. I. M. Craik). Erlbaum, Hillsdale, NJ.
Bregman, A. S. (1977). *Cogn. Psychol.* **9**, 250–92.

Broadbent, D. E. (1958). *Perception and communication*. Pergamon Press, London.
—— (1963). *J. verb. Learn. verb. Behav.* **2**, 34–9.
—— and Broadbent, M. H. P. (1980). In *Attention and performance VIII* (ed. R. Nickerson). Erlbaum, Hillsdale, NJ.
Brown, A. L. (1975). In *Advances in child development and behavior*, Vol. 10 (ed. H. W. Reese). Academic Press, New York.
Brown, J., Lewis, V. J., and Monk, A. F. (1977). *Q. Jl exp. Psychol.* **29**, 461–73.
Brown, R. and McNeill, D. (1966). *J. verb. Learn. verb. Behav.* **5**, 325–37.
Brown, W. (1923). *J. exp. Psychol.* **6**, 377–82.
Bruce, D. and Cofer, C. N. (1967). *J. exp. Psychol.* **75**, 283–9.
Bruner, J. S. (1969). In *The pathology of memory* (ed. G. A. Talland and N. C. Waugh), Academic Press, New York.
Bryan, W. L. and Harter, N. (1897). *Psychol. Rev.* **4**, 27–53.
Buschke, H. (1963).*Science, NY* **140**, 56–7.
—— (1974). *Science, NY* **184**, 579–81.
Caine, E. D., Ebert, M. H., and Weingartner, H. (1977). *Neurology, Minneap.* **27**, 1087–92.
Cannell, C. F. (1977). Vital and health statistics: Series 2, Data evaluation and methods research No. 69. US Department of Health, Education, and Welfare.
Cattell, J. McK. (1887). *Mind* **12**, 68–74.
Cermak, L. S. (1981). *Human memory and amnesia*. Erlbaum, Hillsdale, NJ.
Chalmers, T. (1833). *On the adaptation of external nature to the intellectual constitution of man*. Carey, Lea, & Blanchard, Philadelphia.
Chase, W. G. and Ericsson, K. A. (1981). In *Cognitive skills and their acquisition* (ed. J. R. Anderson). Erlbaum, Hillsdale, NJ.
Claparède, E. (1911). *Arch Psychol.* **11**, 79–90. [Translated in *Organization and pathology of thought* (ed. D. Rapaport). Columbia University Press, New York (1951).]
Clifford, W. K. (1890). *Seeing and thinking*. Macmillan, London.
Cofer, C. N (1960). *Ann, NY Acad. Sci.* **91**, 94–107.
—— (1969). In *The pathology of memory* (ed. G. Talland and N. C. Waugh). Academic Press, New York.
Cohen, B. H. (1963). *J. exp. Psychol.* **66**, 227–34.
Cohen, N. J. and Squire, L. R. (1980). *Science, NY* **210**, 207–9.
Collingwood, R. G. (1945).*The idea of nature*. Clarendon Press, Oxford.
Collins, A. M. and Loftus, E. F. (1975). *Psychol. Rev.* **82**, 407–28.
—— and Quillian, M. R. (1972). In *Organization of memory* (ed. E. Tulving and W. Donaldson). Academic Press, New York.
Conrad, C. (1974). *Memory Cogn.* **2**, 130–8.
Craik, F. I. M. (1973). In *Communication and affect: language and thought* (ed. P. Pliner, L. Krames, and T. Alloway). Academic Press, New York.
—— (1979). In *Levels of processing in human memory* (ed. L. S. Cermak and F. I. M. Craik). Erlbaum, Hillsdale, NJ.
—— (1981). In *Attention and performance IX* (ed. A. D. Baddeley and J. Long). Erlbaum, Hillsdale, NJ.
—— and Jacoby, L. L. (1975). In *Cognitive theory*, Vol. 1 (ed. F. Restle, R. M. Shiffrin, N. J. Castellan, H. R. Lindman, and D. B. Pisoni). Erlbaum, Hillsdale, NJ.
—— —— (1979). In *Levels of processing in human memory* (ed. L. S. Cermak and F. I. M. Craik). Erlbaum, Hillsdale, NJ.
—— and Lockhart, R. S. (1972). *J. verb. Learn. verb. Behav.* **11**, 671–84.

—— and Tulving, E. (1975). *J. exp. Psychol.: Gen.* **104**, 268–94.

—— and Watkins, M. J. (1973). *J. verb. Learn. verb. Behav.* **12**, 599–607.

Craik, K. (1943). *The nature of explanation.* Cambridge University Press.

Cramer, P. (1968). *Word association.* Academic Press, New York.

Cross, R. (1974). *Evidence.* Butterworths, London.

Crovitz, H. F. and Schiffman, H. (1974). *Bull. psychonom. Soc.* **4**, 517–18.

Crowder, R. G. (1976). *Principles of learning and memory.* Erlbaum, Hillsdale, NJ.

Darley, C. F. and Murdock, B. B. (1971). *J. exp. Psychol.* **91**, 66–73.

de Schonen, S. (1968). *Ann. Psychol.* **2**, 1–17.

Dong, T. (1972). *J. exp. Psychol.* **93**, 123–239.

Douglas, R. J. (1975), In *The hippocampus*, Vol. 2 (ed. R. L. Isaacson and K. H. Pribram). Plenum Press, New York.

Drachman, D. A. and Leavitt, J. (1972). *J. exp. Psychol.* **93**, 302–8.

Eagle, M. and Ortof, E. (1967). *J. verb. Learn. verb. Behav.* **6**, 226–31.

Earhard, M. (1967*a*). *J. verb. Learn. verb. Behav.* **6**, 257–63.

—— (1967*b*). *Can. J. Psychol.* **21**, 15–24.

—— (1969). *J. exp. Psychol.* **80**, 412–18.

—— (1977). *Can. J. Psychol.* **31**, 139–50.

Ebbinghaus, H. (1885). *Über das Gedächtnis.* Duncker and Humblot, Leipzig. [*English translation*, Dover Press, New York.]

Ehrlich, S. (1979), In *Memory organization and structure* (ed. C. R. Puff). Academic Press, New York.

Eich, J. E. (1975). *J. verb. Learn. verb. Behav.* **14**, 408–17.

—— (1977). In *Alcohol and human memory* (ed. I. M. Birnbaum and E. S. Parker). Erlbaum, Hillsdale, NJ.

—— (1980). *Memory Cogn.* **8**, 157–73.

—— Weingartner, H., Stillman, R. C., and Gillin, J. C. (1975). *J. verb. Learn. verb. Behav.* **14**, 408–17.

Entwistle, D. R. (1966). *J. verb. Learn. verb. Behav.* **5**, 558–65.

Erdelyi, M. H. and Becker, J. (*1974*). *Cogn. Psychol.* **6**, 159–71.

—— Buschke, H., and Finkelstein, S (1977). *Memory Cogn.* **5**, 283–6.

Estes, W. K. (1959). In *Psychology: a study of a science*, Vol. 2 (ed. S. Koch). McGraw-Hill, New York.

—— (1960). *Psychol. Rev.* **67**, 207–23.

—— (1972). In *Coding processes in human memory* (ed. A. W. Melton and E. Martin). Winston, Washington, DC.

—— (1976*a*). *Psychol. Rev.* **83**, 37–64.

—— (1976*b*). In *1977 Yearbook of science and the future* (ed. D. Calhoun). Encyclopedia Britannica, Chicago.

—— (1978). In *Handbook of learning and cognitive processes*, Vol. 6. (ed. W. K. Estes). Erlbaum, Hillsdale NJ.

—— (1980). *Am. Scient.* **68**, 62–9.

—— and DaPolito, F. (1967). *J. exp. Psychol.* **75**, 18–26.

Evans, F. J. and Thorn, W. A. F. (1966). *Int. J. clin. exp. Hypnosis* **14**, 162–79.

Eysenck, M. W. (1975). *J. Geront.* **30**, 174–80.

—— (1978). *Br. J. Psychol.* **68**, 157–69.

—— (1979). In *Levels of processing in human memory* (ed. L. S. Cermak and F. I. M. Craik). Erlbaum, Hillsdale, NJ.

Feigenbaum, E. A. (1961). *Proc. West. Joint Computer Conf.* **19**, 121–32.

Fisher, R. P. and Craik, F. I. M. (1977). *J. exp. Psychol.: Hum. Learn. Memory* **3**, 701–11.

Flavell, J. H. and Wellman, H. M. (1977). In *Perspectives on the development of memory and cognition* (ed. R. V. Kail Jr and J. W. Hagen). Erlbaum, Hillsdale, NJ.

Flexser, A. J. and Tulving, E. (1978). *Psychol. Rev.* **85**, 153–71.

Fox, P. W., Blick, K. A., and Bilodeau, E. A. (1964). *J. exp. Psychol.* **68**, 321–2.

Fraisse, P. (1963). *The psychology of time*. Harper & Row, New York.

Frase, L. T. and Kammann, R. (1974). *Memory Cogn.* **2**,181–4.

Furlong, E. J. (1951). *A study in memory*. T. Nelson, London.

Galton, F. (1880). *Brain* **2**, 149–62.

Gardiner, J. M. and Tulving, E. (1980). *J. verb. Learn. verb. Behav.* **19**, 194–209.

—— and Watkins, M. J. (1979). *Bull. psychonom. Soc.* **13**, 108–10.

Garner, W. R. (1980). In *Attention and performance VIII* (ed. R. S. Nickerson). Erlbaum, Hillsdale, NJ.

Garofalo, J. and Hindelang, J. (1977). US Department of Justice, Analytic Report SD-VAD-4.

Geiselman, R. E. and Bjork, R. A. (1980). *Cogn. Psychol.* **12**, 188–205.

—— and Glenny, J. (1977). *Memory Cogn.* **5**, 499–504.

Gibson, E. J. (1953). *Psychol. Bull.* **50**, 401–31.

—— (1969). *Principles of perceptual learning and development*. Appleton-Century-Crofts, New York.

Gilhooly, K. J. and Gilhooly, M. L. (1979). *Memory Cogn.* **7**, 214–23.

Glanzer, M. (1969). *J. verb. Learn. verb. Behav.* **8**, 105–11.

—— and Duarte, A. (1971). *J. verb. Learn. verb. Behav.* **10**, 625–30.

Godden, D. R. and Baddeley, A. D. (1975). *Br. J. Psychol.* **66**, 325–31.

Greenwald, A. G. (1981). In *The psychology of learning and motivation*, Vol. 15. Academic Press, New York.

Grice, H. P. (1941). *Mind* **50**, 340.

Hall, T. S. (1969). *History of general physiology*, Vols. I and II. University of Chicago Press.

Hamilton, W. (1859). *Lectures on metaphysics and logic*. William Blackwood, Edinburgh.

Hardin, G. (1961). *Nature and man's fate*. New American Library, New York.

Harris, R. J. and Monaco, G. E. (1978). *J. exp. Psychol.: Gen.* **107**, 1–22.

Hart, J. T. (1965). *J. educat. Psychol.* **56**, 208–16.

Hasher, L. and Griffin, M. (1978). *J. exp. Psychol.: Hum. Learn. Memory* **4**, 318–30.

Herrmann, D. J. and Harwood, J. R. (1980). *J. exp. Psychol.: Hum. Learn. Memory* **6**, 467–78.

—— and McLaughlin, J. P. (1973). *J. exp. Psychol.* **99**, 174–9.

Hilgard, E. R (1956). *Theories of learning*, 2nd edn. Appleton-Century-Crofts, New York.

—— (1977). *Divided consciousness*. Wiley, New York.

Hintzman, D. L. (1978). *The psychology of learning and memory*. Freeman, San Francisco.

Hirst, W., Spelke, E. S., Reaves, C. C., Caharack, G., and Neisser, U. (1980). *J. exp. Psychol.* **109**, 98–117.

Hollan, J. D. (1975). *Psychol. Rev.* **82**, 154–5.

Hollingworth, H. L. (1913). *Am. J. Psychol.* **24**, 532–44.

—— (1928). *J. gen. Psychol.* **1**, 79–90.

Holton, G. and Brush, S. G. (1973). *Introduction to concepts and theories in physical science*, 2nd edn. Addison Wesley, Reading, Mass.

Honig, W. K. (1978). In *Cognitive aspects of animal behavior* (ed. S. H. Hulse,

W. K. Honig, and H. Fowler).Erlbaum, Hillsdale, NJ.

Hoppe, R. B. and Dahl, P. R. (1978).*Psychol. Rec.* **28**, 219–29.

Humphreys, M. S. (1978). *J. verb. Learn. verb. Behav.* **17**, 175–88.

—— and Bowyer, P. A. (1980). *Memory Cogn.* **8**, 271–7.

—— and Galbraith, R. C. (1975). *J. exp. Psychol.: Hum. Learn. Memory* **1**, 702–10.

Hunt, R. R., Elliott, J. M., and Spence, M. J. (1979). *J. exp. Psychol.: Hum. Learn. Memory* **5**, 339–47.

Hyde, T. S. and Jenkins, J. J. (1969). *J. exp. Psychol.* **82**, 472–81.

Indow, T. (1980). In *Attention and performance VIII* (ed. R. S. Nickerson). Erlbaum, Hillsdale, NJ.

Ingvar, D. H. (1979). In *Perspectives on memory research* (ed. L. -G. Nilsson). Erlbaum, Hillsdale, NJ.

Isen, A. M., Shalker, T. E., Clark, M., and Karp, L. (1978). *J. Personal. Soc. Psychol.* **36**, 1–12.

Jacoby, L. L. (1973). *J. verb. Learn. verb. Behav.* **12**, 674–82.

—— (1974). *J. verb. Learn. verb. Behav.* **13**, 483–96.

—— (1978). *J. verb. Learn. verb. Behav.* **17**, 649–67.

—— and Craik, F. I. M. (1979). In *Levels of processing in human memory* (ed. L. S. Cermak and F. I. M. Craik). Erlbaum, Hillsdale, NJ.

—— and Dallas, M. (1981). *J. exp. Psychol.: Gen.* **110**, 306–40.

James, W. (1890). *Principles of psychology*. Holt, New York.

Jaynes, J. (1976). *The origin of consciousness in the breakdown of the bicameral mind*. Houghton Mifflin, Boston, Mass.

Jenkins, J. J. (1974*a*). In *Theories in cognitive psychology: the Loyola Symposium*. Erlbaum, Potomac, Md.

—— (1974*b*). *Am. Psychol.* **29**, 785–95.

—— (1979). In *Levels of processing in human memory* (eds. L. S. Cermak and F. I. M. Craik). Erlbaum, Hillsdale, NJ.

—— Wald, J., and Pittenger, J. B. (1978). In *Minnesota studies in the philosophy of science*, Vol. 9 (ed. C. W. Savage). University of Minnesota Press, Minneapolis.

Johnson, M. K. and Raye, C. L. (1981). *Psychol. Rev.* **88**, 67–85.

Johnson-Laird, P. N., Gibbs, G., and De Mowbray, J. (1978). *Memory Cogn.* **6**, 372–5.

Jones, G. V. (1976). *J. exp. Psychol.: Gen.* **105**, 277–93.

—— (1978*a*). *Psychol. Rev.* **85**, 464–9.

—— (1978*b*). *Br. J. Math. statist. Psychol.* **31**, 1–10.

——(1979). In *Tutorial essays in psychology* (ed. N. S. Sutherland). Erlbaum, Hillsdale, NJ.

—— (1980). In *Attention and performance VIII* (ed. R. S. Nickerson). Erlbaum, Hillsdale, NJ.

Jung, C. G. (1973). In *The collected works of C. G. Jung*, Vol. 2. Kegan Paul, London. [*Originally published 1909.*]

Keenan, J. M. and Baillet, S. D. (1980). In *Attention and performance VIII* (ed. R. S. Nickerson). Erlbaum, Hillsdale, NJ.

Kihlstrom, J. F. (1980). *Cogn. Psychol.* **12**, 227–51.

—— and Evans, F. J. (eds.) (1979). *Functional disorders of memory*. Erlbaum, Hillsdale, NJ.

King, H. E. (1972). In *Psychopathology* (ed. M. Hammer, K. Salzinger, and S. Sutton). Wiley, New York.

Kinsbourne, M. and Wood, F. (1975). In *Short-term memory* (ed. D. Deutsch and

J. A. Deutsch). Academic Press, New York.
Kinsbourne, M. and Wood, F. (1982). In *Human memory and amnesia* (ed. L. S. Cermak). Erlbaum, Hillsdale, NJ.
Kintsch, W. (1968). *J. exp. Psychol.* **78**, 481–7.
—— (1970). In *Models of human memory* (ed. D. A. Norman). Academic Press, New York.
—— (1972). In *Origanization of memory* (ed. E. Tulving and W. Donaldson). Academic Press, New York.
—— (1974). *The representation of meaning in memory*. Erlbaum, Hillsdale, NJ.
—— (1978). *Psychol. Rev.* **85**, 464–9.
—— (1980). In *Attention and performance VIII* (ed. R. S. Nickerson) Erlbaum, Hillsdale, NJ.
Klein, K. and Saltz, E. (1976). *J. exp. Psychol.: Hum. Learn. Memory* **2**, 671–9.
Kochevar, J. W. and Fox, P. W. (1980). *Am. J. Psychol.* **93**, 355–66.
Koestler, A. (1969). In *The patholody of memory* (ed. G. A. Talland and N. C. Waugh). Academic Press, New York.
Koffka, K. (1935). *Principles of Gestalt psychology*. Harcourt, Brace, New York.
Köhler, W. (1941). *Proc. Am. phil. Soc.* **84**, 489–502.
Kolers, P. A. (1975*a*). *J. exp. Psychol.: Hum. Learn. Memory* **1**, 689–701.
—— (1975*b*). *Cogn. Psychol.* **7**, 289–306.
—— (1976). *J. exp. Psychol.: Hum. Learn. Memory* **5**, 554–65.
—— (1979).In *Levels of processing in human memory* (ed. L. S. Cermak and F. I. M. Craik). Erlbaum, Hillsdale, NJ.
—— and Palef, S. R. (1976). *Memory Cogn.* **4**, 553–8.
—— and Smythe, W. E. (1979). *Can. J. Psychol.* **33**, 158–84.
Kosslyn, S. M. (1976). *Cogn. Psychol.* **7**, 341–70.
Kuhn, T. S. (1962). *The structure of scientific revolutions*. University of Chicago Press.
Lachman, R. (1973). *J. exp. Psychol.* **99**, 199–208.
—— and Field, W. H. (1965). *Psychon. Sci.* **2**, 225–6.
—— Lachman, J. L., and Butterfield, E. C. (1979). *Cognitive psychology and information processing*. Erlbaum, Hillsdale, NJ.
—— Shaffer, J. P., and Hennrikus, D. (1974). *J. verb. Learn. verb. Behav.* **13**, 613–25.
—— and Tuttle, A. V. (1965). *J. exp. Psychol.* **70**, 386–93.
Landauer, T. K. (1975). *Cog. Psychol.* **7**, 495–531.
Langley, P. and Simon, H. A. (1981). In *Cognitive skills and their acquisition* (ed. J. R. Anderson). Erlbaum, Hillsdale, NJ.
Lashley, K. S. (1950). In *Society of experimental biology symposium. No. 4: Physiological mechanisms in animal behaviour*. Cambridge University Press.
Laughery, K. R., Alexander, J. F., and Lane, A. B. (1971). *J. appl. Psychol.* **55**, 477–83.
LeCocq, P. and Tiberghien, G. (1981). *Memoire et decision*. Presses Universitaires de Lille.
Ley, R. (1977). *Memory Cogn.* **5**, 523–8.
Lichtenstein, E. H. and Brewer, W. F. (1980). *Cogn. Psychol.* **12**, 412–45.
Light, L. L. (1972). *J. exp. Psychol.* **96**, 255–62.
—— and Carter-Sobell, L. (1970). *J. verb. Learn. verb. Behav.* **9**, 1–11.
—— Kimble, G. A., and Pellegrino, J. W. (1975). *J. exp. Psychol.: Gen.* **104**, 30–6.
Linton, M. (1979). *Psychology Today*. **13**, 81–86.
Lloyd, G. G. and Lishman, W. A. (1975). *Psychol. Med.* **5**, 173–80.

Locke, J. (1690). *Essay on the human understanding*. Thos. Basset, London.
Lockhart, R. S., Craik, F. I. M., and Jacoby, L. (1976). In *Recall and recognition* (ed. J. Brown).Wiley, London.
—— and Murdock, B. B. Jr (1970). *Psychol. Bull.* **74**, 100–9.
Loftus, E. F. (1975). *Cogn. Psychol.* **7**, 560–72.
—— (1977). *Memory Cogn.* **5**, 696–9.
—— and Loftus, G. R. (1980). *Am. Psychol.* **35**, 409–20.
—— Miller, D. G., and Burns, H. J. (1978). *J. exp. Psychol.: Hum. Learn. Memory* **4**, 19–31.
—— and Palmer, J. C. (1974). *J. verb. Learn. verb. Behav.* **13**, 585–9.
—— and Zanni, G. (1975). *Bull. psychonom. Soc.* **5**, 86–8.
Loftus, G. R. (1978). *Memory Cogn.* **6**, 312–19.
Luria, A. R. (1976). *The neuropsychology of memory*. Winston, Washington, DC.
McClelland, A. G. R., Rawles, R. E., and Sinclair, F. E. (1981). *Memory Cogn.* **9**, 164–8.
McCloskey, M. and Santee, J. (1981). *J. exp. Psychol.: Hum. Learn. Memory* **7**, 66–71.
McCormack, P. D. (1972). *Can. J. Psychol.* **26**, 19–41.
McFarland, C. E., Frey, T. J., and Rhodes, D. D. (1980). *J. verb. Learn. verb. Behav.* **19**, 210–25.
McGeoch, J. A. (1942). *The psychology of human learning*. Longmans Green, New York.
—— and Irion, A. L. (1952). *The psychology of human learning*. Longmans, Green, New York.
McGovern, J. B. (1964). *Psychol. Monogr.* 78, No. 16. [Whole No. 593.]
McKoon, G. and Ratcliff, R. (1979). *J. verb. Learn. verb. Behav.* **18**, 463–80.
Madigan, S. (1976). *Memory Cogn.* **4**, 233–6.
Mair, W. G. P., Warrington, E. K., and Weiskrantz, L. (1979). *Brain* **102**, 749–83.
Malcolm, N. (1942). *Mind* **51**, 18–46.
Mandler, G. (1975). *Mind and emotion*. Wiley, New York.
—— (1979). In *Perspectives on memory research* (ed. L. -G. Nilsson). Erlbaum, Hillsdale, NJ.
—— (1980). *Psychol. Rev.* **87**, 252–71.
—— Pearlstone, Z., and Koopmans, H. S. (1969). *J. verb. Learn. verb. Behav.* **8**, 410–23.
Mandler, J. M. and Johnson, N. S. (1977). *Cogn. Psychol.* **9**, 111–51.
Marcel, A. J. and Steel, R. G. (1973). *Q. Jl exp. Psychol.* **25**, 368–77.
Marcel, T. (1980). In *Attention and performance VIII* (ed. R. S. Nickerson). Erlbaum, Hillsdale, NJ.
Martin, E. (1975). *Psychol. Rev.* **82**, 150–3.
Masson, M. E. J. (1979). *J. verb. Learn. verb. Behav.* **18**, 173–86.
Mathews, R. (1954). *J. exp. Psychol.* **47**, 241–7.
Mathews, R. C. (1977). *J. exp. Psychol.: Hum. Learn. Memory* **3**, 160–73.
—— and Tulving, E. (1973). *J. verb. Learn. verb. Behav.* **12**, 707–21.
Melton, A. W. (1963). *J. verb. Learn. verb. Behav.* **2**, 1–21.
—— (1967). *Science, NY* **158**, 532.
—— (1970). *J. verb. Learn. verb. Behav.* **9**, 596–606.
—— and Martin, E. (1972). *Coding processes in human memory*. Winston, Washington, DC.
Meyer, D. E. (1973). In *Attention and performance IV* (ed. S. Kornblum). Academic Press, New York.

—— and Schvaneveldt, R. W. (1976). *Science, NY* **192**, 27–33.
—— —— and Ruddy, M. G. (1974). *Memory Cogn.* **2**, 309–21.
Miller, G. A. (1956*a*). *IRE Trans. inform. Theory* **2**, 129–37.
—— (1956*b*). *Psychol. Rev.* **63**, 81–96.
—— (1969). *J. math. Psychol.* **6**, 169–91.
—— (1972). *Proc. Am. phil. Soc.* **116**, 140–4.
—— Galanter, E., and Pribram, K. H. (1960). *Plans and the structure of behavior.* Holt, New York.
—— and Johnson-Laird, P. N. (1976). *Language and perception.* Belknap, Cambridge, Mass.
Moeser, S. D. (1976). *J. verb. Learn. verb. Behav.* **15**, 193–212.
—— (1977). *Can. J. Psychol.* **31**, 41–70.
—— (1979). *Can. J. Psychol.* **33**, 185–92.
Morris, C. D. (1978). *Memory Cogn.* **6**, 354–63.
—— Bransford, J. D., and Franks, J. J. (1977). *J. verb Learn. verb. Behav.* **16**, 519–33.
Morton, J. (1970). In *Models of human memory* (ed. D. A. Norman). Academic Press, New York.
—— (1979). In *Processing of visible language* (ed. P. A. Kolers, M. E. Wrolstad, and H. Bouma). Plenum Press, New York.
Moscovitch, M. and Craik, F. I. M. (1976). *J. verb. Learn. verb. Behav.* **15**, 447–58.
Munsat, S. (1966). *The concept of memory.* Random House, New York.
Murdock, B. B. Jr (1961). *J. exp. Psychol.* **62**, 618–625.
—— (1965). *Br. J. Psychol.* **56**, 413–19.
—— (1967). *Br. J. Psychol.* **58**, 421–33.
—— (1968). *J. exp. Psychol.* **77**, 79–86.
—— (1974). *Human memory : theory and data.* Erlbaum, Potomac, Md.
—— (1975). In *Information processing and cognition: the Loyola symposium* (ed. R. L. Solso). Erlbaum, Hillsdale, NJ.
—— (1979). In *Perspectives on memory research* (ed. L.-G. Nilsson). Erlbaum, Hillsdale, NJ.
—— and Anderson, R. E. (1975). In *Information processing and cognition: The Loyola symposium* (ed. R. L. Solso). Erlbaum, Hillsdale, NJ.
Muter, P. (1978). *Memory Cogn.* **6**, 9–12.
Natsoulas, T. (1970). *Psychol. Bull.* **73**, 89–111.
—— (1978). *Am. Psychol.* **33**, 906–14.
Naus, M. J. and Halasz, F. G. (1979). In *Levels of processing in human memory* (ed. L. S. Cermak and F. I. M. Craik). Erlbaum, Hillsdale, NJ.
Neely, J. H. (1977). *J. exp. Psychol.: Gen.* **106**, 226–54.
Neisser, U. (1967). *Cognitive psychology.* Appleton-Century-Crofts, New York.
—— (1972). In *The functions and nature of imagery* (ed. P. W. Sheehan).Academic Press, New York.
—— Novick, R., and Lazar, R. (1963). *Percept. Mot. Skills* **17**, 955–61.
Nelson, D. L. (1979). In *Levels of processing in human memory* (ed. L. S. Cermak and F. I. M. Craik) Erlbaum, Hillsdale, NJ.
—— and McEvoy, C. L. (1979). *J. exp. Psychol.: Hum. Learn. Memory* **5**, 292–314.
—— Walling, J. R., and McEvoy, C. L. (1979). *J. exp. Psychol.: Hum. Learn. Memory* **5**, 24–44.
Nelson, K. and Brown, A. L. (1978). In *Memory development in children* (ed. P. A. Ornstein). Erlbaum, Hillsdale, NJ.

Nelson, T. O. (1977). *J. verb. Learn. verb. Behav.* **16**, 151–71.

Nemiah, J. C. (1979). In *Functional disorders of memory* (ed. J. F. Kihlstrom and F. J. Evans). Erlbaum, Hillsdale, NJ.

Newell, A. and Rosenbloom, P. S. (1981). In *Cognitive skills and their acquisition* (ed. J. R. Anderson). Erlbaum, Hillsdale, NJ.

Nilsson, L. -G. and Shaps, L. P. (1981). *Acta psychol.* **47**, 25–37.

Norman, D. A. (1968). *Psychol. Rev.* **75**, 522–36.

—— and Bobrow, D. G. (1979). *Cogn. Psychol.* **11**, 107–23.

Ogilvie, J. C., Tulving, E., Paskowitz, S., and Jones, G. V. (1980). *J. verb. Learn. verb. Behav.* **19**, 405–15.

Ojemann, G. A. (1978). *Brain Lang.* **5**, 331–40.

Olton, D. S., Becker, J. T., and Handelmann, G. E. (1979). *Behav. brain Sci.* **2**, 313–65.

—— —— —— (1980). *Physiol. Psychol.* **8**, 239–46.

—— and Feustle, W. A. (1981). *Exp. Brain Res.* **41**, 380–9.

—— and Papas, B. C. (1979). *Neuropsychologia* **17**, 669–82.

Ortony, A. (1975). In *Theoretical issues in natural language processes* (ed. R. C. Schank and B. L. Nash-Webber). Bolt Beranek & Newman, Cambridge, Mass.

Osgood, C. E. (1949). *Psychol. Rev.* **56**, 132–43.

Ozier, M. (1978). *J. exp. Psychol.: Hum. Learn. Memory* **4**, 469–85

Paivio, A. (1976). In *Recall and recognition* (ed. J. Brown). Wiley, London.

—— (1977). In *Images, perception, and knowledge* (ed. J. M. Nicholas). Reidel, Dordrecht, Holland.

—— and Csapo, K. (1973). *Cogn. Psychol.* **5**, 176–206.

Parker, E. S., Morihisa, J. M., Wyatt, R. J., Schwartz, B. L., Weingartner, H., and Stillman, R. C. (1981). *Psychopharmacologia* in press.

Parkin, A. J. (1979). *Q. Jl exp. Psychol.* **31**, 175–95.

Pellegrino, J. W. and Salzberg, P. M. (1975). *J. exp. Psychol.: Hum. Learn. Memory* **1**, 538–48.

Penfield, W. (1975). *The mystery of the mind.* Princeton University Press, NJ.

—— and Perot, P. (1963). *Brain* **86**, 595–695.

Perlmutter, J., Harsip, J., and Myers, J. L. (1976). *Memory Cogn.* **4**, 361–8.

Peterson, L. R. (1965). *Psychon. Sci.* **2**, 167–8.

—— (1967). In *Concepts and the structure of memory* (ed. B. Kleinmuntz). Wiley, New York.

—— (1969). *Psychol. Rev.* **76**, 376–86.

——Saltzman, D., Hillner, K., and Land, V. (1962). *J. exp. Psychol.* **63**, 396–403

Petrey, S. (1977). *Cognition* **5**, 57–71.

Pezdek, K. (1977) *J. exp. Psychol.: Hum. Learn. Memory* **3**, 515–24.

Piaget, J. (1946). *Le dèvelopment de la notion de temps chez l'enfant.* Presses Universitaires de France, Paris

Platt, J. R. (1964). *Science, NY* **146**, 347–53.

Posner, M I, (1980). *Chronometric explorations of mind.* Erlbaum, Hillsdale, NJ.

—— and Warren, R. E. (1972). In *Coding processes in human memory* (ed. A. W. Melton and E. Martin). Winston, Washington, DC

Postman, L. (1961). In *Verbal learning and verbal behavior* (ed. C. N. Cofers). McGraw-Hill, New York.

—— (1963b). In *Verbal behavior and learning* (ed. C. N. Cofer and B. S. Musgrave). McGraw-Hill, New York.

—— (1964). In *Categories of human learning* (ed. A. W. Melton). Academic Press, New York.

—— (1971). In *Experimental psychology* (ed. J. W. Kling and L. A. Riggs). Holt, Rhinehart & Winston, New York.

—— (1975*a*). *Memory Cogn.* **31**, 663–72.

—— (1975*b*) *Ann. Rev. Psychol.* **26**, 291–335.

—— Adams, A., and Phillips, L. W. (1955). *J. exp. Psychol.* **49**, 1–10.

—— Jenkins, W. O., and Postman, D. L. (1948). *Am. J. Psychol.* **61**, 511–19.

—— Keppel, G., and Stark, K. (1965). *J. exp. Psychol.* **69**, 111–18.

—— Thompkins, B. A., and Gray, W. D. (1978). *J. verb. Learn. verb. Behav.* **17**, 681–705.

Potter, M. C. (1976). *J. exp. Psychol.: Hum. Learn. Memory* **2**, 509–22.

Pryor, W. A. (1970). *Scient. Am.* **223**, 70–83.

Puff, C. R. (1979). *Memory organization and structure*, Academic Press, New York.

Quillian, M. R. (1966). Semantic memory. Ph.D. dissertation, Carnegie Institute of Technology.

Raaijmakers, J. G. W. and Shiffrin, R. M. (1980). In *The psychology of learning and motivation*, Vol. 14 (ed. G. H. Bower). Academic Press, New York.

—— —— (1981). *Psychol. Rev.* **88**, 93–134.

Rabinowitz, J. C., Mandler, G., and Barsalou, L. W. (1977). *J. verb. Learn. verb. Behav.* **16**, 639–63.

—— —— —— (1979). *J. verb. Learn. verb. Behav.* **18**, 57–72.

—— —— and Patterson, K. E. (1977). *J. exp. Psychol.: Gen.* **106**, 302–29.

Raffel, G. (1934). *J. exp. Psychol.* **17**, 828–38.

Ramon Y Cajal, S. (1937). *Recollections of my life* (trans. E. H. Craigie). MIT Press, Cambridge, Mass.

Rapaport, D. (1950). *Emotions and memory*. International Universities Press, New York.

Ratcliff, R. (1978). *Psychol. Rev.* **85**, 59–108.

—— and Murdock, B. B. Jr (1976). *Psychol. Rev.* **83**, 190–214.

Reder, L. M., Anderson, J. R., and Bjork, R. A. (1974). *J. exp. Psychol.* **102**, 648–56.

Reid, T. (1970). *An inquiry into the human mind*. University of Chicago Press.

Reiff, R. and Scheerer, M. (1959).*Memory and hypnotic age regression*. International Universities Press, New York.

Robinson, J. A. (1976). *Cogn. Psychol.* **8**, 578–95.

Rock, I. (1957). *Am. J. Psychol.* **70**, 186–93.

Roediger, H. L. III (1980). *Memory Cogn.* **8**, 231–46.

—— and Adelson, B. (1980). *Memory Cogn.* **8**, 65–74.

—— and Thorpe, L. A. (1978). *Memory Cogn.* **6**, 296–305.

—— and Tulving, E. (1979). *J. verb. Learn. verb. Behav.* **18**, 60–16.

Rosch, E. and Mervis, C. B. (1975). *Cogn. Psychol.* **7**, 573–605.

Rozin, P. (1976). In *Neural mechanisms of learning and memory* (ed. M. R. Rosenzweig and E. L. Bennett). MIT Press, Cambridge, Mass.

Rubenstein, H., Garfield, L., and Millikan, J. A. (1970). *J. verb. Learn. verb. Behav.* **9**, 487–94.

Rumelhart, D. E., Lindsay, P. H., and Norman, D. A. (1972). In *Organization of memory* (ed. E. Tulving and W. Donaldson). Academic Press, New York.

Rundus, D. (1971). *J. exp. Psychol.* **89**, 63–77.

Russell, B. (1921). *The analysis of mind*. George Allen & Unwin, London.

—— (1920). *Introduction to mathematical philosophy*, 2nd edn. Macmillan, New York.

—— (1948). *Human knowledge: its scope and limits.* George Allen & Unwin, London.

Russell, P. N. and Beekhuis, M. E. (1976). *J. abnorm. Psychol.* **85**, 527–34.

Russell, W. A. (1961). In *Verbal learning and verbal behavior* (ed. C. N. Cofer). McGraw-Hill, New York.

Salzberg, P. M. (1976). *J. exp. Psychol .: Hum. Learn. Memory* **2**, 586–96.

Santa, J. L. and Lamwers, L. L. (1974). *J. verb. Learn. verb. Behav.* **13**, 412–23.

—— —— (1976). *J. verb. Learn. verb. Behav.* **15**, 53–7.

Sarton, G. (1959). *A history of science.* Harvard University Press, Cambridge, Mass.

Scarborough, D., Cortese, C., and Scarborough, H. (1977). *J. exp. Psychol.: Hum. Learn. Memory* **3**, 1–17.

—— Gerard, L., and Cortese, C. (1979). *Memory Cogn.* **7**, 3–12.

Schachtel, E. G. (1947). *Psychiatry* **10**, 1–26.

Schacter, D. L. (1981). Unpublished Ph. D. thesis, University of Toronto.

—— (1982). *Stranger behind the engram.* Erlbaum, Hillsdale. NJ.

—— Eich, J. E., and Tulving, E. (1978). *J. verb. Learn. verb. Behav.* **17**, 721–43.

—— and Tulving, E. (1981). In *Human memory and amnesia* (ed. L. S. Cermak). Erlbaum, Hillsdale, NJ.

—— —— (1982). In *Expression of knowledge* (ed. R. L. Isaacson and N. E. Spear). Plenum Press, New York.

—— Wang,. P. L., Tulving, E., and Freedman, M. (1982). *Neuropsychologia* (In press.)

Schank, R. C. (1975). In *Representation and understanding* (ed. D. G. Bobrow and A. M. Collins). Academic Press, New York.

—— and Abelson, R. (1977). *Scripts, plans, goals and understanding.* Erlbaum, Hillsdale, NJ.

—— and Kolodner, J. (1979). Yale University, Dept. of Computer Science, Research Report #159, January.

Scheffler, I. (1965). *Conditions of knowledge.* Scott, Foreman, Glenview, Ill.

Schulman, A. I. (1974). *Memory Cogn.* **2**, 47–52.

Schvaneveldt, R. W., Meyer, D. E., and Becker, C. A. (1976). *J. exp. Psychol: Hum. Percept. Psychophys.* **2**, 243–56.

Semon, R. (1904). *Die Mneme als erhaltendes Prinzip im Wechsel des organischen Gesechehens.* William Engelmann, Leipzig.

—— (1921). *The mneme.* George Allen & Unwin, London.

Shallice, T. (1972). *Psychol. Rev.* **79**, 383–93.

—— (1978). In *The stream of consciousness* (ed. K. S. Pope and J. L. Singer). Plenum Press, New York.

Shepard, R. N. (1961). *Psychometrika* **26**, 185–203.

—— (1975). In *Information processing and cognition* (ed. R. L. Solso). Erlbaum, Hillsdale, NJ.

—— (1978). *Am. Psychol.* **33**, 125–37.

—— and Chang, J. -J. (1963). *J. verb. Learn. verb. Behav.* **2**, 93–101.

—— and Teghtsoonian, M. (1961). *J. exp. Psychol.* **62**, 302–9.

Shiffrin, R. M. (1970). In *Models of human memory* (ed. D. A. Norman). Academic Press, New York.

—— and Atkinson, R. C. (1969). *Psychol. Rev.* **76**, 179–93.

Shoben, E. J., Wescourt, K. T., and Smith, E. E. (1978). *J. exp. Psychol.: Hum. Learn. Memory* **4**, 304–17.

Shoemaker, S. S. (1959). *J. Phil.* **56**, 868–82.

Simon, E. (1979). *J. exp. Psychol.: Hum. Learn. Memory* **5**, 115–24.

Simon, H. A. (1972). In *Cognition in learning and memory* (ed. L. W. Gregg). Wiley, New York.

Slamecka, N. J. (1966). *J. exp. Psychol.* **71**, 822–8.

Smith, B. (1966). *Memory*. George Allen & Unwin, London.

Smith, E. E. (1978). In *Handbook of learning and cognitive processes*, Vol. 6 (ed. W. K. Estes). Erlbaum, Hillsdale, NJ.

—— Rips, L. J., and Shoben, E. J. (1974). In *The psychology of learning and motivation*, Vol. 8. Academic Press, New York.

—— Shoben, E. J., and Rips, L. J. (1974). *Psychol. Rev.* **81**, 214–41.

Smith, S. M., Glenberg, A., and Bjork, R. A. (1978). *Memory Cogn.* **6**, 342–53.

Solso, R. L. (1974). In *Theories in cognitive psychology* (ed. R. L. Solso). Erlbaum, Potomac, Md.

Spelke, E., Hirst, W., and Neisser, U. (1976). *Cognition* **4**, 215–30.

Squire, L. R. (1982). *Ann. Rev. Neuroscience* **5**, 271–73.

Stein, B. S. (1978). *J. verb. Learn. verb. Behav.* **17**, 165–74.

Sternberg, R. J. (1979). In *Human intelligence* (ed. R. J. Sternberg and D. K. Detterman). Ablex, Norwood, NJ.

—— and Detterman, D. K. (eds.) (1979). *Human intelligence*. Ablex, Norwood, NJ.

Stevens, S. S. (1951).In *Handbook of experimental psychology* (ed. S. S. Stevens).Wiley, New York.

Teasdale, J. D. and Fogarty, F. J. (1979). *J. abnorm. Psychol.* **88**, 248–57.

Thomson, D. M. (1972). *J. verb. Learn. verb. Behav.* **11**, 497–511.

—— and Tulving, E. (1970). *J. exp. Psychol.* **86**, 255–62.

Tiberghien, G. (1976). In *La memoire semantique* (ed. S. Ehrlich and E. Tulving). Bulletin de Psychologie, Paris.

Till, R. E. (1977). *J. exp. Psychol.: Hum. Learn. Memory* **3**, 129–41.

—— and Walsh, D. A. (1980). *J. verb. Learn. verb. Behav.* **19**, 1–16.

Toulmin, S. (1961). *Foresight and understanding*. Harper & Row, New York.

Tresselt, M. E. and Mayzner, M. S. (1960). *J. Psychol.* **50**, 339–47.

Tulving, E. (1962*a*). *Psychol. Rev.* **69**, 344–54.

—— (1962*b*). *Can. J. Psychol.* **16**, 185–91.

—— (1964). *Psych. Rev.* **71**, 219–37.

—— (1967). *J. verb. Learn. verb. Behav.* **6**, 175–84.

—— (1968*a*). In *Verbal behavior and general behavior theory* (ed. T. R. Dixon and D. L. Horton). Prentice-Hall, Englewood Cliffs, NJ.

—— (1968*b*). *Psychon. Sci.* **10**, 53–4.

—— (1969). *Science*, NY **164**, 88–90.

—— (1972). In *Organization of memory* (ed. E.Tulving and W. Donaldson). Academic Press, New York.

—— (1974*a*). *Am. Scien.* **62**, 74–82.

—— (1974*b*). *J. exp. Psychol.* **102**, 778–87.

—— (1976). In *Recall and recognition* (ed. J. Brown). Wiley, London.

—— (1979*a*). In *Perspectives on memory research: essays in honor of Uppsala University's 500th anniversary* (ed. L. G. Nilsson). Erlbaum, Hillsdale, NJ.

—— (1979*b*). In *Levels of processing in human memory* (ed. L. S. Cermak and F. I. M. Craik). Erlbaum, Hillsdale, NJ.

—— (1981). *J. verb. Learn. verb. Behav*, **20**, 479–96.

—— and Bower, G. H. (1974). In *The psychology of learning and motivation*, Vol. 8 (ed. G. H. Bower). Academic Press, New York.

—— and Donaldson, W. (1972). *Organization of memory*. Academic Press, New York.

—— and Madigan, S. (1970). *A. Rev. Psychol.* **21**, 437–84.

—— and Osler, S. (1968). *J. exp. Psychol.* **77**, 593–601.

—— and Patkau, J. E. (1962). *Can. J. Psychol.* **16**, 83–95.

—— and Pearlstone, Z. (1966). *J. verb. Learn. verb. Behav.* **5**, 381–91.

—— and Psotka, J. (1971). *J. exp. Psychol.* **87**, 1–8.

—— Schacter, D. L., and Stark, H. A. (1982). *J. exp. Psychol.: Learning, Memory, and Cognition.* **8**, 000–000.

—— and Thomson, D. M. (1971). *J. exp. Psychol.* **87**, 116–24.

—— —— (1973). *Psychol. Rev.* **80**, 352–73.

—— and Thornton, G. B. (1959).*Can. J. Psychol.* **13**, 255–65.

—— and Watkins, M. J. (1973). *Am. J. Psychol.* **86**, 739–48.

—— —— (1975). *Psychol. Rev.* **82**, 261–75.

—— and Watkins, O. C. (1977). *Memory Cogn.* **5**, 513–22.

—— and Wiseman, S. (1975). *Bull. Psychonom. Soc.* **6**, 79–82.

Tversky, A. (1977). *Psychol. Rev.* **84**, 327–52.

Tzeng, O. J. L. and Cotton, B. (1980). *J. exp. Psychol.: Hum. Learn. Memory* **6**,705–16.

Underwood, B. J. (1957). *Psychol. Rev.* **64**, 49–60.

—— (1965). *J. exp. Psychol.* **70**, 122–9.

—— (1969). *Psychol. Rev.* **76**, 559–73.

—— (1972). In *Coding processes in human memory* (ed. A. W. Melton and E. Martin). Winston, Washington,DC.

—— (1977). *Temporal codes for memories: issues and problems*. Erlbaum, Hillsdale, NJ.

—— Boruch, R. F., and Malmi, R. A. (1978). *J. exp. Psychol.: Gen.* **107**,393–419.

—— and Keppel, G. (1962). *J. verb. Learn. verb. Behav.* **1**, 1–13.

—— Runquist, W. N., and Schulz, R. W. (1959). *J. exp. Psychol.* **58**, 70–8.

Underwood, G. (1979). In *Aspects of consciousness* (ed. G. Underwood and R. Stevens). Academic Press, London.

Vallery-Radot, R. (1923). *The life of Pasteur* (trans. R. L. Devonshire). Constable, London.

Victor, M., Adams, R. D., and Collins, G. H. (1971). *The Wernicke–Korsakoff syndrome*. F. A. Davis, Philadelphia.

Vining, S. K. and Nelson, T. O. (1979). *Am. J. Psychol.* **92**, 257–76.

Von Leyden, W. (1961). *Remembering, a philosophical problem*. Gerald Duckworth, London.

Wallace, W. P. (1970). *J. verb. Learn. verb. Behav.* **9**, 58–68.

—— (1978). *J. exp. Psychol.: Hum. Learn. Memory* **4**, 441–52.

Warrington E. K. and Weiskrantz, L. (1974). *Neuropsychologia* **12**, 419–28.

—— —— (1978). *Neuropsychologia* **16**, 169–76.

—— —— (1982). *Neuropsychologia,* **20**, 233–47.

Watkins, M. J. (1974). *J. exp. Psychol.* **102**, 161–3.

—— (1979). In *Memory organization and structure* (ed. C. R. Puff). Academic Press, New York.

—— (1981). *Cognition*, in press.

—— and Gardiner, J. M. (1979). *J. verb. Learn. verb. Behav.* **18**, 687–704.

—— Ho, E., and Tulving, E. (1976). *J. verb. Learn. verb. Behav.* **15**, 505–17.

—— and Todres, A. K. (1978). *J. verb. Learn. verb. Behav.* **17**, 621–33.

—— and Tulving, E. (1975). *J. exp. Psychol.: Gen.* **104**, 5–29.

Watkins, O. C. and Watkins, M. J. (1975). *J. exp. Psychol.: Hum. Learn. Memory* **1**, 442–52.

Waugh, N. C. (1963). *J. verb. Learn. verb. Behav.* **2**, 107–12.

—— and Norman, D. A. (1965). *Psychol. Rev.* **72**, 89–104.

Weingartner, H. and Faillace, L. A. (1971). *J. nerv. ment. Dis.* **153**, 395–406.

Weiskrantz, L. and Warrington, E. K. (1979). *Neuropsychologia* **17**, 187–94.

Wickelgren, W. A. (1977). *Learning and memory*. Prentice-Hall, Englewood Cliffs, NJ.

Wickens, D. D. (1970). *Psychol. Rev.* **77**, 1–15.

—— (1972). In *Coding processes in human memory* (ed. A. W. Melton and E. Martin). Winston, Washington, DC.

Wigmore, J. H. (1961). *Evidence in trials at common law*. Little, Brown, Boston, Mass.

Williams, M. (1953). *J. Neurol. Neurosurg. Psychiat* **16**, 14–18.

—— and Smith, H. V. (1954). *J. Neurol. Neurosurg. Psychiat.* **17**, 173–82.

Williamsen, J. A., Johnson, H. J., and Eriksen, C. W. (1965). *J. abnorm. Psychol.* **70**, 123–31.

Winnick, W. A. and Daniel, S. A. (1970). *J. exp. Psychol.* **84**, 74–81.

Winocur, G. and Weiskrantz, L. (1976). *Neuropsychologia* **14**, 97–110.

Winograd, E. (1968). *J. exp. Psychol. Monog.* Suppl. 76 (February, Part 2), 1–18.

Winograd, T. (1975). In *Representation and understanding* (ed. D. G. Bobrow and A. Collins). Academic Press, New York.

Wiseman, S. and Tulving, E, (1975). *J. verb. Learn. verb. Behav.* **14**, 370–81.

—— —— (1976). *J. exp. Psychol.: Hum. Learn. Memory* **2**, 349–61.

Wood, et al 1982.

Wood, F., Taylor, B., Penny, R., and Stump, D. (1980). *Brain Lang.* **9**, 113–22.

Wood, F., Ebert, V., and Kinsbourne, M. (1982). In *Human memory and amnesia* (ed. L. S. Cermak). Erlbaum, Hillsdale, NJ.

Wood, G. (1970). *J. verb. Learn. verb. Behav.* **9**, 327–33.

Woodward, A. E., Bjork, R. A., and Jongeward, R. H. (1973). *J. verb. Learn. verb. Behav.* **12**, 608–17.

Woozley, A. D. (1949). *Theory of knowledge*. Hutchinson, London.

Yarmey, A. D. (1979). *The psychology of eyewitness testimony*. The Free Press, New York.

Zajonc, R. B. (1980). *Am. Psychol.* **35**, 151–75.

Author index

Subject index